OVERLORD
THE D-DAY LANDINGS

OSPREY
PUBLISHING

OVERLORD
THE D-DAY LANDINGS

KEN FORD · STEVEN J. ZALOGA

First published in Great Britain in 2009 by Osprey Publishing.
This paperback edition published in 2011 by Osprey Publishing.
Midland House, West Way, Botley, Oxford OX2 0PH, United Kingdom.
44-02 23rd Street, Suite 219, Long Island City, NY 11101, USA.
Email: info@ospreypublishing.com

Previously published as *Campaign 1: Normandy 1944* by Stephen Badsey,
Campaign 100: D-Day 1944 (1) and *Campaign 104: D-Day 1944 (2)*
by Steven J Zaloga, *Campaign 105: D-Day 1944 (3)* and *Campaign 112:
D-Day 1944 (4)* by Ken Ford.

A CIP catalog record for this book is available from the British Library.

ISBN: 978 1 84908 478 9

Page layout by Myriam Bell
Index by Glyn Sutcliffe
Typeset in Sabon, Quay Sans ITC and Minion Pro
Originated by PPS Grasmere Ltd, Leeds, UK
Printed in China through Bookbuilders

11 12 13 14 15   11 10 9 8 7 6 5 4 3 2 1

Osprey Publishing is supporting the Woodland Trust, the UK's leading woodland
conservation charity, by funding the dedication of trees.

www.ospreypublishing.com

Imperial War Museum Collections
Many of the photos in this book come from the Imperial War Museum's huge
collections which cover all aspects of conflict involving Britain and the
Commonwealth since the start of the twentieth century. These rich resources are
available online to search, browse and buy at www.iwmcollections.org.uk. In addition
to Collections Online, you can visit the Visitor Rooms where you can explore over
8 million photographs, thousands of hours of moving images, the largest sound
archive of its kind in the world, thousands of diaries and letters written by people in
wartime, and a huge reference library. To make an appointment, call (020) 7416 5320,
or e-mail mail@iwm.org.uk.
Imperial War Museum www.iwm.org.uk

Front cover image: "No time to paddle" (Getty Images)

CONTENTS

INTRODUCTION *with Stephen Badsey*

The battle of Normandy was the last great set-piece battle of the Western world. Between June and August 1944, after the greatest amphibious invasion in history, armies comprising more than a million men fought in the tourist spots and picturesque farmland of northwestern France to decide the fate of Europe. For probably the last time in history, a British general led a mighty land army coalition into battle against an enemy that threatened the very existence of the European social order. If the Allies won, then the German occupation of France, which had lasted more than four years, would be over, and with it any chance of victory for Adolf Hitler's Germany. If the Germans could force a stalemate at Normandy, or even drive the Allies back to the sea, they would have at least a year in which to strengthen their defenses, turn against the advancing armies of the Soviet Union on the Eastern Front, and develop the secret weapons to which Hitler attached such importance. At worst, Hitler's Germany might, like Imperial Germany in 1918, sue for an armistice. At best, it might win World War II. What happened in Normandy would decide all this: history has nothing to offer more dramatic.

Like many other great wars of history, World War II was actually a series of interlocking conflicts, which began and ended at different times and for different reasons. For most Europeans, it began through the attempts of Adolf Hitler, elected Chancellor of Germany in 1933, to extend German rule across Europe in a new empire, his "Third Reich," which by summer 1939 had already absorbed Austria and Czechoslovakia. On September 1, 1939, German troops invaded Poland, and two days later Britain and France declared war on Germany. British defense thinking before 1939, however, had been chiefly based on naval and air power; for most of its land forces it expected to rely, as at the start of World War I, on the French Army. France in turn had adopted a defensive strategy based on the Maginot Line, a formidable belt of fortifications built along its frontier with Germany. There was nothing that Britain and France could do to save Poland from occupation. After a failed attempt by British naval and amphibious forces

On the way to Utah Beach. Task Force U sets sail for Normandy on June 5 with a flotilla of LCIs ahead, as seen from the bridge of an LST. *(NARA)*

to intervene against a German attack on Denmark and Norway in April 1940, the British government fell, to be replaced on May 10 by a coalition government under Winston Churchill as prime minister.

By an improbable coincidence, it was also on May 10 that Germany launched a major attack on France through neutral Holland and Belgium, outflanking the Maginot Line. In the face of this onslaught, the French Army, and with it British strategy for the war, collapsed in four weeks. By June 3 the last of the small British army had been evacuated from France, mainly through the port of Dunkirk, and on June 22 France, uniquely among the countries defeated by Germany, signed an armistice. German troops would occupy northern France and the entire French coast, but the French colonies would continue to be governed by an unoccupied French state allied to Germany, with the town of Vichy in southern France as its capital.

The French collapse was the origin of the battle of Normandy. If France were to be liberated, the British and their allies would have to re-invade and defeat the German occupation forces. Unfortunately, in 1940 the British Empire had no allies, and only the German failure to win the Battle of Britain saved Britain itself from invasion, while Australia, New Zealand, and India were all at risk from a potentially hostile Japan in the Far East.

On June 10, 1940, Italy, under Benito Mussolini, declared war against the collapsing France and against Britain, threatening Egypt and the Suez Canal from the Italian colony of Libya. Fighting in the Western Desert of Libya became, after the Germans reinforced the Italians with the Afrika Korps under Erwin Rommel, the major British land commitment, absorbing most of the British Army's fighting forces for the next three years. In April 1941 the Germans, having signed agreements with Hungary, Bulgaria, and Romania, invaded Yugoslavia and Greece. As a result, most of Europe came under German domination, with only Ireland, Sweden, Switzerland, Spain, Portugal, and Turkey remaining neutral. The British, although receiving arms and support from the neutral United States, were not remotely strong enough to consider an offensive strategy. Even if they had, there was no land front on which to conduct one except the strategically isolated Western Desert. The last, and by far the largest, battle of the desert war, at El Alamein in October 1942, between the forces of Generalfeldmarschall Erwin Rommel and Lieutenant-General Sir Bernard Montgomery, was fought by no more than 11 divisions each side.

Hitler's Nazi party was ideologically deeply opposed to Joseph Stalin's Soviet Union both on political and racial grounds. Nevertheless, in 1939 the two had signed a pact of friendship, and Soviet troops had participated in the invasion of Poland. Yet on June 22, 1941, Germany, in company with all its allies, invaded the Soviet Union, occupying most of the country west of Moscow by Christmas. But the political collapse that had accompanied military defeat in other countries attacked by Germany did not happen.

Instead, for the next three years, more than 200 divisions a side fought a bitter, often stalemated war for the occupied territories on a front stretching from the Baltic to the Crimea. It was here, on the Eastern Front, that the main land battles of World War II took place, leaving the Germans short of troops and equipment to deploy elsewhere. Neither side had any significant naval power or strategic aircraft, and virtually all their resources went into troops, tanks, and guns. Almost at once, Stalin began to press the British for a "Second Front" to ease the pressure on his own forces.

On December 7, 1941, the Japanese attacked Pearl Harbor, declaring war on the United States and Britain. The Soviet Union remained at peace with Japan (not declaring war until a few days before the conflict ended in August 1945), but on December 12 Adolf Hitler, in one of the great strategic blunders of history, declared war on the United States. At the Anglo-American "Arcadia" Conference over Christmas 1941, the Americans decided that their war strategy would give priority to the defeat of Germany rather than Japan.

The events of late 1941 gave the remainder of the war against Hitler its structure. Germany was committed to total war on several fronts against the Soviet Union, the world's largest land power, against the United States, the world's strongest industrial power, and against Britain, still the largest empire in history. The disparity in resources was such that no military skill could overcome it, and the political behavior of the Nazi Party made a separate negotiated peace with any one of the Allies almost impossible. After

Infantry storm ashore from landing craft during an exercise in early 1944. Several full-scale exercises were conducted before the invasion, involving long sea journeys prior to an amphibious landing against simulated opposition. *(Imperial War Museum, H38244)*

9

Pearl Harbor the defeat of Germany, as Churchill put it, was merely the proper application of overwhelming force. This impressed itself deeply on the senior Allied commanders. By taking risks they laid themselves open to the sudden attacks of which the Germans were masters; but by caution – by never giving the Germans an opening – they were bound to win in the end.

The Germans, Soviets, and Americans, sharing a common strategic heritage, saw the obvious Allied strategy as an invasion of France in 1942, or 1943 at the latest. The British opposed this notion of an early Second Front on both military and political grounds. Britain was already fully committed on four fronts: the battle of the Atlantic, the war against Japan in Southeast Asia, the strategic bombing offensive against Germany, and the Western Desert campaign. Neither the British nor the Americans had the trained troops and equipment to undertake such a venture so early. Nor indeed had Churchill any desire to repeat the kind of losses that the British had suffered conducting a major land campaign in France in World War I. Instead, Churchill and his commanders convinced the Americans that the war should be fought where British troops were already deployed. In November 1942, just as Montgomery was driving Rommel back from El Alamein, American and British forces landed in French North Africa, deep in Rommel's rear. In response, the Germans occupied the Vichy state, and its troops overseas joined the Free French as one of the Allies. By May 1943, the German and Italian forces had been pushed into northern Tunisia and forced to surrender. The American commander for the operation – a position that had involved difficult negotiations with the French as well as the British – was Major-General Dwight D. Eisenhower.

Whether an invasion of France could have been mounted or successful in 1943 remains controversial. Regardless, at the "Symbol" Conference in Casablanca in January 1943, the British again committed the Americans to a Mediterranean strategy. The Allies also agreed on a war aim of unconditional surrender for Germany. In June 1943 they invaded Sicily; Mussolini was overthrown by a *coup d'état*, and in September, as the Allies landed in southern Italy, the new Italian government surrendered. German troops in Italy, however, took over the defense of the country against the Allied advance, which was stopped south of Rome in November.

Also in January 1943, the Soviets forced the surrender of the German Sixth Army at Stalingrad (modern Volgograd), and in July they blunted the last great German offensive at Kursk. From then on they were able to maintain the offensive, gradually driving the Germans back. American war production, meanwhile, had reached full capacity, and trained American troops were pouring into Britain. Although Churchill continued to press for a Mediterranean strategy, with British manpower reserves at breaking point and the US Army expected to provide the majority of forces for operations in France, Britain was losing its role as the senior partner in the Allied coalition, and the American strategic viewpoint for an invasion of northern France prevailed. At the "Trident" Conference in Washington in May 1943, a tentative date of a year ahead was set for the invasion, code-named Operation *Overlord*. At the "Eureka" Conference with the Soviets in Tehran in November 1943, the Americans and British committed themselves fully to *Overlord*, coupled with a second invasion of southern France shortly afterwards. Finally, at the "Sextant" Conference in Cairo in December, the Allies named the now full general Eisenhower as Supreme Commander for *Overlord*, to take up his post immediately.

A cross-Channel invasion by British and American forces now became inevitable, since it would provide the shortest and most effective route into Germany's heartland, though Churchill argued for a traditional maritime strategy of peripheral attack through Italy and the Balkans. While the decision to drive for Germany through France and the Low Countries was the most sensible and desirable, Britain claimed that it would be impossible to mount such an amphibious attack until many seemingly insurmountable problems had been solved.

The most serious problem was the lack of sufficient shipping to carry the assault forces, especially the dearth of landing craft. Shipyards in Britain and America worked to full capacity to produce them, but even by the date of the planned invasion, totals still fell well short of demand. There was

Crews from infantry landing craft come alongside a Landing Barge, Kitchen (LBK). This converted Thames barge was equipped to provide hot meals for ferry craft crews. On D-Day alone, this barge served over 1,000 meals to the sailors and marines who operated the exposed assault landing craft. The inclusion of LBKs in the invasion fleet demonstrates the amount of attention to detail that was required during the planning of Operation *Neptune*. *(Imperial War Museum, A24017)*

also no suitable plan for the invasion available, nor a proven set of tactics by which to launch the assault. Even four years into the war, in 1943 amphibious warfare was still very much in its infancy. There had been a few combined operations raids on enemy shores, but none on a scale that provided pointers for the size of the invasion that was envisaged. A raid in force on the French coastal town of Dieppe in August 1942 did, however, provide valuable information regarding the problems of attacking an enemy-held port. The attempted landings were not a success. The troops that arrived on the main beach were pinned down on the shoreline and the tanks that were landed to support them could not cross the seawall and floundered on the loose shingle. On either flank the story was basically the same: beach defenses kept the troops confined to the water's edge and enemy machine-gun fire decimated them as they lay trapped in the open.

The lessons of Dieppe were put to good use during the planning for Operation *Overlord*, and by 1944 the Allies had further amphibious experience, including the landings in North Africa in November 1942 and the Sicily, Salerno, and Anzio landings in Italy in 1943–44. The key factors were as follows: first, the assault would have to be made over open beaches and not against a fortified port area; second, support from naval guns and aircraft was essential to eliminate all enemy strongpoints; and third, specialized weapons and armor designed for beach operations would have to be developed, to allow tanks and infantry to get off the beach and move inland. It was clear that the invasion would have to be a massive combined operation, rather than a series of battles fought by the three different services.

In May 1943, the Chief of Staff, Supreme Allied Command (COSSAC), headed by Lieutenant-General Frederick Morgan, was set up to plan the cross-Channel invasion, taking into account all of the problems that had been raised and the solutions offered to overcome them. Morgan and his team's task was to begin the critical initial planning for the invasion until the appointment of a Supreme Commander for the campaign.

In studying the possible sites for the assault, it soon became clear to COSSAC that the area of Normandy in the Bay of the Seine, between the estuary of the River Orne and the base of the Cotentin Peninsula, would be the most suitable location for the amphibious forces to come ashore. In arriving at this decision, Morgan had to take into account many factors; most significantly, he had to consider the radius of supporting air cover from bases in England, then about 150 miles. Other important elements were: the length of the sea crossing; the strength of enemy defenses; the availability of suitable beaches; and the proximity of usable ports to help with the build-up of men and matériel once the landings had taken place. The choice really came down to just four areas: the Pas-de-Calais, Normandy, the Cotentin Peninsula, and Brittany. Many commanders favored the short sea crossing

The Atlantic Wall in France, 1944

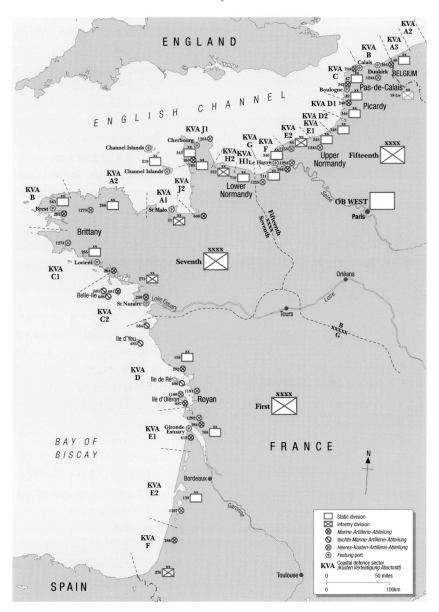

to the Pas-de-Calais. The enemy, however, had also recognized that this area was an obvious target for an assault and the German defences in the Pas-de-Calais were the most formidable along the whole of the Channel. Brittany had several excellent ports, including Brest, but the Breton peninsula was more distant from English ports than either the Pas-de-Calais or Normandy. In addition, had the Allies landed in Brittany, German forces might have contained their advance by sealing off the relatively narrow exit from the

Breton peninsula. As a result, Morgan and his staff quickly rejected the Pas-de-Calais and Brittany as being unsuitable, choosing Normandy instead. The problem in the invasion area was the lack of ports like Le Havre or Calais, but British naval planners had already begun to develop an ingenious artificial harbor that could provide a logistical base until neighboring ports such as Cherbourg were seized.

The first draft of the *Overlord* plan was completed in July 1943, and approved by the Combined Joint Chiefs of Staff in August. *Overlord* consisted of four phases. Operation *Pointblank* was already under way through the efforts of the United States Army Air Force (USAAF) and the British Royal Air Force (RAF), which were aimed at gaining air superiority over the future battlefield by destroying the Luftwaffe and crippling Germany's ability to manufacture, maintain, and fuel its aircraft. The other element of the first phase – Operation *Fortitude* – was an attempt to deceive the Germans about the location of the actual landing site. The second preparatory phase was aimed at isolating the battlefield by air attacks against communication centers, and road and rail networks that linked the Normandy area to potential reinforcements. Since air attacks limited to Normandy would give away the location of the planned invasion, more missions were actually flown against the Pas-de-Calais, as part of an effort to reinforce the Operation *Fortitude* deception. The third phase was Operation *Neptune* itself, the amphibious landings in Normandy. The fourth phase was the follow-up and build-up phase, aimed at reinforcing the bridgehead in preparation for the campaign in France.

Overlord called for British, American, and Canadian forces to land in sufficient numbers to create a beachhead through which would pass the whole of the Allied 21st Army Group. In the British sector were "Gold," "Juno" and "Sword" beaches; in the American area were "Utah" and "Omaha." Ten divisions would come ashore on D-Day: three airborne divisions to protect the flanks of the lodgement, six infantry divisions across the beaches, and one specialized armored division to stiffen the initial assault.

The American First Army, landing on the right of the attack, would come ashore either side of the River Vire with the object of closing the base of the Cotentin peninsula and isolating the important port of Cherbourg. Troops landed on Utah Beach would then turn northwards to secure the port itself. The Omaha Beach landings would build a bridgehead of sufficient depth to allow the concentration of the forces necessary to make a break out toward the Loire and Brittany. The British Second Army would land on the left and make immediately for Caen. The city would be taken with a frontal assault from Sword Beach and a flanking movement from Juno Beach. The landings over Gold Beach would take Bayeux and then link with Juno and Sword to form a lodgement from which operations would be developed to the southeast toward Paris.

The build up of troops and equipment for D-Day was a massive undertaking. Every available space in southern England was put to good use to store stockpiles of vehicles and equipment ready for the invasion. This picture taken on May 15, 1944, shows unmarked Churchill and Cromwell tanks lined up along the Winchester by-pass, 15 miles from Southampton Docks, in preparation for their move to France. *(Imperial War Museum, H38510)*

To make the assault, the British Second Army would rely on a mix of high motivation and experience. Its 50th Division, with a fine record of service in North Africa and Sicily, would land on Gold, while the inexperienced but well-trained Canadian 3rd and British 3rd Divisions would assault Juno and Sword. Both of these divisions had been preparing in England for over three years, and their training in the last year had focused specifically on making an assault landing from the sea.

Under the plan, Operation *Neptune* into northern France would take place in May 1944 and Operation *Anvil*, a second invasion through the French Mediterranean coast, would follow as soon as it was possible to shift the necessary naval amphibious forces from the English Channel to the Mediterranean.

From the German perspective, 1944 was the year of decision. The Wehrmacht had lost the strategic initiative in 1943 following its failed summer offensive at Kursk and the Allied offensive in Italy. Hitler believed that a stout defense in 1944 would lead to cracks in the Allied coalition that might provide the Wehrmacht with opportunities to reverse Germany's declining fortunes on the battlefield. The defeat of an Allied landing attempt in France was a prime opportunity. Hitler's strategic outlook was colored by his experience as a soldier in World War I, where there was no higher objective than the stalwart defense of every last inch of ground. By the beginning of 1944, German forces were scattered all over Europe from Norway and Finland in the north to Greece and the Balkans in the south, and from the Channel Islands in the west to the steppes of Ukraine in the east. "Who defends everything, defends nothing" is a military adage that Hitler ignored at Germany's peril. The Wehrmacht was stretched thin everywhere and Hitler rebuffed attempts to pull troops out of the peripheries to reinforce the most vital sectors. He took ill-advised comfort in the bloated Wehrmacht order of battle, ignoring the reality that his army had become a hollow force.

Worn down by the precarious situation on the Eastern Front, the Wehrmacht's innovative traditions in the art of war had stagnated and been overtaken by the Allies' more advanced approach. While some senior German commanders who had fought Britain and the United States had some appreciation of the new style of deep battle, most did not. The Anglo-American style of war emphasized the use of airpower both as a third dimension in the land battle and as a means to deepen the battlefield. At the strategic level, long-range bombers weakened the military might of Germany by attacking its military industries, fuel production, and infrastructure. At the operational level, Allied medium bombers isolated the battlefield by destroying the road and rail networks feeding the forward edge of battle, sapping the Wehrmacht of its mobility and preventing reinforcement. At the tactical level, fighter-bombers outflanked ground formations from the air, extended the firepower of the Allies beyond the range of traditional artillery, and disrupted the conduct of Wehrmacht operations with their ability to strike unexpectedly practically anytime, anywhere. The decay of the Luftwaffe undermined attempts to resist the forthcoming invasion of France. Rommel grimly noted that "even with the most modern weapons, anyone who has to fight against an enemy in complete control of the air, fights like a savage against modern European troops, under the same handicaps and with the same chance of success".

The decline of the Luftwaffe also helped blind German intelligence to the Allied build-up in the ports of southern England facing Normandy. Photo-reconnaissance missions over Britain were almost impossible and only two photos of British ports were obtained in the spring of 1944. Other intelligence means proved even more dangerous to German strategy, as British counter-intelligence had managed to capture every agent dropped into Britain and had turned many into double agents. Berlin was fed a string of false reports reinforcing their mistaken beliefs about the invasion focus on the Pas-de-Calais and Picardy coastlines. The British success in breaking the German Enigma codes provided a vital source of information on German activities, but a most dangerous security breach was the US decryption of the code used by the Japanese embassy in Berlin. Ambassador

Oshima Hiroshi reported on his frequent meetings with senior Nazi leaders, providing not only insight into Hitler's strategic views, but details of German dispositions as when he undertook an inspection tour of German defenses on the French coast in November 1943. The failures of German intelligence and counter-intelligence left the senior German leadership blind, while at the same time exposing a remarkably complete picture of German plans to the Allies.

The consensus among German military leaders was that the main attacks would take place against the Pas-de-Calais or Picardy coast. The landings at Anzio on January 22, 1944, led a growing number of German commanders to believe that the Allies would launch several smaller amphibious attacks to draw off German reserves from the main landing. This belief greatly confused German defense plans and restricted the actions of German theater commanders because Berlin was increasingly unwilling to commit any reserves until it was evident that an Allied landing was in fact a major operation and not merely another diversion.

CHRONOLOGY

1943

April Generalmajor Wilhelm Richter takes command of German 716th Infantry Division occupying Sword Beach region

April 23 Lieutenant-General Frederick Morgan appointed to head COSSAC to plan for the invasion of mainland Europe

May 2 Major-General Richard Gale appointed to raise and command British 6th Airborne Division for the invasion of Europe

July First draft of *Overlord* plan completed by COSSAC

Canadian 3rd Infantry Division selected as one of the assault divisions for *Overlord*

August *Overlord* plan approved by Combined Joint Chiefs of Staff

November 3 Führer Directive 51 gives priority to reinforcing Western Front

November 6 Rommel appointed to lead Army Group for Special Employment; British 50th Division arrives home from Sicily to begin preparations for its role as one of the assault divisions for *Overlord*

December Lieutenant-General Dwight D. Eisenhower appointed as Supreme Commander for Operation *Overlord*

General Sir Bernard Montgomery given command of 21st Army Group, which contains all the land forces that will be used in the invasion

December 12 Major-General Tom Rennie takes command of British 3rd Division for the invasion of Europe

1944

January Eisenhower and Montgomery propose that two further landing beaches, Utah and Sword, be added to the *Overlord* plan

January 19 Major-General Douglas Graham takes over command of 50th Division for the invasion

April British 6th Airborne Division begins its concentration in camps close to the airfields from where its forces will leave for France

British 50th and Canadian 3rd divisions begin exercises in the Channel

April 7 Montgomery presents the *Overlord* plan to Churchill, King George VI, and to all military commanders at St Paul's School in London

	British 3rd Division moves south to Hampshire from its training ground in Scotland and undertakes exercises in the Channel
May 8	The date of the invasion, D-Day, is fixed for Monday June 5, 1944
May 26	Troops of the British 3rd Division are sealed in their camps and briefing begins on their role in the invasion. French francs and phrase books are issued, last-minute preparations made, and detailed models of the landing beaches inspected
May 28	Landing zone (LZ) for 82nd Airborne Division shifted from St Saveur to River Merderet
June 3	Office of Strategic Services (OSS) teams drop into Normandy to set up beacons for pathfinders; assault divisions begin embarkation onto ships for Channel crossing
June 4	Poor weather forces cancellation of attack on Monday June 5
	Luftwaffe meteorologists forecast rough seas and gale-force winds throughout June
June 5	Eisenhower decides that weather will permit execution of *Neptune* on June 6
	Force S, the invasion fleet destined to land on Sword Beach, and Forces G and J, the invasion fleets set to land on Gold and Juno beaches, sail for France from Portsmouth and Southampton.
	British 6th Airborne Division's advance parties and Major John Howard's *coup de main* party take off from airfields in southern England as the spearhead of the invasion

June 6 D-Day

0015hrs	Pathfinders begin landing in Normandy to set up beacons for air drops
0016hrs	The first glider of Major Howard's force touches down in Normandy close to the bridge over the Caen Canal at Bénouville
0030hrs	Caen Canal bridge and the nearby bridge over the River Orne are captured intact;
	Minesweepers clear channel to Omaha beachhead
0050hrs	Main body of Allied paratroops lands east of the River Orne and on Cotentin peninsula
0100hrs	German units alerted due to reports of Allied paratroopers
0130hrs	Albany mission begins and 101st Airborne paratroopers start landing in Normandy
0230hrs	Boston mission begins and 82nd Airborne paratroopers start landing in Normandy
	Task Force U arrives off Utah Beach, anchors in transport area
0300hrs	Task Force O arrives off Omaha Beach, anchors 25,000 yards from beach;
	Allied air forces begin their final aerial bombardment of the Atlantic Wall defenses prior to the landings
0310hrs	General Marcks orders LXXXIV Corps reserve, Kampfgruppe Meyer, to move to junction between Omaha and Utah beaches to deal with paratroopers
0320hrs	Major-General Gale, his HQ, and divisional heavy weapons arrive in Normandy with the main glider landings
0330hrs	Naval Forces S, G, and J, and the shore bombardment fleet arrive off the coast of Normandy
0400hrs	Chicago mission begins: 101st Airborne gliders start landing
0407hrs	Detroit mission begins: 82nd Airborne gliders start landing

0415hrs	Troops from assault waves begin loading in landing craft
0430hrs	Cavalry detachment lands on St Marcouf island off Utah Beach, finds it deserted
0505hrs	German coastal batteries begin engaging Allied warships
0530hrs	DD tanks begin swim to Omaha Beach
	Troops begin to disembark from the transport ships into assault craft bound for the landing sites on Sword Beach, Queen Red and White sectors
0545hrs	Naval bombardment group begins shelling Omaha Beach – firing ends at 0625hrs
0550hrs	Naval bombardment group begins shelling Utah Beach
0600hrs	Naval bombardment of German coast defenses and gun batteries on Sword Beach begins
0605hrs	Bomber attacks on Utah Beach begin
0629hrs	First wave of tanks begins landing on Omaha Beach
0630hrs	Assault waves begin landing on Utah Beach
0631hrs	First wave of assault troops and Gap Assault Teams begin landing on Omaha
0700hrs	Tide turns, obstacles gradually submerged by 0800hrs
0700–0730hrs	Second wave of troops lands on Omaha Beach
0710hrs	Rangers arrive at Pointe-du-Hoc 40 minutes late; reach summit by 0725hrs
0720hrs	First advance over the bluffs by group under Lieutenant Spalding, E/16th Infantry
0725hrs	Assault companies of 8th Brigade, British 3rd Division, land on Queen Red and White sectors, supported by armor of 27th Armoured Brigade and specialized tanks from 79th Armoured Division
0730hrs	Assault companies of 69th and 231st Brigades, British 50th Division, touch down on King and Jig sectors, supported by armor from 8th Armoured Brigade and the specialized tanks of 79th Armoured Division
0749hrs	Canadian 7th Brigade lands the leading companies of its first assault battalion, Winnipeg Rifles, to the west of Courseulles on Mike Red and Green sectors to begin Canadian 3rd Division's attack on Juno Beach
0750hrs	Advance over the bluffs begins by 116th Infantry led by General Norman Cota and Colonel Charles Canham
	1st Hampshires and 1st Dorsets take heavy casualties from German fire from the Le Hamel strongpoint and are pinned down on Jig sector. On King sector, 6th Green Howards gets some troops off the beach and moves against objectives, while 5th East Yorks gradually moves on La Rivière
0755hrs	Canadian 8th Brigade begins its landings, with the assault companies of the Queen's Own Rifles of Canada landing on Nan White and the North Shore Regiment landing on Nan Red
0800hrs	Admiral Bryant orders destroyers to close on Omaha Beach to provide fire support
	The first of Brigadier Lord Lovat's commandos arrive over Queen sector when 4 Commando comes ashore to attack the gun batteries at Ouistreham and the Casino at Riva Bella
0810hrs	Advance by 5th Rangers over the bluffs begins
	The Regina Rifles of the Canadian 7th Brigade lands its assault companies at Courseulles on Nan Green sector on the eastern side of the River Seulles

0815hrs	Follow-up battalions of 2nd Devons and 7th Green Howards arrive over Jig and Mike sectors and begin to move inland
0820hrs	Regimental HQ of 16th Regimental Combat Team lands
0830hrs	Beachmaster orders no further vehicles to be landed at Omaha due to congestion
	8th Brigade clears the beaches and begins moving inland toward Hermanville
	47 Royal Marine Commando arrives on Jig sector and moves inland to the west on its mission to take Port-en-Bessin and join up with the Americans from Omaha Beach
	The German 441st Ost Battalion, 716th Division, has borne the brunt of the British attack on Gold Beach and is giving way all along the beach, but pockets continue to hold on to most of the strongpoints
	Canadian 7th Brigade lands its follow-up battalion, Canadian Scottish Rifles, on Mike sector and the battalion moves inland toward St-Croix-sur-Mer
0835hrs	Generalleutnant Dietrich Kraiss directs Kampfgruppe Meyer to stop British advance from Gold Beach, except for one battalion aimed at the Colleville penetration
	48 Royal Marine Commando lands on Nan Red, losing almost half its men in the process
0840hrs	Canadian 8th Brigade lands its reserve battalion, La Régiment de la Chaudière, on Nan White sector
0900hrs	WN60 strongpoint falls to L/16th Infantry
	Combat Team 8 begins moving off Utah Beach via Exit 2
	Generalleutnant Kraiss at the HQ of German 352nd Division receives permission from General Marcks, Commander LXXXIV Corps, to release the corps reserve against the British on Gold Beach
0915hrs	WN70 strongpoint abandoned due to advance by Cota's force on Vierville
0930hrs	All assault battalions are off Juno beach and moving inland. Canadian 7th Brigade expands the right flank, but the Regina Rifles and 8th Brigade are heavily occupied in clearing the towns of Courseulles and Bernières
	All assault and follow-up battalions have men off Gold Beach and are attacking targets inland
0945hrs	48 Royal Marine Commando regroups its surviving men and starts the advance on the Langrune strongpoint from Juno Beach
1000hrs	18th Infantry and 115th Infantry move toward Omaha Beach in LCIs; they are delayed by lack of clear lanes
	185th Brigade, 3rd Division's intermediate brigade, starts to come ashore, along with more tanks from 27th Armoured Brigade, and begin their drive to Caen
1100hrs	LCI-554 and LCT-30 force their way through to Omaha Beach, restoring momentum to the landings
	Kampfgruppe Meyer moves toward the British on Gold Beach
	Follow-up brigades of 50th Division – 56th and 151st Brigades – begin to land and assemble on Gold Beach before moving inland
1130hrs	E-1 St Laurent draw opened; first exit cleared on D-Day
	Canadian 9th Brigade now lands behind 8th Brigade and begins to create an enormous traffic jam as troops and vehicles all try to exit Juno Beach through Bernières

1200hrs	Kampfgruppe Meyer is attacked by Allied fighter-bombers during its advance to the area of Gold Beach
1300hrs	Hour-long naval bombardment of D-1 Vierville draw concludes; survivors surrender
	9th Brigade, the 3rd Division's reserve brigade, lands over Sword Beach and starts its drive on Caen, but is soon thrown into some disarray by the loss of its commander
	Engineers complete makeshift road over bluff near E-1 St Laurent draw; vehicle assembly area completed by 1500hrs
	Expansion of Juno and Gold beachheads is underway, but progress inland is slow, as some of the enemy gradually falls back into prepared defensive positions, while others are in full retreat
1310hrs	British 1st Special Service Brigade arrives from Sword Beach to link up with the 6th Airborne Division at the Bénouville bridges
1335hrs	Kraiss reports to LXXXIV Corps HQ that invasion force stopped except at Colleville
1500hrs	3rd Division's advance on Caen begins to falter when 1st Suffolks gets bogged down clearing the Morris and Hillman strongpoints
1600hrs	German 21st Panzer Division launches a counterattack against the Sword beach landings and immediately runs into the 1st King's Shropshire Light Infantry supported by tanks of the Staffordshire Yeomanry
	Kampfgruppe Meyer arrives near Villiers-le-Sec and meets the advancing British 69th Brigade, which is supported by tanks and fighter-bombers. The two sides clash and in the ensuing action Meyer is killed and most of his battlegroup wiped out
1630hrs	E-3 Colleville draw finally taken
	Canadian 3rd Division has all three of its brigades advancing on their objectives, but all begin to stall when the tanks of German 21st Panzer Division attack along its eastern flank on their drive to the coast
1700hrs	Tanks begin moving through E-1 St Laurent draw
1800hrs	D-1 Vierville draw finally opened by engineers
1825hrs	Kraiss orders 1st Company, Grenadier Regiment 914 (1./GR.914) to retake Pointe-du-Hoc
1900hrs	After losing many tanks during the advance, elements of 21st Panzer Division reach the sea between Lion and Luc-sur-Mer, but few reinforcements arrive to help the enemy exploit the gap between Sword Beach and the Canadian landings on Juno Beach
2000hrs	D-3 Les Moulins draw declared open
	Engineers begin clearing path through E-3 Colleville draw, opens at 0100hrs on D+1
	British 50th Division advances on Bayeux and the road and railway line linking Bayeux with Caen, but stops short of its objectives and digs in, preparing to resume the advance the next day
2100hrs	Elmira mission delivers glider reinforcements to LZ W; Keokuk mission to LZ E
	6th Airlanding Brigade arrives by gliders to join the remainder of British 6th Airborne Division and sets down on LZ W, west of the Orne
	21st Panzer Division withdrawn back onto the high ground north of Caen, where it digs in for the night
2400hrs	With their drive on Caen stalled, 3rd Division's three brigades consolidate their gains and make ready for a resumption of the advance the next day

June 7	Galveston mission delivers gliders to LZ W at 0700hrs; Hackensack mission at 0900hrs
	German counterattack on Ste-Mère-Église repulsed with tank support
June 8	Generalfeldmarschall Erwin Rommel receives set of captured VII Corps orders, and decides to reinforce Cotentin peninsula
June 9	La Fière causeway finally captured by 82nd Airborne Division
June 10	101st Airborne seizes causeway leading to Carentan
	US 90th Division begins attempt to cut off Cotentin peninsula
June 11	Fallschirmjäger Regiment 6 retreats from Carentan
June 12	101st Airborne occupies Carentan in effort to link up with V Corps at Omaha Beach
June 13	Counterattack on Carentan by 17th SS-Panzergrenadier Division fails with heavy losses
June 15	Failure of 90th Division leads to substitution of 9th Division and 82nd Airborne Division in westward attack
June 16	Hitler meets Rommel and Rundstedt in France, insists on last-ditch defense of Cherbourg
June 17	60th Infantry, 9th Division, reaches the sea at Barneville, cutting off Cotentin peninsula
June 19	Final drive on Cherbourg begins as a three-division assault
June 21	US VII Corps reaches outer ring of defenses of Fortress Cherbourg
June 25	US infantry begin entering outskirts of Cherbourg
June 26	Senior Wehrmacht commanders in Cherbourg forced to surrender
June 28	Final outlying German positions in Cherbourg harbor surrender
June 30	Last pocket on Cap de la Hague surrenders to 9th Division
July 1	9th Division reports that all organized German resistance on Cotentin peninsula has ended

BACKGROUND TO D-DAY

THE OPPOSING COMMANDERS

Allied Commanders

At the "Arcadia" Conference of December 1941, the British and Americans had established a joint command structure that was to last for the rest of the war. The service chiefs of both nations met as the Combined Chiefs of Staff and delegated to each of their Supreme Commanders absolute control over ground, air, and naval forces in his theatre of operations, regardless of nationality. For the next three years, the two Allies worked out the practical difficulties of fully integrated staffs. President Franklin D. Roosevelt, as commander-in-chief of US forces, interfered little in the daily running of the war. Winston Churchill, in his self-appointed role as British Minister of Defence, kept in closer touch with events through the Chief of the Imperial General Staff, General Sir Alan Brooke.

General Dwight D. Eisenhower was assigned to command the Supreme Headquarters Allied Expeditionary Force (SHAEF) in December 1943. Eisenhower had served as aide to General Douglas MacArthur in the Philippines in the years leading up to World War II – an invaluable education in the lessons of coalition building and the impact of politics on military planning. Although he was assigned to a regimental command on his return to the United States in 1940, his reputation as one of the US Army's rising stars led the War Department to transfer him to War Plans in Washington DC. His performance as the chief of staff of the Third Army in the Louisiana maneuvers in the autumn of 1941 caught the attention of the army's chief of staff, George C. Marshall, and ignited his meteoric rise. Eisenhower played a central role in strategic decision-making during the early years of the war, and was put in command of US forces for the amphibious landings in North Africa in 1942. In contrast to the disjointed German command structure, the Allied command structure was far more centralized. One of the first challenges to

Greenham Common airfield, UK, June 5, 1944: one of the famous sequence of photos showing the Supreme Commander Allied Expeditionary Forces, General Dwight D. Eisenhower, with men of the 101st Airborne Division. Speaking here to a lieutenant, "Ike" wears the jacket he made famous; the paratroopers wear their M1942 uniforms, with the tactical helmet markings – here the white heart of the 502nd Parachute Infantry Regiment. The right-hand man has a general-purpose ammo bag slung on his chest.

Eisenhower's authority was the resistance of senior USAAF generals to the diversion of their long-range bombers from their strategic missions against Germany to the tactical operations to isolate the battlefield in France prior to D-Day. Although his critics have pointed to Eisenhower's lack of tactical battlefield experience, his visionary views on combined arms warfare, as well as his astute political skills, made him an ideal commander for a coalition force depending on tri-service cooperation by two Allied armed forces.

With Eisenhower appointed as Supreme Commander of Allied Forces for the invasion, it was thought proper to have British commanders for the air, sea, and land components of the landings: Air Chief Marshal Sir Trafford Leigh Mallory was made Allied Expeditionary Air Force Commander, Admiral Sir Bertram Ramsay was appointed as the Allied naval commander-in-chief, and General Sir Bernard Montgomery was given the task of leading the 21st Army Group, which contained British, Canadian, and American land forces. Fifty-seven years old, Montgomery was a precise, methodical commander who believed in giving the enemy no chance at all. He had yet to lose a major battle and had already beaten Rommel three times. Vain and boastful, Montgomery infuriated others by often living up to his own boasts. His appointment reflected his reputation as the foremost fighting

British D-Day commanders: Lieutenant-General John Crocker of I Corps; Lieutenant-General Sir Miles Dempsey, Second Army; and Lieutenant-General Gerard Bucknall, XXX Corps. *(Imperial War Museum, B5325)*

General Montgomery, Commander Allied 21st Army Group, in conversation with Major-General Graham, Commander British 50th Infantry Division. *(Imperial War Museum, B5787)*

commander in the British Army. The weak link in this chain of command was between SHAEF and the 21st Army Group. The autocratic Montgomery believed in being allowed to concentrate on the battle, and from his small headquarters he paid little attention to superiors. Although he recognized Eisenhower's administrative abilities, Montgomery also held his ability as a strategist in low esteem. Once the invasion began, and the English Channel separated Montgomery from SHAEF, the potential existed for much misunderstanding.

British and Canadian forces for the landings were combined in British Second Army, commanded by Lieutenant-General Sir Miles Dempsey. It contained two corps: British XXX Corps (Lieutenant-General Gerard Bucknall) and British I Corps (Lieutenant-General John Crocker). The landings on Gold Beach were the responsibility of XXX Corps, which chose to use an enlarged British 50th Division for the attack. The Canadian 3rd Division on Juno Beach was under the command of I Corps, which also controlled the British 3rd Division on Sword Beach.

Dempsey was 48 years old and had previously served with Montgomery on a number of occasions. In World War I he had been awarded a Military Cross (MC) as a young subaltern and rose to the rank of lieutenant-colonel between the wars. In 1939 he took his battalion to France and later commanded a brigade at Dunkirk. Back in England he was promoted to major-general and commanded both the 46th Infantry and 42nd Armoured Divisions before joining Eighth Army as a corps commander in 1942. He planned and executed the British assaults in the invasions of both Sicily and mainland Italy, where his XIII Corps fought with great distinction. At Montgomery's insistence he was brought back from Italy to take command of Second Army for Operation *Overlord*.

Dempsey's two corps commanders, Bucknall and Crocker, were also men who had worked closely with Montgomery in the Mediterranean. Bucknall was two years older than Dempsey and had served throughout World War I. Between the wars he was appointed to a number of staff posts before being given the 5th Division in Sicily in 1943. He fought with the division in Italy and impressed Montgomery so much that he was brought home to command

XXX Corps for the invasion, even though the Chief of the Imperial General Staff, General Sir Alan Brooke, thought Bucknall was not suited for higher command. Crocker enlisted as a private in World War I, was later commissioned into the Machine Gun Corps and won both a Distinguished Service Order (DSO) and MC on the Western Front. He left the British Army in 1919, but later joined the Royal Tank Regiment (RTR) and rose to become the highest-ranking World War II commander to have come from that regiment. Crocker was a great trainer of men and rose rapidly to become lieutenant-general and took command of IX Corps in Tunisia. In August 1943, he was given I Corps with the express purpose of training it for *Overlord*.

The tactical commander of the US Army in *Overlord* was Lieutenant-General Omar Bradley, commander of the First US Army (FUSA). Bradley had been a classmate of Eisenhower's at the US Military Academy at West Point in the class of 1915. Bradley's performance at the infantry school in the early 1930s and his work on the General Staff in 1938 attracted Marshall's attention. Bradley raised the new 82nd Division that would later fight as an airborne division in Normandy, and afterwards became deputy commander of General George S. Patton's II Corps in the North African campaign. Marshall favored intelligent, conservative planners like Bradley over charismatic leaders like Patton for senior commands, and Bradley received the nod to lead FUSA in August 1943.

The American assault force consisted of V Corps at Omaha Beach and VII Corps at Utah Beach. VII Corps was commanded by Major-General J. Lawton Collins, better known by his nickname, "Lightning Joe." Collins graduated

The senior American commanders on D-Day are seen here left to right: Lieutenant-General Omar Bradley (First US Army); Major-General Leonard Gerow (V Corps); General Dwight Eisenhower (SHAEF); General J. Lawton Collins (VII Corps). *(NARA)*

The first major American victory in France was the capture of Cherbourg, and "Lightning Joe" Collins is seen here on a hill overlooking the port talking to Captain Kirkpatrick from the 79th Division. *(MHI)*

from West Point in April 1917, but did not arrive in Europe until after the Armistice. He received a divisional command in May 1942, taking over the 25th Division in the Pacific. Formed from cadres of the peacetime Hawaiian Division, this unit had a poor reputation. Collins whipped it into shape for its first assignment, relieving the 1st Marine Division on Guadalcanal in early 1943. The codename for the division headquarters on Guadalcanal was "Lightning," from which Collins picked up his nickname. He had been brought back from the Pacific theater to provide combat experience. Bradley described him as "independent, heady, capable, and full of vinegar," and he would prove to be one of the most aggressive and talented US field commanders in Europe. He later served as the US Army chief of staff during the Korean War.

The force assaulting Omaha Beach came from V Corps, led by Major-General Leonard Gerow. He was older than either Eisenhower or Bradley, Virginia Military Institute class of 1911, and commanded Eisenhower in 1941 while heading the War Plans division of the General Staff. Gerow was regarded by many as the quintessential staff officer, comfortable with planning combat operations but not leading them. Patton despised him, calling him one of the most mediocre corps commanders in Europe and later calling his appointment to head the War College after the war "a joke." But Gerow had Marshall and Eisenhower's confidence, and was given command of the corps in July 1943 after having led the 29th Division. Bradley had brought in more experienced corps commanders from other theaters, including Collins from the Pacific, to lead at neighboring Utah Beach and probably would not have chosen Gerow had the choice been his. But as his V Corps was the first US tactical formation in the UK and because he had the support of Eisenhower, Gerow would lead the attack. Gerow locked horns with Bradley over many details of the Omaha Beach assault plans and several of his improvements would later prove vital in the success of the operation.

German Commanders

The Wehrmacht had developed a hard-won reputation for tactical excellence during World War II, due in large measure to a style of war epitomized by

Aufträgtaktik: senior commanders briefed their subordinate commanders on the goals of the mission, and then permitted them to carry out the assignment as they saw fit, allowing them considerable tactical flexibility. This flexibility was eroded as the conflict dragged on, particularly in the final year of the war. By 1944, the Wehrmacht's capabilities in the field were degraded by an increasingly Byzantine command structure. At the strategic level, Hitler had gradually usurped more and more command authority due to his growing distrust of the professional army officers. He made all major strategic decisions, but interfered at the tactical level as well. Given the sheer complexity of modern industrial war, management of combat operations was beyond the capabilities of a single great commander as might have been possible in earlier centuries. Hitler's interference was erratic and episodic. He would allow the usual chains of command to exercise control over most operations, but became involved in some operations at his whim. Hitler's leadership style was more feudal than modern, encouraging the dispersion of power away from professional organizations like the General Staff and into the hands of enthusiastic amateurs like himself, cronies such as the Luftwaffe head Reichsmarschall Hermann Göring, and the SS chief, Heinrich Himmler. Hitler's meddling also encouraged the formation of competing factions in the military and the government. This was all too evident in the failed attempts to create a unified command in France, where not only was there the usual inter-service rivalries between the navy, army, and air force, but also between those branches of service and the Waffen-SS and the Organization Todt paramilitary construction service. The armed forces high command, Oberkommando der Wehrmacht (OKW), headed by Generalfeldmarschall Wilhelm Keitel, was a nominal joint staff, but in fact the Luftwaffe and Kriegsmarine (navy) were represented by junior officers, and Göring and Admiral Raeder circumvented the OKW when it suited them.

The commander-in-chief in the West (OB West) from March 1942 was Generalfeldmarschall Gerd von Rundstedt. The revered victor of the 1940 battle of France was described by one of his Panzer commanders as "an elderly man ... a soldier of thorough training with adequate

Generalfeldmarschall Gerd von Rundstedt, Commander-in-Chief (West), was head of all German forces in northwest Europe. He advocated that Panzer divisions should be held back from the beaches well inland, with the intention of massing them for a concerted counterattack against any landings at a time and place of his choosing. *(Imperial War Museum, MH10132)*

experience in practical warfare, but without an understanding of a three-dimensional war involving the combined operations of the Heer [army], Kriegsmarine and Luftwaffe. He was a gentleman and had the personal confidence and respect of his subordinate commanders and his troops. His authority was limited and quite handicapped. His chief of staff [Blumentritt] was not a suitable complement, either as to capability or character." A post-war US Army study concluded that the lack of unified command in France was a more serious weakness than shortages of troops and equipment.

While Rundstedt commanded army units, Generalfeldmarschall Hugo Sperrle was in charge of the air units of Luftflotte 3, including the III Flak Corps and the Luftwaffe paratroop and field divisions. Admiral Theodor Krancke commanded Navy Group West along the French coast, including the coastal artillery batteries that would shift to army jurisdiction only after the invasion had begun. German security troops used for occupation duty were under the control of the two military governors. Tactical control was supposed to shift to OB West once the invasion started, but the disjointed command before the invasion hampered coordinated preparation of defenses and complicated control of the forces during the critical first hours of the invasion.

Rundstedt's limited control was evident in the construction of the Atlantic Wall, a series of coastal fortifications started on Hitler's insistence after the St Nazaire and Dieppe raids of 1942. The fortifications were the responsibility of the Organization Todt paramilitary construction force, which reported to armament minister Albert Speer, not to the army. Furthermore, the navy was responsible for most of the fortified coastal guns, which were positioned as they saw fit. Army artillery officers derided them as "battleships of the dunes," located on the coast vulnerable to Allied bombardment instead of being sheltered further to the rear. Hitler wanted 15,000 concrete strongpoints manned by 300,000 troops by May 1943 – an impossible target. The focus was on the Pas-de-Calais and in the summer of 1943 further emphasis was placed on this sector due to Hitler's decision to locate the new V-1 and V-2 missile bases in this area. In spite of the rhetoric about an impregnable "Fortress Europe," the poor state of defenses prompted Rundstedt to send a special report to Hitler in October 1943, which led to Führer Directive 51 on November 3, 1943. This reversed former priorities and recognized the need to strengthen defenses in the West in view of the likelihood of a 1944 Allied attack. The most tangible outcome of this debate was the assignment of Generalfeldmarschall Erwin Rommel to head the newly created Army Group for Special Employment (later Army Group B), a post directly under OKW for direction of the invasion front.

Rommel's new post partly duplicated Rundstedt's, but both officers attempted to make the best of a confused situation. Rommel's first activities involved an inspection of the Atlantic Wall construction and he

Generalfeldmarschall Erwin Rommel, Commander German Army Group B, during an inspection of the coastal defenses of Hitler's Atlantic Wall. Rommel was convinced that the best hope of defeating the Allied invasion lay in crushing it on the beaches before the Allies could establish a viable bridgehead. To do this coastal fortifications needed to be as strong as possible. *(National Archives, Washington)*

invigorated the effort in previously neglected sectors such as Normandy and Brittany. Rommel's appointment brought to a head the debate about the deployment of forces to repel the expected invasion. Rommel argued that the invasion had to be stopped cold on the beaches. It was, therefore, essential that reserves, especially the Panzers, be kept close enough to the beaches for them to intervene promptly. The commander of Panzer Group West, General Leo Freiherr Geyr von Schweppenburg, argued vociferously that the Panzer divisions and the Luftwaffe should be held back from the coastal zone and kept in reserve to form a counter-attack force that would strike after the Allies had landed. Geyr cited the examples of Sicily, Salerno, and Anzio, where German Panzer forces committed to the coastal battle had been stopped by heavy naval gunfire. Geyr argued that the landings could not be stopped, and that the beach defenses should only be an economy-of-force effort – enough to delay and disrupt significantly, but not so much as to drain forces from the decisive battle inland. Rommel retorted that, given Allied air superiority, the Panzers would never be able to mass for a counterattack and to permit the Allies to win a firm lodgment ensured disaster. The matter came to a head in March 1944, when Rommel asked Hitler for expanded powers to unify the command under his control. Hitler agreed to a compromise, putting three of Geyr's Panzer divisions under Rommel's operational control as the Army Group B reserve, but leaving three other Panzer divisions under Rundstedt's OB West command and the remaining four under direct OKW control as strategic reserves. As a result, the German strategy for Normandy remained a jumble of Rommel's scheme for an immediate defense of the beach and Rundstedt and Geyr's plans for a decisive battle after the landings. On D-Day Rommel was in Germany, hoping to persuade Hitler to give him control of more Panzer divisions.

General forces in Normandy were part of the Seventh Army, which controlled German Army units on the neighboring Cotentin peninsula and Brittany as well. The Seventh Army was commanded by Generaloberst Friedrich Dollman. He had won the Iron Cross in World War I, and commanded a corps in Poland and the Seventh Army in the battle of France in 1940. While he was a highly competent officer, he spent most of the war on occupation duty and many battle-hardened veterans of the Eastern Front were skeptical that his staff was up to the task. Dollman died of a heart attack on June 28, 1944, less than a month after D-Day.

The Normandy sector was the responsibility of the LXXXIV Infantry Corps commanded by General der Artillerie Erich Marcks. He was widely regarded as one of the best General Staff officers and served early in the war

General der Artillerie Erich Marcks, commander of the German LXXXIV Corps, controlled the divisions manning the Normandy coastline in June 1944. He lost a leg while serving as a divisional commander in Russia. Considered by many to be one of the better German general officers in Normandy, General Marcks was killed on June 12 by Allied fighter-bombers on the road near St Lô. *(Bundesarchiv, 183/L19841)*

with an army corps in Poland, and with the Eighteenth Army in France in 1940. He was involved in the planning for Operation *Barbarossa*, and commanded the 101st Jäger Division at the time of the invasion of the Soviet Union in 1941. After he lost a leg in combat in March 1942, he was reassigned to the command of the 337th Infantry Division following his recuperation. His skills as a divisional commander led to his elevation to army corps command, first the LXVI Corps in September 1942, then the LXXXVII Corps. The Nazis considered him politically suspect, as he had been an aide to General von Schleicher, murdered by the SS in 1934, and he was passed over by Hitler for army command. Instead, he was assigned to the LXXXIV Corps in France on August 1, 1943, as part of the process to refresh the command structure in France with Eastern Front veterans. Marcks did not agree with Rommel over tactics to defeat an amphibious landing, since he felt that his corps was far too weak and thinly spread to defend the extensive coastline it had been assigned. He favored the construction of a string of field fortifications in modest depth, but relying on a corps reserve of mobile infantry and Panzers within a day's march of the coast to carry out the burden of the defense. Due to the expected bad weather, the Seventh Army had scheduled a series of anti-invasion staff exercises for senior commanders in Rennes for June 6, with Marcks assigned the role of the senior Allied commander. At 0100hrs on June 6, as the Allied paratroopers were approaching their objectives, Marcks was celebrating his birthday with his staff at St Lô, planning to depart a few hours later for Rennes. He was killed in Normandy during an air attack on June 12, 1944.

One of the abiding myths about the Third Reich is that it was brutal but efficient. In fact, Hitler actively encouraged bureaucratic conflict within the Nazi state in order to increase his own political control. By 1944, Germany's armed forces resembled not those of a single power, but of an alliance whose members functioned together rather less well than those of its enemies.

THE OPPOSING ARMIES

The opposing forces in Normandy had many features in common. With some exceptions, troops on both sides were uniformed, disciplined conscripts in their twenties, each side sharing its own common language and culture. Whatever his specialization, every man in the respective armies was trained as an infantryman. The basic infantry weapons were bolt-action or self-loading rifles with ranges and rates of fire exceeding the needs of most firefights, which generally took place at under 300 yards. Only a minority of riflemen ever actually opened fire in combat. The basic social and tactical unit was a squad or section of about ten such riflemen plus a light or medium machine-gun with a practical rate of fire of 200 rounds per minute. The most important administrative unit, the focus of the soldier's immediate loyalty, was the battalion, of about 800 men plus about 50 tanks for armor, 12 guns for artillery, and other vehicles according to specialization. The basic operational formation was the division of between 10,000 and 20,000 men, the smallest formation of all arms that could function independently on the battlefield. Divisions were switched as required between army corps, which had no fixed organization. Divisional structure was usually "triangular," with each formation commanding three lower formations. Fewer than half the members of a division belonged to the fighting arms, and very few troops of an army engaged in direct combat. A British infantry division at full strength of 18,400 all ranks needed 24,000 further troops at army corps level and higher to support it, but on the attack, "two up and one back," its actual frontline would consist of 32 infantry sections, or fewer than 300 men.

The most numerous tanks in the Normandy campaign, the German Panzer IV, the American M4 Sherman, and the British Cromwell, were all of broadly equal fighting value. All armies also had some form of slower, more heavily armored tank or self-propelled gun for direct infantry support.

Artillery was one of two main types: direct-fire antitank weapons with solid shot to penetrate the tank's armor, and indirect-fire high-explosive for general use. The infantry also carried shaped-charge weapons, such as the American bazooka or German Panzerfaust, which could penetrate a tank's hull but had ranges of less than 100 yards. Direct air support was provided by single-seat propeller-driven fighter-bomber aircraft with an ordnance load of under 2,000lb and top speeds of 400mph. Linking the whole structure together were portable radios, first used at platoon level in the previous year, enabling higher commanders to "listen" to a battle far too vast for one man to see. Electronic warfare was in its infancy, however, and nighttime or bad weather seriously reduced the fighting power of all ground and air forces.

Allied Forces

The American fighting doctrine was that wars were won by administration and organization. The best American troops went to rear-area positions, the less good to the fighting arms, the worst of all to the infantry. American training, firepower, and industry, the latter of which was outproducing Germany in tanks four to one, helped compensate for this deficiency. Divisions were designed to be as "lean" as possible for highly mobile offensive operations. The basic American infantry divisional organization was triangular, with three regiments each of three battalions and an artillery regiment plus one heavy artillery battalion – in all numbering some 14,000 men. An armored division (including the 2nd French Armored equipped by the Americans) was three battalions of M4 Sherman tanks, three infantry battalions in halftracks, and three battalions of self-propelled artillery, plus supporting arms that included a battalion of light tanks – in total 11,000 men and 248 tanks. The division provided three Combat Command headquarters (CCA, CCB, and CC for Reserve), enabling its battalions to combine into two or three battlegroups as necessary. American doctrine retained a central pool of independent battalions of armor, infantry, or artillery to be allocated to divisions as necessary, so that most divisions in Normandy were actually overstrength by two or three battalions. Infantry regiments often combined with armored battalions into "regimental combat teams" or RCTs. The American antitank artillery was about 40 percent towed guns and the remainder was tracked self-propelled guns, both in independent battalions.

The British formations that led the invasion of Normandy on June 6, 1944, were well trained, well equipped, well supported and well led. Their morale was sky high. Since the defeat in France in 1940, which had forced the evacuation of its Expeditionary Force from Dunkirk, there had been revolutionary changes in Britain's fighting arms. The British Army's return to France was made by units that had learned much from the actions of other divisions in theaters all over the world.

The British Army had no fighting doctrine as such, and an eccentric divisional organization. Principally a collection of independent infantry battalions as an armed police force for the British Empire, it recognized no real loyalty above the battalion's parent administrative organization, the regiment, which was not a fighting formation. Three battalions from different regiments combined into a brigade, and three brigades plus an artillery brigade into an infantry division of 18,400 all ranks. The armored division of 286 tanks (chiefly Shermans and Cromwells) and 15,000 men was divided into an infantry brigade of three motorized battalions and an armored brigade of three armored battalions – usually called regiments – plus infantry battalions in halftracks. A law unto themselves, individual battalions might be good or bad, and a commander who was skilled and lucky enough might combine them into a good division. But cooperation between battalions, and between infantry and armor, was notoriously poor. British close support for the infantry came from heavily armored Churchill tanks and from specially equipped tanks grouped administratively into the 79th Armoured

An assault section/boat team clambering down into an LCVP. They carry only light combat packs; note, ahead of the coxswain at the right stern, long engineer pole charges. *(NARA)*

Division, but dispersed throughout the Second British Army. The most efficient and successful of the British arms was the artillery, organized so that even junior officers could bring down the fire of all guns within range upon a given target. The Canadians, who were all volunteers, and the 1st Polish Armoured Division, shared the British divisional structure.

German Forces

At the time of the landings, there were 60 German divisions in the West waiting for the Allies to strike. It sounds like an impressively large force, but these divisions were manning a coastline that stretched from Denmark to the Spanish border. They also guarded the French Mediterranean coast, as well as garrisoning the interior of the occupied territories of France, Belgium, Holland, and Denmark. Of these divisions, 20 were static formations, raised to hold a sector of the coast. They were not easily moved, as they lacked any

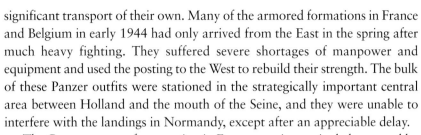

significant transport of their own. Many of the armored formations in France and Belgium in early 1944 had only arrived from the East in the spring after much heavy fighting. They suffered severe shortages of manpower and equipment and used the posting to the West to rebuild their strength. The bulk of these Panzer outfits were stationed in the strategically important central area between Holland and the mouth of the Seine, and they were unable to interfere with the landings in Normandy, except after an appreciable delay.

The German army of occupation in France was increasingly hampered by the destruction of its internal communications by Allied bombing and acts of sabotage committed by the French Resistance. Roads, railways, rivers, canals, and depots were, by June 1944, in a very poor state, and their condition severely restricted the transportation of fuel and supplies. Open movement of military convoys became increasingly difficult as the date of the invasion approached, especially as a result of the strafing tactics employed by low-flying British and American fighter-bombers. The Allied dominance of the air meant that few massed troop movements could be undertaken in daylight, further restricting Germany's ability to react quickly to the Allied landings.

A German infantry squad takes part in invasion drills prior to D-Day. The troops in the background are installing steel beams used to block the roadway from tanks while they are overwatched by a machine-gunner armed with an MG15. *(MHI)*

In contrast to the readiness of the Allies, the German forces in Normandy needed at least another year before they could hope realistically to repulse an amphibious landing. On paper they were ready, for the propaganda machine had almost convinced everyone that the great Atlantic Wall of fortifications was strong enough to keep out any invader, but the reality was very different. During 1942 and 1943, work on the wall had often taken second place to other construction projects and it was not until Rommel was appointed in late 1943 to inspect the effectiveness of the fortifications, that construction work increased in pace and quality. Even then, only a fraction of the strongpoints, minefields, and gun sites that were needed were actually constructed. It was an enormous task, for Hitler did not know just where the Allies would make their attack, so the fortification of the coastline had to stretch from Norway to the Spanish border and also along the Mediterranean shores of France.

Even if construction of the defensive wall had been complete, the Germans would still have had great problems. There were simply not enough troops to garrison such a line effectively. The war in Russia dwarfed the conflict in the West and the Eastern Front was consuming huge numbers of men at a horrendous rate. Retaining divisions in static defenses in France and the Low Countries, all while the German forces in the East were bled white and generals were screaming for reinforcements, was unsustainable and little by little the strength of those divisions guarding the coast was whittled away, often to be replaced by old men and conscripted foreigners. Hitler "wanted to be stronger than mere facts" and so the Wehrmacht order of battle became increasingly fanciful in the last year of the war, with impressive paper strength but increasingly emaciated forces. A German division, therefore, could be anything from the five weak Ost (East) battalions and four of sick men with no heavy weapons that comprised the 226th Static Division, to the 21,386 fully equipped 18-year-old volunteers of the "Hitler Jugend" Division.

In response to Rundstedt's strong criticism of the state of the forces in France in October 1943, Hitler issued Führer Directive 51 to reinvigorate the Wehrmacht in the West. Rundstedt's command increased from 46 to

There was no more vivid symbol of the Atlantic Wall than the heavy coastal guns of the Kriegsmarine along the Channel coast, like this one at Le Havre. These batteries were in their densest concentration on the Pas de Calais where the Wehrmacht expected the Allies to land. *(NARA)*

58 divisions, partly from the transfer of burned-out divisions from the Eastern Front to France for rebuilding, and partly from newly formed divisions. The units on the Cotentin peninsula were second-rate formations. In 1942, Rundstedt had initiated the formation of "static" divisions. These were understrength compared to normal infantry divisions, lacked the usual reconnaissance battalion, and had only three battalions of artillery. In addition, their personnel were mostly from older age groups. Through much of the autumn of 1943, the better troops were siphoned off to satisfy the insatiable requirements for more replacements on the Eastern Front. In their place came a steady stream of Ost battalions manned by "volunteers" from Red Army prisoners. Paratrooper Colonel von der Heydte of FJR 6 recalled that: "The troops for a defense against an Allied landing were not comparable to those committed in Russia. Their morale was low; the majority of the enlisted men and noncommissioned officers lacked combat experience; and the officers were in the main those who, because of lack of qualification or on account of wounds or illness were no longer fit for service on the Eastern Front." The weapons were "from all over the world and seem to have been accumulated from all periods of the twentieth century." For example, during the fighting along a 1-mile stretch of the Carentan front, von der Heydte's unit was equipped with four

This propaganda photo of the Atlantic Wall was released by Germany in December 1943. The Cotentin peninsula, especially around Cherbourg, was one of the few portions of the Normandy coast with a substantial number of heavy coastal defense guns like these. (USAOM)

calibers of mortar from 78mm to 82mm, of German, French, Italian, and Soviet design. General Marcks summed up his assessment during the Cherbourg maneuvers in 1944: "Emplacements without guns, ammunition depots without ammunition, minefields without mines, and a large number of men in uniform with hardly a soldier among them."

The occupation divisions were bedeviled by the petty mindset of an army assigned to years of peaceful occupation duty. General Schlieben recalled that "for someone who had served only in the East, the flood of orders, directives, and regulations which continually showered the troops was a novelty for me. This paper flood impressed me more than the tide along the Atlantic coast. Higher headquarters concerned themselves with trivial affairs of subordinate commanders. For example, it became a problem whether a machine-gun was to be placed 20 meters more to the right or the left … A senior commander wanted to have an old ramshackle hut demolished to create a better field of fire so a written application had to be filed with the appropriate area HQ, accompanied by a sketch." This practice began to change in February–March 1944 after Rommel's arrival. Rommel was insistent that beach defenses be strengthened. There were not enough workers from the paramilitary Organization Todt to carry out this work, since they were involved in the construction of a series of massive concrete bases for the secret V-1 and V-2 missiles. Instead, the construction work was carried out by the infantry in these sectors, at the expense of their combat training.

PART I
OMAHA BEACH

OPPOSING COMMANDERS

GERMAN COMMANDER

The 352nd Infantry Division, commanded by Generalleutnant Dietrich Kraiss, defended Omaha Beach. He was a professional soldier, commissioned into the 126th Infantry Regiment in 1909 at the age of 20, and fought in World War I. At the outbreak of World War II he was commander of the 90th Infantry Regiment. His successful leadership in the early campaigns resulted in his appointment to command the 168th Infantry Division in Russia on July 8, 1941, which he led until March 1943. He was transferred to the newly formed 355th Infantry Division, which he commanded until it was disbanded on November 6, 1943, due to the heavy losses it had suffered during the autumn fighting in Russia. Kraiss was then transferred to France to command the newly formed 352nd Infantry Division which was originally earmarked for the Eastern Front. He was wounded during the fighting near St Lô on August 2, 1944, dying of his wounds four days later.

AMERICAN COMMANDERS

Senior US commanders wanted an experienced unit to land at Omaha Beach and, not surprisingly, the "Big Red One" – the 1st Infantry Division – was selected. Led by Theodore Roosevelt Jr and the charismatic general Terry Allen in North Africa and Sicily, the division had developed a cocksure reputation. Its popular definition of the US Army was "the Big Red One and a million frigging replacements." Bradley relieved the popular Allen on Sicily in August 1943, replacing him with Major-General Clarence Huebner. Huebner was a veteran of the 1st Division in World War I, awarded the Distinguished Service Medal (DSM) for his courageous and skilled leadership of the 28th Infantry. Huebner, a strict disciplinarian, had a hard time asserting control after Allen was sacked. He imposed a strict training regime on the division when transferred to Britain and the rambunctious unit was finally won over. Huebner would later command V Corps under Patton in Germany in 1945.

The second Omaha Beach division, the 29th Infantry Division, had been commanded by Gerow until July 1943, when he was replaced by West Pointer and former cavalry officer Major-General Charles Gerhardt, who had been commissioned in 1917 and served on the staff of the 89th Division in World War I. Gerhardt's excellent performance as a cavalry brigade commander in the 1941 Louisiana maneuvers prompted Marshall to give him command of the new 91st Division. Gerhardt was a very traditional officer demanding a high level of discipline. His stern leadership of the 29th Division helped overcome the friction between the National Guard officers and troops, who formed the core of the unit, and the new influx of Regular Army officers and conscripts who had filled out the division for war.

In charge of the Engineer Special Brigades was Brigadier-General William Hoge. His role in the training and planning of the vital engineer operations at Omaha Beach is often overlooked and he would win greater fame for his leadership of Combat Command B of the 9th Armored Division during the battle for St Vith during the Ardennes campaign.

The tactical command of forces landing on D-Day was in the hands of the regimental leaders. The 1st Division's 16th Infantry Regiment was led by Lieutenant-Colonel George Taylor, an experienced veteran who had headed the regiment since the Tunisian campaign. The 29th Division's 116th Regiment was led by Lieutenant-Colonel Charles Canham, a strict, by-the-book West Pointer nicknamed "Stoneface" by his troops. Although widely

Antitank ditches were widely used along the D-Day beaches to channel the armor into killing zones and prevent exit off the beach. They were often filled with water, as seen in this example from Omaha Beach. *(NARA)*

Workers from Organization Todt scramble for cover as a US P-38 Lightning reconnaissance aircraft piloted by Lieutenant Albert Lanker makes a fast pass over the Normandy beaches on May 6, 1944, a month before the landings. The German construction teams continued to install more anti-invasion obstacles on the beaches until D-Day. *(NARA)*

disliked by the enlisted men before D-Day, Canham's heroic performance on Omaha Beach abruptly changed opinions. He had a BAR shot from his hands and fought the rest of the day with one arm in an improvised sling, a .45cal pistol in his good hand. Canham's role has been overshadowed by the presence of the division's assistant commander, Brigadier-General Norman "Dutch" Cota, who landed on the beach early in the day. Cota was the former chief of staff of the 1st Division and had fought in Tunisia. He was a charismatic combat commander, preferring to be in the field leading his troops rather than behind a desk.

Unlike most of the divisional and regimental commanders, the leader of the Ranger Provisional Group, Lieutenant-Colonel James E. Rudder, was not a professional soldier. Rudder had graduated from Texas A&M in 1932 and was commissioned a second lieutenant in the US Army reserves. He was a high school teacher until 1941, when he was called up to active duty and sent to the infantry school at Ft Benning. After further training at the Army Command and General Staff College in the autumn of 1942, he was posted to the 2nd Ranger Battalion, assuming command in the summer of 1943.

OPPOSING PLANS

AMERICAN PLAN

Omaha Beach was selected early in the *Overlord* planning, as at the time it was undefended. On the negative side, the bluffs along the beach formed a significant tactical obstacle and were well suited for defense. Even after Rommel began fortifying the beach in the autumn of 1943 it remained an attractive option, for it offered a deep-water anchorage only three-quarters

The commander of the 352nd Infantry Division defending Omaha Beach was Generalleutnant Dietrich Kraiss. *(NARA)*

of a mile from all parts of the beach with a full 36ft of water at low tide, making it an ideal location for an artificial harbor required for follow-on operations. The terrain behind the beach was much more suitable for motor transport than at neighboring Utah Beach. In February 1944, FUSA conducted a study of Omaha Beach which concluded that, if defended by an infantry regiment, the configuration of the beach would multiply the combat power of the German troops and present a formidable defensive position – assaulting it would likely result in heavy casualties. If it was defended by a full infantry division, it would be impregnable. The US Army, right up to the time of the landings, thought that the beach was only defended by a single, understrength, poor-quality regiment. As will be discussed further, this would prove to be the most significant mistake in the US plan. The German forces on Omaha Beach were more than three times the strength of those anticipated.

The 16th Infantry led the assault on the eastern sector of Omaha Beach, and its officers are seen here shortly before the landings. From left to right are: the regimental commander, Colonel George Taylor, Lieutenant Colonel Gibbs (7th Artillery Battalion), Lieutenant-Colonel Herbert Hicks (2nd Battalion), Lieutenant-Colonel Charles Horner (3rd Battalion), and Major Edmond Driscoll (1st Battalion). (*MHI*)

The critical necessity in the Operation *Neptune* plan was for tactical surprise. Allied planners were very concerned that if the Germans suspected a landing in Normandy, they would reinforce the area to the point where an amphibious assault would be impossible. The need for surprise affected the bombardment of the battlefield in the weeks before the landing. Since the Allies did not want to tip their hand, this precluded any concentrated bombardment of the assault beaches by either sea or air. For every bomb dropped in the Normandy area, two or more were dropped in the Pas-de-Calais and Picardy areas to continue the Operation *Fortitude* ruse. The risk of this strategic choice paid off at all the beaches except Omaha.

Operation *Neptune* contemplated a dawn landing at low tide due to Rommel's new beach defenses, which placed anti-boat obstacles in the water close to shore. A dawn landing would make it less likely that the Germans would discover the invasion fleet during its movement to the beaches. The landings were scheduled to begin on June 5, 1944, but were postponed due to foul weather in the Channel. Eisenhower rescheduled the assault for Tuesday, June 6, 1944, after Allied meteorological services had discovered a break in the weather that would last for several days. By this time, the enormous momentum of the operation also put pressure on Eisenhower to approve the attack, and his decision was reinforced by an intelligence report early in June from the Japanese ambassador in Berlin, which indicated that Hitler was still convinced the attack would come on the Pas-de-Calais.

The amphibious assault was a carefully choreographed plan calling for a series of preliminary though short bombardments of the coast followed by amphibious landings. The initial naval element of Operation *Neptune* at Omaha Beach was Force O. The naval forces for the American beaches were originally named Forces X and Y, but to make them more comprehensible they were switched first to "Omaha" and "Oklahoma," and then to their final names, Omaha and Utah, monikers that applied to the beaches as well. The bombardment ships consisted of two old battleships and three light cruisers, supported by 15 destroyers and numerous smaller ships and craft. The naval bombardment plan had three phases. At first light (0558hrs) the navy would begin the counterbattery phase, attacking all 14 known German artillery positions. Twenty minutes before the landings (H-20) the bombardment would shift to the attack of beach defenses, especially known fortifications. At H-hour, the fire would shift to targets behind the beachhead, or on the flanks. Admiral Hall was not happy with the "shoe-string naval force" allotted to Task Force O and he wanted more destroyers. Due to tidal conditions, the landings would begin at Omaha Beach before other beaches and as a result the naval bombardment would be significantly shorter, only 40 minutes. Task Force O had neither the time nor the resources to fulfill its bombardment mission.

Shortly after the naval bombardment began, the USAAF was scheduled to attack the defenses using heavy bombers. The bluff above the beach, the concrete emplacements in the draws (see below), and the areas behind the beach were the primary targets. Contrary to what many army troops believed, the plan did not call for attacks on the beach obstructions in order to avoid cratering the beach, since this would make it difficult later in the day to move motorized transport off the beach. This decision would prove to be one of the most crucial failures at Omaha Beach on D-Day.

The assistant commander of the 29th Division and one of the most conspicuous heroes of D-Day was Brigadier-General Norman "Dutch" Cota. He was appointed to command another National Guard division, the 28th, in August 1944 and led it during the gruesome Hürtgen forest fighting. He is seen here (right) with Dwight Eisenhower on November 9, 1944, wearing the keystone patch of the 28th Division. (*MHI*)

The Omaha Beach Bombardment Group included ten destroyers. This is USS *Thompson* (DD-627) commanded by Lieutenant-Commander A. L. Gebelin. She is seen here at the end of May 1944 being replenished at sea from the battleship USS *Arkansas* before setting off for Normandy. On D-Day the *Thompson* began by bombarding the Pointe-et-Raz-de-la-Percée and spent the afternoon providing fire support for the Rangers on Pointe-du-Hoc. *(NARA)*

The USAAF liked to advertise its precision bombing capabilities, but in reality the bomber commanders knew that there was still a considerable margin of error in their attacks, especially in poor weather. While collateral damage was of little concern when bombing German industrial targets, it was a significant concern when carrying out heavy strikes near US forces. The bombing mission required good weather for even modest precision and when the weather proved poor the air force changed the bombing tactics to limit any possible short-falls into the landing force. Due to the use of blind bombing (using radar for targeting), the air force commanders ordered the bombardiers to delay their bomb release by 30 seconds once the coast was picked up on radar. This guaranteed that the bombs would fall far from the coastline. The lack of contingency measures, such as the use of bombers under the cloud cover, was a major weakness of the plan, and the army had unrealistic expectations of the air force's capabilities. There were no plans to use the Ninth Air Force in close-support missions against the beach defenses, as the army lacked the communications to call in air strikes and no training had been undertaken.

Since the Allies expected to confront fortifications along the beach, armored support was deemed essential. In theory, each RCT would be preceded onto the beach by three companies of tanks to knock out any remaining bunkers not destroyed by the bomber attack. After the Dieppe experience, the British Army had developed an assortment of specialized tanks, dubbed "Funnies," to aid in amphibious assaults. The myth has developed over the years that the US Army spurned the use of these specialized tanks. In fact, by February 1944 the US Army had submitted a request for 25 Sherman Crab antimine flail tanks, 100 Sherman Crocodile flamethrower tanks, and other Sherman combat engineer equipment for *Overlord*. The original US plans expected the use of the Churchill AVRE (Armoured Vehicle Royal Engineers) to support the engineer breaching operations. None of these were provided in time for D-Day as British industry could barely keep pace with the needs of the British Army. Since it would take time for US industry to manufacture these, priority was given to those items deemed most necessary – the controversial Duplex Drive (DD) tanks. In place of the Churchill AVREs, V Corps was allotted 16 M4 dozer-tanks to assist the engineers.

The DD tank was a cover name for an amphibious version of the Sherman medium tank, and was developed in Britain as a means to bring tanks ashore without the need for landing craft. The attraction of this scheme was that the tanks could be sent ashore in the first waves in a less conspicuous and less vulnerable fashion than by using large landing craft. Buoyancy was provided by a large canvas flotation screen around the tank, which folded like an accordion when not in use. The DD tank's canvas screen had only a foot of freeboard when in the water and anything like rough seas threatened to collapse or swamp the fragile screen. A pair of propellers were added at the rear of the hull that were powered off the tank's engine. Since British firms could not produce these in adequate numbers, conversion kits were built by Firestone in the United States for M4A1 medium tanks. Of the 350 converted, about 80 tanks were transferred to British units to make up for shortages.

In past amphibious landings, such as those at Sicily and Salerno, the US Army had preferred to fit tanks with wading trunks, allowing them to be deposited by landing craft in shallow water beyond any beach obstructions and then drive ashore. This technique also allowed the tanks to fire at beach targets during their run into the beach on the landing craft, and they could remain in the surf, with their submerged hull protected by water, while engaging targets on the beach. The new DD tanks were greeted with skepticism by many US officers, who doubted their seaworthiness. The V Corps commander, Gerow, opposed their use and would have preferred to land both tank battalions on Omaha with wading trunks. As a result of these misgivings, the US tank battalions slated for Operation *Neptune* were mixed formations equipped with two companies of DD tanks to land in the

Omaha Beach – cross-sectional view

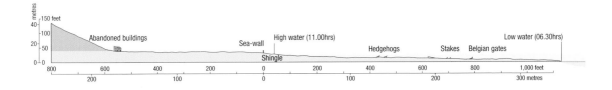

initial waves, and one company of tanks with wading trunks to land shortly afterward from Landing Craft, Tank (LCT) vessels. During pre-invasion exercises at Slapton Sands in Devon, England, a number of DD tanks sank, leading doubtful US Navy officials to insist on guidelines for launching them. An arrangement was reached under which the senior officer (army or navy) aboard the landing craft could make the judgment that the sea was too rough for the DD tanks to swim ashore and land them directly on the beach. The loophole in this procedure was that some of the young tank officers outranked the commanders of the landing craft, but lacked the experience to evaluate the sea conditions.

One mystery has been why the US Army at Normandy did not use amtracs (amphibious tractors) to land troops, as had been done in the Pacific theater since Tarawa in 1943. Bradley had brought back two of the best US divisional commanders from the Pacific to provide some seasoning to the European theater officers, and one of these, J. Lawton Collins, was assigned as the corps commander at the neighboring Utah Beach. The other, Major-General Charles Corlett, had landed with his 7th Division on Kwajalein in February 1944. Corlett arrived in the UK in April and was surprised to see that the landings would rely on Landing Craft, Vehicle, Personnel (LCVP) and Landing Craft, Assault (LCA) landing craft instead of the amtracs now favored in the Pacific. He approached both Eisenhower and Bradley about the issue, but plans were so far along that his opinions were dismissed. The failure to consider the lessons of the Pacific campaign was mainly due to the conviction of the army in Europe that they had much more experience in large-scale amphibious landings than the army in the Pacific or the US Marines. There had been no landings in the Pacific on the scale of North Africa, Sicily, Salerno, or Anzio and there would not be until after the Normandy landings. The amtracs had been used at Tarawa specifically to surmount the coral reef surrounding the atoll, and this was not a feature of the Normandy beaches. What the US Army commanders in Europe failed to realize and their Pacific counterparts had come to recognize was that the amtracs were a necessity when landing on a contested, fortified beach. The amtracs could put the infantry ashore at the seawall, minimizing their exposure to small-arms fire as they struggled from the landing craft, waded through the surf, and raced across hundreds of yards of beach. In fact, the US Army had shipped over 300 amtracs to Europe in 1944, but the lack of demand for their use in the *Overlord* plan meant that they were reserved for Operation *Swordhilt*, a contingency operation in which Patton's uncommitted Third Army was intended to reinforce *Overlord* in the event of a failure at one of the beaches.

American planning for Operation *Neptune* did not pay enough attention to a key difference between Normandy and previous landings in the Mediterranean, namely the fortified coast. None of the 1943 landings were contested on the shoreline and none involved landings against obstructed beaches. Normandy required tactics and equipment comparable to those for operations against fortifications. While considerable effort went into providing large numbers of engineers to tackle the fortifications at Normandy, neither the M4 tanks nor bulldozers were equipped to survive on a constricted beach targeted by numerous antitank guns. In February 1944, the US Army in Europe had requested an assault tank version of the M4A3 medium tank with sufficient armor to confront German bunkers on the Siegfried Line later in the European campaign. This request resulted in the M4A3E2 assault tank, which could withstand frontal hits from 88mm antitank guns, the largest gun encountered in Normandy. These might have made a difference on D-Day had there been more appreciation of the vulnerability of the existing M4 tank to contemporary German antitank guns. As it transpired, the M4A3E2 did not arrive in Europe until the autumn, but did prove very effective in the Siegfried Line campaign. The British already had an effective support tank in their thickly armored Churchill infantry tank and it was used with success on D-Day, including a specialized combat engineer version – the AVRE.

The other specialized forces landing in the first waves were the Gap Assault Teams (GATs), of which 16 were assigned to Omaha Beach. They were to blast gaps 50 yards wide through the beach obstructions to allow landing craft to continue to reach the beach once the tide began to rise. Owing to the rising tide, the plan gave these teams only about 30 minutes to carry out their tasks. Theirs

These US Army combat engineers are seen on the way to their landing craft in England, carrying bangalore torpedoes in their arms along with a pair of satchel charges and reels of primacord. They lack the distinctive Engineer Special Brigade markings on their helmets and so may be from the Gap Assault Teams. *(NARA)*

V Corps D-Day Objectives

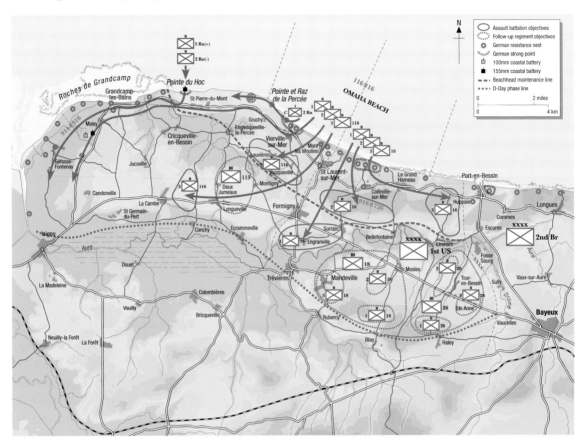

was a vital mission, for if the gaps were not cleared, the underwater obstacles would prevent follow-up landings by later waves of craft.

The main landings were to be conducted by two RCTs each consisting of an infantry regiment with attached engineers and other support troops. The left (eastern) flank would be assaulted by the 16th RCT based around the 16th Infantry Regiment, 1st Division, while the right (western) flank would be assaulted by the 116th RCT, based around the 116th Infantry, 29th Division. The engineers in the first wave were mainly from the divisional engineer battalions, but follow-on waves contained the 5th and 6th Provisional Engineer Brigades to assist in preparing the beach for follow-on forces and supplies. The tasks of the engineers included clearing the beach obstacles (for example, using bangalore torpedoes to open gaps in wire obstructions), clearing lanes through minefields to provide the infantry with exits off the beach, and destroying German fortifications. After the Dieppe experience, the British Army felt that combat engineers required armored support in the form of flail tanks to conduct minefield clearance, and specialized Churchill tanks with petard mortars for demolition work. The US Army ignored the use of armored engineer vehicles, except for armored bulldozers, due to a lack of experience in this type of operation.

The Ranger Provisional Brigade was assigned the most perilous mission of the assault – the capture of the German artillery battery on Pointe-du-Hoc on the western edge of the assault area. This heavily fortified battery could strike both Utah and Omaha Beaches and Bradley deemed it essential that it be eliminated. Unfortunately, it was located on a promontory with cliffs all around. One officer remarked that an attacking force could be swept off the cliffs by "three old women with brooms." Pointe-du-Hoc was scheduled to receive special treatment from the naval bombardment force in advance of the Ranger attack, but American commanders thought it was the single most difficult aspect of the attack on Omaha Beach.

After the first two RCTs landed at dawn, additional reinforcements would arrive in successive waves, bringing the total to four RCTs by midday. Force B would arrive in the afternoon, which would increase the strength on Omaha Beach to two reinforced divisions, with a third division to land on D+1. Allied intelligence had detected the German 352nd Infantry Division around St Lô and anticipated that it would begin to move against the beachhead sometime on D-Day, and might reach the River Aure or even cross it on the afternoon of D-Day. However, the plan expected that it would delay, but not stop the advance to the D+1 positions.

A group from the 2nd Rangers enjoy Red Cross coffee and donuts in Weymouth, England, shortly before loading aboard their landing craft. They have their M5 assault gas-mask bags slung on their chests, a common practice on D-Day. (NARA)

GERMAN PLAN

The defenses along Omaha Beach increased continually after the autumn of 1943 when Rommel was put in charge of reinvigorating the Atlantic Wall. Although Hitler and most senior German commanders expected the main invasion to take place on the Pas-de-Calais, Rommel believed that a case could be made for landings on the Normandy coast, or in Brittany around Montagne d'Aree. As a result, he ordered the construction of defenses along the most likely areas of coastline and increased the forces ready to defend the coast. Defenses in Normandy were initially based around the 716th Infantry Division, a poor-quality, static division. Omaha Beach was patrolled by a single regiment of this division.

Rommel believed that the sea itself was the best defensive barrier and the terrain around Omaha Beach presented ample defensive opportunities. The initial defensive work began at the water's edge with the construction of obstructions against landing craft. The outer barrier, about 100 yards above the low-tide mark and 275yds from the seawall, consisted of a string of steel obstructions, called Cointet gates by the Germans and Belgian gates or Element C by the Allies. These were designed to block landing craft from approaching the beach. The next line of barriers about 30 yards closer to shore were wooden stakes that were planted in the sand facing seaward and buttressed like an enormous tripod. These stakes were usually surmounted by a Tellermine 42 antitank mine – the obstacles were designed to blow holes in the bottom of landing craft. In some sectors these were followed by

Rommel watches as German soldiers construct beach obstacles during a tour of Normandy in March 1944. The lack of enough laborers forced German infantry divisions along the coast to spend more time in the spring of 1944 doing construction work than training. *(MHI)*

Among the most effective defenses on Omaha Beach were the Bauform 667 gun casemates. These bunkers were positioned for enfilade fire along the beach and had a protective wall in front to shield them from bombardment from the sea. This particular example was part of the WN65 strongpoint defending the E-1 St Laurent draw on Easy Red beach and fitted with a 50mm PaK 38 antitank gun. The gouge at the top was caused by naval gunfire, but the gun was knocked out when engaged by a pair of M15A1 multiple gun motor carriage halftracks of the 467th AAA Battalion. (NARA)

Hemmkurven, called ramp obstacles by the Allies, which were curved steel structures designed to obstruct the landing craft. Finally there was a row of hedgehogs of various types. The most common was the *Tschechenigel*, called "Rommel's Asparagus" by the Allies, which was an anti-craft/antitank obstruction made from steel beams. The obstructions on the tidal flats were primarily intended to prevent the approach of landing craft to the seawall during high tide. These were submerged and invisible at high tide, preventing landing craft crews from steering easily through any gaps. There were a total of 3,700 obstacles at Omaha Beach – the highest density of any of the D-Day beaches.

At the high-water mark was a swathe of shingle – round stones the size of golf balls – sometimes backed by a seawall. One or more rows of concertina wire or other barbed-wire obstructions were placed immediately inland from this. Until the autumn of 1943, there were many small beach houses and other structures along the shoreline for vacationers and local residents. These were knocked down to deprive Allied infantry of cover. A few of the more substantial buildings along the shore were left intact, but were converted into infantry strongpoints. The beach area was heavily mined, though gaps that contained no mines were also marked with minefield warnings to confuse Allied troops.

In contrast to the other four Normandy beaches, which are relatively flat, Omaha Beach is characterized by its bluffs rising up to 150ft from the sea, most noticeably on its western side. The edges of these bluffs provide

German Defenses – Omaha Beach

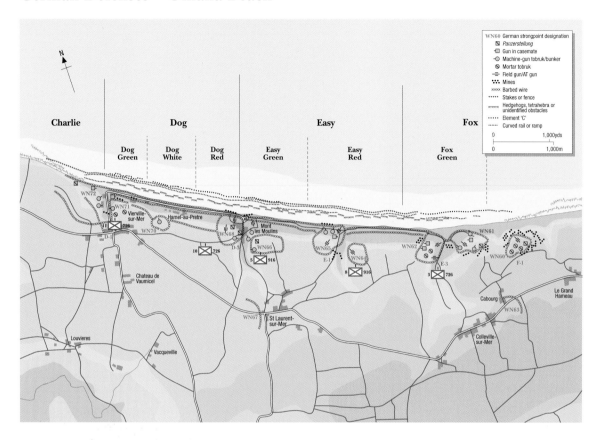

ideal defensive positions for infantry, with clear fields of fire on the exposed troops below. On some of the cliffs on the eastern side of the beach, 240mm artillery shells were dangled over the cliff with trip-wires to serve as booby-traps for any infantry attempting the climb. These were called "roller-grenades" and they were spaced some 330ft apart.

Access from the beach was limited to five gullies (called "draws" by the US Army), and only two of these were readily passable by armored vehicles or motor transport. These became the central focus of German defenses at Omaha Beach. Since the tactical objective of the defense was to prevent the Allies from moving off the beach, all five draws were stiffly defended by establishing a fortified belt in and around them. Fourteen strongpoints (*Wiederstandnester*), numbered WN60 through WN73, were created along the beach. Most of the draws were covered by a strongpoint on the hilltops on either side of the draw. Two other strongpoints were constructed on the Pointe-et-Raz-de-la-Percée promontory on the eastern side of the beach to provide enfilading fire along the beach, and the three other strongpoints were constructed immediately behind the beach, covering the exits from the draws.

The configuration of each of these strongpoints differed according to terrain, and they were still being built when the Allies landed on June 6, 1944. Generally they consisted of small pillboxes, or concrete-reinforced "Tobruk" machine-gun pits, at the base of the bluff obstructing the entrances to the draws. The larger draws were also blocked by barrier walls, antitank ditches, and antitank traps. One of the most effective defenses were the Bauform 667 antitank gun bunkers built into the sides of the bluffs, with their guns pointed parallel to the beach. These bunkers had a defensive wall on the side facing the sea that made it very difficult for warships to engage them with gunfire. By careful positioning they prevented Allied tanks from entering the draw, as they could hit the tanks on their vulnerable side armor from point-blank range and, furthermore, the guns were positioned to fire in defilade down the length of the beach. The bunkers often contained older antitank guns, such as the obsolete PaK38 50mm. However, such weapons were more than adequate to penetrate the side armor of the Sherman tank and they were also effective against landing craft. In total, there were eight antitank gun bunkers along Omaha Beach, including two 88mm guns. Apart from the fully enclosed antitank guns, there were three 50mm antitank guns on pedestal mounts in concrete pits, and ten other antitank guns and field guns in open pits in the various strongpoints. As an additional defensive installation, the turrets from obsolete French and

One of the more common defensive works in Normandy was this type of 50mm gun pit. The obsolete 50mm PaK 38 antitank gun was mounted on a new pintle for easier traverse and deployed within a concrete emplacement. There were three of these along Omaha Beach and many more inland, like this example on the approaches to Cherbourg. (NARA)

The artillery regiment of the 352nd Infantry Division was deployed in field emplacements about 6 miles behind the beach, as was the case with this 105mm leFH 18/40. Pre-sighted on targets along the beach, they proved to be one of the German defenders' most effective weapons on D-Day. *(NARA)*

German tanks were mounted over concrete bunkers. There were five of these on Omaha Beach, the heaviest concentration being in WN66/68 covering the D-3 Les Moulins draw. Generally, the strongpoints had a mixture of these types of firing positions. For example, the WN61/62 strongpoint at the E-3 Colleville draw had two 75mm PaK 40 antitank guns in casemates to enfilade the beach, two 50mm antitank guns on pedestals in open concrete emplacements, a 50mm mortar Tobruk, and six machine-gun Tobruks.

Around these fortifications, the German infantry dug out a series of trenches as a first step to creating a series of interlocking shelters and protected passages. However, the shortage of concrete in the spring of 1944 meant that only a small portion of these trench lines were concrete-reinforced. The construction of these defenses was hampered by the haphazard priorities of the Wehrmacht, Luftwaffe, and Organization Todt. The Luftwaffe, for example, built an elaborate concrete shelter for its radar station on the neighboring Pointe-et-Raz-de-la-Percée that was absolutely useless in protecting the radar from any form of attack. At the same time, many key infantry trenches on the bluffs, lacking concrete reinforcement, flooded during spring rain and were rendered useless by the time of the attack.

Of all the defenses near Omaha Beach, by far the most fortified was the Pointe-du-Hoc. The site was originally constructed to contain six 155mm guns in open gun emplacements, but the defense was being reconstructed to protect

Normandy had lower priority than the Pas-de-Calais for concrete, so many of the German infantry positions were ordinary slit trenches, like these from the WN66 strongpoint on the east shoulder of D-3 Les Moulins draw. *(NARA)*

each gun with a fully enclosed Bauform 671 ferro-concrete casemate. In addition, the site contained a fully enclosed artillery observation point on the seaward side of the promontory and fully protected crew shelters and ammunition bunkers.

Due to Rommel's tactical approach, most of the German tactical defenses were spread as a thin crust along the shoreline with very modest reserve forces behind the main line of resistance. On D-Day itself the tactical plan would simply be to hold the invading force on the beach with the resources at hand.

The most powerful weapons on Omaha Beach were two 88mm PaK 43/41 *Scheunentor* ("barn door") guns. These were located in casemates, but one was moved out of the bunker after the landings, as seen here. *(NARA)*

OPPOSING ARMIES

GERMAN FORCES

The 716th Infantry Division had garrisoned Omaha Beach, called the Grandcamps sector by the Germans, since June 1942. This understrength, static division was spread from Carentan to the Orne estuary and, therefore, was defending all of the Normandy beaches except Utah in the west. The 726th Grenadier Regiment (GR.726) was responsible for covering the Omaha Beach area in 1942–43. Of the 58 divisions under OB West on June 6, 1944, 33 were static or reserve divisions. The troops in these static divisions tended to be older conscripts, typically about 35 years old. The fourth battalion of the GR.726 was the 439th Ost Battalion, made up of former Red Army troops. The division was significantly understrength, with only about 7,000 troops compared to a nominal strength of over 12,000. On the other hand, most of its forces were deployed in bunkers or field fortifications with a large number of supplementary weapons, including 197 machine-gun pits, 12 antitank rifles, 75 medium mortars, and 249 flamethrowers.

On March 15, 1944 the 352nd Infantry Division was ordered to take over defense of the Bayeux sector of the Normandy beaches as part of Rommel's effort to strengthen the defenses in this sector. This division had been formed in December 1943 near St Lô from the remnants of the battered 321st Infantry Division, which had been sent back from Russia to rebuild. The new division was organized as a Type 44 infantry division and most of its personnel were recent conscripts from the classes of 1925/26, meaning young men 18–19 years old. Unlike the old 716th Infantry Division, the 352nd Infantry Division was at full strength. It consisted of three infantry regiments, each with two rifle battalions with their companies numbered 1 through 4 and 5 through 8 respectively. The 13th Company was a cannon company for direct-fire support; it was equipped with two 150mm and six 75mm infantry howitzers. The 14th Company in each regiment was an antitank unit with Panzerschreck antitank rocket launchers. The 1944 divisional structure substituted a fusilier regiment for the old reconnaissance battalion, with one company on bicycles and one company motorized. The division's artillery regiment had four battalions, three with 12 105mm howitzers each and the fourth with 12 150mm guns. The division's antitank battalion had a company with 14 PzJg 38(t) Ausf. M Marder III tank-destroyers, another with ten StuG III assault guns, and a third with improvised 37mm guns on Opel trucks. Divisional training was hamstrung by the lack of fuel and ammunition as well as by the need to divert the troops to work on field fortifications to reinforce the Atlantic Wall. There was little opportunity for training above company level. This unit was reasonably well trained by German 1944 standards, though not by US Army standards. The 1944 German infantry division had less manpower than its US counterpart, but more firepower, especially in automatic weapons.

The reconfiguration of the defenses along the Bayeux coast in late March 1944 more than tripled their strength. The Omaha Beach area that had been held by two battalions from GR.726 was now reinforced by two regiments of

German Forces in the Grandcamps Sector, 6 June 1944

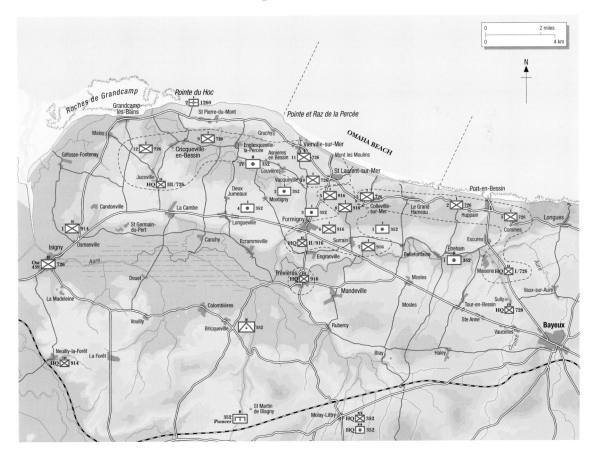

A young German infantryman enjoys a cup of coffee while on the way to a POW camp in England after having been captured in Normandy. The troops of the 352nd Infantry Division were mostly 18–19-year-old conscripts, with their tactical training cut short by the need to do construction work on beach defenses for the three months they were stationed along the Atlantic coast prior to D-Day. *(NARA)*

the 352nd Infantry Division along the coastline and a reinforced regiment as corps reserve within a few hours' march of the coast. The two battalions of GR.726 in the Omaha Beach sector were subordinated to the headquarters of the 352nd Infantry Division and retained their mission of manning the coastal emplacements and trenches along the beach. The GR.914 was responsible for the Isigny/Pointe-du-Hoc sector west of Omaha Beach, while GR.916 was responsible for the Omaha Beach sector as well as the eastern section of Gold Beach. The third regiment, GR.915, and the division's 352nd Fusilier Battalion, were formed into Kampfgruppe Meyer and stationed behind the coast near St Lô to serve as the corps reserve.

The reinforced 352nd Infantry Division, however, was responsible for defending 33 miles of coastline, far beyond what was considered prudent in German tactical doctrine. This led to a number of arguments between Rommel and the divisional commander, Generalleutnant Kraiss. Rommel wanted all of the infantry companies deployed along the main line of resistance so they could fire on landing Allied troops. Kraiss wanted to adopt a more conventional defense with a relatively thin screen along the beach and most of the companies held in reserve behind the bluffs from where they could counterattack any penetrations. In the end a compromise was reached. In the Omaha Beach sector one of its infantry battalions moved up to the coastline and deployed two of its companies in the forward defenses alongside GR.726, with the other companies in the villages a few miles from the beach. The other battalion formed a reserve for the regimental sector along with the division's self-propelled antitank battalion.

In terms of artillery support, Omaha Beach was also covered by I Battalion, 352nd Artillery Regiment (I./AR.352) headquartered at Etreham with three batteries of 105mm howitzers. This battalion had forward observation posts located in bunkers along the coast, significantly enhancing the deadliness of their guns when employed against targets on Omaha Beach. The II./AR.352, headquartered to the east at St Clement, also had Omaha Beach in range. The artillery battalions were provided with only one unit of fire, meaning 225 rounds per 105mm howitzer and 150 rounds for each 150mm gun. No resupply was available for a few days. The final element of the artillery in this sector was added on May 9, 1944 when a battery of heavy artillery rockets (*Nebelwerfer*) of the 84th Werfer Regiment was positioned in this sector. Behind the 352nd Infantry Division was the 1st Flak-Sturm Regiment of the Luftwaffe 11th Flak Division, adding 36 88mm guns to the defense of this sector.

Allied intelligence personnel believed that the entire 352nd Infantry Division was in corps reserve around St Lô when in fact only one of its three infantry regiments was in reserve on June 6, 1944. To explain its appearance in the fighting on Omaha Beach on D-Day, the myth developed that the

German Forces, Grandcamps Sector, June 6, 1944

German Supreme Commander – Adolf Hitler
German Commander-in-Chief (West) – Generalfeldmarschall Gerd von Rundstedt
German Army Group B – Generalfeldmarschall Erwin Rommel
German Seventh Army – Generaloberst Freidrich Dollmann

352nd Infantry Division – Generalleutnant Dietrich Kraiss

914th Grenadier Regiment – Oberstleutnant Ernst Heyna
    I Battalion
    II Battalion
915th Grenadier Regiment – Oberstleutnant Karl Meyer
(detached to corps reserve)
    I Battalion
    II Battalion
916th Grenadier Regiment – Oberstleutnant Ernst Göth
    I Battalion
    II Battalion
726th Infantry Regiment – Oberstleutnant Walter Korfes
(from 716th Infantry Division)
    I Battalion
    III Battalion
    439th Ost Battalion
352nd Artillery Regiment – Oberstleutnant Karl Ocker
    I Battalion
    II Battalion
    III Battalion
    IV Battalion

352nd Fusilier Battalion (detached to corps reserve)
352nd Panzerjäger Battalion
352nd Pioneer Battalion

division had been deployed near the beach to conduct training a few days before D-Day. This was not the case; the division had been in place near Omaha Beach for more than two months before D-Day.

On the Pointe-du-Hoc promontory between Omaha and Utah beaches was the 2nd Battery of the 1260th Army Coastal Artillery Regiment (2./HKAA.1260) equipped with six French 155mm guns and five light machine-guns. By June 1944, four of six casemates for the guns had been completed, but heavy Allied bombing raids had reduced the ground around the batteries to a lunar landscape of craters. After the April 25, 1944, bombing, the battery had withdrawn its guns from the casemates to an orchard south of the point. In their place the crews had fabricated dummy guns from timbers that fooled Allied intelligence into thinking the guns were still present. At the time of the invasion the concrete emplacements around the forward observation bunker were reinforced by a company from GR.726.

Luftwaffe support for the beach defenses was nonexistent. On June 4, 1944, Luftflotte 3 had 183 day-fighters in northern France of which 160 were serviceable. There were few ground-attack aircraft due to the policy of hoarding these units on the Eastern Front. Allied air attacks on forward airfields were so intense that on June 5, 124 fighters were withdrawn from the coast to bases further inland and the supplies and support for these aircraft were not available until June 6 or 7.

A young GI from the 1st Infantry Division on the way to Normandy. He is wearing the distinctive assault jacket worn by the initial waves at Omaha Beach, and his M1 carbine is in plastic wrap to protect it from water. To the left is a pole charge for attacking pillboxes while to the right is an M1A1 bazooka. In front of him are pack charges and behind him bangalore torpedoes, all tied to inflated life belts to provide buoyancy in the water. *(NARA)*

AMERICAN FORCES

The US plan for Omaha Beach began with an attack by a single division which would expand to two divisions by the afternoon. Rather than land the two divisions in column, the left flank of the assault force was the 16th RCT from the 1st Infantry Division, while the right flank was the 116th RCT from the 29th Division, but subordinated for the initial phase of the operation to the 1st Infantry Division.

The 1st Infantry Division, named "Big Red One" after its shoulder patch, was the army's most experienced division and had been personally selected for the landings by Bradley. The division had already fought in North Africa and on Sicily and was one of the few divisions in the UK with any combat experience. In view of its

An assault section of the 16th RCT, 1st Division loads onto its LCVP on the USS *Samuel Chase* on D-Day. The assault waves were rail loaded on the assault transports rather than using rope ladders due to the weight of equipment they carried. Judging from the light, this is probably the second assault wave. *(NARA)*

excellent performance in repulsing a German Panzer attack on the Gela beachhead on Sicily a year before, the 16th Infantry was a natural choice for the initial assault wave.

The 29th Division was nicknamed the "Blue and Gray" for its shoulder patch, symbolizing an amalgamation of the Union and Confederate traditions. This National Guard division was headquartered in Baltimore, Maryland, which as a mid-Atlantic border state between north and south meant that the division drew its units from both Maryland and Virginia. As with nearly all National Guard divisions, the Regular Army insisted on filling out its senior command posts with professional officers, as the National Guard had the reputation for granting ranks as political sinecures. It was also necessary to flesh out the division with conscripts. There was some friction in the unit between the Guardsmen, who were often neighbors with years of peacetime service together, and the new influx of Regular Army officers and conscripts. Gebhardt's strict training regimen in the UK before D-Day was intended to forge the division into a cohesive fighting force and the 29th Division proved to be one of the better National Guard divisions during the subsequent fighting in France. Each RCT was allotted a tank battalion for fire support, the 741st Tank Battalion in support of the 16th RCT and the 743rd Tank Battalion supporting the 116th RCT.

The task of eliminating the German artillery battery on Pointe-du-Hoc was assigned to the Provisional Ranger Group, consisting of the elite 2nd and 5th Ranger Battalions. Since the battery was located on a clifftop the battalion developed a number of unique solutions for quickly scaling the cliffs under fire. Ladders were fitted inside the cargo holds of DUKW

Order of Battle: US Forces, Omaha Beach

Allied Supreme Commander – General Dwight D. Eisenhower

V Corps – Major-General Leonard T. Gerow

>1st Infantry Division – Major-General Clarence R. Huebner
>29th Infantry Division – Major-General Charles H. Gebhardt
>Provisional Ranger Group – Lieutenant-Colonel James Rudder
>5th Engineer Special Brigade - Colonel William Bridges
>6th Engineer Special Brigade - Colonel Paul Thompson

Force O

16th Regimental Combat Team

>16th Infantry Regiment – Colonel George Taylor
>741st Tank Battalion
>Special Engineer Task Force (b)
>7th Field Artillery Battalion
>62nd Armored Field Artillery Battalion
>197th Antiaircraft Battalion (AWSP)
>1st Engineer Battalion
>5th Engineer Special Brigade (-)
>20th Engineer Combat Battalion
>81st Chemical Weapons Battalion (motorized)

116th Regimental Combat Team

>116th Infantry Regiment – Colonel Charles Canham
>2nd Ranger Battalion
>5th Ranger Battalion
>743rd Tank Battalion
>Special Engineer Task Force
>58th Armored Field Artillery Battalion
>111th Field Artillery Battalion
>6th Engineer Special Brigade (-)
>112th Engineer Combat Battalion
>121st Engineer Battalion
>81st Chemical Weapons Battalion
>467th Automatic Antiaircraft Weapons Battalion (SP)
>461st Amphibious Truck Company

18th Regimental Combat Team

>18th Infantry Regiment – Colonel George Smith Jr
>745th Tank Battalion
>32nd Field Artillery Battalion
>5th Field Artillery Battalion
>5th Engineer Special Brigade (-)

Force B

115th Regimental Combat Team
115th Infantry Regiment – Colonel Eugene Slappey
110th Field Artillery Battalion

175th Regimental Combat Team

175th Infantry Regiment – Colonel Paul Goode

26th Regimental Combat Team

26th Infantry Regiment–Colonel John Seitz
33rd Field Artillery Battalion

amphibious trucks. These ladders were difficult to operate unless located firmly against the base of the cliff, so the Rangers also developed a rocket-fired grapnel hook using standard 2in rockets and portable projectors. The assault teams also carried climbing rope and lightweight ladders. The main assault would be conducted by the 225 men of Force A, with Companies E and F, 2nd Rangers, scaling the eastern side of Pointe-du-Hoc, and Company D on the western side. Force B, based on D/2nd Rangers, would scale the cliffs on the neighboring Pointe-et-Raz-de-la-Percée promontory to eliminate German positions there. Force C, consisting of the remainder of 2nd Rangers and the 5th Rangers, would remain offshore during the initial assault, reinforcing Force A if the mission proceeded according to plan, but landing with the 116th RCT if the mission failed in order to assault Pointe-du-Hoc from the landward side. The Pointe-du-Hoc mission was widely considered the most dangerous of any assignment on D-Day – the reason the Rangers were given the job.

The other key elements in the assault waves were the GATs of the Special Engineer Task Force. Each of these 16 teams was formed by combining a 13-man Naval Combat Demolition Unit (NCDU) with a 28-man army engineer unit. The latter were drawn from the two units supporting the assault wave: the 146th and 299th Engineer Combat Battalions. The task of each team was to blow a gap 50 yards wide in the beach obstructions to permit later waves of landing craft to pass through the obstacles when the tide rose. Each team was allotted an M4 tank-dozer that arrived separately on an LCT.

D-DAY ON OMAHA

THE INITIAL OPERATIONS

D-Day was originally scheduled to begin on June 5, but the appalling weather in the Channel forced a postponement until June 6. The German meteorology service in the Atlantic had been rolled-up by determined Allied action in the preceding months and most senior German commanders were convinced that any landing operations would be impossible for several days until the weather cleared. As a result, Rommel was in Germany and a number of senior commanders were away from their posts conducting staff exercises. Generaloberst Dollman had lowered the alert status of all of his troops, believing that the foul weather would preclude any Allied activity.

Around 2215hrs on June 5, the intelligence sections of several German headquarters picked up a coded radio message to the French Resistance indicating that the invasion would begin in the next 48 hours. Some reconnaissance aircraft were sent to sweep the Channel, but many officers thought it was a false alarm. Seventh Army in Normandy was not alerted.

At 0030hrs Allied minesweepers began to clear paths through anticipated minefields, guided by markers placed on the beaches by midget submarines. In fact, the Germans had not yet established any significant minefields off Omaha Beach. At 0300hrs Task Force O arrived 25,000 yards off Omaha Beach and dropped anchor to prepare the landing craft. At 0330hrs the assault troops were called to their debarkation posts on the assault transports and loaded into the landing craft at 0415hrs. The landing craft gradually set off from the assault transports over the next hour, aiming to arrive at the rendezvous point by 0600hrs. The sea was choppy, with 3–4ft waves and an occasional interference wave as high as 6ft. The wind was gusting from the northwest at 10–18 knots. As a result, more than half of the assault troops were seriously seasick even before the final approach to the beach.

Wehrmacht units were alerted at 0100hrs when LXXXIV Corps headquarters first learned of paratroop drops in neighboring sectors of the

LCVPs begin the move to shore on D-Day under the watchful eye of the USS *Augusta*, flagship of the Western Task Force. The landing craft had a 12-mile run to shore in seas with 3–4ft waves. The navy censor has partly obscured the cruiser's radar masts in this photo. *(NARA)*

716th Infantry Division. Although Omaha Beach was not in the landing zone of the 82nd or 101st Airborne Divisions, the dispersion of the drop resulted in small numbers of paratroopers landing in the GR.914 positions west of Omaha Beach and near the artillery batteries of II./AR.352 behind the beach. Through the early morning hours, reports flowed in of paratroop and glider landings in neighboring sectors. At 0310hrs General Marcks ordered the corps reserve, Kampfgruppe Meyer, to begin moving toward Montmartin-Deville in order to keep open the routes between the 709th Division at Utah Beach and the 352nd Division at Omaha. The decision to send the reserves after the paratroopers proved to be premature and a serious mistake. Later in the morning the force would be badly needed in the opposite direction. As a result, Kampfgruppe Meyer spent most of the morning marching westward, only to have its orders changed a few hours later, whereupon it had to about turn and march eastward, all the while under air attack. The division's artillery positions began to come under air attack around 0320hrs, with especially heavy attacks on Pointe-du-Hoc around 0335. Darkness shrouded the Allied naval force and visibility was only about 10 miles, not enough to see the anchorage. The first reports of Allied naval vessels came from the right flank of the division positions at 0502hrs and by 0520hrs large numbers of Allied naval vessels had been spotted moving over the horizon.

Task Force O began to approach Omaha Beach and the battleships and destroyers began the preliminary naval bombardment at 0545hrs, lasting until 0625hrs. Many inland German positions reported these as air attacks. The initial targets were behind the beach and at dawn the warships shifted their sights to specific targets along the beach. Aerial bombardment of positions behind the beach was scheduled to begin at 0600hrs, but the decision to delay bomb release for 30 seconds after passing over the coast

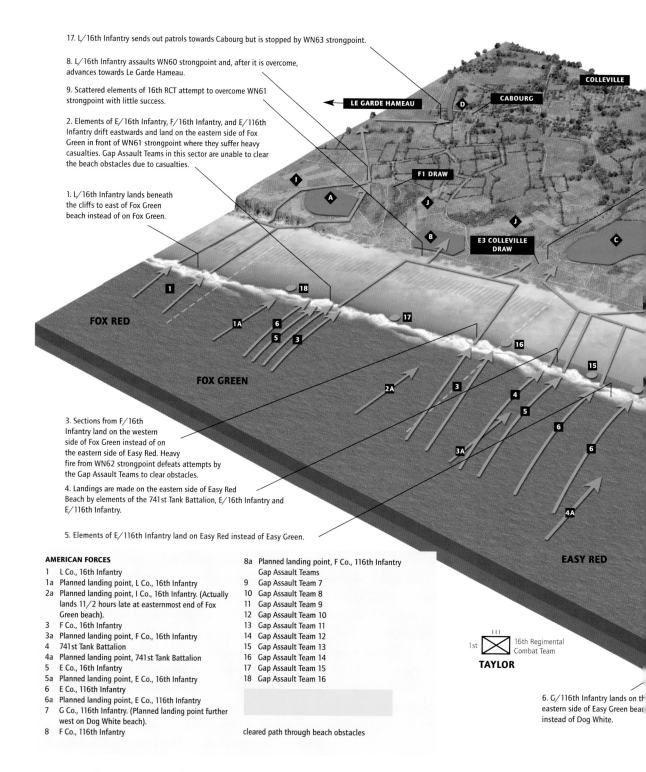

17. L/16th Infantry sends out patrols towards Cabourg but is stopped by WN63 strongpoint.

8. L/16th Infantry assaults WN60 strongpoint and, after it is overcome, advances towards Le Garde Hameau.

9. Scattered elements of 16th RCT attempt to overcome WN61 strongpoint with little success.

2. Elements of E/16th Infantry, F/16th Infantry, and E/116th Infantry drift eastwards and land on the eastern side of Fox Green in front of WN61 strongpoint where they suffer heavy casualties. Gap Assault Teams in this sector are unable to clear the beach obstacles due to casualties.

1. L/16th Infantry lands beneath the cliffs to east of Fox Green beach instead of on Fox Green.

3. Sections from F/16th Infantry land on the western side of Fox Green instead of on the eastern side of Easy Red. Heavy fire from WN62 strongpoint defeats attempts by the Gap Assault Teams to clear obstacles.

4. Landings are made on the eastern side of Easy Red Beach by elements of the 741st Tank Battalion, E/16th Infantry and E/116th Infantry.

5. Elements of E/116th Infantry land on Easy Red instead of Easy Green.

COLLEVILLE

CABOURG

LE GARDE HAMEAU

F1 DRAW

E3 COLLEVILLE DRAW

FOX RED

FOX GREEN

EASY RED

AMERICAN FORCES

1	L Co., 16th Infantry
1a	Planned landing point, L Co., 16th Infantry
2a	Planned landing point, I Co., 16th Infantry. (Actually lands 1 1/2 hours late at easternmost end of Fox Green beach).
3	F Co., 16th Infantry
3a	Planned landing point, F Co., 16th Infantry
4	741st Tank Battalion
4a	Planned landing point, 741st Tank Battalion
5	E Co., 16th Infantry
5a	Planned landing point, E Co., 16th Infantry
6	E Co., 116th Infantry
6a	Planned landing point, E Co., 116th Infantry
7	G Co., 116th Infantry. (Planned landing point further west on Dog White beach).
8	F Co., 116th Infantry

8a	Planned landing point, F Co., 116th Infantry Gap Assault Teams
9	Gap Assault Team 7
10	Gap Assault Team 8
11	Gap Assault Team 9
12	Gap Assault Team 10
13	Gap Assault Team 11
14	Gap Assault Team 12
15	Gap Assault Team 13
16	Gap Assault Team 14
17	Gap Assault Team 15
18	Gap Assault Team 16

cleared path through beach obstacles

1st ⊠ 16th Regimental Combat Team

TAYLOR

6. G/116th Infantry lands on the eastern side of Easy Green beach instead of Dog White.

Omaha Beach 16th Regimental Combat Team Sector

June 6, 1944, 0630hrs onwards, viewed from the northwest showing 16th RCT's landings on "Fox" and "Easy" beaches, the eastern sector of Omaha Beach. The first wave suffers heavy casualties but with the arrival of the second wave US troops begin to climb the bluffs and overcome the German defenses.

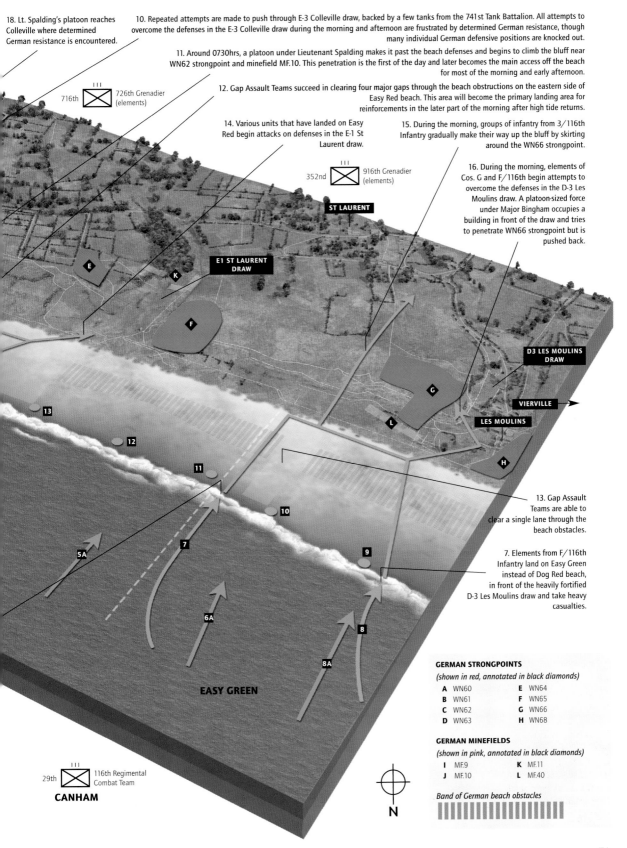

18. Lt. Spalding's platoon reaches Colleville where determined German resistance is encountered.

10. Repeated attempts are made to push through E-3 Colleville draw, backed by a few tanks from the 741st Tank Battalion. All attempts to overcome the defenses in the E-3 Colleville draw during the morning and afternoon are frustrated by determined German resistance, though many individual German defensive positions are knocked out.

11. Around 0730hrs, a platoon under Lieutenant Spalding makes it past the beach defenses and begins to climb the bluff near WN62 strongpoint and minefield MF.10. This penetration is the first of the day and later becomes the main access off the beach for most of the morning and early afternoon.

12. Gap Assault Teams succeed in clearing four major gaps through the beach obstructions on the eastern side of Easy Red beach. This area will become the primary landing area for reinforcements in the later part of the morning after high tide returns.

14. Various units that have landed on Easy Red begin attacks on defenses in the E-1 St Laurent draw.

15. During the morning, groups of infantry from 3/116th Infantry gradually make their way up the bluff by skirting around the WN66 strongpoint.

16. During the morning, elements of Cos. G and F/116th begin attempts to overcome the defenses in the D-3 Les Moulins draw. A platoon-sized force under Major Bingham occupies a building in front of the draw and tries to penetrate WN66 strongpoint but is pushed back.

716th ╫ 726th Grenadier (elements)

352nd ╫ 916th Grenadier (elements)

ST LAURENT

E1 ST LAURENT DRAW

E

K

F

D3 LES MOULINS DRAW

G

VIERVILLE

L

LES MOULINS

H

13. Gap Assault Teams are able to clear a single lane through the beach obstacles.

7. Elements from F/116th Infantry land on Easy Green instead of Dog Red beach, in front of the heavily fortified D-3 Les Moulins draw and take heavy casualties.

13

12

11

10

5A

7

9

6A

8

8A

EASY GREEN

29th ╫ 116th Regimental Combat Team

CANHAM

GERMAN STRONGPOINTS

(shown in red, annotated in black diamonds)

A	WN60	E	WN64
B	WN61	F	WN65
C	WN62	G	WN66
D	WN63	H	WN68

GERMAN MINEFIELDS

(shown in pink, annotated in black diamonds)

I	MF.9	K	MF.11
J	MF.10	L	MF.40

N

Band of German beach obstacles

meant that none of the bombs fell on their intended targets. Most exploded harmlessly in the pastures south of the landing beaches. Of the 446 B-24 bombers taking part, 329 dropped 13,000 bombs. At 0610hrs five LCG(L) monitors approached the beach and added their gunfire to the naval bombardment. A few moments before H-hour, nine LCT(R)s approached the beach and fired 9,000 rockets. These were a major disappointment due to their poor accuracy – none were seen to hit the beach.

THE FIRST ASSAULT WAVE, 0530–0700HRS

The four companies of DD tanks were supposed to be launched from LCTs around 0530hrs to give them time to swim the 5,000 yards to shore by H-Hour – 0630hrs. The naval officer in charge of the eight craft carrying the DD tanks of the 743rd Tank Battalion was convinced that the water was too rough for the tanks to swim ashore and reached agreement with the tank commander to land the tanks directly onto the beach. The LCTs landed the DD tanks on Dog Green and Dog Red sectors starting at 0629hrs. Company B, coming into the beach at the Vierville draw (Exit D-1), came under heavy antitank gunfire. The LCT carrying the company commander was sunk immediately offshore and four other tanks from the company were disabled before reaching the beach. Machine-gun fire from the German pillboxes damaged several other LCTs, but all withdrew safely. Company A with the normal M4 tanks with wading trunks landed about the same time, so that 40 out of 48 tanks made it to shore.

To the west the situation was much worse. The two captains from the 741st Tank Battalion outranked the senior naval officers and insisted that

An LCVP from the USS *Samuel Chase* with Coxswain D. Nivens at the helm was raked by German machine-gun fire as it approached the beach. The fire detonated explosives being carried by the infantry and started a fire, but the craft landed safely and later returned to the transport. *(NARA)*

the DD tanks be launched as ordered 5,000 yards offshore at 0540hrs. The DD tanks immediately encountered problems on entering the water, a few sinking immediately when their fragile canvas screens collapsed. The rest valiantly tried to swim ashore, but the combination of wind, sea conditions, and tidal currents sank all but two tanks from Company B. Of the tank crews' personnel, 33 drowned while the rest were rescued by accompanying vessels. Having watched the first of the four DD tanks on his craft sink immediately after leaving the ramp, the young skipper of LCT-600 decided to drop the remaining three on the beach. As a result, of the 32 DD tanks of the 741st Tank Battalion only five made it to shore on Easy Red sector. Following the two doomed companies of DD tanks was Company A with M4A1 tanks with wading trunks; each LCT carried two regular tanks and a dozer-tank. The luckless 741st lost two M4s and an M4 dozer-tank when their LCT struck a mine and sank. As a result, only 18 of its 48 tanks reached shore and three were knocked out by antitank guns almost immediately. In spite of their losses, the tanks attempted to carry out their mission and began engaging the various bunkers and defensive works.

The first assault wave, consisting of 1,450 men in eight infantry companies and the GATs, began landings at 0631hrs. Each LCVP or LCA usually carried 31 men and an officer, with six landing craft to a company. Few of the LCVPs made dry landings, with most grounding on sandbars 50–100 yards out. As the ramps dropped, the landing craft were subjected to a fusillade of gunfire. Some GIs had to wade through neck-deep water under savage fire the entire way. The troops in the assault wave had been issued much more equipment than normal infantry, including explosive charges and additional supplies, which made the passage through the surf

The final approach to the beach by LCVPs carrying the 16th RCT from the USS *Samuel Chase* during the second wave on D-Day around 0730hrs. The troops on the craft ahead have already disembarked and are wading to shore. *(NARA)*

73

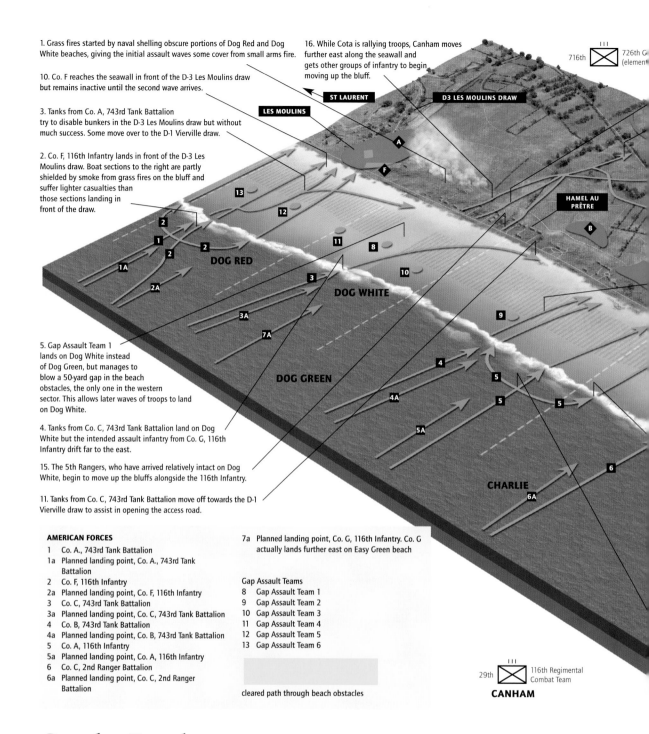

1. Grass fires started by naval shelling obscure portions of Dog Red and Dog White beaches, giving the initial assault waves some cover from small arms fire.

10. Co. F reaches the seawall in front of the D-3 Les Moulins draw but remains inactive until the second wave arrives.

3. Tanks from Co. A, 743rd Tank Battalion try to disable bunkers in the D-3 Les Moulins draw but without much success. Some move over to the D-1 Vierville draw.

2. Co. F, 116th Infantry lands in front of the D-3 Les Moulins draw. Boat sections to the right are partly shielded by smoke from grass fires on the bluff and suffer lighter casualties than those sections landing in front of the draw.

16. While Cota is rallying troops, Canham moves further east along the seawall and gets other groups of infantry to begin moving up the bluff.

716th / 726th G (element

ST LAURENT

LES MOULINS

D3 LES MOULINS DRAW

A

F

HAMEL AU PRÊTRE

B

13

12

2

1

2

2

DOG RED

11

8

1A

3

10

2A

DOG WHITE

3A

7A

9

5. Gap Assault Team 1 lands on Dog White instead of Dog Green, but manages to blow a 50-yard gap in the beach obstacles, the only one in the western sector. This allows later waves of troops to land on Dog White.

DOG GREEN

4

5

4A

5

5

4. Tanks from Co. C, 743rd Tank Battalion land on Dog White but the intended assault infantry from Co. G, 116th Infantry drift far to the east.

5A

6

15. The 5th Rangers, who have arrived relatively intact on Dog White, begin to move up the bluffs alongside the 116th Infantry.

CHARLIE

6A

11. Tanks from Co. C, 743rd Tank Battalion move off towards the D-1 Vierville draw to assist in opening the access road.

AMERICAN FORCES

1   Co. A., 743rd Tank Battalion
1a   Planned landing point, Co. A., 743rd Tank Battalion
2   Co. F, 116th Infantry
2a   Planned landing point, Co. F, 116th Infantry
3   Co. C, 743rd Tank Battalion
3a   Planned landing point, Co. C, 743rd Tank Battalion
4   Co. B, 743rd Tank Battalion
4a   Planned landing point, Co. B, 743rd Tank Battalion
5   Co. A, 116th Infantry
5a   Planned landing point, Co. A, 116th Infantry
6   Co. C, 2nd Ranger Battalion
6a   Planned landing point, Co. C, 2nd Ranger Battalion

7a   Planned landing point, Co. G, 116th Infantry. Co. G actually lands further east on Easy Green beach

Gap Assault Teams
8   Gap Assault Team 1
9   Gap Assault Team 2
10   Gap Assault Team 3
11   Gap Assault Team 4
12   Gap Assault Team 5
13   Gap Assault Team 6

cleared path through beach obstacles

29th / 116th Regimental Combat Team

CANHAM

Omaha Beach
116th Regimental Combat Team Sector

June 6, 1944, 0629hrs onwards, viewed from the northwest showing 116th RCT's landings on "Dog" and "Charlie" beaches, the western sector of Omaha Beach. As in the eastern sector, the troops in the first assault wave suffer heavily. However, the efforts of General Norman "Dutch" Cota and Lieutenant-Colonel Charles Canham help restore momentum to the US troops and they begin to press inland.

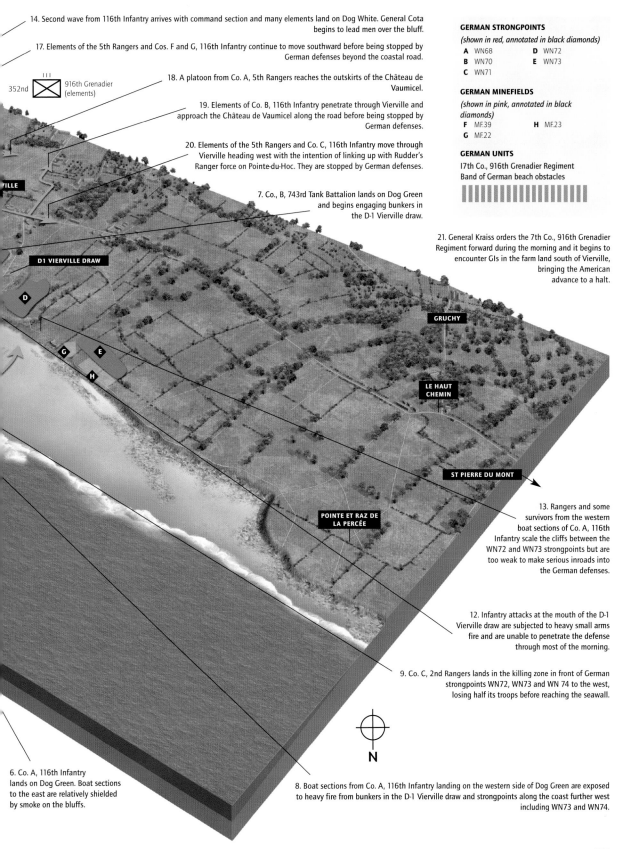

14. Second wave from 116th Infantry arrives with command section and many elements land on Dog White. General Cota begins to lead men over the bluff.

17. Elements of the 5th Rangers and Cos. F and G, 116th Infantry continue to move southward before being stopped by German defenses beyond the coastal road.

18. A platoon from Co. A, 5th Rangers reaches the outskirts of the Château de Vaumicel.

352nd | 916th Grenadier (elements)

19. Elements of Co. B, 116th Infantry penetrate through Vierville and approach the Château de Vaumicel along the road before being stopped by German defenses.

20. Elements of the 5th Rangers and Co. C, 116th Infantry move through Vierville heading west with the intention of linking up with Rudder's Ranger force on Pointe-du-Hoc. They are stopped by German defenses.

7. Co., B, 743rd Tank Battalion lands on Dog Green and begins engaging bunkers in the D-1 Vierville draw.

GERMAN STRONGPOINTS
(shown in red, annotated in black diamonds)

A	WN68	D	WN72
B	WN70	E	WN73
C	WN71		

GERMAN MINEFIELDS
(shown in pink, annotated in black diamonds)

F	MF.39	H	MF.23
G	MF.22		

GERMAN UNITS

17th Co., 916th Grenadier Regiment
Band of German beach obstacles

21. General Kraiss orders the 7th Co., 916th Grenadier Regiment forward during the morning and it begins to encounter GIs in the farm land south of Vierville, bringing the American advance to a halt.

VILLE

D1 VIERVILLE DRAW

D

G E

H

GRUCHY

LE HAUT CHEMIN

ST PIERRE DU MONT

13. Rangers and some survivors from the western boat sections of Co. A, 116th Infantry scale the cliffs between the WN72 and WN73 strongpoints but are too weak to make serious inroads into the German defenses.

POINTE ET RAZ DE LA PERCÉE

12. Infantry attacks at the mouth of the D-1 Vierville draw are subjected to heavy small arms fire and are unable to penetrate the defense through most of the morning.

9. Co. C, 2nd Rangers lands in the killing zone in front of German strongpoints WN72, WN73 and WN 74 to the west, losing half its troops before reaching the seawall.

N

6. Co. A, 116th Infantry lands on Dog Green. Boat sections to the east are relatively shielded by smoke on the bluffs.

8. Boat sections from Co. A, 116th Infantry landing on the western side of Dog Green are exposed to heavy fire from bunkers in the D-1 Vierville draw and strongpoints along the coast further west including WN73 and WN74.

The deadliest sectors of Omaha Beach for the initial wave were at the western end, Charlie and Dog Green. This aerial view taken in 1945 shows how the German strongpoints on the cliffs of Pointe-et-Raz-de-la-Percée (to the right) could cover the beach with enfilading fire. At the very top of the picture is the D-1 Vierville draw. *(MHI)*

especially difficult. Exhausted and seasick, when the survivors reached the water's edge there was little refuge. The expected bomb craters were nowhere to be seen and it was a 200-yard dash to the only reliable cover – the shingle and seawall. Many troops simply collapsed, or tried to find cover behind the numerous beach obstructions.

The conditions varied from sector to sector. G/116th RCT, landing west of the D-3 Les Moulins draw, faced far less gunfire than on other beaches, as grass fires started by the naval bombardment helped obscure the landing area. Company F, landing immediately in front of the D-3 Les Moulins draw, was partly shielded by the smoke, but the three sections furthest east were exposed and suffered 50 percent casualties by the time they reached the cover of the shingle. A/116th RCT, and C/2nd Rangers, landing furthest west on Dog Green opposite the D-1 Vierville draw, were slaughtered by the most intense fire encountered in any landing area in the 116th RCT sector. Not only was there a concentration of fortifications in the draw itself, but there was enfilading fire from the WN72 and WN73 strongpoints on the Pointe-et-Raz-de-la-Percée promontory on their right flank. The first Company A landing craft grounded about 1,000yds from shore in deep water and few men made it to the beach. One LCA was hit by four mortar rounds in rapid succession and disintegrated. Every single soldier in the company commander's LCA was killed. Within moments most of the company's officers and NCOs were dead or wounded and two-thirds of A/116th Infantry, were casualties. The 1/116th Infantry lost three of its four company commanders and 16 junior officers before even reaching the shoreline. Leaderless and under intense fire, the survivors clung to any protection available, mainly the beach obstacles. The company from the 2nd Rangers lost 35 of its 64 men before reaching the base of a cliff at the eastern edge of the beach. (The slaughter depicted in the opening sequence of the film *Saving Private Ryan* depicts this beach sector.)

On the beaches to the east assaulted by the 16th RCT, the situation was bloody chaos. Problems with the control craft and the strong current caused many landing craft to drift eastward and many units landed far from their objectives. The landings on Easy Red between the St Laurent and Colleville draws were the most weakly defended, and two sections of E/16th RCT, made it to the shingle with modest losses but with few items of heavy equipment, which were abandoned while swimming ashore. A section from Company F landing further east came under heavy fire when disembarking from its LCVP in neck-deep water and only 14 men reached the shore. The fire was much more intense on Fox Green sector to the east, where F/16th RCT put ashore opposite the heavily defended E-3 Colleville draw. Most of the casualties occurred after the ramps were dropped, when machine-gun fire from the bunkers cut a swathe through the disembarking troops. On one LCVP only seven of the original 32 GIs reached the beach. Within moments Company F had lost six officers and half its troops. E/116th RCT had the misfortune of being further from their assigned beach than any other, and landed on Fox Green. It lost a third of its men, including the company commander, before reaching the shingle.

L/16th Infantry drifted far east of their intended landing and ended up on the eastern end of Omaha Beach below the cliffs near Fox Green. The company commander was killed, but other officers rallied the unit to attack he WN60 strongpoint on the cliffs above. *(NARA)*

Assault Landing Plan, 116th RCT, Omaha Beach (West)

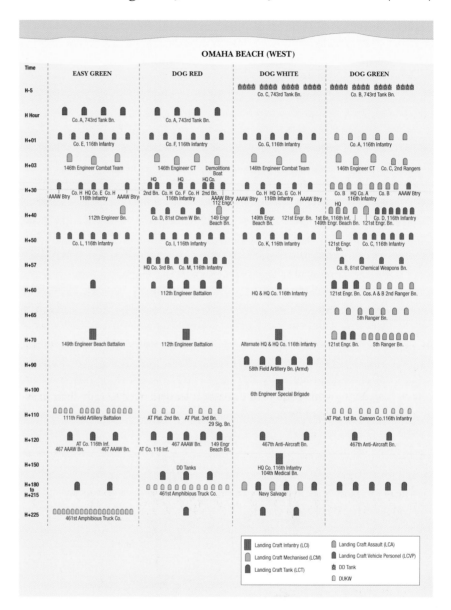

The two other companies of the 16th RCT were also scheduled to land on Fox Green, but Company L wandered too far east and arrived 30 minutes late at the eastern extreme of Fox Green. Although suffering 35 percent casualties, it was the only company of the first assault wave to remain a coherent unit. Company I became even more disoriented and drifted much too far east before its navigation was corrected. It landed 1½ hours late in front of the cliffs at the easternmost edge of Fox Green.

The heavy losses among the infantry were also suffered by the critical GATs. Team 11 landed in front of the E-1 St Laurent draw and, while dragging ashore its rubber boat loaded with explosives, artillery hit the demolition charges, obliterating the team. Team 15 near the E-3 Colleville draw suffered the same fate, and an artillery round struck the explosives of the neighboring Team 14 while still aboard the LCM, killing the entire navy contingent. Team 12 managed to plant its explosives on the obstacles on Easy Red beach, but hesitated to detonate them due to the many wounded infantrymen near them. A mortar round hit some primacord, setting off the charges and killing or wounding most of the team and many of the nearby infantry. Team 13 was working on obstacles when German fire set off some of the charges, killing the Navy section of the team. Team 7 was ready to breach a set of obstacles when an LCM crashed into the outer barrier, setting off seven Teller mines. Although these teams were supposed to be supported by M4 dozer-tanks, only six of the 16 made it ashore safely and three of these were quickly knocked out. By the end of the day only one dozer-tank was still operational. In spite of the heavy losses in front of the E-3 Colleville draw, several gap teams landed further east than planned due to the tides and so helped blow four adjacent gaps along the beach between the E-1 and E-3 exits. This accomplishment would prove crucial later in the day, as this was the only gap wide enough to accommodate a large number of landing craft.

The first infiltrations through the German defenses were made here around 0720hrs. Courage is not the absence of fear, but the ability to act in spite of fear. Many young squad and platoon leaders tried to rally their men, but most were cut down by intense small-arms fire. After engineers breached

A machine-gun team from L/16th Infantry moves under the protective cover of the cliffs on the eastern side of Omaha Beach during the initial effort to push through the F-1 draw and capture the WN60 strongpoint. *(NARA)*

some wire obstructions, Sergeant Philip Streczyk from E/16th RCT ran through a gap at the base of the bluff west of the E-3 Colleville draw. Under covering fire from Company G, Lieutenant John Spalding rallied a platoon-sized force and followed. Spalding's small force began to attack strongpoint WN62 from behind. In the meantime, the battered F/16th RCT had begun to attack the WN62 pillboxes from the front, putting one out of action with a bazooka. There were also penetrations into the F-1 draw by scattered groups of GIs who attacked the WN61 strongpoint from both front and rear. At 0720hrs an M4A1 tank of the battered 741st Tank Battalion managed to knock out the 88mm gun casemate at WN61. Around 0745hrs another M4A1 knocked out the top casemate at WN62 on the west side of the E-3 Colleville draw. The commander of GR.726 in this sector radioed back to 352nd Infantry Division HQ that his telephone lines had been disrupted by the attack and asked for a counterattack to throw back the American penetration. The divisional commander, Generalleutnant Kraiss, radioed to the LXXXIV Corps HQ, as his GR.915 was in corps reserve as Kampfgruppe Meyer. At 0735hrs the request for a counterattack was granted and at 0750hrs Kampfgruppe Meyer began dispatching a battalion toward Colleville that was scheduled to arrive around 0930hrs. It was so far west chasing paratroopers that it did not arrive until the afternoon. While it was not apparent at the time, the German defenses had already begun to crumble.

The gap teams were far less successful in the 116th RCT sector, in part due to the eastward drift of some landing craft. Team 1 inadvertently missed the killing zone on Dog Green, landing on Dog White instead. They blew a 50-yard gap in textbook fashion in only 20 minutes. The neighboring Teams 2 to 5 had little or no success. Team 2 arrived too late, while Team 3 suffered a direct artillery hit on its LCT and only one of the 40-man team survived. Team 4 suffered heavy casualties in front of the D-3 Les Moulins draw. Team 5 managed to plant its charges, but by the time it was ready to detonate them, so many infantry had huddled around the obstacles for shelter that only a few could be blown. Team 6 landed east of the D-3 Les Moulins draw and managed to create a gap in spite of the infantry using the obstacles for cover. Teams 7 and 8 had an impossible time clearing the obstructions, in part due to casualties and in part due to the recurring problem of the infantry using the obstacles as cover from the deadly German small-arms fire. The two narrow gaps in the 116th RCT sector, while not as wide as the gaps to the east, would become the only means for reinforcement during much of the morning. Casualties among the GATs in both sectors were 41 percent, and some of the teams were virtually wiped out.

By 0700hrs the sea's tide had turned and the obstacle belt was slowly inundated, drowning the badly wounded who had taken shelter near the beach obstructions. The surviving members of the eight infantry and one Ranger companies hid behind the shingle and seawalls along 7,000 yards of beach, losing more and more men as German mortar and machine-gun fire took their toll. Many of the GIs had a difficult time engaging the German positions, as their rifles had become fouled with seawater or sand. Of the troops who landed in the first wave, more than a third were casualties within the first hour and most units were leaderless, their officers and NCOs dead or wounded.

THE SECOND ASSAULT WAVE, 0700–0800HRS

The second assault wave was supposed to land at 0700hrs in the midst of an advancing tide. It had as many navigation problems as the first wave, exacerbated by the remaining, partly submerged obstacles. B/116th RCT, landing on Dog Green, took heavy casualties like the first wave. Company C landed on Dog White, enjoying the cover provided by the grass fires. Company D lost several LCVPs on the way into the beach and landed in a disorganized fashion with heavy casualties. The HQ company landed at the extreme western area of the beach near the foot of the cliffs and was pinned

GIs look warily toward the beach during landings on Omaha later on D-Day morning. The beach is already littered with vehicles and tanks knocked out earlier in the day. *(NARA)*

A USAAF reconnaissance aircraft provides a bird's-eye view of Omaha Beach on D-Day. In the center is an LCI(L) while to either side are LCTs. There is a string of DUKW amphibious trucks moving in column ashore. (NARA)

down by sniper fire for most of the day. Company H and the 2/116th Infantry HQ company landed on either side of the D-3 Les Moulins draw. Casualties among the officers of 2/116th Infantry were particularly heavy, with two of the company commanders dead and another wounded. While the second wave landed, the tanks tried to reduce the German strongpoints. Three M4 tanks from the 743rd Tank Battalion began to crawl up the bluff near WN70, while three more began an assault on WN68 on the western side of the D-3 Les Moulins draw, penetrating the first layer of the defenses.

The 3/116th RCT was scheduled to follow around 0730hrs. Aside from Companies A and B, 2nd Rangers, which landed in the killing zone near Dog Green, most of the later infantry companies and the 5th Rangers made it to shore with fewer casualties than the preceding waves and were soon crowding the beaches on either side of the D-3 Les Moulins draw. Around 0730hrs the regimental command parties began arriving, including Colonel Canham and Brigadier-General Cota. Two LCIs bringing in the alternative HQ for 116th RCT were hit by artillery fire around 0740hrs and they burned for the rest of the day. To further add to the confusion on the beach, the second-wave landings also brought to shore an increasing number of vehicles, which bunched up along the shoreline and became easy targets for German gunners. By 0800hrs the tide had risen by 8ft, covering many obstacles and drowning many of the severely wounded.

Cota and Canham walked along the beach, cajoling the men to move toward the bluffs above. After a breach was made in the concertina wire beyond the seawall, around 0750hrs Cota led forward a small group of men from C/116th Infantry. They waded through tall reeds and marsh grass at the base of the bluffs, finally finding their way up onto the bluffs themselves, using the terrain to avoid the German machine-gun positions. Ragged columns of troops followed, some being hit by sniper fire or wandering onto mines. Further east along Dog Red sector, Canham led a similar column from Companies F and G, 116th Infantry, over the bluffs. Around 0810hrs the neighboring 5th Ranger Battalion blew four gaps in the wire. It made its way to the top of the bluffs by 0900hrs, parallel to Cota's and Canham's growing bands. As the groups reached the crest of the bluff, they began to coalesce and send out patrols. A small group of Rangers under Lieutenant Charles Parker set off for Château-de-Vaumicel to carry out their mission at Pointe-du-Hoc. Sometime after 1000hrs, once enough troops had finally gathered, Cota ordered C/116th Infantry and a platoon from 5th Rangers into the village of Vierville while other elements of the 5th Rangers moved to the southwest to cut the roads leading out of Vierville.

The first attempt to climb the bluffs east of the D-3 Les Moulins draw failed. Major Sidney Bingham, the 2nd Battalion commander, whose own companies had been decimated by the bunkers in the Les Moulins draw, tried rallying the leaderless men of Company F who had landed in the first wave. He led them in the capture of a house in the mouth of the D-3 Les Moulins draw and then attempted to attack the WN66 strongpoint on the eastern shoulder of the draw. However, the German defensive positions were too strong and the GIs had to retreat to the protection of the house and neighboring trenches. A number of squads from Company G had more success on the bluffs east of Les Moulins draw by skirting behind the WN66 strongpoint. When the 3/116th RCT landed relatively unscathed in this area, it provided the momentum to finally push inland and by 0900hrs there were portions of three companies over the bluffs between the D-3 and E-1 draws. By late morning there were about 600 GIs over the bluffs advancing southward. The scattered tanks fought a day-long battle with the

The entrance to the D-3 Les Moulins draw was dominated by this solid house. It was captured by a group under Major Sidney Bingham, but they were unable to overcome strongpoint WN66 at the top of the draw, seen here in the distance beyond the barbed-wire. (NARA)

Landings at Easy Red Sector, 0730hrs

This boat section of assault troops from 1/16th Infantry huddle inside their LCVP as it approaches Easy Red sector around 0730hrs during the second wave of landings. The tide has already started to turn, and some of the beach obstructions are already awash. A M4A1 medium tank with the number 10 on its wading trunk can be seen in the water to the left. The intended tactic for these tanks was to remain in the water with only the turret exposed, thereby protecting the hull from German antitank gun fire. In the event, most tanks drove onto the beach. Each LCVP carried one officer and 31 enlisted men. The standard loading pattern in the craft was for three men abreast in 11 rows. The first two rows were the boat team leader, in this case a young lieutenant, and rifle team armed with M1 Garand rifles. They were followed by a four-man wire-cutting team, two BAR automatic weapons teams, a four-man 60mm mortar team, two two-man bazooka teams, a two-man flamethrower team, a five-man demolition team, and the assistant boat team leader (a sergeant) in the rear. The positioning of the lieutenant in the front of the craft proved disastrous in the initial assault waves, as so many of the young lieutenants were the first men killed when the ramp went down, exposing the craft hold to German machine-gun fire. The green brassard on the rifleman in the center is a chemically impregnated panel that would change color if exposed to chemical weapons. There was considerable concern that the Germans would attempt to repel the landings using gas weapons, so the troops in the assault waves wore battledress impregnated with a special (and uncomfortable) gas-resistant substance and carried a gas mask. Rifles were protected by a plastic wrap, though some troops removed this before disembarking. Many of the landing craft were crewed by the Coast Guard, one of whom can be seen to the right. *(Howard Gerrard © Osprey Publishing Ltd)*

This photograph was taken after the war looking directly into the D-3 Les Moulins draw. Several of the small structures at the opening of the draw were added after the landings. The numerous bunkers that so effectively resisted the US advance down the access road are difficult to identify due to their small size. *(MHI)*

German beach fortifications. Major Bingham later said that the tanks of the 743rd Tank Battalion had "saved the day. They shot the hell out of the Germans and got the hell shot out of them."

In the 16th RCT sector to the east, Easy Red held out the most promise, as there were a few M4A1 tanks from the 741st Tank Battalion providing covering fire, and this area included the only major gap through the obstacles. Company G came in first in the second wave and suffered 30 percent casualties before reaching the shingle. But in contrast to the first wave, this company was still functional. H/116th RCT landed late a little further west and took the heaviest casualties in those boat sections landing nearest the E-1 draw. Three more companies from 1/116th Infantry landed between 0740hrs and 0800hrs, followed by two more from 3/116th Infantry. By 0800hrs there were elements of eight infantry companies on Fox Green, mainly concentrated in the area where the gaps in the obstacles had been made between the E-1 and E-3 draws. Several defensive positions were created behind the protection of shingle, and some light machine-guns and 60mm mortars were in action. Company G began another wary advance through the minefields at the base of the bluff and eventually managed to join Spalding's group from Company E on the crest. Company A tried to follow but suffered heavy losses after wandering into a minefield. These scattered units spent most of the morning advancing slowly southward and dealing with German snipers. Strongpoint WN64 was cleared around 1000hrs, although a lone pillbox at the head of the draw remained in German control until the evening.

Further to the east, strongpoint WN60 was captured by Company L around 0900hrs, this being the first of the defensive positions to fall. The companies from 3/116th RCT began to push further into the F-1 draw toward the village of Cabourg, but were halted by the WN63 strongpoint.

The command post for the 16th RCT landed around 0820hrs on Easy Red, along with the much-needed regimental medical section. Colonel George Taylor gathered the battalion and company commanders together and prodded them to get their troops off the beach. "Two kinds of people are staying on the beach, the dead and those who are going to die – now let's get the hell out of here!" Taylor continued down the beach, urging the infantrymen forward. At 1100hrs Colonel Taylor ordered the decimated 741st Tank Battalion to shift all of its tanks to attack the fortifications in the E-3 Colleville draw. Three M4A1 tanks entered the draw and two were knocked out in duels with the antitank guns in the bunkers. Apart from the tanks, the engineers' D-7 armored bulldozers were very active in trying to clear beach obstacles to assist the infantry in their attacks.

From the perspective of Generalleutnant Kraiss, the situation on Omaha Beach was far less worrying than that on neighboring Gold Beach, where British tanks had already comprehensively penetrated the defenses by early morning. Since his division was committed to defending the western side of Gold Beach as well as Omaha Beach, he decided to commit his reserves to stemming the more dangerous British advances. At 0835hrs he asked permission from the LXXXIV Corps HQ to shift all of Kampfgruppe Meyer to the eastern sector against the British, with the exception of the single battalion already promised for the repulse of the American penetrations in front of Colleville. Corps headquarters agreed with this plan. Shortly after these decisions had been made, the reports from Omaha Beach began to

The critical link between the army units ashore and the navy destroyers were the Naval Shore Fire Control Parties. One is seen in operation using an SCR-284 with hand-operated generator while the soldier to the right is using an SCR-586 handie-talkie. *(NARA)*

Dog Red Sector, 0740hrs

The 29th Division's assistant commander, Brigadier-General Norman "Dutch" Cota, and the 116th Infantry commander, Lieutenant-Colonel Canham, landed on Dog White with the second assault wave. They found the troops from the first wave leaderless due to the heavy losses among officers and NCOs. Canham moved westward, prodding his 116th Infantry troops along Dog White to move forward, while Cota headed eastward along Dog White and Dog Red. Cota cajoled the troops, "Don't die on the beaches, die up on the bluff if you have to die. But get off the beaches or you're sure to die!" On meeting Captain John Raaen of the 5th Rangers nearby, he uttered the phrase that would go down in Ranger legend: "We're counting on you Rangers to lead the way!" Here Cota is seen talking to some soldiers from the 116th Infantry, distinguished by the blue and gray divisional insignia painted on their helmets and worn as a patch on the left shoulder above the rank insignia. To the right are two soldiers from the 5th Rangers, evident from the yellow rhomboid painted on the backs of their helmets. The 29th Division rifleman in the right of the scene can be seen still wearing the olive-green anti-gas brassard and he still carries the chemical protective mask bag on his chest, as does the lieutenant left of Cota. The weapons of many of the GIs had become fouled with sand or seawater during the chaotic landings and the rifleman is attempting to clean his using a toothbrush. On the ground to the right of Cota is a set of bangalore torpedoes. These were tubes filled with high explosive that would be joined end to end, and then pushed under wire obstructions. Once in place, they would be detonated to clear a path through the wire. A helmet belonging to a member of one of the Engineer Special Brigades, with its distinctive crescent marking, lies on the beach behind Cota. Around 0750hrs, small groups of soldiers from C/1st Battalion, 116th Infantry began moving through a gap in the seawall toward the bluff in an area out of sight of the German machine-gun teams. A private placed a bangalore torpedo under a wire obstruction blocking their path, but was killed by sniper fire. A platoon leader, Lieutenant Stanley Schwartz, replaced him and detonated the charge, blowing a wide gap. The first man trying to run through the gap was hit by the sniper and his agonized cries demoralized the troops following. Realizing that the advance was faltering, Cota raced through the gap, shouting back: "C'mon! If an old buzzard like me can do that so can you!" The infantry, with Cota at the lead, waded through tall reeds and marsh grass at the base of the bluffs, finally finding their way to the bluffs. It was the first advance off the beach in the 116th RCT sector. *(Howard Gerrard © Osprey Publishing Ltd)* give cause for concern as US troops continued to penetrate over the bluffs. At 0915hrs GR.916 reported that WN65 to WN68 and WN70 had been captured. From east to west these strongpoints stretched from the west shoulder of the E-1 St Laurent draw across to the west side of the D-3 Les Moulins draw. In fact, only WN70 had been abandoned due to the presence of General Cota's force. The battalion from Kampfgruppe Meyer due to make the counterattack toward Colleville had not yet returned from its dawn odyssey to the west.

STALEMATE ON THE BEACH

Although the first penetrations of the German defensive line were well under way by 0900hrs, the Operation *Neptune* plan was already hours behind schedule. The inability of the GATs to clear and mark sufficient paths through the beach obstructions had caused considerable problems when the tide turned after 0800hrs. There were too few safe approaches to the beach for landing craft and those exits that had been cleared were soon jammed with vehicles that could not move off the beach. At 0830hrs the beachmaster ordered that no landing craft with vehicles should land. Even the troop-laden LCTs and LCIs could find no marked lanes to enter, so around mid-morning landings ground to a gradual halt. The senior commanders offshore did not appreciate the status of the forces on the beach due to the loss of so many radios during the landings, as well as the generally chaotic situation ashore. However, the evidence of heavy casualties and burning equipment, apparent even from offshore, allowed little doubt that the landing was in jeopardy.

Around 0800hrs the destroyers began moving dangerously close to shore to provide more fire support to the beleaguered troops. Around 0830hrs

When the tide turned after 0800hrs the inbound LCIs had a difficult time landing since few marked channels through the obstacles were visible. After milling around for much of mid-morning, the LCIs began heading toward shore around 1000hrs, hoping to find gaps in the obstacles like these two craft, LCI-430 and 496, approaching Fox Green. Smoke can be seen coming from a house in the E-3 Colleville draw, which the German troops of WN62 on the neighboring hillside had used as a canteen. *(NARA)*

USS *McCook* arrived off Vierville and began pounding the D-1 Vierville draw, as well as the WN73 strongpoint on Pointe-et-Raz-de-la-Percée that had been inflicting so many casualties on Charlie and Dog Green beaches. After about 15 minutes of fire one of the gun emplacements on the cliff fell into the sea and the other exploded. Around 0950hrs Admiral Bryant radioed the destroyers: "Get on them, men! Get on them! They're raising hell with the men on the beach, and we can't have any more of that! We must stop it!" By 1030hrs the *McCook* took up stations a mere 1,300 yards from shore, in only three fathoms of water, and spent most of the day firing at targets of opportunity. Starting around 0800hrs, USS *Carmick* began a pass offshore from Pointe-et-Raz-de-la-Percée toward Fox Red, eventually approaching within 900 yards of shore. With only intermittent contact with shore fire-control parties, the destroyer was close enough that the officers watched where tanks and infantry were firing, and then responded with their own 5in gunfire. Near the D-3 Les Moulins draw, for example, a tank from the 743rd Tank Battalion began engaging targets on the bluff and then the destroyer eliminated the targets with 5in shells. When Bingham's small detachment became trapped in the house at the base of the draw, the *Carmick* began smashing up the WN68 and WN66 strongpoints overlooking the draw. USS *Carmick* was soon joined by USS *Doyle*, which spent much of the day shelling the D-3 Les Moulins draw area. In one of the more famous incidents, Admiral Bryant ordered the USS *Emmons* to eliminate a German artillery spotter in the steeple of the Colleville church, toppling the belfry with the 13th round. Several other destroyers took part in fire-support missions during the course of the day and they provided what little artillery support was available to the army. One of Gerow's first messages to Bradley after arriving on the beach later in the day was "Thank God for the Navy!"

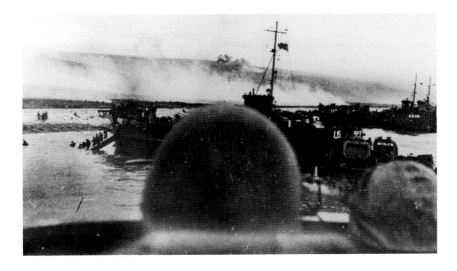

Around 1100hrs LCI-554 and LCT-30 charged Fox Green sector and successfully crashed through the obstacles, encouraging other skippers to follow suit. LCI-553 came ashore almost in front of the WN62 strongpoint on the western shoulder of the Colleville draw, but struck two mines during the approach. It was later hit by artillery fire and was abandoned on the beach. *(NARA)*

LCI-83 carrying troops of the 20th Engineer Battalion first tried landing at 0830hrs but was unable to do so, instead transferring some of the troops to shore via LCVPs. Another attempt around 1115hrs, seen here, was more successful but the craft was struck by an artillery round, killing seven and damaging a ramp. Two of the M4A1 tanks of A/741st Tank Battalion can be seen further down the beach. *(NARA)*

In spite of the beachmaster's cancellation of any further vehicle landings after 0830hrs, there was a dire need to reinforce the infantry ashore. The next two regiments scheduled to land were the 115th RCT from the 29th Division and the 18th RCT from the 1st Division. These regiments were already onboard the larger Landing Craft Infantry (Large) – LCI(L) – "Elsies" and began moving toward the beach around 1000hrs, very behind schedule. The 115th RCT was supposed to land around the D-3 Les Moulins draw, but fire from that area was still so intense the landing site was shifted eastward toward the E-1 St Laurent draw. Not only was this area less subject to German fire, but the 115th could follow behind the penetrations already made in this sector. Although there was some sporadic mortar fire during the landings, the regiment suffered relatively light casualties. The WN65 strongpoint on the western side of the draw had been mostly eliminated when G/116th Infantry had advanced over the bluff and tanks and destroyer fire reduced WN64. The 2/115th RCT had to clear a few remaining defenses in WN64, but by 1130hrs the E-1 St Laurent draw had been opened. As a result the 1st and 2nd Battalions, 115th Infantry actually advanced through the draw, while the 3/115th Infantry advanced over the bluff behind the WN64 strongpoint. The Engineer Special Brigade moved into action with bulldozers around 1200 and the E-1 St Laurent draw became the single most important exit route from the beachhead on D-Day.

The situation for the 18th RCT proved somewhat more complicated. Although a gap in the beach obstacles had been made on the eastern side of Easy Red sector, it was poorly marked and by late morning the obstacles were completely submerged. The strongpoints around the E-3 Colleville draw had still not been silenced. For nearly two hours the LCIs carrying the 18th RCT had tried in vain to find clear channels to the beach. Finally, around 1100hrs the two young skippers on LCT-30 and LCI-554 decided to try to crash through the obstructions and they headed in to Fox Green sector under a hail of gunfire. They began to engage the German gun pits with their own 20mm cannon and .50cal machine-guns and one of the nearby destroyers moved over to provide fire support. Both craft made it to the beach safely and disembarked their troops. LCT-30 was so smashed up by gunfire that it had to be abandoned. LCI-554 managed to pull away from the beach, evacuating a number of wounded at the same time. The example of these two craft convinced other LCI skippers to make an attempt and within moments the shoreline was again swarming with landing craft and the 18th RCT was finally ashore. Casualties were relatively light, but a total of 22 LCVPs, two LCIs, and four LCTs were put out of action by beach obstacles while carrying the 18th RCT ashore.

From the German perspective, the defense of Omaha Beach appeared to be holding. Telephone connections to GR.916 were severed at 0855hrs and contact was intermittent through the day. At 1140hrs GR.726 reported that the E-1 St Laurent draw had been breached. However, Kraiss' attention was focused on neighboring Gold Beach as a result of the rapid advance of British units there. At 1225hrs LXXXIV Corps agreed to transfer the 30th Mobile Brigade to the landing area to be committed opposite Gold Beach. At 1235hrs GR.726 reported that Colleville had fallen into American hands, which was only partly true, and that WN61 on the eastern side of the E-3 Colleville draw was occupied by US troops, which was not true. Through the morning Kraiss had received reports that various strongpoints had fallen to the Americans, to learn moments later that in fact they had not been lost – their communications had simply been cut. He was completely unaware

Later waves of troops approach Easy Red sector on D-Day. The cloudy weather gave way to sunshine after 1100hrs and so this section from the 18th RCT of the 1st Infantry Division is probably heading inshore in the late morning or early afternoon. *(NARA)*

A view from Easy Red sector eastward toward Fox Green and the E-3 Colleville draw shows an LCVP from the *Samuel Chase* in the foreground, and the damaged LCI-553 behind. On the beach are several vehicles including a few tanks from the 741st Tank Battalion.

of the penetrations around Vierville by the 116th RCT. By late morning Kraiss concluded that the Allied plan was a two-pronged attack on Bayeux with one arm of the assault emanating out of the St Laurent/Colleville area and the other out of the British sector. Resources to blunt the attack in the Grandcamps/Omaha Beach sector were limited. He ordered forward the 14 PzJg 38(t) Ausf. M Marder III tank destroyers of his antitank battalion, as well as 7./GR.916, which was stationed south of the beach near Trevieres. These forces converged on the area behind the D-3 Les Moulins draw around noon. In the sector south of the St Laurent and Colleville draws he alerted the 5./GR.916 to move forward from its barracks in Surrain and also directed the II./GR.915 from Kampfgruppe Meyer to conduct the counterattack that had been delayed by the difficulties in moving to the beach. By early afternoon, Kraiss believed that the situation on Omaha Beach was under control and at 1335hrs he contacted LXXXIV Corps with the news that the invading forces had been thrown back into the sea except at Colleville, but that his forces were counterattacking there. This report was forwarded to Army Group B and was one of the few bright spots in view of the dire circumstances on the other Normandy beaches.

Although out of touch with Kraiss and the divisional headquarters, companies of GR.916 were firmly holding defensive positions behind the bluffs, mainly along the road that paralleled the beach. The American infiltrations at this time were not strong enough to overcome these defenses and there were numerous skirmishes through the early afternoon.

The senior US commanders waiting anxiously on ships off the coast were even more confused about the real situation than were the German

With vehicle landings on the beach suspended in the later part of the morning, the early afternoon landings brought more vehicles ashore. This is a contingent from 2/18th RCT landing on Easy Red, the main access area for most of the afternoon of D-Day. On the beach is an antitank company with M2A1 halftracks towing 57mm antitank guns. *(NARA)*

commanders. Although the situation in the late morning was actually improving on the beach, the news arriving on board the ships reflected the despair of mid-morning. Bradley dispatched an aide by DUKW toward the beach, who sent back alarming reports of the congestion, casualties, and disorder along the beach, concluding at 1130hrs that "Disaster lies ahead." In fact, by late morning the situation on Omaha Beach was rapidly improving. The reinforcements from the 115th and 18th RCTs, although slow in moving off the beach, solidified the four penetrations over the dunes. The naval gunfire from the destroyers was wreaking havoc on the German strongpoints and, furthermore, the German gunners were running out of ammunition after the intense firing of earlier in the morning. While the situation was far from secure, the momentum was shifting in favor of the American assault.

THE RANGERS AT POINTE-DU-HOC

The most isolated skirmish of the morning was fought by the three companies of the 2nd Rangers under Lieutenant-Colonel James Rudder that had been sent to silence the guns on Pointe-du-Hoc. The rocky promontory had been thoroughly pulverized by naval gunfire and bombers prior to the mission, including 698 tons of bombs in the early morning hours. The assault force of about 200 Rangers was loaded into ten British LCAs escorted by several other craft. The mission began badly when the waterlogged LCA carrying the Company D commander sank in the assembly area along with a supply craft. The remainder of the flotilla, led by a Royal Navy Fairmile motor-launch and escorted by a pair of British LCS fire-support craft, set off for the

The 2nd Rangers at Pointe-du-Hoc

The original plan for the Ranger landing at Pointe-du-Hoc was to land two companies on the east side of the cliffs, and one on the west side. Due to the delays caused by a navigational error all three companies landed on the east side. LCA-888 carrying a section from Company D landed along the cliffs where the preparatory naval bombardment had collapsed a large slab of the rock-face, creating a heap of spoil about 40ft high. This spoil and the shell craters along the beach prevented the DUKW amphibious trucks from placing their ladders up against the cliff. But the spoil allowed the Rangers from Company D to climb almost half way up the cliff without the need for ropes or assault ladders. The first ropes were launched over the edge of the cliff using rocket-propelled grappling hooks. Once the first fire teams had reached the top, they dropped additional ropes down the cliff to the troops below. In this scene, the Rangers are continuing to climb the cliffs after the first teams have established a toehold above. Many of the Rangers, like the first wave of assault troops, wore the distinctive assault jacket, best seen on the lieutenant at the left. The Rangers at the right are wearing the distinctive insignia of the Rangers including the blue and yellow Ranger rhomboid patch on their left shoulder and yellow/orange rhomboid with the battalion number superimposed in black painted on the rear of the M1 steel helmet. The horizontal white stripe on the back of the helmet is a standard US Army marking, indicating an NCO. Officers' helmets were painted with a vertical white stripe. The British Commando with the bandaged head is serving as a liaison with the Rangers for the mission. He is armed with a Sten gun and wears British battledress with the distinctive Commando insignia on his shoulder. *(Howard Gerrard © Osprey Publishing Ltd)*

A section from the 2nd Rangers is seen loaded in the hold of their LCA in Weymouth, England, before setting out across the Channel for Pointe-du-Hoc. The diamond-shaped Ranger insignia can be seen on the back of several helmets. There is a BAR gunner to the left and a bazooka gunner to the far right. *(NARA)*

The German artillery battery had withdrawn their guns from Pointe-du-Hoc after a series of intense Allied bomber raids in late April 1944. They substituted crude decoys made from timber for the real guns, which proved convincing enough in aerial photos. *(MHI)*

objective. The guide boat became disoriented and led the flotilla toward Pointe-et-Raz-de-la-Percée to the east of Pointe-du-Hoc before Rudder realized the mistake and ordered the flotilla westward. The navigation error cost the Rangers about 40 minutes and they had to run a gauntlet of fire from the cliffs. A DUKW and an LCS were sunk by 20mm cannon fire. During the lull between the naval bombardment and the arrival of the landing craft, the German garrison on top of Pointe-du-Hoc exited their concrete bunkers and made their way to the edge of the cliffs.

The nine LCAs landed along the eastern side of Pointe-du-Hoc, with the crews setting off the grappling rockets on touchdown. The early-morning naval bombardment by the battleship USS *Texas* had caused a large slab of cliff to fall off, creating a 40ft mound of spoil. This was both a blessing and a curse. It prevented the DUKWs from deploying their scaling ladders, but nearly half the height of the cliff could be climbed without ropes or ladders. German troops began appearing along the edge of the cliffs as the Rangers landed, firing small-arms and causing about 15 casualties. The destroyer *Satterlee* came in close to shore and swept the clifftop with fire, forcing the German garrison back into the shell craters and bunkers. Within five minutes of landing, the first Rangers were on top of the cliffs. The promontory was a lunar landscape of deep bomb and shell craters that provided the Rangers with ample cover. But the terrain was so pockmarked that the Rangers had a difficult time assembling or communicating. By the time the main body of Rangers ascended the cliff, the survivors of the German garrison had withdrawn into the surviving bunkers. Prior to the bombardment the German garrison on Pointe-du-Hoc consisted of about 125 troops of the 716th Division manning the defensive positions, as the 85 artillerymen had withdrawn off the point three days before.

There had been some hints the night before the landing that Allied intelligence had learned that the guns had been withdrawn. When the Rangers reached the casemates they found that this was indeed the case. The only "guns" on Pointe-du-Hoc were a number of dummies made from timber. At least two significant concentrations of German troops remained on the point for much of the morning, the most dangerous being an antiaircraft position at the southwest corner of the artillery position that resisted repeated Ranger attacks. The observation bunker at the tip of the point was defended by a handful of German troops and there were several small groups of German soldiers in the ruins of the ammunition and troop bunkers. A German strongpoint on a cliff to the east continued to rake the point with harassing fire for much of the morning until a British destroyer spotted it and blasted it into the sea.

Small groups of Rangers gradually set out southward to secure the point and about 50 men reached the highway by 0800hrs after a firefight near two German defensive positions on the southern edge of the base. Small patrols infiltrated south through the farm fields looking for the missing guns. A two-man patrol finally found them, completely unguarded but ready to fire, in an

When the Rangers reached the crest of Point du Hoc, they were surprised to find that the Bauform 771 casemates were empty. The site has been preserved and this casemate was photographed by the author in the 1980s. *(Author)*

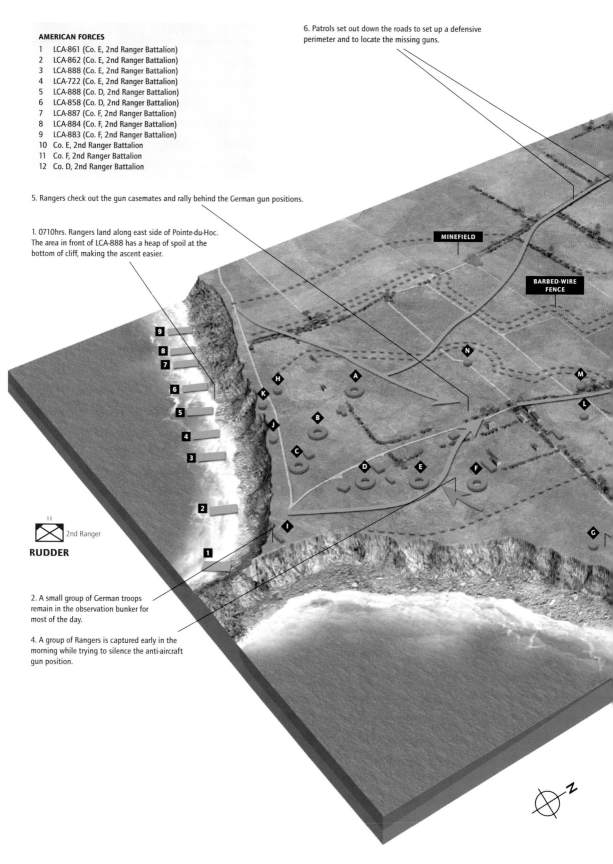

AMERICAN FORCES

1 LCA-861 (Co. E, 2nd Ranger Battalion)
2 LCA-862 (Co. E, 2nd Ranger Battalion)
3 LCA-888 (Co. E, 2nd Ranger Battalion)
4 LCA-722 (Co. E, 2nd Ranger Battalion)
5 LCA-888 (Co. D, 2nd Ranger Battalion)
6 LCA-858 (Co. D, 2nd Ranger Battalion)
7 LCA-887 (Co. F, 2nd Ranger Battalion)
8 LCA-884 (Co. F, 2nd Ranger Battalion)
9 LCA-883 (Co. F, 2nd Ranger Battalion)
10 Co. E, 2nd Ranger Battalion
11 Co. F, 2nd Ranger Battalion
12 Co. D, 2nd Ranger Battalion

6. Patrols set out down the roads to set up a defensive perimeter and to locate the missing guns.

5. Rangers check out the gun casemates and rally behind the German gun positions.

1. 0710hrs. Rangers land along east side of Pointe-du-Hoc. The area in front of LCA-888 has a heap of spoil at the bottom of cliff, making the ascent easier.

MINEFIELD

BARBED-WIRE FENCE

2nd Ranger

RUDDER

2. A small group of German troops remain in the observation bunker for most of the day.

4. A group of Rangers is captured early in the morning while trying to silence the anti-aircraft gun position.

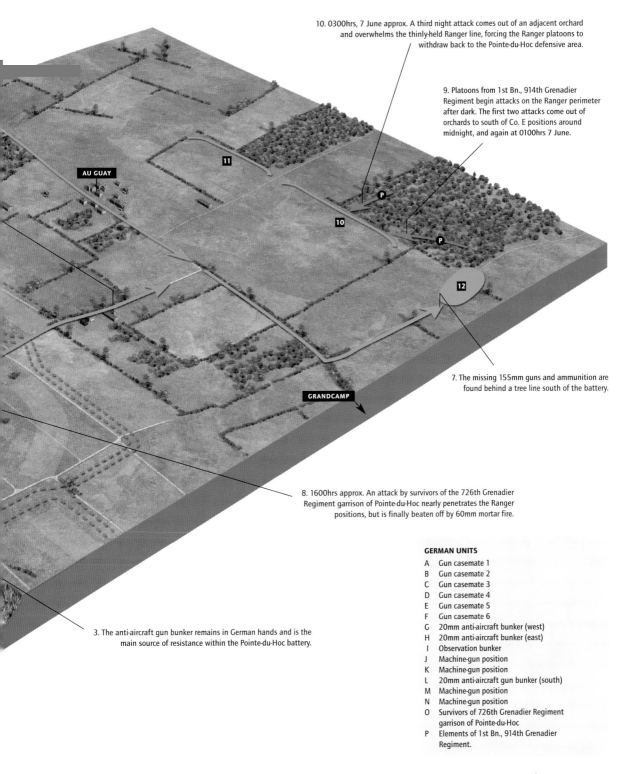

10. 0300hrs, 7 June approx. A third night attack comes out of an adjacent orchard and overwhelms the thinly-held Ranger line, forcing the Ranger platoons to withdraw back to the Pointe-du-Hoc defensive area.

9. Platoons from 1st Bn., 914th Grenadier Regiment begin attacks on the Ranger perimeter after dark. The first two attacks come out of orchards to south of Co. E positions around midnight, and again at 0100hrs 7 June.

AU GUAY

11

P

10

P

12

GRANDCAMP

7. The missing 155mm guns and ammunition are found behind a tree line south of the battery.

8. 1600hrs approx. An attack by survivors of the 726th Grenadier Regiment garrison of Pointe-du-Hoc nearly penetrates the Ranger positions, but is finally beaten off by 60mm mortar fire.

GERMAN UNITS
A   Gun casemate 1
B   Gun casemate 2
C   Gun casemate 3
D   Gun casemate 4
E   Gun casemate 5
F   Gun casemate 6
G   20mm anti-aircraft bunker (west)
H   20mm anti-aircraft bunker (east)
I   Observation bunker
J   Machine-gun position
K   Machine-gun position
L   20mm anti-aircraft gun bunker (south)
M   Machine-gun position
N   Machine-gun position
O   Survivors of 726th Grenadier Regiment garrison of Pointe-du-Hoc
P   Elements of 1st Bn., 914th Grenadier Regiment.

3. The anti-aircraft gun bunker remains in German hands and is the main source of resistance within the Pointe-du-Hoc battery.

2nd Rangers at Pointe-du-Hoc

0710hrs June 6–0300hrs June 7, 1944, viewed from the northwest showing the successful assault on the Pointe-du-Hoc battery by Lieutenant Colonel James E. Rudder's 2nd Ranger Battalion.

The 2nd Rangers landing at Pointe-du-Hoc were led by Lieutenant-Colonel James Rudder. He is seen here at his command post at the edge of the cliff a few days after the landing with an EE-84 signal lamp behind him, which was used to communicate with ships at sea due to the loss of most of the unit's radios. (MHI)

apple orchard in Criqueville-en-Bessin about 600 yards south of the battery positions. They were pointed toward Utah beach, with ammunition at the ready. The first patrol placed thermite grenades in two guns and smashed the sights, and further damage was done when a second patrol arrived with more grenades. The Rangers had accomplished their mission.

The other elements of the Provisional Ranger Group still at sea remained unaware of Rudder's success. Although a message at 0725hrs that the Rangers were up the cliffs was acknowledged, a second message at 0745hrs that the point had been taken was not acknowledged. As a result of Rudder's force landing 40 minutes late, the remainder of the Provisional Ranger Force assumed that the mission had failed and went ashore with the 116th RCT at 0730hrs. This would pose a major problem to Rudder's force as by 0830hrs it was barely at company strength and attracting an increasing amount of German attention. About 60 Rangers remained in and around the point, establishing a lightly defended skirmish line near the southern edge of the battery positions. At the same time Rudder sent out a number of small patrols, about a half-dozen men each, to scout and clear out isolated pockets of German troops who had withdrawn from the battery positions due to the bombardment.

The headquarters of the German 352nd Infantry Division knew about the attack almost from the outset, but the news was not particularly alarming in view of the disturbing events elsewhere. At 0805hrs GR.916 reported to divisional headquarters that a "weak force" had penetrated into Pointe-du-Hoc and that a platoon from 9./GR.726 was being sent to counterattack. The German resistance forced the Rangers to set up a defensive line south and east of the Pointe-du-Hoc fortifications. The first

The 2nd Rangers take a break near the unit headquarters on Pointe-du-Hoc after a relief column from the 116th RCT had reached them on D-Day +2. Note the British Commando in the lower right of the photo. *(MHI)*

significant counterattack by 9./GR.726 came out of St-Pierre-du-Mont to the eastern side of the Ranger defensive line in the early afternoon. It was repulsed by rifle fire. A more dangerous attack began around 1600hrs on the western edge of the defenses near the antiaircraft pit. This attack was finally broken up by the Ranger's sole surviving 60mm mortar. The V Corps headquarters knew nothing of the fate of the Rangers until the afternoon when a message was passed via the *Satterlee*, which remained off the point for most of the day providing fire support. The message was simple and to the point: "Located Pointe-du-Hoc – mission accomplished – need ammunition and reinforcements – many casualties."

The Rangers on Pointe-du-Hoc remained isolated for most of the day, expecting the planned relief force from the 116th RCT and 5th Rangers to arrive at any time. At dusk around 2100hrs, a patrol of 23 soldiers from A/5th Rangers led by Lieutenant Charles Parker made its way into the defensive line. Parker's group had been with the force that had made the penetration into Vierville earlier in the day and, facing modest resistance, they gradually infiltrated through German defenses to Pointe-du-Hoc.

In view of the lack of success of GR.726 in overcoming the Rangers, at 1825hrs Kraiss ordered 1./GR.914 to regain control of Pointe-du-Hoc. Nightfall came late, around 2300hrs, and the Ranger defensive line of about 85 soldiers stretched along a series of hedgerows south of the battery complex and the hamlet of Au Guay. German infantry began probing the defenses shortly after dark and skirmishing began in earnest around 0100hrs. A concerted German attack around 0300hrs overwhelmed a portion of the defensive line, capturing 20 Rangers. This forced the Rangers in the outlying positions to withdraw from the orchards and into the battery positions behind the road. By dawn on D+1 Rudder's force had been reduced to 90 Rangers capable of bearing arms and several dozen wounded. Naval gunfire kept the 1./GR.914 at bay and in the afternoon a landing craft finally arrived with provisions, ammunition, and a relief platoon. But throughout D+1 the Rangers on Pointe-du-Hoc could do little more than hold on for the relief force to arrive. During the night of D+1 a patrol from the relief force arrived, by which time the 116th RCT had reached St-Pierre-du-Mont only 1,000 yards away. The relief of the Rangers at Pointe-du-Hoc finally came on the morning of D+2, spearheaded by tanks of the 743rd Tank Battalion.

CONSOLIDATING THE BEACHHEAD

The senior US commanders did not have an accurate appreciation of the situation on the beach until well into the afternoon of D-Day. The first favorable reports by Colonel Talley of the Forward Information Detachment did not arrive at Gerow's V Corps HQ on the USS *Ancon* until 1225hrs and spoke vaguely of "men advancing up slopes" and "men believed to be ours on skyline." At 1309hrs Talley sent the first optimistic report back to the ships: "Troops formerly pinned down on beaches Easy Red, Easy Green, Fox Red advancing up heights behind beaches."

As the second group of regiments landed in late morning, the situation along the beach was shifting from total chaos to mere disorder. By noon the Engineer Special Brigades had enough troops ashore to begin the complicated task of preparing the beachhead for subsequent waves of troops

The first exit to be opened was the E-1 St Laurent draw, locally known as the Ruquet Valley. This was the site of the first penetration of the bluffs in the 16th RCT sector by Lieutenant Spalding's group toward the right side of this photo. Here we see a column of German prisoners of war evacuating their wounded to landing craft on the shore for transit back to camps in the UK. The area under the blimp was the site of the WN65 strongpoint. *(NARA)*

One of the most valuable types of vehicle on the beach in the first few hours of D-Day was the D-7 armored bulldozer. These were used by the engineers to clear beach obstructions, fill in antitank ditches, and perform a multitude of other tasks, while constantly under fire. This one is seen in a Norman town a few days after D-Day. *(NARA)*

and equipment. Some significant portions of the beach, especially in the Easy Red sector, were relatively free of small-arms fire, although still subject to occasional mortar and artillery fire. The beaches were littered with the dead and wounded, smashed and burning equipment, and a significant traffic jam of troops and vehicles unable to move off the beach. None of the draws had been cleared sufficiently to permit traffic off the beach and the troops moving inland were all walking over the bluffs.

One of the engineers' first tasks was to finish removing the beach obstructions. High tide was around 1100hrs and then the sea began to recede, making it easier to tackle the obstacle problem. The areas along the bluffs were still heavily mined and these minefields had to be cleared to permit troops to pass safely southward. The worst sectors of the morning had been Charlie and Dog Green to the west. Like the infantry landing there, the engineers had taken heavy casualties. By late morning, C/121st Engineers had landed along with bulldozers and explosives. Between 1200 and 1300hrs navy shore fire-control parties directed four salvoes from the battleship USS *Texas* against surviving bunkers in the D-1 Vierville draw. Stunned by the barrage, about 30 surviving German soldiers exited the bunkers and surrendered. A few moments later General Cota walked down the draw from the other side to try to get more troops moving to Vierville. At 1400hrs, as he watched, the engineers breached the antitank wall there with a half-ton of explosives. The road to Vierville was finally open around 1800hrs although still subject to artillery fire. The D-3 Les Moulins draw remained the most stubborn of the defenses and no progress was made until late evening when it was declared

open at 2000hrs. The E-1 St Laurent draw had been one of the first German strongpoints overcome in the morning, but progress was slow in clearing the many minefields, filling in antitank ditches, clearing barbed-wire obstructions, and removing accumulated debris. Under continual sniper fire, bulldozers plowed a new road up the bluff west of the draw by 1300hrs. The availability of a road off the beach led the beachmaster to open Easy Red and Easy Green to vehicles again, the first DUKWs arriving around 1400hrs.

The E-3 Colleville draw was strongly defended and the last pillbox was not silenced by tank fire until 1630hrs. The draw remained dangerous through most of the evening as it was registered for artillery fire, with salvoes arriving every 15–20 minutes. Engineer work to clear the obstructions at the front of the draw began around 2000hrs when artillery fire slackened. Tanks began moving through the draw around 0100hrs on D+1, but wheeled vehicles did not use the exit until dawn. By the evening of D-Day the engineers had fully cleared 13 of the 16 gaps that planners had expected to be open after the first wave landed. About 35 percent of the beach obstacles had been cleared as well.

TOP:
Following the landings, engineers were kept very busy clearing the beaches and the immediate coastal areas of the thousands of mines that the Germans had laid. This engineer is using the standard SCR-625 mine-detector near the beach on June 13, 1944. The painted insignia on his helmet identifies him as belonging to one of the Engineer Special Brigades.

RIGHT:
Engineers from the 5th Engineers Special Brigade come ashore from LCT-538 on Easy Red around 1130hrs. The engineers had the distinctive crescent marking on their helmets, as seen here. The photographer who took this photo, Captain Herman Wall of the 165th Photographic Company, was wounded shortly after this picture was taken. (NARA)

Efforts to land artillery on the beach for fire support proved frustrating. The field artillery battalions attached to the infantry regiments had their 105mm howitzers on DUKWs. But these amphibious trucks were heavily loaded and in rough seas they began to ship water. All but one of the DUKWs of the 111th Field Artillery Battalion, 116th RCT, sank. The 7th Field Artillery Battalion, 16th RCT, lost six on the way in and the remaining six were unable to land in mid-morning due to the beach congestion. The two armored field artillery battalions with M7 105mm self-propelled howitzers participated in the early bombardment from offshore and had no more luck landing. Five of the LCTs of the 58th Armored Field Artillery Battalion struck mines or were sunk and the 62nd Armored Field Artillery Battalion was unable to land. The 7th Field Artillery Battalion plus a single 105mm howitzer from the 111th Field Artillery Battalion fired their first mission from the beach at 1615hrs against German machine-gun nests near Colleville. Six M7 howitzers from the 62nd Armored Field Artillery Battalion finally made it ashore by 1830hrs, but were not ready for action on D-Day. Seven M7 howitzers of the 58th Armored Field Artillery Battalion arrived in the afternoon and were sent to support the fighting near St Laurent. In total, five artillery battalions were eventually landed on D-Day, but lost 26 of their 60 howitzers and saw very little use.

Medical treatment for the wounded on the beach improved in the afternoon when sniper fire slackened. Aid stations were set up near the seawall to provide a little cover, as artillery and mortar rounds continued to land well into the evening. *(NARA)*

Antitank ditches at the base of the bluffs were also turned into aid stations on the afternoon and evening of D-Day. Once stabilized, the wounded were sent back to ships for further medical treatment or evacuation to Britain. *(NARA)*

THE BATTLES FOR THE VILLAGES

Throughout the afternoon a series of skirmishes raged all along the coastal road, centered on the small villages located behind the bluffs. The first of these to be taken was Vierville on the western side of Omaha Beach. The American control of the Vierville sector remained precarious throughout D-Day due to the extremely heavy losses suffered by the units landing on Charlie and Dog Green beaches and the diversion of the reinforcing wave of the 115th RCT to beaches further east. In addition, the German 352nd Infantry Division had an unbloodied regiment west of Pointe-et-Raz-de-la-Percée. A company from the 5th Rangers and 116th Infantry headed west out of Vierville around noon but were stopped by German defensive positions. The remainder of the Ranger force arrived by late afternoon, but the 116th RCT commander, Colonel Canham, decided against pushing on to Pointe-du-Hoc that day due to the weakness of his force. This was a realistic assessment, as the German forces opposite Vierville were the strongest in any sector. To the immediate south of Vierville was III./GR.726, which was reinforced by elements of the 352nd Infantry Division's engineer battalion and 7./GR.916 later in the day. To the west were two companies of GR.726 and a battalion of GR.914, reinforced late in the day by a battalion from the 30th Mobile Brigade.

V Corps D-Day Operations, June 6, 1944

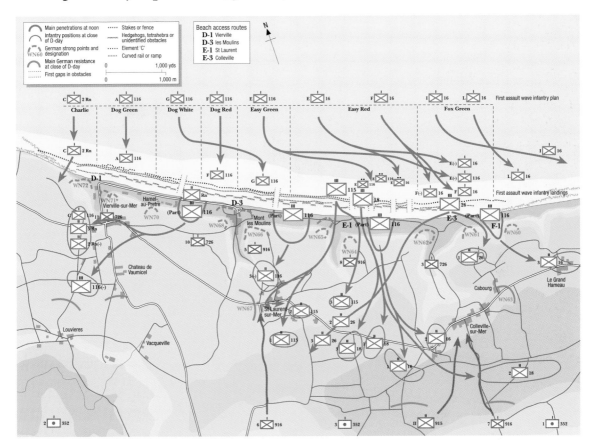

With the D-1 Vierville draw finally cleared by late afternoon, the surviving 17 tanks of the 743rd Tank Battalion moved into Vierville for the night. US tank losses on D-Day were 79 and if it had not been for the four reserve tanks landed later in the day, the 741st Tank Battalion would have been without tanks. Several of the disabled tanks were put back into service over the next few days.

The advance toward St Laurent in the center had progressed more slowly, even though there were about five battalions of US infantry in the immediate area. The hedgerows and orchards made the area well suited for defense and the US units were scattered and uncoordinated. To deal with the US attack, Kraiss ordered his dozen 75mm Marder III tank destroyers forward to support local counterattacks by 7./GR.916. The tank destroyers were spotted by naval observation aircraft and pummeled by naval gunfire well south of the beach. Their attack came to an end before reaching US lines. The two companies of 3/116th Infantry fought a number of skirmishes with the newly arrived 7./GR.916 and their advance slowed as a result. In addition,

A/741st Tank Battalion provided the 16th RCT with critical fire support against German strongpoints during the morning of D-Day. This tank, A-13 "Adeline II," was hit on the rear bogie by a 50mm antitank gun during fighting against the bunkers in the E-1 St Laurent draw. The tank could still move in spite of the damage, but it could not surmount the seawall to exit the beach. It was later recovered by the battalion's T2 tank recovery vehicle and is seen being towed through Colleville after D-Day for repair. (NARA)

strongpoint WN67 covered the crossroads where the road from the beach intersected the coastal road. Unknown to 3/116th Infantry, 2/115th Infantry was advancing southward along the eastern side of St Laurent and spent most of the afternoon skirmishing with German troops inside the village. The area was hit by a naval barrage around dusk, which halted the US attack. Around 1700hrs, four M4A1 tanks from the 741st Tank Battalion were ordered through the E-1 St Laurent draw to reinforce the attack on the village but, not finding the infantry, they formed a defensive line on the eastern side of the village. By this time 1/115th Infantry had bypassed St Laurent and bedded down in the fields south of the village. The 2/115th Infantry joined them there by nightfall. The tanks finally linked up with some scattered infantry units, and conducted a few missions with the infantry to clear out snipers and machine-gun nests shortly before nightfall.

Reinforcements continued to arrive through D-Day and this platoon is seen moving through a mine-cleared lane west of the E-1 St Laurent draw. The engineers marked lanes with white tape as seen here. (NARA)

Scattered platoons from the 16th Infantry began the fighting for Colleville in mid-morning. Around noon the US forces had coalesced into a force of about 150 men and began moving into the western side of the village. While this was taking place, elements of II./GR.915 from Kampfgruppe Meyer appeared on the scene and began to reinforce the German positions around Colleville. G/16th Infantry was forced onto the defensive until the arrival of 2/18th Infantry around 1500hrs. The counterattack ordered by Kraiss earlier in the morning was

The headquarters of the German 352nd Infantry Division got the first clear glimpse of the enormity of the Allied landings in the late morning of D+1, when Oberst Fritz Ziegelmann reached a strongpoint still in German hands on the Pointe-et-Raz-de-la-Percée promontory on the western side of the beach. The scene he saw was something like this, although this view is from the eastern side of the beach. *(NARA)*

not well organized, and failed to push back the US penetration as planned. Further American penetration into the village was halted when naval gunfire hit the village in the late afternoon. The 2/18th Infantry made its way south of Colleville, while the three understrength battalions of the 16th Infantry were deployed in a band along the coastal highway southwest of Colleville. The situation in this area was extremely confused, as not only were the US units facing local attacks by II./GR.915, but numerous small groups of German troops were retreating from the defensive works near the beach and bumping into US patrols.

On the eastern side of the beach, the small village of Le Garde Hameau was taken early in the day and occupied by 3/16th Infantry. When the third regiment of the 1st Infantry Division began arriving later in the day one of its battalions, 1/26th Infantry, was sent through the F-1 draw and bivouacked north of Cabourg, while the other two battalions went over the bluff west of the E-3 Colleville draw to secure the area between the 1st and 29th Divisions between St Laurent and Colleville.

US troops spent the next few days after D-Day clearing up isolated pockets of German troops and snipers in the countryside around the beach. This soldier's choice of a surrender flag was maybe not the best, but seems to have worked. *(NARA)*

PART II

UTAH BEACH AND THE US AIRBORNE LANDINGS

INTRODUCTION

The plans for the US Army at Utah Beach were a bold attempt to use airborne units to overcome the difficult terrain behind the beachhead. In the largest combat airdrop yet seen, two airborne divisions were delivered at night behind enemy lines to secure key bridges and access points. Due to the risks of such a night operation, the paratroopers were very scattered and unable to carry out many of their specific missions. Yet in spite of these problems, the gamble paid off. The landings at Utah Beach were never in doubt, and within a day the US Army had a firm foothold in Normandy.

Normandy had few large port facilities except for Cherbourg on the Cotentin peninsula. Nevertheless, it was attractive for its proximity to the English Channel ports and the relatively weak German defenses in the region, especially in mid-1943 when Allied planning started in earnest. A two-step solution was found to the problem of port facilities. Initially, the Allies would rely on two artificial harbors that would be constructed at the landing beaches. The next objective would be to seize suitable port facilities. This was a task assigned to the US Army: first, the seizure of Cherbourg and then the Breton ports. Utah Beach was selected with this objective in mind. It was the westernmost of the five D-Day landing beaches, at the base of the Cotentin peninsula, offering the best access toward Cherbourg.

The German defense of the Cotentin peninsula was based on the mistaken assessment that the main Allied effort would be against the Pas-de-Calais. As a result, German defensive efforts in 1943 concentrated on developing the "Atlantic Wall" along this stretch of coastline. The Allied landings in Italy, particularly at Anzio in January 1944, convinced senior German commanders that the Allies would use several smaller landings to draw off German reserves and weaken the main defenses. As a result, the German strategy was to deploy second-rate units behind mediocre beach defenses on other areas of the French coast, such as Normandy and Brittany, as an economy-of-force approach. These forces would prevent an uncontested Allied landing and would be reinforced in early 1944 as resources permitted.

OPPOSING COMMANDERS

GERMAN COMMANDERS

Utah Beach fell within the defense zone of the 709th Infantry Division, commanded by Generalleutnant Karl Wilhelm von Schlieben. He was appointed to command the division in December 1943 as part of the process to refresh occupation forces in France with hardened veterans from the Eastern Front. He was not the most likely officer to be assigned to a static division, having spent most of the war in the Panzer forces. He had commanded a Panzergrenadier regiment, a rifle brigade, and then the 18th Panzer Division in two-and-a-half years of fighting in Russia. The western side of the Cotentin peninsula was defended by another static division, the 243rd Infantry Division, commanded by Generalleutnant Heinz Hellmich. The division had been raised in July 1943, and Hellmich was its second commander, assigned on January 10, 1944. Hellmich was killed in action on June 17, 1944. A third division, the newly formed 91st Luftlande Division, was sent to the Cotentin peninsula in May 1944 and had been commanded by Generalleutnant Wilhelm Falley since April 25, 1944.

Of the three divisional commanders in this sector, two were in Rennes on D-Day

The hapless 91st Luftlande Division had three commanders within a few days after Generalleutnant Wilhelm Falley was killed by paratroopers on D-Day. He was finally succeeded by Generalmajor Eugen König, seen here. *(NARA)*

participating in a *Kriegsspiel* (wargame) along with many of their staff. Schlieben did not arrive back at his command post in Valognes until noon, and Falley was killed by US paratroops near Picauville while returning to his headquarters around dawn. Command of the 91st Luftlande Division was temporarily taken over by Generalmajor Bernhard Klosterkemper later on D-Day, awaiting the arrival of a new commander, Generalmajor Eugen König, who was assigned the post on June 7. He arrived at the command post on the afternoon of June 10.

AMERICAN COMMANDERS

With few exceptions, Major-General Collins of VII Corps was blessed with excellent commanders. Not surprisingly, the two airborne division commanders stood out. The 82nd Airborne Division had been commanded by Major-General Matthew Ridgway from June 1942, when it had first converted from a regular infantry division into a paratroop division. Ridgway had led the unit during its first major combat jump over Sicily in 1943, and after the Normandy operation would be pushed upstairs to lead the XVIII Airborne Corps in time for Operation *Market Garden* in September 1944. He would go on to a distinguished career after the war as NATO supreme commander and army chief of staff. The 101st Airborne Division was led by Major-General Maxwell Taylor, who had served as the artillery commander of the 82nd Airborne Division during the Sicily campaign. Taylor became best known for a cloak-and-dagger affair in 1943 when he was smuggled into Rome to confer with Italian officers about a plan to land the 82nd Airborne Division to capture the city. He quickly appreciated that the hare-brained scheme would lead to the destruction of the division, and he was able to avert it in the nick of time. He also enjoyed a distinguished post-war career, and was the army chief of staff in the mid-1950s after Collins.

The infantry division leading the assault on Utah Beach was the 4th Infantry Division, commanded by Major-General Raymond "Tubby"

Barton since July 1942. Barton led the division through the autumn campaign, culminating in the ferocious Hürtgen Forest campaign that gutted the division. He was relieved for medical reasons by George Patton in December 1944. His assistant divisional commander was Brigadier-General Theodore Roosevelt Jr, son of former president Teddy Roosevelt, and a distinguished soldier in his own right. Roosevelt had been assistant commander of the 1st Infantry Division in North Africa and Sicily, and when the divisional commander was relieved in 1943 due to personality conflicts with Bradley, Roosevelt was given the boot as well. He was reassigned to the 4th Division, where he proved to be a popular and effective leader. He died in Normandy from a heart attack, but his inspirational leadership at Utah Beach led to his posthumous decoration with the Medal of Honor.

Following the initial phase of the Utah Beach operation, the 82nd and 101st Airborne Divisions were withdrawn to Britain for refitting. Three other infantry divisions would play a central role in the fighting on the Cotentin peninsula. The 9th Infantry Division, headed by Major-General Manton Eddy, was a veteran formation of the North Africa and Sicily fighting and was widely regarded as one of the army's best divisions. Eddy was a particularly capable officer and in August was given command of the XII Corps in Patton's Third Army. The 79th Division was commanded by Major-General Ira Wyche, West Point class of 1911. Wyche had served in the field artillery until assigned to command the 79th Division in May 1942, leading it in its combat debut in 1944. Of all the divisions in Collins' VII Corps, the only one to suffer from serious leadership problems was the 90th Division, led by Major-General Jay MacKelvie. An artilleryman by training, MacKelvie had little feel for infantry operations and was relieved by Collins on June 12 after five days of combat, along with two of his regimental commanders.

The 82nd Airborne Division was led by the veteran paratrooper commander Major-General Matthew Ridgway, seen here in his paratrooper battledress after being decorated with the Distinguished Service Cross. *(MHI)*

OPPOSING ARMIES

GERMAN FORCES

The 709th Infantry Division defending Utah Beach provides a clear example of the problems facing the German armed forces. The division had been formed in May 1941 as an occupation division and in November 1942 it was converted into a static division. One of its battalions was sent to Russia in October 1943, and in June 1944 three of its infantry battalions were manned by former Red Army prisoners of war. Two of these were attached Ost battalions formed from various Red Army prisoners, while another was recruited from Georgian prisoners. (The Georgian volunteers numbered 333 men; the Red Army POWs 1,784.) The division was further weakened by the incorporation of a high percentage of troops recruited from Volkliste III, mostly Poles from border areas incorporated into Germany after 1939. The divisional commander later noted that their reliability in combat was doubtful, and he did not expect that the eastern battalions would "fight hard in cases of emergency." German troops in the division were aging, with an average of 36 years. In spite of the mediocre quality of the troops, the division was relatively large for a static division with 12,320 men, and it had 11 infantry battalions instead of the nine found in the new-pattern 1944 infantry divisions.

The workhorse of the German infantry divisions was the StuG III Ausf. G assault gun, which combined the excellent 75mm antitank gun on the old PzKpfw III chassis. This one was knocked out in the fighting with the 82nd Airborne Division near Ste-Mère-Église. *(NARA)*

The divisional artillery had three battalions; one with mixed French/Czech equipment, the second with French guns, and the third with Soviet guns. For antitank defense, it had 12 towed 75mm antitank guns and nine self-propelled 75mm tank-destroyers. Tank support was provided by Panzer-Abteilung 101, a training unit weakly equipped with ten Panzerjäger 35R, an improvised combination of Czech 47mm antitank guns on obsolete French Renault R-35 chassis.

Originally the division was spread along the entire Cotentin coastline, a distance of some 150 miles. With the arrival of the 243rd Infantry Division in May, its frontage was reduced. It still stretched from Utah Beach all the way to the northern coast around Cherbourg, a distance of about 60 miles. As a result, its defenses were simply a thin crust along the shore, with very little depth. Rommel hoped to compensate for the paucity of men with concrete defenses, but the construction along the Cotentin coast received less priority than in other sectors.

The 243rd Infantry Division was formed in July 1943 as a static division and reorganized in January 1944. Two of its infantry battalions were converted from static units to bicycle infantry, though in the process the division lost an infantry battalion. The division was originally in reserve, but in late May was shifted to defend the western coast, taking over from the over-extended 709th Infantry Division. On D-Day it included about 11,530 troops, a complement that was somewhat understrength. Its artillery was mostly captured Soviet types, but it had a self-propelled tank destroyer battalion with 14 75mm Marder III and ten StuG III assault guns. The division was reinforced by Panzer-Abteilung 206, equipped with a hodgepodge of old

German Defenses – Utah Beach

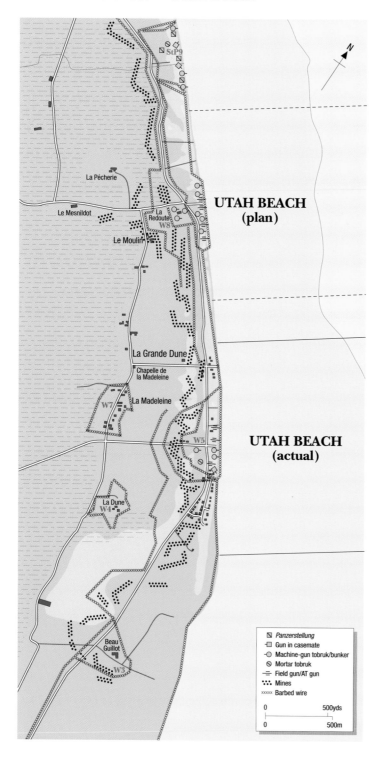

La Pécherie

Le Mesnildot

La Redoute

Le Moulin

UTAH BEACH (plan)

W8

La Grande Dune

Chapelle de la Madeleine

W7

La Madeleine

UTAH BEACH (actual)

W5

La Dune

W4

Beau Guillot

W3

StP9

Symbol	Description
	Panzerstellung
	Gun in casemate
	Machine-gun tobruk/bunker
	Mortar tobruk
	Field gun/AT gun
	Mines
xxxxx	Barbed wire

0 — 500yds

0 — 500m

French tanks, including 20 Hotchkiss H-39, 10 Somua S-35, 2 Renault R-35, and 6 Char B1 bis. This unit was deployed on the Cap de la Hague on the northwestern tip of the Cotentin peninsula.

The 91st Luftlande Division was formed in January 1944 to take part in Operation *Tanne* ("Pine Tree"), an aborted airborne operation in Scandinavia planned for March 1944. When this mission fell through, the partially formed division was transferred to Normandy, arriving in May 1944 to reinforce the two static divisions. At the time of the invasion, it was understrength, with only two infantry regiments and a single fusilier battalion, and numbered about 7,500 men. However, FJR 6 from the 2nd Fallschirmjäger Division was attached to the division during the Normandy fighting. Colonel von der Heydte of FJR 6 considered that the combat efficiency of the division was poor, especially compared to his elite Luftwaffe troops. The division artillery was based around the 105mm Gebirgs-haubitze 40 mountain gun, which did not share the same type of ammunition as the normal 105mm divisional gun. Once the division had expended its one basic load of ammunition, its guns were useless. During the course of the fighting, its artillery regiment was re-armed with a mixture of captured artillery types, including Czech and Soviet guns. Panzer-Abteilung 100, headquartered at Château-de-Francquetot, provided armored support. It had a motley collection of captured French tanks, including 17 Renault R-35, 8 Hotchkiss H-39, one Somua S-35, 1 Char B1 bis, and 1 PzKpfw III.

There were a number of smaller formations in the area as well. Sturm-Abteilung AOK 7 was an assault infantry battalion attached to the Seventh Army headquarters. On D-Day, it was redeployed from Cherbourg to the 701st Infantry Division during its actions near the River Vire.

Even if the German units on the Cotentin peninsula were not the best in the Wehrmacht, they were still a credible fighting force. Training and tactics were based on hard-won battle experience, and there were Eastern Front veterans in many of the divisions. During the fighting, General Barton visited one of his battalions that had been stalled by the German defenses and assured the officers that the German troops facing them were second-rate. A young lieutenant replied: "General, I think you'd better put the Germans on the distribution list. They don't seem to realize that!"

Many German units on the Cotentin peninsula were over-extended, second-rate units. The lack of motor transport led to expedients such as the use of bicycles in some units such as the 243rd Infantry Division. This is a bicycle-borne Panzerschreck antitank rocket unit. Note that the lead bicycle carries spare rockets in a seat over the rear wheel. *(MHI)*

German Defenses on the Cotentin Peninsula, June 6, 1944

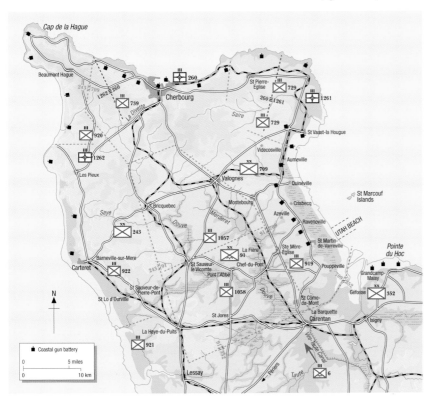

German units in France exploited the large inventory of captured French armored vehicles to flesh out their meager armored reserves. The small Renault R-35 infantry tank was fitted with a Czech 47mm antitank gun, resulting in a lightly armed and thinly armored tank destroyer. On the Cotentin peninsula, these vehicles served with Panzer-Abteilung 101, a training unit attached to the 709th Infantry Division. *(NARA)*

German Forces, Cotentin Peninsula, June 6, 1944

German Supreme Commander – Adolf Hitler
German Commander-in-Chief (West) – Generalfeldmarschall Gerd von Rundstedt
German Army Group B – Generalfeldmarschall Erwin Rommel
German Seventh Army – Generaloberst Friedrich Dollmann

LXXXIV Corps – General der Artillerie Erich Marcks

709th Infantry Division – Generalleutnant Karl von Schlieben
     729th Grenadier Regiment
     739th Grenadier Regiment
     919th Grenadier Regiment

243rd Infantry Division – Generalleutnant Heinz Hellmich
     920th Grenadier Regiment
     921st Grenadier Regiment
     922nd Grenadier Regiment

91st Luftlande Division – Generalmajor Wilhelm Falley
     1057th Grenadier Regiment
     1058th Grenadier Regiment
     6th Fallschirmjäger Regiment

Coastal Artillery Units
     1261st Army Coastal Artillery Regiment – Oberst Gerhard Triepel
     1262nd Army Coastal Artillery Regiment
     260th Naval Artillery Regiment – Korvettenkapitän Karl Weise
     608th Naval Artillery Regiment – Korvettenkapitän Hubbert

German Panzer forces on the Cotentin penisula were mostly composed of training units equipped with obsolete, captured French tanks. The Hotchkiss H-39s of Panzer-Abteilung 100 would figure prominently in the fighting against the paratroopers around Utah Beach. *(NARA)*

Apart from the infantry formations, there were a significant number of coastal gun batteries located around the Cotentin peninsula. The army controlled two coastal artillery regiments (Heeres-Küsten-Artillerie-Abteilungen): HKAA 1262 on the west coast of the peninsula and HKAA 1261 on the east coast. Some of these took part in the later land actions, most notably the Azeville and Crisbecq battery of HKAA 1261 near St Marcouf. The navy's Marine-Artillerie-Abteilung (MAA) 260 was responsible for the seven naval batteries located mainly in the area around Cherbourg while MAA 608 protected the port of Granville on the western side of the peninsula.

Some paratroopers of the 506th PIR, 101st Airborne Division, decided to get Mohican haircuts and daub their faces with their idea of Indian warpaint. This is demolition specialist Clarence Ware applying the finishing touches to Private Charles Plaudo. The censor has obscured the "screaming eagle" divisional patch on his shoulder. *(NARA)*

AMERICAN FORCES

The US units taking part in the initial landings contained the two best light infantry divisions in the US Army: the 82nd and 101st Airborne Divisions. The 82nd Airborne Division had already seen combat in Sicily and Italy, though in June 1944 more than half of its paratroopers were replacements. Normandy was the first combat jump for the 101st Airborne Division, but like the 82nd it was formed on the basis of volunteer troops and had exceptionally thorough training. In addition, its officer ranks were stiffened by transferring veterans from the 82nd Airborne Division. Both were elite units in the true sense of the word.

Tank support for Combat Team 8 came from the 70th Tank Battalion. Several M4 and M4A1 medium tanks of Company C are seen here fitted with deep wading trunks for the Utah Beach landing while in the background, one of the unit's T2 tank recovery vehicles backs on board the landing craft before setting off from Kingswear, Devon, England. *(NARA)*

A large group of GIs from the 4th Infantry Division are seen on the deck of an assault transport on the way to Utah Beach in June 1944. *(NARA)*

The 4th Infantry Division had been reactivated in 1940 and at first was equipped as a motorized infantry division. This concept was eventually dropped, and the division reverted back to a conventional organization in August 1943 prior to being sent to England. While Bradley had insisted on using at least one experienced division in the assault at neighboring Omaha Beach, Utah Beach was viewed as a less demanding mission. Nevertheless, it required the use of a well-trained and ably led division, and the 4th Division was chosen. The assault would be conducted by Combat Team 8 (CT8) with the division's 8th Infantry Regiment forming its core.

Armored support for CT8 came from the 70th Tank Battalion, the most experienced separate tank battalion in the US Army, which had previously seen combat as a light tank battalion in North Africa and Sicily. For D-Day, two of its companies were equipped with M4A1 DD amphibious tanks. In order to deal with beach obstacles, especially the seawall, there were plans to equip the third medium tank company with 7.2in demolition rockets in a T40 launcher over the turret. The first four rocket launchers were delivered in May and tested against simulated beach obstructions. The rockets were not particularly effective, but the tank crews

US Forces, Cotentin Peninsula, June 6, 1944

Allied Supreme Commander – General Dwight D. Eisenhower

VII Corps – Major–General J. Lawton

4th Division – Major-General Raymond Barton
> 8th Infantry – Colonel James Van Fleet
> 12th Infantry – Colonel Russell Reeder
> 22nd Infantry – Lieutenant-Colonel James Luckett

9th Division – Major-General Manton Eddy
> 39th Infantry – Colonel Harry Flint
> 47th Infantry – Colonel George Smythe
> 60th Infantry – Colonel Frederick de Rohan

79th Division – Major-General Ira Wyche
> 313th Infantry – Colonel Sterling Wood
> 314th Infantry – Colonel Warren Robinson
> 315th Infantry – Colonel Poter Wiggins

82nd Airborne Division – Major-General Matthew Ridgway
> 505th Parachute Infantry – Colonel William Ekman
> 507th Parachute Infantry – Colonel George Millett Jr
> 508th Parachute Infantry – Colonel Roy Lindquist
> 325th Glider Infantry – Colonel Harry Lewis

90th Division – Brigadier-General Jay MacKelvie
> 357th Infantry – Colonel Philip Ginder
> 358th Infantry – Colonel James Thompson
> 359th Infantry – Colonel Clarke Fales

101st Airborne Division – Major-General Maxwell Taylor
> 501st Parachute Infantry – Colonel Howard Johnson
> 502nd Parachute Infantry – Colonel George Moseley Jr
> 506th Parachute Infantry – Colonel Robert Sink
> 327th Glider Infantry – Colonel George Wear

4th Cavalry Group – Colonel Joseph Tully
> 4th Cavalry Squadron – Lieutenant-Colonel E. C. Dunn
> 24th Cavalry Squadron – Lieutenant-Colonel F. H. Gaston Jr

6th Armored Group – Colonel Francis Fainter
> 70th Tank Battalion – Lieutenant-Colonel John Welbron
> 746th Tank Battalion – Lieutenant-Colonel C. G. Hupfer

Additional armored support for Utah Beach came from the 899th Tank Destroyer Battalion, which later played a role in the efforts to overcome the German coastal fortifications at Crisbecq and Azeville. Here a number of M10 3in Gun Motor Carriages with deep wading trunks are loaded aboard LSTs in England for the D-Day operation. *(NARA)*

showed that two or three high-explosive rounds from the tank's 75mm gun were adequate to breach seawalls. As a result, Company C was landed without the rocket launchers. The battalion's light tank company was landed later on D-Day and assigned to support the 82nd Airborne Division.

In the build-up immediately after D-Day, three more infantry divisions were gradually injected into the Cotentin fighting. The 90th Division was based around National Guard units raised in the Texas–Oklahoma area, hence its nickname "Tough Ombres." It developed a bad reputation in Normandy due to poor leadership, which in turn led to poor training. It went through a series of leadership changes and by the fall the problems had been largely corrected. It fought with distinction with Patton's Third Army in Lorraine in September 1944. In contrast, the 9th Division was widely regarded as one of the army's best infantry divisions, with previous combat experience in North Africa and Sicily. It would play a critical role in the capture of Cherbourg. The 79th Division was activated in 1942 and shipped to Britain in April 1944. It was a fairly typical US infantry division, with good training and leadership.

One of the most significant Allied advantages was the availability of continual air support. At this stage of the war, cooperation between ground and air units was still in a formative stage, and did not come to fruition until late July during Operation *Cobra*. Nevertheless, continual air operations over the Cotentin peninsula by roving fighter-bombers made any concentrated daytime movement by German units impossible. Some measure of air power's impact can be surmised from the significant percentage of senior German commanders killed by air attack while trying to move between their units.

OPPOSING PLANS

AMERICAN PLAN

The original Operation *Overlord* plans did not envision any Allied landings to the west of the River Vire at the base of the Cotentin peninsula. In January 1944, when General Montgomery was first briefed, he insisted that the frontage of the assault be widened. Montgomery was not entirely convinced of the viability of the artificial harbors and wanted a landing west of the Vire to facilitate an early capture of Cherbourg. The preliminary Operation *Neptune* plan of February 1, 1944, and the FUSA plan of February 25 expanded the US beachheads to two, one in the Grandcamps sector (Omaha), and one further east near Les Dunes-de-Varreville (Utah).

Although many beaches on the eastern Cotentin coast were suitable for landing, the areas behind the beach were a problem, as many had been

Eisenhower visited with the paratroopers of the 502nd PIR at Greenham Common airbase on the evening of June 5, 1944. The division used playing card symbols on the sides of their helmets to identify the various battalions, the white heart indicating the 502nd PIR. The white cloth band around the left shoulder is believed to be a recognition sign for 2/502nd PIR. *(MHI)*

flooded by the Germans. Access between the beach and inland areas was over a small number of narrow causeways that could be defended easily by small German detachments. The second problem was the terrain of the peninsula itself. The River Douve runs through the center of the peninsula, and the low-lying areas of the peninsula were naturally marshy. The Germans exploited this terrain to reduce the number of possible airborne landings by using locks to flood many lowland fields. The planners wanted a beach with at least four causeways to permit the transit of a single division off the beach on D-Day, compared to two on neighboring Omaha Beach. The coast immediately west of Omaha Beach was the obvious solution.

To make certain that the causeways remained open, an airborne division would be landed behind the beach before H-Hour on D-Day. Many planners were reluctant to place too much faith in paratroop operations, especially in light of the fiasco on Sicily in 1943. On that occasion the aircraft transporting the 82nd Airborne Division came under fire from enemy naval forces, and the paratroopers subsequently landed in widely scattered and ineffective groups. However, Eisenhower believed that the Sicily operation had merely shown that the airborne force had to land in a more concentrated fashion, and he agreed with General Ridgway to expand the existing US airborne divisions. The initial plan in February envisioned using the 101st Airborne Division immediately behind Utah Beach to secure the causeways. Bradley's FUSA planners wanted the 82nd Airborne dropped further west to permit a rapid cutoff of the Cotentin peninsula, preventing the Germans from reinforcing Cherbourg.

These plans were viewed as extremely risky but Eisenhower decided that they were essential to the operation and that the risks would have to be accepted. The plans continued to evolve well into May, only days before D-Day. Allied intelligence learned of the move of the German 91st Luftlande

Division into the central Cotentin peninsula in mid-May. This made the planned landing of the 82nd Airborne Division around St Sauveur-le-Vicomte too risky. Instead, its drop zone (DZ) was shifted to the River Merderet area, and the 101st Airborne DZ was shifted slightly south so that both divisions would control an easily defensible area between the beaches and the Douve and Merderet rivers.

GERMAN PLAN

As we have seen, German defensive plans were in a state of flux due to serious disagreements between Rundstedt and Rommel over the deployment and control of the Panzer reserve. To some extent this debate was irrelevant to the Cotentin peninsula, since no senior German commander was particularly concerned that this area would be the focus of an Allied invasion. Until May 1944, the defense of the entire 155 miles of coastline on the Cotentin peninsula was the responsibility of a single second-rate division. The western coast was lightly guarded, as the navy had argued that the heavy seas off the west coast, as well as the heavily defended Channel Islands, made amphibious landings unlikely. In mid-May, the navy staff had a change of heart, and began to suggest that the Allies might land on both the east and west coasts, with simultaneous attacks on either side of Cherbourg. Shortly afterwards, Rommel visited the area, and later had a conference with Dollman and Marcks about the state of defenses in this sector. Von Schlieben argued that the port facilities in Cherbourg should be sabotaged immediately to make the port an unattractive target, and to permit units to withdraw to the base of the Cotentin peninsula rather than becoming trapped. The navy would not even consider such a plan and the proposal was ignored. Instead, the defenses of the Cotentin peninsula were

One of the most effective types of bunker on the Normandy coast was the Bauform 667 casemate, which were positioned parallel to the shore to permit enfilade fire along the beach. This Bauform 667 casemate of the W5 strongpoint at Utah Beach was armed with a 50mm antitank gun, and it was knocked out by tank gunfire directed against the embrasure from close range. *(NARA)*

substantially increased. The 243rd Infantry Division was shifted from its location further south in reserve, and placed along the west coast. The partially formed 91st Luftlande Division was placed at the base of the peninsula to back up the two static divisions.

Defense of the Cotentin coast did not have as high a priority as other sectors further east, which were judged to be more likely objectives for an Allied amphibious assault. The forces along the coast were spread very thin, locally concentrated in strongpoints. Defenses were not particularly heavy along Utah Beach, as it was presumed that such a beach would be an unattractive objective given the tidal marshes behind it. Two battalions of GR.919 held a total of 25 strongpoints from Le Grand Vey in the south to the Aumeville beach in the north, a distance of about 15 miles. The strongpoints were categorized into two types: as well as the *Wiederstandnest* there was also *Stutzpunkt* (StP = support position). These strongpoints typically consisted of a platoon of 40 troops with several small bunkers, a few machine-gun pits or concrete-reinforced Tobruks, and a few antitank guns or obsolete field guns. To make up for the shortage of troops, the formations along the coast had more firepower than a normal infantry unit, even though the weapons were a motley selection of obsolete or captured types.

The strongpoint that figured most directly in the subsequent fighting was WN5. It was manned by a platoon from 3./GR.919 and was commanded by Leutnant Arthur Jahnke, a young veteran of the Eastern Front and holder of the Knight's Cross. It included a 50mm antitank gun in a Bauform 667 casemate, two 50mm antitank guns in open concrete pits, one French 47mm antitank gun in a concrete pit, a Bauform 67 with a French tank turret and 37mm gun, four mortar and machine-gun Tobruks, and a half-dozen other bunkers and shelters. One of the platoon's more exotic weapons was a group of Goliath remote-control demolition vehicles, a type of wire-guided tracked vehicle designed to be used like a land torpedo to attack high-value targets such as tanks and landing craft. These were deployed from small caves facing the beach. A second strongpoint, WN4, was located immediately to the west of WN5, covering the main access causeway off the beach.

The regimental commander, Oberstleutnant Gunther Keil, did not agree with Rommel's tactic of placing all of his troops in the forward bunkers. Instead, he placed a minimal number of troops on the coast, and the rest of each platoon as an "alert unit" (*Alarmeinheit*) in the buildings behind the beach. Artillery in this sector included a battery from Sturm-Abteilung AOK 7 west of Foucarville, and a battery of multiple rocket launchers from I./100th Nebelwerfer Regiment south of Brucheville. There were also three batteries from an army coastal artillery regiment (HKAA.1261) in this sector; the 1./HKAA.1261 in St-Martin-de-Varreville with four ex-Soviet 122mm guns, the 2./HKAA.1261 in Azeville with four French Schneider 105mm guns, and the 3./HKAA 1261 in Crisbecq with three massive 210mm Skoda guns.

Unlike neighboring Omaha Beach, the Utah Beach sector was relatively flat, not affording the excellent fields of fire to be found further east on the coast. The beach obstacles in front of WN5 were far less extensive than those at Omaha, and the obstacles largely petered out in the area in front of Grande Dune where the landings actually occurred. Although GR.919 had attempted to reinforce these defenses, the tidal conditions simply washed many of the obstacles ashore. The main reserve in this sector was the Georgian Battalion 795 Ost, which was located further west near Criqueville, and GR.1058 from the 91st Luftlande Division located in the central peninsula in the LZ of the 82nd Airborne Division.

The Kriegsmarine lacked sufficient forces to entertain seriously the idea of repelling the Allied invasion at sea. Marinegruppe West, under Vizeadmiral Theodor Krancke, was divided into sectors with Konteradmiral Rieve's Channel Coast responsible for the Normandy coast through to the Dutch border. The port nearest to Utah Beach was Cherbourg, which contained two torpedo flotillas, totaling 16 S-boats. Krancke had attempted to inhibit the invasion activities by a program of minelaying off the Normandy coast to coincide with Rommel's fortification efforts. Unknown to him, the Allies were aware of the location of nearly all of these minefields due to the breaking of the Enigma codes. In addition, Enigma allowed the Royal Navy to disrupt minelaying in the weeks before D-Day. Attempts to mine the Seine bay on May 24 were met by a force of British torpedo boats and Coastal Command aircraft that put an end to any further attempts. The lack of bombproof U-boat shelters along the Channel inhibited Krancke from deploying submarines in the invasion area.

The Luftwaffe played virtually no role in the fighting in the Cotentin sector during June. Allied air superiority was so great, and the Luftwaffe so weak, that there was little hope for conducting Luftwaffe operations so far west from the air bases near Paris.

On June 4, 1944, Major Lettau, the chief Luftwaffe meteorologist in Paris, released a forecast indicating that the Allies were unlikely to launch an invasion over the next fortnight due to rough seas and gale-force winds that were unlikely to weaken until mid-June. This forecast convinced OB West that it would be an appropriate opportunity to conduct a major command wargame in Rennes to study possible counter-strokes against Allied airborne attacks in Normandy. As a result, about half the divisional commanders and a quarter of the regimental commanders were on their way to a wargame in Rennes. Indeed, the weather forecast was so bad that many units were using the opportunity to give their men rest from the strenuous construction program along the coast. Rommel used the spell of bad weather to visit Germany, hoping to convince the Führer to release more Panzers to his control for a forward defense of the coast.

D-DAY

The first troops to land in France in preparation for Operation *Neptune* were Office of Strategic Services (OSS) teams, usually consisting of two US soldiers trained in the operation of signal devices, teamed with three British commandos for site security. A half-dozen of these teams were flown into France around 0130hrs on June 3 to mark airborne DZs for later pathfinder teams who would bring in more extensive marking equipment.

The troops of the two airborne divisions began final preparations for the Normandy airdrops on June 5 at 15 separate airfields in southern England. The air delivery of the two divisions was assigned to the IX Troop Carrier Command. Mission "Albany," the delivery of the 101st Airborne Division, was assigned to the 50th Troop Carrier Wing and Mission "Boston," the delivery of the 82nd Airborne Division, was assigned to the 52nd Wing. The initial wave used 821 troop-laden C-47 and C-54 transports. Each aircraft carried a "stick" of paratroopers, usually 18–20 per aircraft in most aircraft, but 9–10 in parachute artillery units due to the amount of other equipment carried.

Troops of the 325th Glider Infantry prepare to board Horsa gliders at an airfield in England. The US airborne units were provided with the British Horsa gliders to carry larger loads than the Waco CG-4. *(NARA)*

To conduct a nighttime drop, the transport pilots were dependent on visual and radar signals to locate the DZ. Pathfinders were parachuted into the DZs ahead of the main wave to set up both types of signal – a set of seven color-coded Aldis lamps in the shape of a "T" and an AN/PPN-1 "Eureka" radar beacon. The Eureka set was a useful aid for the approach to the DZ, but became less effective about 2 miles out, requiring the use of the Aldis signal lamps for the final approach. Nineteen aircraft carrying the pathfinders departed before midnight and they began landing in France around 0015hrs on June 6, 1944. The following waves of C-47 transports were fitted with a "Rebecca" system to pick up the signal emitted from the Eureka ground beacon, and some were also fitted with "Gee" navigation aids.

On approaching the DZs, the pathfinder aircraft encountered an unexpected bank of cloud that created navigational problems. In the 101st Airborne sector, only the teams allotted to DZ C parachuted close to the target. Likewise, in the 82nd Airborne Division sector only one batch of pathfinders was accurately dropped into DZ O. In the case of the other four drop zones, the pathfinders were dropped so far away from their targets that they did not have enough time after their landing to reach their designated DZ. As a result, some of the pathfinder teams set up their landing beacons in areas away from the planned DZs, while other teams were able to set up only the Eureka beacons, as the presence of German troops nearby made it impossible to set up the Aldis lamps.

The main wave of C-47 transports began taking off from England around midnight. The two skytrains coalesced over the English Channel, and then followed a route around the Cotentin peninsula, passing between the Channel Islands, and entering enemy airspace over the west Cotentin coast, heading northeastward toward the DZ, and exiting over Utah Beach. In parallel, a force of RAF Stirling bombers flew a diversionary mission, dropping chaff to simulate an airborne formation and dropping dummy paratroopers and noisemakers into areas away from the actual DZs. The weather conditions were a full moon and clearing skies. The flight proved uneventful until the coast, and the aircraft flew in tight

Like a medieval knight, a fully loaded paratrooper sometimes needed help simply to move due to the enormous weight of gear and equipment he carried. This is T/4 Joseph Gorenc of the 506th PIR climbing aboard a C-47 on the evening of June 5, 1944. *(NARA)*

D-Day Airlift Operations, IX Troop Carrier Command

Mission	Albany	Boston	Total
Aircraft sorties	433	378	811
Aborted sorties	2	1	3
Aircraft lost or missing	13	8	21
Aircraft damaged	81	115	196
Aircrew killed or missing	48	17	65
Aircrew wounded	4	11	15
Troops carried	6,928	6,420	13,348
Troops dropped	6,750	6,350	13,100
Howitzers carried	12	2	14
Cargo carried (tons)	211	178	389

formation in a "V-of-Vs." On reaching the coast, the problems began. The aircraft encountered the same dense cloud that had frustrated the pathfinders. The pathfinder transports had not radioed back a warning about this due to the need for radio silence. The clouds created immediate dangers due to the proximity of the aircraft in formation, and C-47s began to maneuver frantically to avoid mid-air collisions. Some pilots climbed to 2,000ft to avoid the clouds, others descended below the cloud bank to 500ft, while some remained at the prescribed altitude of 700ft. This cloud bank

Paratroopers of the 101st Airborne have their chutes and equipment checked by Lieutenant Bobuck prior to boarding their C-47 for the flight to Normandy. The C-47 in the background has had the black and white D-Day invasion stripes hastily painted on. (NARA)

completely disrupted the formation and ended any hopes for a concentrated paratroop drop.

Antiaircraft fire began during the final approach into the DZs near the coast. Although they had been instructed to maintain a steady course, some pilots began jinking their aircraft to avoid steady streams of 20mm cannon fire. It was an inauspicious start for an inherently risky mission.

Paratroopers sit on the canvas benches along the fuselage of the C-47 during the trip to Normandy with a captain closest to the camera. These men are probably from the 82nd Airborne, which was not as keen on facial camouflage as the 101st Airborne. *(MHI)*

MISSION ALBANY

The 101st Airborne Division was the first to land around 0130hrs on June 6, 1944. Its primary objective was to seize control of the area behind Utah Beach between St-Martin-de-Varreville and Pouppeville to facilitate the exit of the 4th Infantry Division from the beach later that morning. Its secondary mission was to protect the southern flank of VII Corps by destroying two bridges on the Carentan highway and a railroad bridge west of it, gaining control of the Barquette lock, and establishing a bridgehead over the River Douve northeast of Carentan.

The 502nd Parachute Infantry Regiment (PIR) and 506th PIR (less one battalion) were assigned to the primary objective. The first wave of the

502nd PIR consisted of the 2/502nd PIR and HQ/502nd PIR. The transport aircraft carrying these units were scattered by cloud cover and flak, landing far from DZ A. Most of the 2/502nd PIR was dropped compactly but inaccurately on the far edge of DZ C, 3 miles south of intended DZ A. The battalion landed in an area divided up by a maze of dense hedgerows, the Normandy *bocage*, and had a great deal of difficulty assembling and orienting themselves. These units spent most of D-Day regrouping and took no part in the initial fighting.

The 3/502nd PIR landed in very scattered fashion to the east of Ste-Mère-Église. The battalion commander, Lieutenant-Colonel Robert Cole, gathered about 75 men and began moving on the coastal battery at St-Martin-de-Varreville. They found that the guns had been removed and the position deserted due to pre-invasion bombardment, so they moved on to their next objective, the western side of Audouville–La Hubert causeway (Exit 3), arriving there around 0730hrs. German troops of I./GR.919 abandoning strongpoint WN8 began retreating across this causeway around 0930hrs and were ambushed by the concealed paratroopers, the Germans losing 50–75 men. The US battalion also attempted to clear Exit 4, and while they found it undefended, the location of the nearby German batteries made this causeway unusable for exiting the beach. Contact was made with the 4th Infantry Division around 1300hrs, and the battalion spent the rest of the day collecting their scattered and missing men.

Lieutenant-Colonel Patrick Cassidy's 1/502nd PIR landed near St-Germain-de-Varreville, with 20 of the 36 aircraft within a mile of the beacon. One group led by Cassidy moved toward the stone buildings near

James Flanagan of C/502nd PIR displays a German flag captured during the fighting on D-Day. This scene was photographed at "Stopka strongpoint," the Marmion farm south of Ravenoville where "Mad Major" John Stopka was trying to gather troops from the 502nd and 506th PIR who had landed nearby. (NARA)

Mésières, the garrison for the German coastal battery at St-Martin-de-Varreville. Cassidy's group occupied the crossroads outside Mésières and determined that the two northern exits assigned to his battalion were clear. On meeting another group of about 45 men from his unit, he ordered them north to create a defensive perimeter near Foucarville. Cassidy kept about a company of troops near the crossroads to prevent any intervention against the beach from the west, and sent a squad to the eastern side of Mésières to clean out any German troops. A team led by Staff-Sergeant Harrison Summers killed or captured about 150 German troops in a series of one-sided encounters. As this action was winding down, the regimental commander, Lieutenant-Colonel John Michaels, arrived with 200 men. This freed up the remainder of Cassidy's men at the crossroads, who then followed the other paratroopers to the Foucarville area. Cassidy's force advanced to the west, since a secondary mission of his unit was to link up with the 82nd Airborne Division that was scheduled to land near Ste-Mère-Église. In doing so, a company became engaged in a series of encounters with German infantry around the village of Fournel that lasted through much of D-Day. The 1/502nd PIR held the northern perimeter throughout D-Day without serious challenge from the Germans except at Fournel.

Of all the units in this sector, the 377th Parachute Field Artillery, with 12 75mm pack howitzers, was the most badly dispersed, with some even landing near the marshes around St Marcouf, and others far north around Valognes. This meant there was no artillery fire support in this sector except for a single howitzer.

Paratroopers of the 101st Airborne cluster around a Renault UE armored tractor that had been pressed into service to help carry supplies from the drop zone to the "Stopka strongpoint" near Ravenoville on D-Day. The troops with the circle insignia on their helmets to the left are from the divisional artillery while the paratrooper in the center with the white spade insignia is from the 506th PIR. (NARA)

The southern sector was the responsibility of the two battalions of the 506th PIR, landing in DZ C. The cloudbank disrupted the C-47s, and some aircraft passed over a concentration of German flak near Etienville; six aircraft were shot down and 30 damaged. In spite of the fire, some drops were concentrated, with one serial of 14 aircraft dropping almost on top of

US Airborne Landings, June 6, 1944

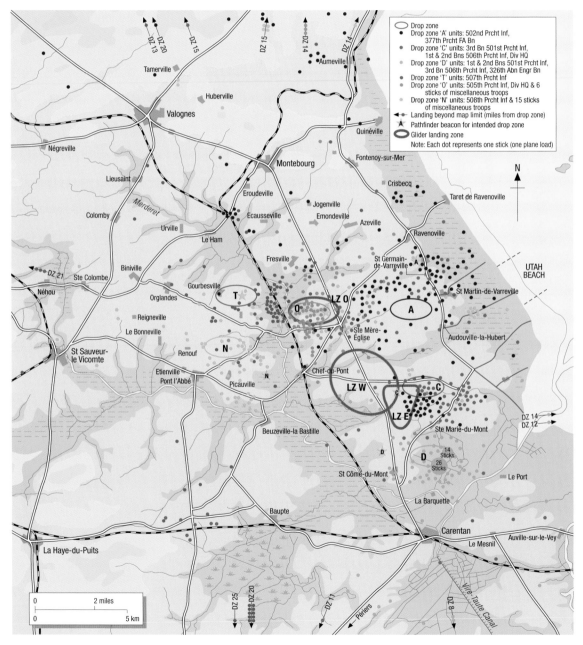

DZ C and another serial of 13 bunching their sticks a mile-and-a-half east and southeast of the DZ. But the other serials were much further from their intended targets due to confusion over the beacons. About 140 men of the HQ and 1/506th PIR assembled in the regimental area in the first hours of the landing, including the regimental commander, Colonel Sink.

The 2/506th PIR landed north of the DZ in the same area as the 501st PIR, but Lieutenant-Colonel Robert Strayer managed to collect about 200 men by 0330hrs. Strayer's group began moving south to seize the areas behind the Houdienville (Exit 2) and Pouppeville (Exit 1) causeways. Sink had no idea where Strayer's men had landed, and so instructed the assembled paratroopers of Lieutenant-Colonel William Turner's 1/506th PIR to take control of the Pouppeville causeway. Strayer's men were delayed by persistent German small-arms fire and did not arrive at the Houdienville causeway until early afternoon, by which time the access road had already been overrun by troops from the 4th Infantry Division moving inland. Turner's column also had tough going and it took several hours to reach the Poupeville causeway.

Next to land were the 3/501st PIR and the divisional HQ, which was to control the planned glider-landing area near Hiesville. The 3/501st PIR lost three aircraft to flak on the approach. A force of about 300 paratroopers from the HQ and Lieutenant-Colonel Julian Ewell's 3/501st PIR congregated near Hiesville. General Taylor, not knowing what was happening with Strayer's and Turner's two columns, decided to ensure that the southernmost Poupeville causeway was under US control, and so dispatched Colonel Ewell with 40 of his men around 0600hrs. This was the first of the three paratrooper columns to reach the causeway, around 0800hrs. The 2/GR.919 manned the WN6 strongpoint covering the western end of the causeway and

A patrol from the 101st Airborne tows supplies from the drop zone on D-Day. The paratrooper to the right has used a captured German belt to carry a pair of German "potato masher" hand-grenades, while one of his comrades carries what appears to be a German officer's service cap. (NARA)

WN2a on the beach itself. The defenses were poorly organized, but it took nearly four hours for the outnumbered paratroopers to overcome the German defenders in house-to-house fighting. The Germans surrendered around noon after suffering 25 casualties; 38 surrendered and the remainder who tried to escape across the causeway toward strongpoint WN2a on the beach were captured by advancing infantry of the 4th Division. About half of Ewell's men were casualties, but they made contact with the 2/8th Infantry at Exit 1.

Fighting flared up near the divisional command post (CP) in DZ C due to the presence nearby of troops from the German 191st Artillery Regiment centered around Ste-Marie-du-Mont. The paratroopers gradually eliminated the batteries, and the town was finally cleared of German troops by mid-afternoon when they were reinforced by GIs from the 8th Infantry advancing from the beaches.

The final groups to land were the 1/501st PIR, elements of the 2/501st PIR, the 3/506th PIR, as well as engineer and medical personnel. These forces were earmarked for DZ D, the southernmost of the DZs. The approach to the DZ was hot, with a considerable amount of light flak, searchlights, and magnesium flares. Six C-47s were shot down and 26 damaged. These drops were among the most successful in putting the paratroopers near their intended objective, but this was not entirely fortuitous, as the Germans had assumed that this area could be used for airborne landings. As this was the last of the divisional landings, the German troops in the sector were alerted and had troops near the LZ. The 1/501st PIR commander was killed and his executive officer captured. The regimental commander, Colonel Johnson, landed near the center of the zone and was able to rally about 150 paratroopers. He immediately set off for the primary objective, La Barquette locks controlling the flooding of the areas along the River Douve. The force brushed aside the German sentries and occupied the locks, but was soon under fire from German artillery. With the situation at the locks in hand, around 0900hrs Johnson and about 50 paratroopers returned to the LZ to seek reinforcements. About half of 2/501st PIR was engaged in a sharp firefight around the village of Les Droueries, and had been unable to disengage and move south to the objective. Instead of encountering the single platoon expected in this sector, they were confronted by an entire battalion, III./GR.1058. They spent most of the day fighting around the town of St-Côme-du-Mont. Johnson was able to collect a few additional paratroopers and set off to seize or destroy the bridges over the River Douve below its junction with the River Merderet.

The third unit landing in DZ D, the 3/506th PIR, had the roughest time. German troops were waiting in the landing area and had soaked a wooden building with fuel. They set the building on fire, illuminating the descending paratroopers. The battalion commander and his executive officer were among those killed in the first moments. Captain Charles Shettle, the battalion S-3,

A pair of 82nd Airborne paratroopers from the 505th PIR eye a rabbit, though it is unclear whether they view it as a potential pet or potential lunch. This photo was taken near Ste-Mère-Église on D-Day and provides some details of the paratroopers' specialized garb, including the jump gloves and scarves made from camouflage fabric. *(NARA)*

landed away from the main DZ and set off to the Le Port bridge with about 15 men. This small group gradually increased in size as it attracted scattered paratroops, and emplaced itself at two of the bridges by 0430hrs. They were forced back by German counterattacks around 0630hrs as they were nearly out of ammunition. They took up positions near the bridges, however, and were able to keep the Germans at bay. Ironically, the next day Shettle was able to call in a P-47 strike in hopes of attacking the German positions, but due to confusion, the P-47s skip-bombed the bridges instead.

MISSION BOSTON

The 82nd Airborne Division revised its plans on May 28 due to the discovery that the 91st Luftlande Division had moved into its planned landing area. The 82nd Airborne's new assignment was to land two regiments on the western side of the River Merderet, and one regiment on the eastern side around Ste-Mère-Église to secure the bridges over the Merderet. The landings of the 82nd Airborne were even more badly scattered than those of the 101st Airborne and, as a result, only one of its regiments was able to carry out its assignment on D-Day. The 82nd Airborne began landing about an hour after the 101st Airborne, around 0230hrs.

The 505th PIR was assigned to land on DZ O to the northwest of Ste-Mère-Église. Unlike many other transport serials, those flying to DZ O spotted the cloudbank early and managed to fly over it in coordinated

Mission Boston – 82nd Airborne Division over Drop Zone T, 0240hrs, D-Day

Based at Fulbock in England, the 442nd Troop Carrier Group was attached to the 52nd Wing for the D-Day airlift. The group's four squadrons made up Serial 26 of Mission Boston and arrived over Drop Zone T between 0239 and 0242hrs on D-Day. The serial carried 45 sticks of paratroopers: 36 from the rifle companies of 1/507th PIR, and nine sticks of the HQ company. The group lost one aircraft on the approach to the DZ, and suffered damage to 31 of its aircraft due to flak over the DZ. This shows aircraft from the 305th Troop Carrier Squadron (TCS), which carried the codes 4J on the nose (the other squadrons were J7: 303rd TCS; V4: 304th TCS; 7H: 306th TCS). The C-47 was a military derivative of the Douglas DC-3 civil airliner. The main structural difference between the two types was the use of a large cargo door on the left rear side of the C-47 fuselage. The C-47 had simple, folding bench seats in the main cabin instead of conventional passenger seats. On paratrooper missions such as this, the typical load was one "stick" of paratroopers, which usually totaled 18 to 20 paratroopers. Alternatively, fewer paratroopers and more cargo could be air-dropped. The paratrooper in the foreground, a Tech 5 from the 507th PIR, is seen moments after jumping from the aircraft. After leaving the C-47, the aircraft's slipstream tended to blow the paratrooper backward and curl him up. As the static line opened up the T-5 parachute pack, the olive-drab canopy began to deploy. The large surface area of the deploying canopy tended to swing the paratrooper around again, and within seconds, the shroud lines cleared the pack and the canopy blossomed, giving the paratrooper a hard jolt. Quick deployment of the parachute was essential, as the drops were conducted from only 700ft. US paratroopers also carried a reserve chute on their chest. This paratrooper is armed with a .45cal. Thompson submachine-gun, which has been tucked under the waist web of the T-5 parachute harness to keep it in place. The paratroops carried a good deal of equipment into combat. Just visible under the harness is his yellow "Mae West" life vest. His musette bag hangs under the reserve chute, an ammunition bag from his right hip, and an assault gas mask in waterproof bag from his left hip (not visible). He has a fighting knife strapped to his right leg above his jump boots. Although not visible here, he also carries a .45cal automatic in a holster on his hip with a folding knife in its scabbard in front of this. On his chest is a TL122C flashlight. Paratroopers on D-Day wore the M1942 paratroop battledress with its distinctive pockets. The paratrooper's M1C helmet resembles the normal GI helmet, but has a modified liner and chinstrap to absorb the shock of the opening parachute. The first aid packet taped to the front of the helmet for ready access contained a field dressing, tourniquet, and morphine. Many paratroopers wore gloves to protect their hands during the jump. *(Howard Gerrard © Osprey Publishing Ltd)*

A patrol of paratroopers from the 508th PIR, 82nd Airborne, moves through the churchyard of St Marcouf on D-Day. (NARA)

fashion. The only cloud problems were over the DZ itself, forcing some C-47 pilots to initiate the drop higher than usual at 1,000ft. The pathfinders had done such a thorough job marking it that many aircraft circled back over the area to drop the paratroopers more accurately. This was the most precise series of jumps of any that night. Lieutenant-Colonel Edward Krause's 3/505th PIR was assigned to take the town of Ste-Mère-Église and managed to assemble about 180 paratroopers. The town had been garrisoned by the supply element of the divisional antiaircraft unit Flak Regiment Hermann, but most of the 200 men of the unit left the town before the arrival of the paratroopers. Krause ordered his men into the town with explicit instructions to limit their actions to knives, bayonets, and grenades to make it easier to distinguish German defenders. Krause's group quickly seized the town, killing about ten German troops and capturing 30 others.

Lieutenant-Colonel Benjamin Vandervoort's 2/505th PIR collected about half its troops and set out to establish a defense line north of the DZ as planned. At 0930hrs, however, the German GR.1058 staged a counterattack against Ste-Mère-Église from the south. The regimental commander, Colonel William Ekman, ordered Vandervoort to return back southward to assist in the defense. Before doing so, he broke off a platoon to remain at Neuville and carry out the battalion's original mission. It proved to be a crucial decision. Shortly after establishing a defensive perimeter north of the town, Lieutenant Turner Turnbull's platoon was hit by a German infantry company, but managed to hold its position during an eight-hour struggle. Only 16 of the 44 paratroopers in Turnbull's platoon survived the fighting, but the platoon's defense shielded the battalion while it faced an even greater threat to the south.

The 2/505th PIR arrived in Ste-Mère-Église around 1000hrs and took over part of the perimeter defense. The first German attack consisted of two companies from the 795th Georgian Battalion and troops of the 91st Luftlande Division with a few of the division's StuG IIIs. It was repulsed by the 3/505th PIR. Colonel Krause ordered a counterattack and about 80 men from Company I advanced southward along the road, hitting one of the retreating German convoys with a grenade attack. This was the one and only German attack of the day against the town.

The 1/505th PIR landed with the HQ, including General Ridgway. Around 0400hrs, Company A under Lieutenant John Wisner set off for the La Fière bridge with about 155 paratroopers. This group increased in size as it approached the bridge, picking up stragglers from the 507th and 508th PIR. The advance on the bridge was slowed by frequent encounters with German troops. An initial attempt to rush the bridge failed due to entrenched German machine-gun teams, the first of several attempts that day in a confusing series of engagements.

The two other regiments of the 82nd Airborne Division landing in DZs T and N on the west side of the River Merderet were hopelessly scattered. Pathfinders had been unable to mark the DZs, in some cases due to the proximity of German troops. The transport aircraft were disrupted by the coastal cloudbank, and after arriving over the drop area, the pilots had searched in vain for the signals, or in some cases homed in on the wrong beacon. Although the 507th PIR dropped in a tighter pattern than the 508th, much of the 507th PIR was dropped into the the swampy fringes of the River Merderet east of DZ T, while the 508th was dropped south of DZ N. The swamps were deep and many of the heavily laden paratroopers drowned before they could free themselves of their equipment. In addition, a large amount of important equipment and supplies landed in the water, and valuable time had to be spent trying to retrieve this equipment. About half of the 508th PIR landed within 2 miles of the DZ, but the remainder landed on the other side of the River Merderet or were scattered to even more distant locations. The most noticeable terrain feature in the area of the 507th PIR drop was the railroad line from Carentan on an embankment over the marshes. Many paratroopers gathered along the embankment.

LA FIÈRE BRIDGE

One of the missions of the 507th PIR was to seize the western approaches to the La Fière bridge, which connected the DZs west of the River Merderet with Ste-Mère-Église and the paratroopers on the east side. The bridge was a small stone structure over the River Merderet, but the farmland on the west side of the river had been flooded by the Germans to prevent its use as

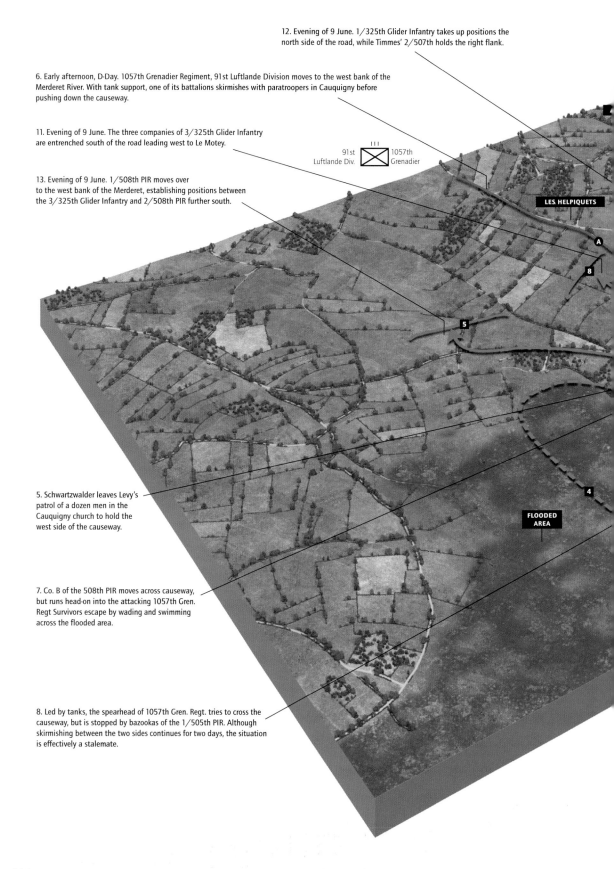

12. Evening of 9 June. 1/325th Glider Infantry takes up positions the north side of the road, while Timmes' 2/507th holds the right flank.

6. Early afternoon, D-Day. 1057th Grenadier Regiment, 91st Luftlande Division moves to the west bank of the Merderet River. With tank support, one of its battalions skirmishes with paratroopers in Cauquigny before pushing down the causeway.

11. Evening of 9 June. The three companies of 3/325th Glider Infantry are entrenched south of the road leading west to Le Motey.

13. Evening of 9 June. 1/508th PIR moves over to the west bank of the Merderet, establishing positions between the 3/325th Glider Infantry and 2/508th PIR further south.

91st
Luftlande Div.

1057th
Grenadier

LES HELPIQUETS

A

8

5

4

FLOODED AREA

5. Schwartzwalder leaves Levy's patrol of a dozen men in the Cauquigny church to hold the west side of the causeway.

7. Co. B of the 508th PIR moves across causeway, but runs head-on into the attacking 1057th Gren. Regt Survivors escape by wading and swimming across the flooded area.

8. Led by tanks, the spearhead of 1057th Gren. Regt. tries to cross the causeway, but is stopped by bazookas of the 1/505th PIR. Although skirmishing between the two sides continues for two days, the situation is effectively a stalemate.

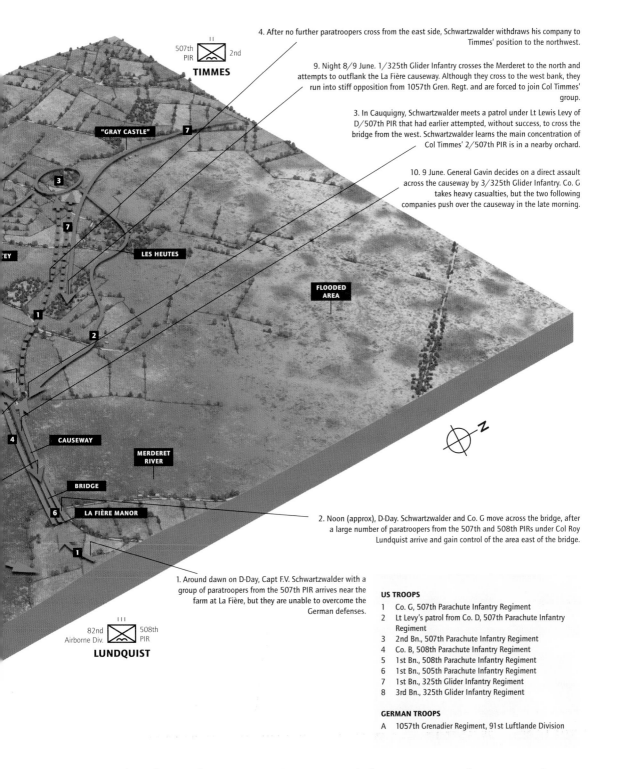

4. After no further paratroopers cross from the east side, Schwartzwalder withdraws his company to Timmes' position to the northwest.

9. Night 8/9 June. 1/325th Glider Infantry crosses the Merderet to the north and attempts to outflank the La Fière causeway. Although they cross to the west bank, they run into stiff opposition from 1057th Gren. Regt. and are forced to join Col Timmes' group.

3. In Cauquigny, Schwartzwalder meets a patrol under Lt Lewis Levy of D/507th PIR that had earlier attempted, without success, to cross the bridge from the west. Schwartzwalder learns the main concentration of Col Timmes' 2/507th PIR is in a nearby orchard.

10. 9 June. General Gavin decides on a direct assault across the causeway by 3/325th Glider Infantry. Co. G takes heavy casualties, but the two following companies push over the causeway in the late morning.

507th PIR — TIMMES — 2nd

"GRAY CASTLE"

LES HEUTES

FLOODED AREA

CAUSEWAY

MERDERET RIVER

BRIDGE

LA FIÈRE MANOR

2. Noon (approx), D-Day. Schwartzwalder and Co. G move across the bridge, after a large number of paratroopers from the 507th and 508th PIRs under Col Roy Lundquist arrive and gain control of the area east of the bridge.

1. Around dawn on D-Day, Capt F.V. Schwartzwalder with a group of paratroopers from the 507th PIR arrives near the farm at La Fière, but they are unable to overcome the German defenses.

82nd Airborne Div. — 508th PIR — LUNDQUIST

US TROOPS
1   Co. G, 507th Parachute Infantry Regiment
2   Lt Levy's patrol from Co. D, 507th Parachute Infantry Regiment
3   2nd Bn., 507th Parachute Infantry Regiment
4   Co. B, 508th Parachute Infantry Regiment
5   1st Bn., 508th Parachute Infantry Regiment
6   1st Bn., 505th Parachute Infantry Regiment
7   1st Bn., 325th Glider Infantry Regiment
8   3rd Bn., 325th Glider Infantry Regiment

GERMAN TROOPS
A   1057th Grenadier Regiment, 91st Luftlande Division

Battle for the La Fière Bridge, Merderet River

June 6–9, 1944, viewed from the southeast, showing the bitter 4-day struggle for the La Fière bridge. This small bridge and its associated causeway over the Merderet River proved crucial in the early operations beyond Utah Beach as they were the main link between the separated elements of the 82nd Airborne Division.

an airborne LZ. The connection between the bridge and the hamlet of Cauquigny over the flooded area was a long, tree-lined causeway.

After the first attempt by Lieutenant Wisner of A/505th PIR to rush the bridge, the eastern approaches became a collection point for paratroopers trying to make their way to the west side of the River Merderet, having been wrongly dropped on the eastern side. By mid-morning about 600 paratroopers had coalesced and a force under Captain F. "Ben" Schwarzwalder from the 2/507th PIR began a house-to-house skirmish to clear the manor farm on the eastern side of the bridge. When General Gavin arrived later, he split the growing force, sending a team of 75 paratroopers south to find another crossing point, while leading a second group of 75 to the bridge at Chef-du-Pont. General Ridgway arrived afterwards, and ordered Colonel Lindquist of the 508th PIR to organize the various groups near La Fière and capture the bridge.

Unknown to the force on the east side of the La Fière bridge, about 50 paratroopers of the 2/507th PIR had attempted to cross the bridge earlier in the morning from the western side. After being forced back by machine-gun fire, they established a defensive position in the Cauquigny church on the other end of the causeway. The attack against the bridge from the east side began around noon and about 80 paratroopers under Schwarzwalder pushed over the causeway and linked up with the platoon on the western side. Schwarzwalder's men were not followed by any other troops, and he decided that they should join up with the rest of their battalion under Lieutenant-Colonel Charles Timmes in an orchard in Amfreville to the northwest of Cauquigny. Schwarzwalder left behind about a dozen paratroopers, believing they would be adequate to hold the bridge until other paratroopers from the east side passed over. However, before the force on the eastern side moved

Troops disembark from the large side access door of a Horsa glider. These large British gliders were preferred for carrying heavier supply loads. *(NARA)*

more paratroopers across, GR.1057 of the 91st Luftlande Division attacked with the support of a few Hotchkiss H-39 light tanks of Panzer-Abteilung 100, quickly regaining control of the western side of the causeway in Cauquigny. As a result, the bridgehead over the Merderet was lost for the next two days and would be the scene of intense fighting.

The group under General Gavin that split off to seize the Chef-du-Pont bridge had no success. The bridge was stubbornly defended by a small number of German troops dug in along the causeway. Gavin's force was ordered back to La Fière to reinforce the main effort, and he left behind an understrength platoon commanded by Captain Roy Creek to cover the bridge. This unit was nearly overwhelmed by a later German counterattack, but it was rescued in the nick of time by the unanticipated arrival of a glider carrying a 57mm antitank gun, followed by reinforcements from La Fière. The reinforcements allowed Creek's force to clear the Germans off the bridge and cross the river to the west side.

One of the few other coherent operations of the early morning on the west bank of the Merderet involved a force assembled by Lieutenant-Colonel Thomas Shanley of the 2/508th PIR near Picauville. His unit's assignment was to destroy the Douve bridge at Pont l'Abbé, but his force quickly came in to contact with a German infantry battalion from GR.1057 involved in sealing off the west bank of the Merderet. Shanley withdrew his

The plywood construction of the Horsa made it vulnerable to break-up during hard landings as is all too evident in this case. The combination of poor light and confined landing fields led to many crashes on D-Day. *(NARA)*

D-Day Glider Missions, IX Troop Carrier Command

Mission	Chicago	Detroit	Keokuk	Elmira	Galveston	Hackensack	Total
Mission date:	D-Day	D-Day	D-Day	D-Day	D+1	D+1	
Mission time	0400hrs	0407hrs	2100hrs	2100hrs	0700hrs	0900hrs	
Landing zone	LZ E	LZ O	LZ E	LZ W	LZ W	LZ W	
Tow aircraft sorties	52	52	32	177	102	101	516
Aborted sorties	1	0	0	2	2	0	5
Aircraft lost or missing	1	1	0	5	0	0	7
Aircraft damaged	7	38	1	92	26	1	165
Horsa sorties	0	0	32	140	20	30	222
Horsa sorties aborted	0	0	0	2	2	0	4
Waco sorties	52	53	0	36	84	70	295
Waco sorties aborted	1	1	0	0	2	0	4
Aircrew killed or missing	4	4	0	1	0	0	9
Aircrew wounded	1	3	0	8	0	0	12
Glider pilots dispatched	104	106	64	352	208	200	1,034
Glider pilots lost	14	13	0	26	0	3	56
Troops carried	155	220	157	1,190	968	1,331	4,021
Troops landed	153	209	157	1,160	927	1,331	3,937
Waco casualties*	27	30	0	15	35	16	123
Horsa casualties*	0	0	44	142	80	74	340
Artillery carried	16	16	6	37	20	0	95
Vehicles carried	25	27	40	123	41	34	290
Cargo carried (tons)	14	10	19	131	26	38	238

*troops injured or killed during landing

force to the battalion assembly area on Hill 30 and they fought a day-long engagement, shielding the operations of the forces near La Fière.

By the afternoon of D-Day, there were three separated groups of paratroopers in the area around La Fière bridge: about 300 paratroopers with Shanley, 120 with Timmes and Schwarzwalder, and 400 with Colonel George Millett of the 507th PIR on the east side of La Fière. All three groups were short on ammunition, and under intense pressure from GR.1057. As will be detailed later, the fighting for La Fière continued for three days.

GLIDER REINFORCEMENTS

The next airborne missions in the early hours of D-Day were the glider reinforcement flights: Mission "Detroit" for the 82nd Airborne Division and Mission "Chicago" for the 101st Airborne Division. Mission Detroit left England at 0120hrs with 52 Waco C-4A gliders carrying 155 troops, 16 57mm antitank guns, and 25 jeeps. One of these gliders, carrying the division's SCR-499 long-range radio, was lost shortly after take-off.

A second aircraft and glider were lost before reaching LZ E. The overloaded glider carrying the 101st Airborne deputy commander, Brigadier-General Donald Pratt, crashed on landing, killing the general. The nighttime landings at 0345hrs were almost as badly scattered as the paratroopers, with only 6 gliders on target, 15 within three-quarters of a mile, ten further west, and 18 further east. Nevertheless, casualties were modest with 5 dead, 17 seriously injured, and 7 missing.

The 46 Waco CG-4A gliders of Mission Detroit landed at 0410hrs near the 82nd Airborne's LZ O, carrying 220 troops as well as 22 jeeps and 16 antitank guns. About 20 of the gliders landed on or near the LZ, while seven were released early (five disappearing) and seven more landed on the west bank of the Merderet. The rough landings in this sector led to the loss of 11 jeeps and most of the gliders, but troop losses were less than expected: 3 dead and 23 seriously injured.

The extreme congestion in the glider landing zones is made very evident in this overhead view of some of the gliders east of Les Forges. *(NARA)*

THE GERMAN REACTION

German forces on the Cotentin peninsula were not on alert on the night of June 5/6, 1944 due to the weather conditions mentioned earlier. The first hint of activity came into German intelligence around 2300–2400hrs on June 5 when signals units picked up a coded message to the French Resistance. Around 2330hrs, an aircraft warning station at Cherbourg alerted the local command that ship activity and the concentration of transport aircraft at British airfields suggested an invasion was underway. This set in train a number of alerts. The first news of paratroop jumps began arriving at headquarters around 0130hrs from the area around the River Vire. These alerts increased in number through the early morning hours. One of the sticks of pathfinders landed on top of the regimental HQ of GR.919, located in a quarry on the road between Quineville and Montebourg. Oberstleutnant Gunther Keil commanded the battalions along the coastline, and found a map on one of the paratroopers that indicated that the main drop would be around Ste-Mère-Église. At first, the regimental HQ believed that the paratroopers were part of a raid, and not a major drop. The 795th Georgian Battalion located east of Ste-Mère-Église reported around 0300hrs that the battalion was surrounded, but Keil was a bit skeptical as the messengers had arrived at the command post without difficulty and an officer of the Georgian battalion arrived safely by car. He gave more credence to a report from a company of the divisional engineers who reported that thousands of paratroopers were landing.

At LXXXIV Corps headquarters, General Marcks became concerned that the paratroopers might create a gap between the 709th Division at Utah Beach and the 352nd Division at Omaha. The only major corps reserve was Kampfgruppe Meyer of the 352nd Infantry Division near St Lô. At 0310hrs, Marcks ordered Meyer to advance toward the junction of the two divisions between Utah and Omaha beaches. The decision to send the reserves after the paratroopers proved to be premature and a serious mistake. Later in the morning, the force would be badly needed in the opposite direction. As a result, Kampfgruppe Meyer spent most of the morning marching westward, only to have their orders changed a few hours later and shifted in the opposite direction, all the while under air attack.

US paratroopers landed mainly in the deployment area of the 91st Luftlande Division. The reaction of the division was confused, in part due to the absence of senior divisional commanders at the Rennes wargame. General Falley was alerted to the paratrooper landings early in the morning and set out by car to return to his unit. Around dawn, his car was intercepted before reaching his command post by a paratrooper patrol and he was killed after a short skirmish near Picauville. Unaware of Falley's fate and unable to contact him, the division's operations officer, General Bernhard Klosterkemper, took temporary command. On learning that the Americans had seized Ste-Mère-Église, he ordered GR.1057 to begin to move east over the Merderet via the La Fière bridge, where the regiment would become entangled with the 82nd Airborne Division over control of the River Merderet crossings.

In the meantime, Oberstleutnant Keil had asked permission from LXXXIV Corps headquarters to use Major Moch's battalion from GR.1058 of the 91st Luftlande Division located at St-Côme-du-Mont to assist him in his own efforts to regain control of Ste-Mère-Église from the north. Permission was granted by corps HQ at 0330hrs and Keil hoped that Moch's battalion would arrive at Ste-Mère-Église by 0800hrs. Instead of moving on the town, Moch's battalion was still in its garrison north of Ste-Mère-Église at 0800hrs and Keil again ordered him to attack the town, without result. Finally, around 1100hrs, Moch sent a message indicating that the battery at Azeville had been captured and asking Keil if he should retake it. At the end of his patience, Keil told him to follow the previous orders but Moch's battalion did not reach the outskirts of the town until 1300hrs. By the afternoon, a perimeter defense had already been established and Moch's battalion reinforced the units assaulting Lieutenant Turnbull's platoon outside Neuville, but were unable to overcome the outnumbered but tenacious paratroopers.

The German troops south of Ste-Mère-Église, including the remnants of the 795th Georgian Battalion, were pressed into a pocket by the paratrooper attacks from the north, and the advance of 4th Division troops from the beaches later in the day. This pocket continued to block the road south of Ste-Mère-Église through D-Day.

While Moch's battalion was sluggishly approaching Ste-Mère-Église, the corps HQ ordered a second battalion from GR.1058 to follow it southward to the town. It became bottled up around Montebourg, however. The corps headquarters also activated the Sturm-Abeilung AOK 7 and sent it along the road from St Floxel to Beuzeville-au-Plain, eventually attacking the US positions on the eastern side of Ste-Mère-Église in the afternoon. Elements of the 709th Panzerjäger Company accompanied it, but were lost in the fighting with the paratroopers around Beuzeville-au-Plain.

FJR 6 near Périers was alerted around midnight, and began encountering paratroopers who had landed far south of the intended landing areas. Von der Heydte tried reaching higher command, but telephone lines in the area had been cut, probably by the French Resistance. The 3./FJR 6 engaged in skirmishes with US paratroopers in the pre-dawn hours, being pushed to the southeast. Von der Heydte finally managed to reach Marcks around 0600hrs by using telephones at the St Lô post office, and he was ordered to clear the Carentan area of paratroopers and begin moving his regiment northward toward Ste-Mère-Église with the objective of eliminating the paratrooper concentrations there. In the days prior to the invasion, Rommel had ordered units in areas vulnerable to paratroop landing to disperse their garrison, and as a result, FJR 6 had a difficult time assembling its troops. Von der Heydte passed through Carentan ahead of his troops, finding the town devoid of German or American troops, and he reached a German

German Counterattack on the River Merderet, 1400hrs D-Day

Around 1300hrs, the 1057th Grenadier Regiment of the 91st Luftlande Division began a counterattack toward the La Fière causeway through Cauquigny. A company of Hotchkiss H-39 tanks of Panzer-Abteilung 100 spearheaded the attack, but two were disabled in the first attack, which was beaten off. The surviving pair of Hotchkiss tanks again took up the lead, accompanied by infantry. Company A, 1/505th PIR had set up a defensive position on the east side of the La Fière bridge and earlier in the morning the paratroopers had placed a string of antitank mines in plain sight on top of the road as a deterrent to the Panzers. The Hotchkiss tanks sped ahead of the accompanying infantry, and approached to within 40ft of the mines. The paratroopers had two bazooka teams in ambush position and they immediately hit the first tank. The second tank had no room to maneuver on either side of the causeway, and backed away. An infantry attack by GR.1057 followed, which was stopped by small-arms fire and the support of some 60mm mortars. Attacks continued through the day, with the paratrooper positions pounded by German artillery. During a truce late in the day to recover the wounded, a paratrooper surveyed the German positions on the causeway and estimated they had suffered about 200 casualties in their brave but futile counterattacks. The paratroopers had also taken heavy losses, and few of the men holding the east side of the bridge survived D-Day. Around 0200hrs on June 7, the second Hotchkiss returned and attempted to push the derelict tank off the road, but was attacked in the dark by Sergeant William Owens with Gammon grenades, and retreated again. This was the last attempt by GR.1057 to cross the Merderet, but it established blocking positions on the causeway that prevented the paratroopers from crossing as well. The Hotchkiss H-39 tank, dubbed PzKpfw 38H 735(f) in Wehrmacht service, was a French cavalry tank captured in the wake of the 1940 campaign. They were widely used by the Wehrmacht in secondary roles, especially anti-partisan fighting, and saw combat in Finland, Yugoslavia, Russia, and France. The Wehrmacht made several changes to the tanks, most evidently cutting off the top of the turret cupola and replacing it with a split hatch for the tank commander. After being rebuilt in 1941, they were repainted in standard German dark gray, but many were camouflaged later with the newer dark yellow color. Despite its name, the 91st Luftlande Division was a regular army (Heer) division. As a result, its uniforms were typical of those worn by the German Army in the summer of 1944. The Unteroffizier (NCO), riding on the back of the rear tank, is the squad leader (Gruppenführer) and is armed with the ubiquitous 98k rifle, although nominally the squad leader should be armed with a machine pistol. His binoculars and map case set him apart from the rest of the rifle squad. The soldier alongside him on the tank is equipped with an MP40 machine pistol. Following the tank is a Richtschütze armed with a Panzerschreck antitank rocket launcher. A loader, not visible here, would normally accompany him carrying two more rockets. The rest of the squad includes the machine-gun team, consisting of a gunner and assistant gunner and armed with a MG42 machine-gun, and two more riflemen. *(Howard Gerrard © Osprey Publishing Ltd)* battalion dug in near St-Côme-du-Mont. He climbed the village church's steeple, giving him a vista of the battlefield all the way to Utah Beach. The vast armada of US ships was clearly visible, and he later recalled that the scene was oddly tranquil, like a summer's day on the shore of the Wannsee near Berlin with little evidence of fighting. This was the first time that a senior German officer learned that the paratrooper attack had been reinforced by a major amphibious landing. As 3./FJR 6 was still engaged with US forces, the other two battalions reached this assembly area in the early afternoon. The 2./FJR 6 was directed to advance on Ste-Mère-Église along the main road while the 1./FJR 6 would advance further east to shield the column from US troops landing from the sea. The two advancing battalions moved out around 1900hrs and had no serious contact with US forces until after nightfall, when both battalions were heavily disrupted by further airborne landings virtually on top of them.

The fate of the I./GR.919 stationed along Utah Beach was not recorded in detail due to its quick rout. Communications between the battalion and the division headquarters were lost before noon on D-Day as US troops captured most of its strongpoints. Of the 13 strongpoints, WN1 to WN14 along the coast, all of the southern strongpoints closest to the US landings were taken by US forces on D-Day. Those further north on the coast including WN10, WN10a, WN11, and StP12 held out for another day or two, finally surrendering after running out of food and ammunition.

The W5 strongpoint at Utah Beach had a French 47mm Model 1937 antitank gun among its defenses that was knocked out by the preliminary bombardment. The Wehrmacht made extensive use of captured equipment in its Normandy defenses as well as older German equipment deemed obsolete for the Russian front. *(NARA)*

THE AMPHIBIOUS LANDINGS

Task Force U under Rear-Admiral Don Moon reached the transport area off Utah Beach around 0230hrs and the command ship, USS *Bayfield*, dropped anchor. There was no significant German naval activity in the area even though Admiral Krancke had issued orders to repel the invasion force after shore radar had located the oncoming invasion fleet at 0309hrs. Two torpedo boat flotillas operating out of Cherbourg encountered heavy seas, and returned to port before dawn without engaging the Allied landing force. The first actions of the day began around 0505hrs, when German coastal batteries began to open fire on Allied shipping as it crossed the horizon. The Morsalines battery of 6./HKAA.1261 with six French 155mm guns had been located in concrete emplacements near St Vaast, but due to air attacks it was moved to open ground near Videcosville. It began engaging a minesweeper, prompting HMS *Black Prince* to respond. The Marcouf battery of 3./HKAA.1261 and the neighboring 4./HKAA.1261 engaged the destroyers USS *Corry* and *Fitch*. While maneuvering to avoid the fire, the *Corry* struck a mine amidships, cutting it in two. The destroyers *Fitch* and *Hobson* pulled alongside while keeping the coastal batteries under fire. The Marcouf battery was subjected to the most intense fire, first by the cruiser *Quincy* and then by the battleship USS *Nevada*. *Nevada* scored a direct hit on one of the four bunkers with a 5in round, but it was a dud, passing through the bunker and out the other side. The battery lost the first of three guns in the early morning exchange, the second at 1557hrs and the last at 1830hrs.

German resistance on Utah Beach was quickly overwhelmed except for sporadic artillery shelling from distant coastal batteries. This view from a Coast Guard LCVP shows troops wading ashore with an LCI beached to the left. The barrage balloons were intended to prevent low-altitude strafing by German aircraft.

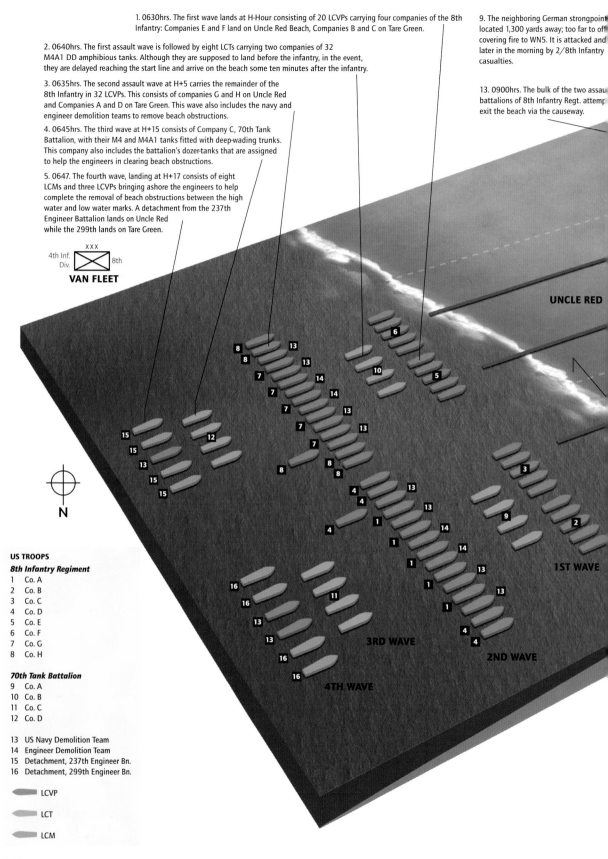

1. 0630hrs. The first wave lands at H-Hour consisting of 20 LCVPs carrying four companies of the 8th Infantry: Companies E and F land on Uncle Red Beach, Companies B and C on Tare Green.

2. 0640hrs. The first assault wave is followed by eight LCTs carrying two companies of 32 M4A1 DD amphibious tanks. Although they are supposed to land before the infantry, in the event, they are delayed reaching the start line and arrive on the beach some ten minutes after the infantry.

3. 0635hrs. The second assault wave at H+5 carries the remainder of the 8th Infantry in 32 LCVPs. This consists of companies G and H on Uncle Red and Companies A and D on Tare Green. This wave also includes the navy and engineer demolition teams to remove beach obstructions.

4. 0645hrs. The third wave at H+15 consists of Company C, 70th Tank Battalion, with their M4 and M4A1 tanks fitted with deep-wading trunks. This company also includes the battalion's dozer-tanks that are assigned to help the engineers in clearing beach obstructions.

5. 0647. The fourth wave, landing at H+17 consists of eight LCMs and three LCVPs bringing ashore the engineers to help complete the removal of beach obstructions between the high water and low water marks. A detachment from the 237th Engineer Battalion lands on Uncle Red while the 299th lands on Tare Green.

9. The neighboring German strongpoint located 1,300 yards away; too far to off covering fire to WN5. It is attacked and later in the morning by 2/8th Infantry casualties.

13. 0900hrs. The bulk of the two assau battalions of 8th Infantry Regt. attemp exit the beach via the causeway.

4th Inf. Div. XXX 8th

VAN FLEET

UNCLE RED

1ST WAVE

2ND WAVE

3RD WAVE

4TH WAVE

N

US TROOPS

8th Infantry Regiment
1   Co. A
2   Co. B
3   Co. C
4   Co. D
5   Co. E
6   Co. F
7   Co. G
8   Co. H

70th Tank Battalion
9   Co. A
10   Co. B
11   Co. C
12   Co. D

13   US Navy Demolition Team
14   Engineer Demolition Team
15   Detachment, 237th Engineer Bn.
16   Detachment, 299th Engineer Bn.

LCVP

LCT

LCM

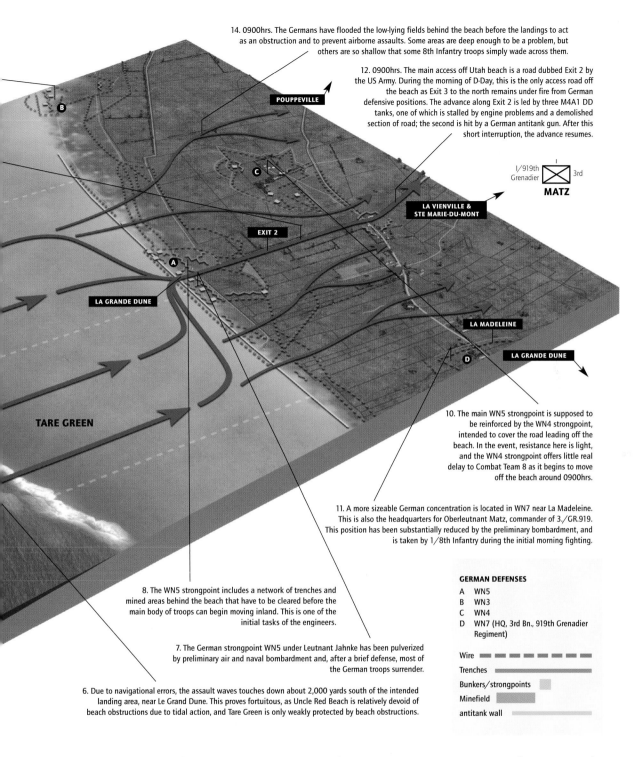

14. 0900hrs. The Germans have flooded the low-lying fields behind the beach before the landings to act as an obstruction and to prevent airborne assaults. Some areas are deep enough to be a problem, but others are so shallow that some 8th Infantry troops simply wade across them.

12. 0900hrs. The main access off Utah beach is a road dubbed Exit 2 by the US Army. During the morning of D-Day, this is the only access road off the beach as Exit 3 to the north remains under fire from German defensive positions. The advance along Exit 2 is led by three M4A1 DD tanks, one of which is stalled by engine problems and a demolished section of road; the second is hit by a German antitank gun. After this short interruption, the advance resumes.

POUPPEVILLE

I/919th Grenadier $\boxed{\times}$ 3rd

MATZ

LA VIENVILLE & STE MARIE-DU-MONT

EXIT 2

LA MADELEINE

LA GRANDE DUNE

LA GRANDE DUNE

TARE GREEN

10. The main WN5 strongpoint is supposed to be reinforced by the WN4 strongpoint, intended to cover the road leading off the beach. In the event, resistance here is light, and the WN4 strongpoint offers little real delay to Combat Team 8 as it begins to move off the beach around 0900hrs.

11. A more sizeable German concentration is located in WN7 near La Madeleine. This is also the headquarters for Oberleutnant Matz, commander of 3./GR.919. This position has been substantially reduced by the preliminary bombardment, and is taken by 1/8th Infantry during the initial morning fighting.

GERMAN DEFENSES

A WN5
B WN3
C WN4
D WN7 (HQ, 3rd Bn., 919th Grenadier Regiment)

Wire	
Trenches	
Bunkers/strongpoints	
Minefield	
antitank wall	

8. The WN5 strongpoint includes a network of trenches and mined areas behind the beach that have to be cleared before the main body of troops can begin moving inland. This is one of the initial tasks of the engineers.

7. The German strongpoint WN5 under Leutnant Jahnke has been pulverized by preliminary air and naval bombardment and, after a brief defense, most of the German troops surrender.

6. Due to navigational errors, the assault waves touches down about 2,000 yards south of the intended landing area, near Le Grand Dune. This proves fortuitous, as Uncle Red Beach is relatively devoid of beach obstructions due to tidal action, and Tare Green is only weakly protected by beach obstructions.

Assault waves, Combat Team 8, Utah Beach

0630–0900hrs, June 6, 1944, viewed from the north. As a result of the offshore current and poor visibility, Combat Team 8's first wave lands 2,000yds south of the intended landing zone. The defenses are less formidable and the assault actually easier. The German strongpoints are rapidly overcome and the troops push inland to link up with troops from the 82nd and 101st Airborne.

The preliminary naval bombardment of the beach began at H-40 (0550hrs). As H-Hour approached, the fire was redirected toward flank targets, especially remaining German naval batteries in the area. Utah Beach was scheduled for a preliminary air bombardment by IX Bomber Command. Although cloud cover threatened to disrupt the bombardment, the attacking B-26 Marauder pilots decided to drop below the prescribed altitude, descending to 3,500–7,000ft. A total of 269 bombers took part, dropping 525 tons of 250lb bombs between 0605 and 0624hrs. This pounding was in complete contrast to Omaha Beach, where the bombers remained above the cloud cover, and ineffectively dropped their bombs far behind the beach using blind-bombing tactics. Apart from the bombardment of the beach itself, a further 33 aircraft dropped 47 tons of bombs on the coastal artillery batteries near Maisy and Gefosse.

The preliminary bombardment proved to be extremely effective in suppressing the German defenses at the WN5 strongpoint. Most of the open gun pits had been knocked out by the attacks, and even some of the enclosed bunkers had collapsed or were seriously damaged. One of the few defense positions intact was the well-protected Bauform 667 casemate on the southern fringe of WN5. Although casualties from the bombardment had been low, many of the German defenders were stunned by the bomb blasts and naval gunfire.

The first landing actually occurred two hours before the main landings. Activity had been spotted on the St Marcouf islands off Utah Beach in May, so a cavalry detachment of 132 men from the 4th and 24th Cavalry Squadrons were sent ashore at 0430hrs. In fact, there were no German troops on the islands, but minefields and later German artillery fire killed two and wounded 17.

As on Omaha Beach, the preliminary force ashore was scheduled to be amphibious Duplex Drive M4A1 medium tanks. The 32 tanks from the 70th Tank Battalion were carried toward their launch point on board eight LCTs. The run toward the beach was slowed by the headwind and steep

Company C of the 70th Tank Battalion goes ashore at Utah Beach in the third wave. The first two companies of the 70th Tank Battalion used DD tanks, while this company used deep-wading trunks. *(NARA)*

Tank casualties on Utah Beach were due almost entirely to mines. This M4 medium tank named "Cannonball" of C/70th Tank Battalion became trapped in a hidden shell crater while driving to the beach from its LCT. The two deep-wading trunks are very evident in this view. *(NARA)*

chop. At 0521hrs, one of the two control craft guiding in the force struck a mine and sank, followed 15 minutes later by an LCT. The naval control officer realized that the force was behind schedule, and to speed up the landing, the LCTs launched the tanks from closer to shore than planned, from about 1,500 yards instead of 5,000 yards. Even so, the 28 DD tanks arrived ten minutes after the first wave of troops.

The assault force for Utah Beach was CT8, formed from the 8th Infantry of the 4th Infantry Division, along with supporting engineers and other specialist troops. The initial two waves consisted of two assault battalions, more heavily equipped than normal infantry, landing in LCVPs. The first wave included 20 LCVPs with 30 troops each. The offshore current pushed the craft somewhat to the south, and the landmarks on shore were difficult to see due to the smoke caused by the heavy bombardment. As a result, the first wave of the assault force landed about 2,000 yards south of the intended objective around Exit 3 and Les Dunes-de-Varreville, landing instead near Exit 2 and the Grande Dune. The navigational error had little effect on the operation, and if anything permitted an easier landing as it transpired that there were fewer beach obstructions in this sector and the German strongpoints were less substantial. Instead of facing two major German strongpoints on the intended beach, the landing faced only a single strongpoint that had been pulverized by the aerial bombing. Several company-sized task forces set about reducing the German strongpoints along the beach, which was accomplished without difficulty, aided by the newly arrived DD tanks. The tanks quickly knocked out the surviving bunkers, and began breaching the seawall using gunfire. The commander of the German defenses, Leutnant Jahnke, ordered the Goliath remote-control

Combat Team 8 on Utah Beach, 0730hrs D-Day

The M4A1 Sherman tanks of C/70th Tank Battalion arrived on Utah Beach in the third wave aboard LCTs at H+15. Unlike the battalion's two other companies of tanks fitted with DD Duplex Drive equipment, which in theory at least allowed them to "swim" ashore, Company C relied on deep-wading trunks to get to the beach. After reaching the shoreline, the crew detached the clumsy upper trunks, but the lower adapter trunks are still evident on this tank. The mission of the tanks on the beach was to help the infantry in overcoming any beach defenses, and to assist in exiting the beach by blasting the seawall with their guns. Here "Colombia Lou," one of the company's M4 medium tanks, engages a German Bauform 667 bunker with GIs from the 8th Infantry taking cover behind the advancing tank. These ferro-concrete bunkers were so thick that naval gunfire or bombs could not easily knock them out. The only effective method to silence them was to engage them at relatively close quarters, firing directly into the bunker's embrasure. Assault troops of the 8th Infantry wore distinctive battledress on D-Day. Due to the suspicion that the Germans might use chemical weapons to defeat the landings, the troops' uniforms were impregnated with a solution that prevented the chemical agent from soaking into the clothing. On Omaha beach, the usual battledress was impregnated with this chemical preparation. On Utah Beach, the assault troops wore a set of chemically impregnated HBT (herringbone twill) battledress over their normal uniforms. They could then discard the HBTs after the landings. The black waterproof bag they are carrying contains an assault gas mask. Another item specially developed for the D-Day landings was the assault vest, which was intended to take the place of normal webbing, ammunition pouches, and musette bags all in a single garment. In the event, the assault vest proved to be cumbersome and unworkable and the concept was discarded. All the members of the fire team seen here are armed with the M1 Garand rifle except for one team member who is armed with a Browning Automatic Rifle (BAR). The GI on the right has a rifle grenade adapter fitted to his rifle, and is preparing to fire a rifle grenade at the German defenses. Due to the recoil from launching these grenades, the prescribed method of firing them was to place the butt of the rifle on the ground. *(Howard Gerrard © Osprey Publishing Ltd)* vehicles to be launched against the tanks and landing craft, but the bombardment had severed the wire guidance cables to their hidden nests.

The first assault wave was followed by 32 more LCVPs containing the remainder of the two assault battalions along with engineer and naval demolition parties. The demolition teams set about destroying beach obstructions to permit the landing of additional craft once the tide had turned. The engineers began to tackle the problem of minefields along the beach, and also used explosive charges to blow gaps in the seawall to allow the troops speedier passage off the beach. The third wave at H+15 consisted of eight more LCTs containing C/70th Tank Battalion using M4 tanks fitted with wading trunks, as well as four dozer-tanks to assist in the beach-clearing operation. The fourth wave consisted mainly of detachments from the 237th and 299th Engineers to assist in clearing the beaches. Two additional battalions, 3/8th Infantry and 3/22nd Infantry, also followed. By this stage, German fire was limited to sporadic artillery. Most of the German defenders surrendered quickly, but Jahnke was not pulled from his command bunker until around noon during the clean-up operations.

The first senior officer on the beach was General Theodore Roosevelt Jr, the 4th Division's assistant commander. On realizing they had landed on the wrong beach, he personally scouted the exits to determine which causeway to use to exit the beach. Roosevelt met with the two infantry battalion commanders and instructed them to eliminate remaining German defenses and move out over the Exit 2 causeway. By 0900hrs, the defenses behind the beach had been reduced and the 8th Infantry was moving inland, led by tanks from the 70th Tank Battalion. On the way down the causeway, the Germans had set off a demolition charge under a small culvert, creating a gap in the road. The lead tank had mechanical problems, stalling the second tank, which was struck by an antitank gun. The third tank quickly eliminated the gun, and engineers from the Beach Obstacle Task Force brought up a length of treadway bridge to cover the gap. Due to congestion on the causeway, some units moved across the flooded tidal pools behind the beach.

The 1/8th Infantry moved north from the causeway and reached Turqueville by evening without encountering any serious resistance. The 3/8th Infantry headed directly west from the causeway, and ran into elements of 14./GR.919, the regimental antitank unit, with a platoon of 75mm antitank guns deployed in field positions along with infantry from the I./GR.919. A short firefight ensued in which about 50 Germans were killed and about 100 surrendered. The battalion reached the area north of Les Forges and sent out a platoon to link up with the 82nd Airborne Division near Chef-du-Pont. The 2/8th Infantry headed south toward Pouppeville along the seawall rather than crossing the causeway. There was almost continuous skirmishing with isolated German riflemen along the coast, but the battalion overwhelmed the weakly defended WN2a strongpoint and made its way to Exit 1 and the road junction near Pouppeville. They linked up with Colonel Ewell of the 3/501st PIR who had already cleared the town of troops from GR.1058. Apart from the actions by the 8th Infantry, A/49th Engineer Combat Battalion was assigned to seize a lock near Grand Vey that controlled the flooding of the tidal pools. In the process, they took about 125 German prisoners.

The remainder of the 4th Infantry Division landed on D-Day, along with the first elements of the 90th Division. Both the 12th and 22nd Infantry were directed toward the northern side of the beachhead area. Starting from a position further south than the planned landing area, they did not reach their objectives on D-Day. They formed a defensive perimeter emanating westward from St-Germain-de-Varreville toward Ste-Mère-Église.

Reinforcement of the airborne divisions continued through the day. Howell Force, a reserve of troops from the 82nd Airborne Division under Colonel E. Raff, landed by sea and followed 3/8th Infantry, planning to join up with its parent unit. On reaching the area near Les Forges where the 3/8th Infantry had set up its nighttime bivouac, Raff was told that the infantry planned to advance no further that night as they were already in possession of their objective and had run into German defenses north of their position. Raff wanted to link up with airborne forces in Ste-Mère-Église, and was also concerned about the safety of LZ W, the destination of Mission "Elmira," another glider supply effort. Attempts to budge the German defenses had not succeeded by the time that the gliders appeared over the LZ around 2100hrs, and the fields were in no-man's land. The first wave consisted of 54 Horsa and 22 Waco CG-4A gliders with 437 troops, 64 vehicles, 13 57mm antitank guns, and 24 tons of supplies. In the declining light, the gliders landed under fire from scattered German positions. The main hazard was the difficulty of landing the gliders in confined farm fields at dusk, and many gliders crashed on landing. The casualties were surprisingly light considering the circumstances. The second wave of the Elmira mission, consisting of 86 Horsa and 14 Waco CG-4A gliders, landed about an hour-and-a-half later in LZ O north of Ste-Mère-Église. The third and smallest glider landing of the evening, "Keokuk," crunched into LZ E, west of Hiesville.

D-DAY AT MIDNIGHT

By midnight on D-Day, Utah Beach was securely in American hands and the 4th Infantry Division had reached its initial objectives, at a very modest cost – only 197 casualties. The startling contrast in the casualties compared to the more than 2,000 suffered on neighboring Omaha Beach was due to the weak defenses on Utah Beach and the total disruption of German defenses by the airborne landings. Omaha Beach was defended by 11 strongpoints instead of the one at Utah, and the defending forces there had 26 antitank guns and field guns aimed at the beach compared to only five at Utah Beach. There was a similar discrepancy in machine-guns and mortars. In addition, the Utah Beach bunkers were heavily damaged by the preliminary bombardment, while the Omaha bunkers were never bombed. Utah Beach was defended by only about a company of infantry, while Omaha Beach had portions of two infantry regiments. Tanks also landed in force on Utah, with nearly three intact companies on the beach in the opening hour of the fighting.

The air landings by the 82nd and 101st Airborne Divisions had not gone according to plan, due to dispersion of the drops. Only about 10 percent of the paratroopers landed on their DZs, a further 25 percent within a mile, and another 20 percent within 2 miles. The remainder were more scattered: about 25 percent were within 5 miles, 15 percent were between 5 and 25 miles from their DZs, and about 5 percent were missing. By dawn, the 82nd Airborne Division had only about 1,500 paratroopers near their divisional objectives and the 101st Airborne had only about 1,100. By midnight, the situation was

Fighting went on for several days to clear the German strongpoints along the coast north of Utah Beach. This is a sniper patrol from 3/22nd Infantry checking out a farm in the Dunes des Varreville area on June 10, 1944. (NARA)

not much better: only about 2,000 under divisional control with the 82nd and 2,500 with the 101st Airborne Division of the 13,350 dropped. While the serious dispersion accounts for the problems in the morning, the continued difficulties collecting troops during the course of the day was due to the unexpected isolation of small groups of paratroopers enforced by the maze of hedgerows and flooded farmlands and the lack of sufficient radios to link the dispersed groups. Casualties sustained by the airborne units on D-Day have never been accurately calculated as so many troops were missing for days afterwards. Nevertheless, it is evident that casualties in these units were considerably higher than those suffered by the 4th Infantry Division during the beach landings. Indeed, total casualties in the Utah sector were comparable to the 2,000 casualties on Omaha Beach, but a significant portion of these casualties were paratroopers captured by the Germans and non-combat injuries sustained during the night drops.

As a result of the difficulties in assembling the paratroopers, the objectives of the airborne divisions were not met on D-Day. The airborne divisions did secure some of the access routes off the beach, but the only causeway that really mattered was seized by the 8th Infantry. Bridges over the Merderet were not secured, and large portions of the 82nd Airborne remained cut off on the west side of the river. Equally worrisome, the airborne divisions did not manage to create an effective defensive screen on the southern edge of the VII Corps lodgment, leaving the bridgehead vulnerable to attack by German reserves. This had no consequence due to the weak German response.

By the perverse logic of war, the airborne assault actually did accomplish its mission even if specific objectives were not achieved. The paratroopers were so widely scattered that they disrupted and tied down most German forces on the eastern side of the Cotentin peninsula. If the US airborne commanders were unhappy over their failures, the German senior commanders were baffled. Some German officers believed that the airborne assault represented a clever new tactical approach they dubbed "saturation attack," intended to disrupt defensive efforts by the German Army rather than to control specific terrain features. Although the Germans may have been impressed by the airborne landings, senior Allied leaders were not. The problems with the Normandy landings convinced them that nighttime landings were inherently too risky given the limitations of contemporary navigation technology, and subsequent Allied airborne operations were conducted in daylight.

German defensive operations on D-Day had been passive and unsuccessful. The vaunted Atlantic Wall in this sector had been breached within an hour with few casualties. The combat performance of German infantry units, not surprisingly, was quite mixed. Some units, such as GR.1057 along the Merderet, attacked and defended with tenacity and skill. Many of the static defense units surrendered to the paratroopers even though they outnumbered

The Georgian Battalion. The 795th Ost was stationed immediately behind Utah Beach and involved in the D-Day fighting. This Georgian captain was captured after their positions were overrun. Curiously enough, he had featured in a series of German propaganda photos taken before D-Day of Hitler's new allies. *(NARA)*

the attackers, especially those with conscripted Poles and "volunteer" Soviet prisoners. In general, the Utah Beach sector received relatively little attention from German corps and army HQs due to the perception that other sectors were far more dangerous, especially the British beaches. Indeed, it was not apparent to senior German commanders until late in the day that a major amphibious landing was under way at Utah Beach.

CONSOLIDATING THE BEACHHEAD

General Collins, commander of VII Corps, realized that his first mission would be to consolidate the beachhead area due to the lingering dispersion of the paratroop forces. He was still not in touch with General Ridgway from the 82nd Airborne Division, and the first communications were not received until late on D+1. The primary mission of the day was to eliminate the German pocket south of Ste-Mère-Église, and to relieve the pressure on the northern sector of the town's defenses. The pocket contained the remnants of the 795th Georgian Battalion and GR.919. By dawn, the 8th Infantry was poised along its southern and eastern flank, and attacks began that morning. Although the Georgians resisted the initial attacks, a Russian-speaking GI was able to convince them to surrender. About 250 troops surrendered to the 1/8th Infantry. The two other battalions of the 8th Infantry had a much harder fight against German units holding a ridge that covered the access road to Ste-Mère-Église, but this was overcome, and the two battalions fought their way into town. In the meantime, Collins had already ordered a column of tanks of C/746th Tank Battalion to Ste-Mère-Église along the eastern road, and these arrived in time to beat back an early afternoon attack by GR.1058, supported by StuG III assault guns. The 82nd Airborne was reinforced during the day by additional air-landings of the 325th Glider Infantry at 0700 and 0900hrs in the Les Forges area. Fighting continued around the La Fière bridge, with the paratroopers repulsing German attacks. But at the end of D+1, a substantial portion of the 82nd Airborne Division remained cut off on the western side of the Merderet. Nevertheless, the fighting on D+1 solidified the 82nd Airborne positions on the eastern bank, with the division now in firm control of Ste-Mère-Église and connected to the seaborne invasion force.

The other two regiments of the 4th Division pushed northward out of the beachhead along the coast. The most difficult fighting took place around the fortified German coastal gun positions at Azeville and Crisbecq. Although the two regiments were able to push about 2 miles northward during the day, they were unable to overcome the two fortified areas and suffered heavy casualties. The 3/22nd Infantry advanced along the coast and reduced the surviving German beach strongpoints. Naval fire-control parties helped direct the gunfire of warships against the bunkers. By the evening of D+1, the battalion had fought its way through all of the German defenses up to WN11 when it was ordered inland to serve as a reserve for the other two battalions of the 22nd Infantry that had been battered that day in the fighting with the coastal artillery fortifications. While moving across the inundated tidal flats westward, a German prisoner reported that most of

A paratrooper patrol moves through the outskirts of Ste-Mère-Église on June 10, clearing out isolated groups of German stragglers still in the town. (NARA)

his comrades in the WN13 strongpoint wanted to surrender after a day of pounding from naval gunfire. As a result, the 3/22nd Infantry swung behind WN11 and occupied WN13 further to the north, leaving behind a company to prevent the garrison of WN11 from escaping. This strongpoint surrendered the following day.

The 101st Airborne Division was involved for most of D+1 in securing the southern flank of the beachhead, especially around St-Côme-du-Mont and the River Douve north of Carentan. Two battalions of German paratroopers from FJR 6 had been advancing through this area on D-Day, with 1./FJR 6

Securing Utah Beach, June 7, 1944

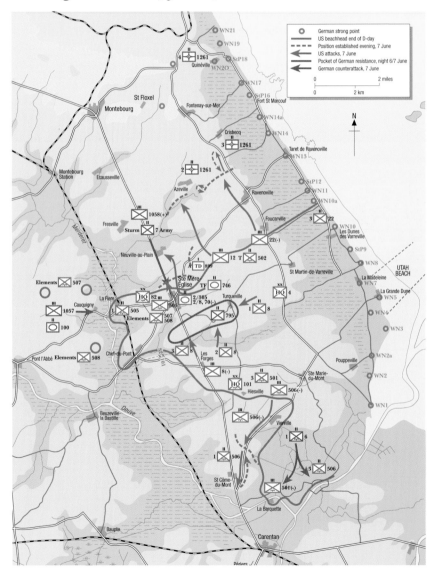

reaching the area of Ste-Marie-du-Mont and 2./FJR 6 reaching within a mile of Ste-Mère-Église from the east. Von der Heydte, after seeing the scale of the American operation, realized that his attack on Ste-Mère-Église with a mere two battalions was a fool's errand, and during the night of June 6/7, ordered both battalions to withdraw. The 2./FJR 6 received the order and withdrew, but the other battalion did not respond. It belatedly withdrew southward during D+1 toward the rear of the defensive positions of the 101st Airborne Division along the River Douve. It nearly bumped into a column from 1/506th PIR heading out of Vierville, but the American column hesitated to fire as the identity of the force was very unclear. By late afternoon, about 300 German paratroopers from the 1./FJR 6 began approaching the rear of Captain Shettle's force of about 100 paratroopers from 3/506th PIR. The American paratroopers responded with a series of aggressive patrols that convinced the Germans they were facing a much superior force. About 40 Germans were killed in the skirmishes, but platoon-sized units began surrendering, eventually totaling 255 men by evening, outnumbering their captors by a large margin. The remainder of the 1./FJR 6, numbering about 500 German paratroopers, began approaching the defensive perimeter held by 250 paratroopers under Colonel Johnson who were positioned near the La Barquette locks and the Le Port bridge. Not realizing that US forces held

Troops from Utah Beach pass through Ste-Mère-Église on June 10 while infantrymen cast a wary glance for snipers. From their uniforms, these are troops of the 4th or 90th Division rather than paratroopers. There were still isolated German soldiers near the beach for several days after the landings. *(NARA)*

the area, the German paratroopers marched carelessly into an ambush and were halted by a blast of small-arms fire at 350 yards. Skirmishing followed, and Johnson finally sent an ultimatum, ordering the Germans to surrender or be annihilated by his "superior forces." Small groups of German paratroopers began surrendering and by nightfall about 150 Germans had been killed or wounded, and another 350 surrendered at a cost of ten US paratroopers killed and 30 wounded. Only 25 German paratroopers survived the chaos and made it over the river to Carentan.

While this fighting was going on, other elements of the 101st Airborne were making their way toward St-Côme-du-Mont in a series of small skirmishes with the Sturm-Abteilung AOK 7 and elements of 3./FJR 6. By the end of the day, the force around St-Côme-du-Mont included five airborne battalions, two artillery battalions, and a company of light tanks. These would form the core of an assault force to strike south to the key town of Carentan to help link up Utah and Omaha beaches.

Although VII Corps had made solid progress on D+1, it was still behind schedule. Under the original plan, Collins had hoped that the 4th Division could rapidly exit the beachhead and begin advancing north toward Cherbourg. However, the fighting was progressing much more slowly than intended due to the inability of the 82nd Airborne Division to control the River Merderet crossings, the unexpected difficulties of infantry combat in the coastal hedgerows, and the long delay in consolidating the badly scattered paratroopers. During a visit to Normandy on D+1, Eisenhower expressed his concern to Bradley that the Germans might exploit the gap between the V Corps on Omaha Beach and the VII Corps on Utah. As a result, Bradley instructed Collins to focus his immediate attention on closing this gap by seizing Carentan.

Rommel had originally believed that the main Allied effort was on the Calvados coast, especially in the British sector around Caen. On June 8 he received a set of orders for the US VII Corps that had been found by a German unit near Utah Beach. This made it clear that the Allies intended to push northward out of Utah Beach toward Valognes and eventually take Cherbourg. As a result, he diverted a first-rate unit, the 77th Infantry Division, which had been intended to prevent the link-up of Omaha and Utah beaches, and ordered it instead into the Cotentin peninsula to reinforce the Cherbourg front. The task of preventing the link-up of the two American beaches in the Carentan sector was assigned to the new and inexperienced 17th SS-Panzergrenadier Division "Gotz von Berlichingen."

THE BATTLE FOR CARENTAN

The force attacking Carentan was placed under command of Brigadier-General Anthony McAuliffe, better known for his later role in the defense of Bastogne. The plan was to seize St-Côme-du-Mont, which controlled the highway to Carentan. The defense of Carentan fell mainly to the two surviving battalions of FJR 6 under Oberstleutnant von der Heydte. He gathered a number of withdrawing German infantry companies to the defense, and on June 9 the corps attached a further two Ost battalions, which he deployed on the eastern side of the town due to their dubious potential.

After a preliminary artillery preparation on the morning of June 8, one glider infantry and three paratroop battalions began the assault. The survivors of Sturm-Abteilung AOK 7 began to retreat out the west side of St-Côme-du-Mont, but then veered southward toward the main road, colliding with the 3/501st PIR. A series of skirmishes ensued that were finally settled when two more paratroop battalions pushed past the town. By the end of the day, McAuliffe's forces had gained control of the northern side of the causeway leading to Carentan over the Douve and Madeleine rivers. The nature of the fighting that ensued was determined by the terrain. The area on either side of the causeway consisted of marshes and flooded farmland that was mostly impassable to infantry. As a result, the fighting had to be conducted down the narrow causeway itself and across each of its four bridges. The retreating German force had blown the first bridge over the River Douve, and so the advance along the bridge did not begin until the night of June 9/10 while the engineers attempted to span the gap. A boat patrol that night reached as far as the fourth and final bridge over the River Madeleine, but came under intense fire from Carentan. An artillery barrage preceded the attack by the 3/502nd PIR in the early evening of June 10. The battalion was stretched out in a thin column from the second to fourth bridge, when German machine-gunners began to open fire. Advance across

Battle for Carentan, June 10–13, 1944

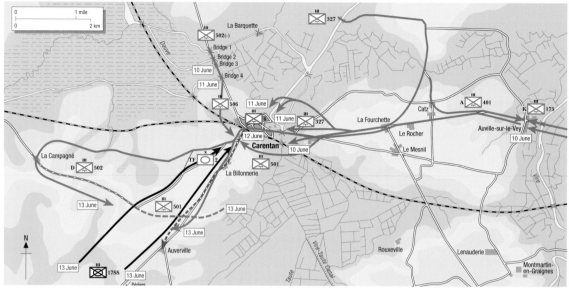

the River Madeleine bridge was inhibited by a Belgian gate obstacle that the paratroopers had managed to move, creating a single 18in gap. As a result, only one soldier at a time could pass over the bridge. The fighting continued after dark, and was marked by a strafing run by two Luftwaffe aircraft, a rare appearance in the Normandy skies.

By dawn, about 250 paratroopers had reached the final Madeleine bridge, which was overlooked by a stone farmhouse. At 0615hrs, Colonel Cole and the battalion executive officer, Major John Stopka, led a bayonet charge by 70 paratroopers into the farm. Although the farm was taken, by this stage the 3/502nd PIR had taken such heavy casualties that the 1/502nd PIR was brought forward to carry on the attack. In fact, the position was so tenuous that the 1/502nd could do no more than reinforce Cole's men to hold the farm against repeated German counterattacks. An afternoon attack almost succeeded in overwhelming the US paratroopers, but an artillery barrage placed almost on top of the American positions broke the German attack. Around 2000hrs, the 2/502nd PIR was brought forward to relieve the other two battered battalions. By now, von der Heydte's German paratroopers were beginning to show the strain of combat as well, experiencing serious shortages of machine-gun ammunition and receiving few reinforcements. All rifle ammunition was collected and turned over to the machine-gun crews, and the paratroopers were forced to rely on pistols, grenades or whatever else was at hand. A request to airlift small-arms ammunition to the beleaguered garrison was granted on June 11, but the DZ was in a field nearly 9 miles behind the front, taking time to collect and distribute.

During the two days of intense fighting by the 502nd PIR along the causeway, the 327th Glider Infantry had crossed the Douve further east in the early morning hours of June 10. It was then reinforced by 1/401st Glider Infantry, which began moving south to seize the roads leading out of Carentan toward the east. One of its companies moved east toward Isigny, meeting up with scouts from the 29th Division, marking the first contact between Utah and Omaha beaches. By the end of June 10, the 327th Glider Infantry set up a defensive perimeter covering the east side of Carentan, where it was joined by elements from the 401st Glider Infantry. In contrast to the frustrating assault over the causeway, this advance proceeded so well that McAuliffe ordered the 501st PIR to reinforce the glider infantry on June 11 in preparation for a final assault on June 12. The situation of the German garrison had become so perilous that on the afternoon of July 11, von der Heydte decided to withdraw his force rather than face certain annihilation. During a lull in the fighting in the late afternoon, the garrison began to slip out to the southwest.

The attack on the city itself in the early morning hours of July 12 consisted of a drive by the glider infantry from the northeast directly into Carentan and a pincer movement by the 501st and 506th PIR to cut the roads to the southwest to prevent the garrison from escaping. The city was captured quickly, but aside from a small rearguard, the garrison had already withdrawn. After Carentan was taken, the VII Corps set about reinforcing the connections with V Corps to the east.

As von der Heydte's paratroopers made their way southwest from Carentan on July 11, they bumped into the lead elements of the 17th SS-Panzergrenadier Division. Von der Heydte later claimed that he had not been informed of the reinforcement, but senior German commanders blamed him for the unauthorized and premature abandonment of the city

Hedgerow defenses, Normandy, 1944. The faint lines are the hedgerows and the double broken lines are sunken roads. This c. 300×900-yard company area was self-contained and could fend off attacks from any direction. The buildings were undefended, as they attracted artillery fire. If the perimeter was penetrated, troops would move to the flanking hedgerows to engage the attackers. There were several positions located in adjacent hedgerows on all sides of this area.

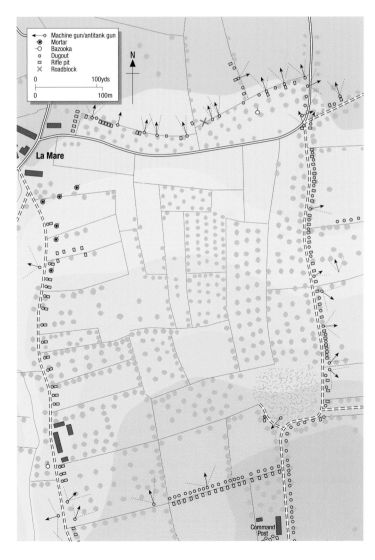

The initial defenders of Carentan were Fallschirmjäger Regiment 6, which had already lost one of its battalions in the first days of fighting against the US paratroopers. This photo shows a team of German paratroopers on an exercise on June 1, 1944 shortly before the invasion, wearing their distinctive helmets. *(MHI)*

after he had been informed several times about the plans. Generalleutnant Max Pemsel, the Seventh Army chief of staff, later wrote that von der Heydte had suffered a temporary mental and physical breakdown due to the savage and uninterrupted fighting of the previous several days. The only reason he was not relieved for such a "misguided" decision was the outstanding performance of his outnumbered regiment up to that point.

The 17th SS-Panzergrenadier Division had been formed in November 1943, and was not complete when sent into action in June 1944. Although near strength in personnel, it had only about 60 percent of its officers and NCOs, and was very short of motor transport. The divisional commander, SS-Gruppenführer Werner Ostendorf, decided to retake Carentan by attacking down two roads on the western side of the city. The attack would not be preceded by reconnaissance or artillery fire in order to gain tactical surprise, and would be spearheaded by SS-Panzer-Abteilung 17 equipped with 48 StuG IV assault guns. Ostendorf felt that the sudden appearance of large numbers of armored vehicles would carry the day as, to date, the fighting in this sector had been conducted by light infantry on both sides with few antitank weapons. The Panzers would serve as the spearhead for the main attack by the 37th SS-Panzergrenadier Regiment.

McAuliffe had planned to deploy the 506th PIR into the same area on the morning of June 13 to deepen the defenses, but they had not begun to advance when the German attack began around 0700hrs. The German columns started from the divisional assembly areas, and due to the congestion on the country roads, the advance was slow in progressing. No contact was made with the paratroopers until around 0900hrs, when the lead StuG IV assault guns had approached to within 875 yards of the southwestern side of Carentan. In the confined terrain southeast of the city, the 506th PIR was able to slow the attack by using the hedgerows to good effect. It was reinforced by the 2/502nd PIR on the right flank.

There had been growing indications from Enigma decryption that Rommel planned to deploy the 17th SS-Panzergrenadier Division against Carentan, prompting Bradley to deploy a task force from the newly arrived 2nd Armored Division, including a company of medium tanks, a company of light tanks, and an armored infantry battalion, into the area. When the paratroopers reported the Panzer attack around 0900hrs, the task force began moving and reached the town around 1030hrs. The German attack petered out by noon. The inexperienced Panzergrenadiers had a hard time adjusting to the *bocage* fighting, and a combination of officer and NCO shortages as well as combat losses left many units leaderless. Some units began to retreat on their own, forcing von der Heydte and his adjutant to round up many of them, sometimes at gunpoint. The left flank of the German attack was supposed to be defended by the surviving Hotchkiss H-39 tanks of Panzer-Abteilung 100, but the battered force evaporated. The US armored counterattack began around 1400hrs down the Carentan–Baupte road. This threatened to cut off the

The 90th Division began to move forward to replace the 82nd Airborne Division once the bridges over the Merderet had been cleared. This is a machine-gun team moving forward, the gunner in front with the .30cal Browning light machine-gun, and his assistant behind carrying the tripod and ammunition. *(NARA)*

A fine character study of a typical young German *Landser* of the 353rd Infantry Division during the Normandy fighting, wearing a shelter segment that doubled as a poncho. In front of him is his entrenching shovel and mess kit. This photo was taken on June 25, 1944, near La Haye-du-Puits during efforts by the Wehrmacht to prevent the American beachhead from pushing south out of the Cotentin peninsula. *(MHI)*

German attack force, especially when it was followed by a second tank/paratrooper thrust down the Carentan–Périers road. Von der Heydte, finding the 37th SS-Panzergrenadier Regiment commander dazed, took command and ordered the Panzergrenadiers as well as his force to withdraw to a line he had reconnoitered earlier. Losses in the 17th SS-Panzergrenadier Division were 79 killed, 316 wounded, and 61 missing. In addition, only about half of the division's 48 StuG IV assault guns were still operational with seven lost, and 13 damaged.

Infuriated by the debacle, Ostendorf attempted to make von der Heydte the scapegoat for his division's failure, and had him arrested and sent before an SS military judge that night. General Meindl, in temporary command of this sector after General Marcks had been killed in an air attack the day before, ordered von der Heydte released. The Seventh Army staff concluded that the counterattack at Carentan had failed due to the 17th SS-Panzergrenadier Division's inexperience. The rebuff of the German counterattack allowed Collin's VII Corps to consolidate the link-up with Gerow's V Corps on 14 June.

CUTTING OFF THE COTENTIN

Although it had been Collins' intention to shift the emphasis of VII Corps to a rapid assault on Cherbourg, by D+3 the focus was changed again. The slow pace of the advance in the *bocage* convinced both Bradley and Collins that a quick capture of Cherbourg was unlikely. Under such circumstances, it became imperative to cut off the Cotentin peninsula from any further German reinforcements. The first issue was completing the link-up of the elements of the 82nd Airborne Division on either side of the River Merderet.

With the positions on the east bank of the Merderet at La Fière bridge secure, on D+1 Gavin sent the 3/508th PIR to Chef-du-Pont to link up with Colonel Shanley's isolated force on the west bank. The fire directed against the causeway during the daylight hours made it impossible to carry out this mission, though Shanley was able to send a patrol across the causeway at night.

A GI from the 9th Division, armed with a .45cal Thompson submachine-gun, moves along a shallow road embankment near St Sauveur-le-Vicomte during the effort to cut off the Cotentin peninsula. *(NARA)*

GIs of the 9th Division use a roadside drainage ditch for cover during a skirmish near St Sauveur-le-Vicomte on June 21, 1944. In the background to the right is their 1½-ton weapons carrier, while to the left is an abandoned German truck. *(NARA)*

On D+2, the focus again returned to La Fière bridge. On the night of June 8, two paratroopers from Colonel Timmes' group found a partially submerged road across the inundated fields north of the bridge, and crossed to the east bank. A plan was developed for Colonel Millett's group to join Timmes' group, and then link up with a battalion from the east bank moving across the newly discovered crossing. Colonel Millett's column began moving before daylight on June 9, but was discovered and raked by German machine-gun fire. Millett was captured and the column retreated. The 1/325th Glider Infantry was able to make it across the inundated river and join Timmes' group, but attempts to push southward to the La Fière bridge were repulsed by German troops in a stone building dubbed the "Gray Castle."

Under growing pressure from senior commanders, Gavin was forced to execute a direct assault across the La Fière causeway from the east bank. He moved a few M5A1 tanks and a company of the 507th PIR to the forward edge of the bridge to provide covering fire. The force chosen for the assault was the 3/325th Glider Infantry. After a preliminary artillery bombardment and under a partial cover of smoke, Company G led the attack at 1045hrs on June 9. The glidermen were told to make the 500-yard crossing in one sprint, but only a handful of men were able to do so in the face of intense German machine-gun fire. Those who hesitated were caught in the open on the exposed stretches of the causeway, and casualties soon mounted. One of the M5A1 light tanks attempted to push across the causeway, but hit a mine. This tank, along with a German Hotchkiss H-39 knocked out in earlier fighting, further congested the narrow passage. Company E tried the crossing next, but along the northern bank of the causeway instead of on top of it. They made their way toward the church in Cauquigny, and the German

The approaches to Cherbourg were studded with bunkers and other fortifications. This team of GIs from the 79th Division poses near a pillbox it had knocked out with a bazooka during the fighting outside the port. *(NARA)*

positions were suppressed by small-arms fire from Timmes' group. After this company made its way over the bridge and began clearing buildings on the north side of the exit, it was followed by Company F, which pushed beyond the bridgehead toward Le Motey. Due to the usual radio problems, Gavin was unsure of the progress of the 3/325th Glider Infantry and ordered his reserve company from the 507th PIR across the causeway. Further advances westward toward Le Motey were brought to a halt when US artillery continued its fire missions into the area, unaware that US troops had pushed that far. In spite of the many problems, the attacks on June 9 finally cleared the La Fière bridge and causeway.

With passage of the Merderet open, Collins moved the 90th Division forward to take over the task of moving westward. On June 10 two regiments of the 90th Division began a westward advance over the La Fière and Chef-du-Pont bridges aiming to establish a bridgehead over the Douve. The 357th Infantry moved over the La Fière bridge but ran into the defenses of GR.1057 past Le Motey. Inexperienced in *bocage* fighting, its lead battalion retreated into the positions of the 325th Glider Infantry. A second attack at dusk by another battalion was equally unsuccessful. The 358th Infantry was assigned to reach Pont l'Abbé, and its lead battalion dug into defensive positions short of the objective after coming under heavy fire. GR.1057 launched a counterattack in mid-afternoon, without success. The attacks continued the following day, with 357th Infantry still unable to overcome the German defensive positions around Les Landes, and the 358th Infantry on the fringe of Pont l'Abbé. The next day, the 359th Infantry rejoined the division from other assignments and reinforced the attack. The June 12 attack was further reinforced by the 746th Tank Battalion and additional artillery fire support.

Cutting off the Cotentin, June 10–18, 1944

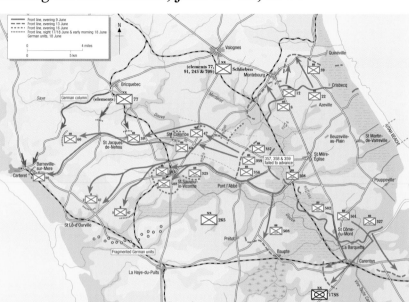

In spite of the reinforcements, the advance on June 12 and 13 was measured in hundreds of yards. In frustration at the slow pace of the advance in four days of fighting, General Collins visited the division on June 13. After visiting the divisional command post, Collins was aggravated when he could find no regimental or battalion HQ, nor much evidence of fighting.

Exasperated by the 90th Division's poor performance, Collins telephoned Bradley about his plans to relieve the division's commander and two regimental commanders. He felt that the main problem was the division's poor training and lackluster leadership. They decided to pull the division out of the line in favor of an experienced unit and Bradley agreed to the use of the 9th Division, regarded as being one of the two best divisions in theater along with the 1st Division at Omaha Beach. This rearrangement delayed the advance, so the attack resumed toward the Douve on June 15 with the 82nd Airborne Division on the left and the 9th Division on the right. The 82nd Airborne Division reached St Sauveur on the Douve on June 16, while the 9th Division's 60th Infantry reached the Douve near Ste Colombe. With German resistance crumbling, Collins urged Eddy to push to the sea as rapidly as possible. During the night of June 16/17, a company from 3/60th Infantry riding on tanks and other armored vehicles reached the hill overlooking the coastal town of Barneville-sur-Mer before dawn. Early in the morning, the company advanced into the town, unoccupied except for a few startled German MPs. The rapid advance by the 9th Division had severed the Cotentin peninsula and cut off Cherbourg.

A squad of GIs advances through a farm field on the outskirts of Cherbourg. They are probably from the 4th Division as the NCO to the left armed with the M1 carbine is still wearing one of the assault vests issued to combat teams involved in the initial D-Day landings. *(NARA)*

The sudden isolation of Cherbourg caused a major row among senior German leaders. Rommel had moved the 77th Infantry Division into the Cotentin peninsula on June 9, but was unwilling to lose the best division in LXXXIV Corps. On June 15 he ordered the amalgamation of the remnants of the 709th Infantry Division and 243rd Infantry Division into Kampfgruppe Schlieben with a mission to defend the port of Cherbourg. The 77th Infantry Division, along with the few surviving elements of the 91st Luftlande Division, were formed into Kampfgruppe Hellmich and instructed to withdraw southward if the Americans cut off the peninsula, with an aim to prevent any further American penetration south. The capture of St Sauveur prompted Rundstedt and Rommel to begin the withdrawal of Kampfgruppe Schlieben into the Cherbourg area.

Rommel and Rundstedt met with Hitler on June 16 at the W2 Battle HQ in Margival, France. Hitler insisted that the largest possible forces be committed to the defense of "Fortress Cherbourg," but he finally agreed to allow Kampfgruppe Hellmich to withdraw southward starting on June 17. The order proved difficult to implement after both General Hellmich and the commander of the 77th Infantry Division, General Rudolf Stegmann, were killed during air attacks on June 17. The first unit to begin the withdrawal was GR.1049, which ran into 1/39th Infantry on the morning of June 18 near St-Jacques-de-Nehou and was stopped. The neighboring GR.1050 had more success, gaining control of a bridge over the River Ollande near St Lô-d'Ourville from the hapless 357th Infantry of the 90th Division, capturing about 100 GIs and breaking out with about 1,300 men before the gap was finally sealed. In the event, this was the only major group to escape the encirclement, and the 77th Infantry Division lost most of its artillery in the breakout attempt.

NORTH TO CHERBOURG

On June 18, 1944, Montgomery laid out the immediate tasks for the Allied forces in Normandy. FUSA was to take Cherbourg while the British Second Army was to take Caen. The breakthrough to the west coast led Bradley to reorganize the forces on the Cotentin peninsula. The new VIII Corps under Major-General Troy Middleton was given the 82nd Airborne and 90th Division with an assignment to defend toward the south and prevent any German forces from reinforcing the Cotentin peninsula. Collins' VII Corps now consisted of three infantry divisions, the 4th, 9th, and 79th Divisions, which had the mission of advancing on Cherbourg. Eddy's 9th Division began an abrupt change in direction from west to north, moving against the western side of Cherbourg. Barton's 4th Division continued its push up along the eastern coast to Cherbourg, while the newly deployed 79th Division would push up the center. The initial aim was to seize the Quineville ridge, which dominated the terrain southward.

The 4th Division had been fighting northward since D-Day, its advance hampered by the presence of many fortified coastal artillery batteries along the eastern coast. On the left flank, 82nd Airborne's 505th PIR and 4th Division's 8th Infantry Regiment finally reached positions from the Montebourg railroad station to the western outskirts of Montebourg by June 11. Barton decided against taking the city for fear of tying down too many troops in street fighting. Instead, on June 13, the 8th Infantry set up defensive positions around the city to contain any German forces within it.

The 22nd Infantry had a much more difficult time, confronting both the Crisbecq and Azeville coastal batteries, which had been reinforced by infantry from the 709th Infantry Division and Sturm-Abteilung AOK 7. After repeated attacks, the Azeville position was finally overwhelmed on the afternoon of June 9 by an attack on the command blockhouse with satchel charges and flame-throwers. Frustrated by the failure of previous attacks on Crisbecq, General Barton formed Task Force Barber from the 22nd Infantry, reinforced with M10 3in tank-destroyers of the 899th Tank Destroyer Battalion, and tanks of the 746th Tank Battalion. He instructed Barber to skirt around Crisbecq and seize the high ground around Quineville after taking Ozeville. The attack was frustrated by the thick *bocage*, heavy German artillery fire, and determined counterattacks. The Crisbecq fortifications finally fell on June 11, when 57mm antitank guns of K/22nd Infantry fired through the embrasures of the two remaining strongpoints. To gain momentum, Collins took the newly arrived 39th Infantry from the 9th Division and sent it to deal with the many strongpoints along the coast. This freed up Task Force Barber to concentrate on positions further inland, and both air support and naval gunfire support resumed after several days of bad weather. Quineville was finally taken on June 14, along with the ridgeline to the west, which had been the anchor of German defenses in this sector. Besides clearing the gateway to Cherbourg on the east coast, the operations in the week after D-Day finally ended the threat of German artillery fire into Utah Beach, which had been hampering unloading operations there.

The drive on Cherbourg began on the evening of June 19 with the 4th Division kicking it off at 0300hrs, followed by the 9th and 79th Divisions at 0500hrs. The 4th Cavalry Group was assigned to protect the right flank of the 4th Division and move up along the eastern coast. German defenses by this stage of the campaign were the disorganized remnants of four

Infantry advance under the cover of an M4 medium tank of the 740th Tank Battalion during the street fighting inside Cherbourg. *(NARA)*

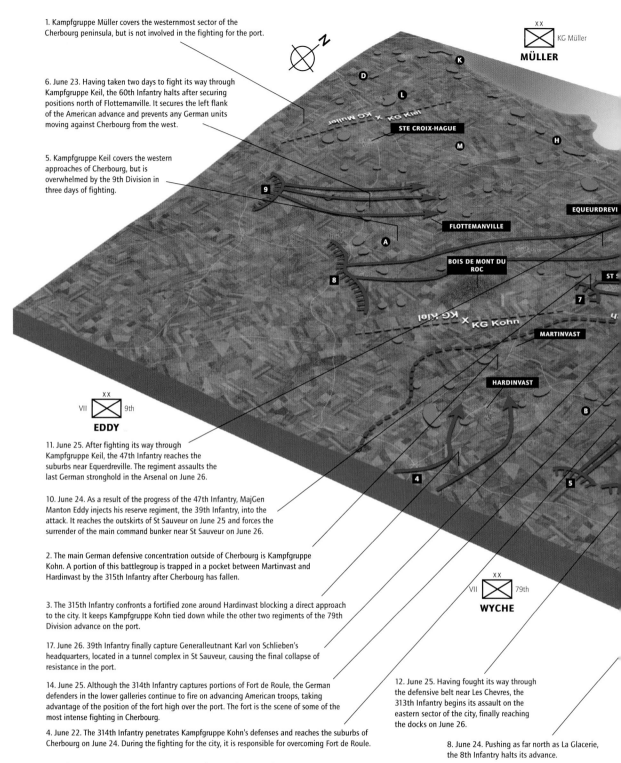

1. Kampfgruppe Müller covers the westernmost sector of the Cherbourg peninsula, but is not involved in the fighting for the port.

6. June 23. Having taken two days to fight its way through Kampfgruppe Keil, the 60th Infantry halts after securing positions north of Flottemanville. It secures the left flank of the American advance and prevents any German units moving against Cherbourg from the west.

5. Kampfgruppe Keil covers the western approaches of Cherbourg, but is overwhelmed by the 9th Division in three days of fighting.

11. June 25. After fighting its way through Kampfgruppe Keil, the 47th Infantry reaches the suburbs near Equerdreville. The regiment assaults the last German stronghold in the Arsenal on June 26.

10. June 24. As a result of the progress of the 47th Infantry, MajGen Manton Eddy injects his reserve regiment, the 39th Infantry, into the attack. It reaches the outskirts of St Sauveur on June 25 and forces the surrender of the main command bunker near St Sauveur on June 26.

2. The main German defensive concentration outside of Cherbourg is Kampfgruppe Kohn. A portion of this battlegroup is trapped in a pocket between Martinvast and Hardinvast by the 315th Infantry after Cherbourg has fallen.

3. The 315th Infantry confronts a fortified zone around Hardinvast blocking a direct approach to the city. It keeps Kampfgruppe Kohn tied down while the other two regiments of the 79th Division advance on the port.

17. June 26. 39th Infantry finally capture Generalleutnant Karl von Schlieben's headquarters, located in a tunnel complex in St Sauveur, causing the final collapse of resistance in the port.

14. June 25. Although the 314th Infantry captures portions of Fort de Roule, the German defenders in the lower galleries continue to fire on advancing American troops, taking advantage of the position of the fort high over the port. The fort is the scene of some of the most intense fighting in Cherbourg.

4. June 22. The 314th Infantry penetrates Kampfgruppe Kohn's defenses and reaches the suburbs of Cherbourg on June 24. During the fighting for the city, it is responsible for overcoming Fort de Roule.

12. June 25. Having fought its way through the defensive belt near Les Chevres, the 313th Infantry begins its assault on the eastern sector of the city, finally reaching the docks on June 26.

8. June 24. Pushing as far north as La Glacerie, the 8th Infantry halts its advance.

XX
KG Müller
MÜLLER

STE CROIX-HAGUE

EQUEURDREVI

FLOTTEMANVILLE

BOIS DE MONT DU ROC

ST S

MARTINVAST

HARDINVAST

VII — 9th
EDDY

XX
VII — 79th
WYCHE

The capture of Cherbourg

June 22–30, 1944, viewed from the southeast, showing the assault on this vital strategic port by US 4th, 9th, and 79th Infantry Divisions. The city was captured amid bitter fighting, but comprehensive destruction of facilities by the German defenders rendered the port of Cherbourg useless to the Allies for many weeks.

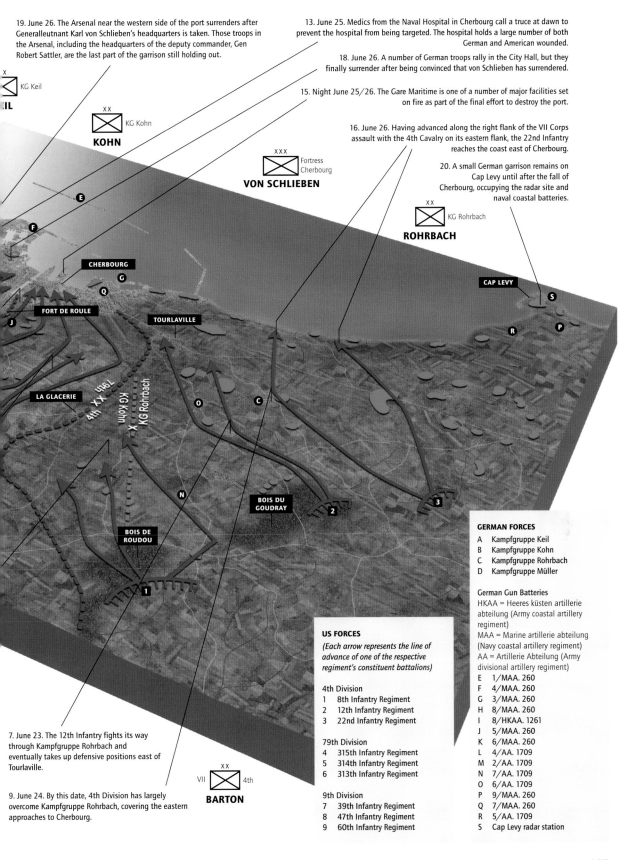

19. June 26. The Arsenal near the western side of the port surrenders after Generalleutnant Karl von Schlieben's headquarters is taken. Those troops in the Arsenal, including the headquarters of the deputy commander, Gen Robert Sattler, are the last part of the garrison still holding out.

13. June 25. Medics from the Naval Hospital in Cherbourg call a truce at dawn to prevent the hospital from being targeted. The hospital holds a large number of both German and American wounded.

18. June 26. A number of German troops rally in the City Hall, but they finally surrender after being convinced that von Schlieben has surrendered.

15. Night June 25/26. The Gare Maritime is one of a number of major facilities set on fire as part of the final effort to destroy the port.

16. June 26. Having advanced along the right flank of the VII Corps assault with the 4th Cavalry on its eastern flank, the 22nd Infantry reaches the coast east of Cherbourg.

20. A small German garrison remains on Cap Levy until after the fall of Cherbourg, occupying the radar site and naval coastal batteries.

7. June 23. The 12th Infantry fights its way through Kampfgruppe Rohrbach and eventually takes up defensive positions east of Tourlaville.

9. June 24. By this date, 4th Division has largely overcome Kampfgruppe Rohrbach, covering the eastern approaches to Cherbourg.

KG Keil

KG Kohn
KOHN

Fortress Cherbourg
VON SCHLIEBEN

KG Rohrbach
ROHRBACH

CAP LEVY

CHERBOURG

FORT DE ROULE

TOURLAVILLE

LA GLACERIE

BOIS DU GOUDRAY

BOIS DE ROUDOU

VII 4th
BARTON

US FORCES

(Each arrow represents the line of advance of one of the respective regiment's constituent battalions)

4th Division
1   8th Infantry Regiment
2   12th Infantry Regiment
3   22nd Infantry Regiment

79th Division
4   315th Infantry Regiment
5   314th Infantry Regiment
6   313th Infantry Regiment

9th Division
7   39th Infantry Regiment
8   47th Infantry Regiment
9   60th Infantry Regiment

GERMAN FORCES

A   Kampfgruppe Keil
B   Kampfgruppe Kohn
C   Kampfgruppe Rohrbach
D   Kampfgruppe Müller

German Gun Batteries
HKAA = Heeres küsten artillerie abteilung (Army coastal artillery regiment)
MAA = Marine artillerie abteilung (Navy coastal artillery regiment)
AA = Artillerie Abteilung (Army divisional artillery regiment)
E   1/MAA. 260
F   4/MAA. 260
G   3/MAA. 260
H   8/MAA. 260
I   8/HKAA. 1261
J   5/MAA. 260
K   6/MAA. 260
L   4/AA. 1709
M   2/AA. 1709
N   7/AA. 1709
O   6/AA. 1709
P   9/MAA. 260
Q   7/MAA. 260
R   5/AA. 1709
S   Cap Levy radar station

A pair of M4 medium tanks advances along the battered Rue du Val-de-Saire in the Tourlaville district of Cherbourg on June 26, 1944. The 746th Tank Battalion supported the 9th Division during the fighting in Cherbourg. *(NARA)*

divisions. The 9th Division was facing portions of GR.920 and GR.921 from the 243rd Infantry Division along with the surviving elements of the 77th Infantry Division that had failed to escape southward during the breakout attempt two days before. The 79th Division in the center faced parts of the 77th Infantry Division as well as remnants of the 91st Luftlande Division. The 4th Division was facing most of the 709th Infantry Division, the survivors of Sturm-Abteilung AOK 7, and large parts of the 243rd Infantry Division.

The initial attacks made steady progress as the German units tended to withdraw after first contact. After the peninsula had been isolated on July 17, the Cherbourg garrison had been cut off from most outside communication. On July 19 General von Schlieben decided to disengage his forces from the front, and pull them back into a fortified zone on the outskirts of Cherbourg in hopes of conducting a protracted defense. As a result, the American advance only encountered rearguard units or outposts that had lost contact with HQ. On June 20, Eddy began steps to cut off the Cap de la Hague peninsula from the rest of the Cherbourg defense. German resistance stiffened considerably, and Eddy realized that the 9th Division had finally run into the main line of defense for Fortress Cherbourg.

Von Schlieben reorganized his disparate forces into four Kampfgruppen that formed a semicircular defensive line outside the city. The German defenses were based on a series of hills and ridges located 4–6 miles from the port. Many of the defenses included bunkers, while others included concrete structures of the abandoned V-1 buzz bomb bases. The attack on Cherbourg was preceded by an intense air preparation conducted by the IX Tactical Air Command. The ground attack on the afternoon of June 22 was preceded at 1240hrs by 25 minutes of rocket attacks and strafing by ten squadrons of Typhoons and Mustangs of the 2nd Tactical Air Force (RAF), 55 minutes of bombing and strafing by 562 P-47s and P-51s, followed at H-Hour (1400hrs) by bombing runs of 11 groups of B-26 Marauders of the Ninth Air Force. The air attacks proved less effective than anticipated, and many infantry units radioed that they were being inadvertently attacked. The best results had been obtained on the western side, where the 9th Division artillery had suppressed German flak positions in anticipation of the air missions. None of the main defenses were cracked on June 22, and it took two days of hard fighting before the first portions of the defensive belt were finally overcome. The first penetrations past the outer defenses took place in the 9th Division's sector near the Flottemanville–Hague strongpoints late in the evening of June 23.

Although von Schlieben was in command of the four divisions holding the city, the actual command of the port was under Generalmajor Robert Sattler until June 23 when Hitler appointed von Schlieben as the commander of Fortress Cherbourg. Requests for further ammunition and reinforcements went unanswered, but senior German commanders felt that the garrison

Some of the most savage fighting for Cherbourg took place in and around Fort de Roule on a hill overlooking the port. Although the 314th Infantry seized control of the upper sections of the fort on June 25, it took another day of fighting to secure the lower galleries. *(MHI)*

Around 1400hrs on June 26, General von Schlieben and the other senior commanders of Cherbourg exited a tunnel of their command bunker to surrender. The soldier to the right is carrying the cap and coat of Admiral Walter Hennecke, the naval commander of Cherbourg. (NARA)

could hold out for months due to the geography and the extensive fortifications around the port.

The final assaults into the town were made by infantry–tank teams, with each of the divisions receiving a separate tank battalion for support. These were essential to deal with the many bunkers and defenses encountered. Although German resistance on June 24 continued to be intense, there was a growing tendency for the defenses to crumble once vigorously assaulted. By the end of the day, breaches had been made in the final layer of outer defenses, allowing the first access to the city itself. At dawn on June 25, a German medical officer accompanied by a captured American pilot came out under a flag of truce to ask that the naval hospital be spared from shelling and for a supply of plasma. They were allowed to return to the city with the plasma, and with a demand for the immediate surrender of the city. By the time the demand had reached von Schlieben, the 314th Infantry was already assaulting Fort de Roule overlooking the city. The intensity of the fighting for the fort is evident from the fact that two Medals of Honor for bravery were awarded for the action. By midnight, the 314th Infantry had broken into the fort and occupied the upper levels, but with German troops still occupying the lower galleries.

The 47th Infantry made the first penetration into the suburbs of Cherbourg on June 25 after overcoming the defenses at Equeurdreville. By nightfall the city was illuminated by the fires of the burning port facilities that the Germans had set as the final stage of the destruction of the port.

The final assault into the city by the 9th and 79th Divisions occurred on June 26. US patrols in the city continued to be harassed by artillery fire from the lower levels of Fort de Roule, which were still in German hands. These lower levels were not immediately accessible to the troops from 2/314th Infantry on top of the fort, and they began to try to lower charges down ventilation shafts. A demolition team snaked its way along the cliff face on the western side of the fort and blasted one of the tunnel openings with pole charges and bazookas. Troops below the fort began firing into the embrasures with 57mm antitank guns. Resistance finally collapsed in the early evening and several hundred prisoners were taken.

Fighting in the city remained intense through the day, and the presence of many large concrete structures and coastal gun positions greatly complicated the American attacks. The 39th Infantry learned from prisoners that General von Schlieben was in a bunker in St Sauveur, and by mid-afternoon Companies E and F had fought their way to the tunnel entrance

A group of GIs and French civilians celebrate the capture of Cherbourg, driving around the city in a captured Renault UE tractor. *(NARA)*

of the command bunker. A prisoner was sent in to demand surrender, which was refused. M10 tank-destroyers were brought forward, and a few 3in high-explosive rounds were enough to cause the Germans to reconsider. About 800 officers and troops began to pour out, including General von Schlieben, Admiral Walter Hennecke, and their staffs. The surrender was made to General Eddy, but von Schlieben refused to order the surrender of the rest of his garrison. Nevertheless, the forces still holding the City Hall surrendered after learning of von Schlieben's surrender. The last major defensive position in the city was the Arsenal, which was protected by a moat and strongly defended by antiaircraft and antitank guns on parapets. The 47th Infantry was assigned to take it on the morning of June 26, and began by picking off two of the 20mm Flak parapets with tank fire. Before the main assault at 0830hrs, a psychological warfare unit brought up a loudspeaker, urging the garrison to surrender. Generalmajor Sattler, now the deputy commander of Cherbourg, agreed to surrender the 400 men under his command, and the rest of the arsenal surrendered by 1000hrs. This ended the organized resistance in the port, though mopping-up operations continued for two days. About 10,000 prisoners were captured on June 25–26. Two more days were spent eliminating outlying forts in the harbor, mainly by air attack and tank gunfire. There were also isolated garrisons on Cap Levy that were taken by the 22nd Infantry, and about 3,000 Germans had retreated to Cap de la Hague. The 9th Division assaulted these positions and overran the final defenses on June 30. A total of 6,000 prisoners were captured in the final operations in late June. On July 1, the 9th Division reported to Collins that all organized resistance on the Cotentin peninsula had ended.

The total casualties of VII Corps from D-Day to the fall of Cherbourg at the end of June numbered about 22,000. The large number of missing was due to scattered airborne landings that accounted for 4,500 of the missing, some of whom were captured. German casualties are not known with any

US VII Corps Casualties D-Day to July 1, 1944

Unit	killed	wounded	missing	captured	Total
4th Div.	844	3,814	788	6	5,452
9th Div.	301	2,061	76		2,438
79th Div.	240	1,896	240		2,376
90th Div.	386	1,979	34		2,399
82nd Abn. Div.	457	1,440	2,571	12+	4,480
101st Abn. Div.	546	2,217	1,907	?	4,670
Corps troops	37	157	49	61	304
Total	2,811	13,564	5,665	79	22,119

precision, although prisoners totaled 39,000. The Allies had hoped to capture Cherbourg by D+15, so its capture on D+21 was not far behind schedule, especially compared to the plans for Caen in the neighboring British sector. The capture of Cherbourg did not provide any immediate benefit to the Allied supply situation, as the Germans had thoroughly demolished the port facilities prior to the surrender. Their one failure in this regard was the large fuel storage facility in the port, which remained intact and was quite valuable to the Allies. It took almost two months to clean up the port, but it was back in operation by September 1944.

The fall of the port shocked Hitler and the senior German leadership, who believed that such a heavily fortified facility could hold out for months. They seriously overestimated the paper strength of their own forces and seriously underestimated combat efficiency of the US Army. With the capture of the Cotentin peninsula, hope evaporated that the Allies could be dislodged from France.

PART III

SWORD BEACH AND THE BRITISH AIRBORNE LANDINGS

INTRODUCTION

The landings on Sword Beach and the battles fought by British paratroopers in the area around the estuary of the River Orne were just a small part of the great Allied liberation of Normandy that began on June 6, 1944. What happened in this left-hand sector of the invasion front was matched with equal and, as we have seen, sometimes greater ferocity by the fighting on four other beaches and on other landing places along a 50-mile stretch of coastline to the west. This chapter will explain why Sword Beach and the British airborne assault were so important to the overall success of the D-Day landings.

In the original plan for the invasion submitted by COSSAC in late 1943, only two British and two American divisions were to land by sea on beaches code-named Omaha, Gold, and Juno. This number was raised after Eisenhower and Montgomery studied the scheme and decided that the proposed attack was to be made on too narrow a front. They suggested two further beaches and proposed that two more divisions should land; one American division on the eastern base of the Cotentin Peninsula, and one British division closer to Ouistreham.

This new British beach was designated Sword Beach, and it stretched from St Aubin-sur-Mer in the west to the mouth of the River Orne in the east. Eight miles up the Orne was the city of Caen, and from the city a network of roads radiated outwards, linking it to all parts of Normandy. The quick capture of Caen, therefore, became of strategic importance in order to give the Allied landings a swift route into the heartland of France. The inclusion of Sword Beach in the invasion plans now made it possible to contemplate seizing Caen on the first day of the landings, before the enemy could mobilize to prevent the city falling to the Allies. Montgomery made it clear that the seizure of Caen was a D-Day objective of the highest order.

To protect Sword Beach and the whole left flank of the landings, it was also decided that an airborne landing would take place to the east of the River Orne during the night before the invasion. This threat to the east of Caen would inevitably split the enemy defenses and allow easier progress toward the city.

PREVIOUS PAGE:
This picture was taken at around 0845hrs near the junction of Queen Red and White beaches opposite German strongpoint 'Cod'. In the foreground are two Royal Engineers from a Beach Group who can be identified by their white banded helmets and their sleeve badges that depict a red anchor on a white background. Troops of 41 Royal Marine Commando assemble in the mid-background ready for their move on Lion sur Mer. In the far background, troops of 2nd Middlesex Regiment, the 3rd Division's machine gun battalion, make their way across the tidal stretch of beach, taking casualties as they move. *(Imperial War Museum, B5114)*

OPPOSING COMMANDERS

Sword Beach was the objective of Major-General Tom Rennie's British 3rd Division. Rennie had been a battalion commander at El Alamein and later headed a brigade of the Highland Division in Sicily. In December 1943 he was promoted to major-general and ordered back to England to take over the 3rd Division and train it specifically for the invasion.

Also at the disposal of Dempsey's British Second Army was the 6th Airborne Division, commanded by Major-General Richard Gale. Gale had served for 17 years in India after World War I and had then been appointed to various staff posts at the War Office. In August 1941 he took command of 1st Parachute Brigade and began a program of rigorous training. In the spring of the following year, he was recalled to the War Office once again, but left in April 1943 to raise the 6th Airborne Division and prepare it for the invasion.

Opposite Sword Beach and astride the River Orne, General Marcks had the German 716th Infantry Division holding 21 miles of coastline onto which the British and Canadian forces would descend. This division was headed by Generalleutnant Wilhelm Richter, an artillery officer and a veteran of many campaigns. Richter had served in the German Army since before World War I and had been an officer since 1914. He later served in Poland, Belgium and Russia and was involved in the final stages of the advance on Moscow. He assumed command of the 716th Division in March 1943.

Major-General Tom Rennie, commander of the British 3rd Division, talks to a tank crew from 27th Armoured Brigade prior to embarkation at Gosport, England. *(Imperial War Museum, H39002)*

Major-General Richard Gale raised and commanded the British 6th Airborne Division ready for the invasion of Europe. The most successful of all of the D-Day generals, his division gained all of its objectives and remained in the line until August 1944. *(Imperial War Museum, B 5352)*

Many miles inland, but also in the sector opposite Sword Beach astride the River Orne, was the German 21st Panzer Division, commanded by Generalmajor Edgar Feuchtinger. This Panzer unit was under the control of Rommel's Army Group B and was located as a mobile reserve, able to strike anywhere in Normandy that an Allied landing might take place. Feuchtinger had fought in the campaigns in the Netherlands, Belgium, and France in 1940 as an artillery regimental commander, and he was later wounded in Russia at the siege of Leningrad in August 1942. Although he had no experience of armored units, he was given command of a re-formed 21st Panzer Division in August 1943. He gained his promotion as a result of political connections, having been a Nazi Party organizer in the 1930s and a friend of Hitler. He was, however, not an inspired choice, and his performance as leader of the 21st Panzer Division was later called into question when he was court-martialed in March 1945.

OPPOSING FORCES

BRITISH FORCES

Destined to land on Sword Beach, the 3rd Infantry Division was as prepared for *Overlord* as it could be. In 1940, commanded by Montgomery, it had been evacuated out of Dunkirk and arrived back in England after fighting many fierce rearguard actions against the advancing Germans. All of its equipment and transport was left in France. The 3rd Division was completely re-equipped and spent the next four years training and preparing itself for a return to war. It was earmarked for several campaigns, including the invasion of Sicily, but remained at home while other divisions achieved fame in North Africa and Italy. In the summer of 1943 its then commander, Major-General Ramsden, secured an undertaking that the 3rd Division would lead the British return to northwest Europe and that it would be the first division ashore. From then on, all training assumed a new focus and Ramsden's division entered a program of preparation that was both vigorous and realistic, concentrating on amphibious assaults and attacks on fixed strongpoints.

The division quickly built up a close relationship with the Royal Navy and began a series of exercises up and down the coast of Scotland. In late 1943 it joined with the naval force that would carry it to the Normandy beaches. Known as Task Force S and commanded by Rear Admiral A. G. Talbot, it was responsible for the seaborne element of the landings on Sword Beach.

In December 1943, Montgomery was appointed head of the 21st Army Group and designated land commander for the invasion. He immediately brought in new commanders for some of the units already allocated to *Overlord*, appointing officers who had previously fought with him in North Africa and in the Mediterranean and in whom he had confidence. In the 3rd Division, Ramsden was replaced by Major-General Tom Rennie.

The British 3rd Infantry Division consisted of three brigades: 8th, 9th, and 185th, each containing three battalions. The 8th Brigade consisted of the 1st Suffolk Regiment, 2nd East Yorkshire Regiment, and 1st South

Lancashire Regiment; the 9th Brigade contained the 2nd Lincolnshire Regiment, 1st King's Own Scottish Borderers (KOSB), and 2nd Royal Ulster Rifles; and the 185th Brigade was made up of the 2nd Royal Warwickshire Regiment, 1st Royal Norfolk Regiment, and 2nd Shropshire Light Infantry. In addition, the division had the usual complement of support troops – 3rd Reconnaissance Regiment Royal Armoured Corps (RAC), 3rd Divisional Engineers, and 3rd Divisional Signals. Heavy machine-gun and mortar support was provided by 2nd Middlesex Regiment.

The 3rd Division's artillery element (7th, 33rd, and 76th Field Regiments) was re-equipped with self-propelled Priest 105mm howitzers, and its 20th antitank Regiment was given Wolverine 3in self-propelled guns (US M10s). This conversion to self-propelled artillery increased the speed with which the guns could be disembarked and allowed them to fire from the decks of landing craft during the run-in to the beaches, thus increasing the artillery support given to the division during the final critical approach to its landing sectors. The 92nd Light Anti-aircraft Regiment, Royal Artillery (RA) completed the heavy firepower of the division.

Joining with Rennie's division were a number of other units that were placed under his command specifically for the assault. These specialized forces included an armored element in the shape of the 27th Armoured Brigade and 5th Assault Regiment Royal Engineers (RE; from 79th Armoured Division);

Allied Forces, Sword Beach, June 6, 1944

Allied Supreme Commander – General Dwight D. Eisenhower
British 21st Army Group – General Sir Bernard L. Montgomery
British Second Army – Lieutenant-General Sir Miles Dempsey

British I Corps – Lieutenant-General John Crocker

British 6th Airborne Division – Major-General Richard N. Gale

    3rd Parachute Brigade – Brigadier James Hill

        8th Parachute Battalion – Lieutenant-Colonel Alistair Pearson

        9th Parachute Battalion – Lieutenant-Colonel Terence Otway

        1st Canadian Parachute Battalion – Lieutenant-Colonel George Bradbrook

    5th Parachute Brigade - Brigadier Nigel Poett

        7th Parachute Battalion – Lieutenant-Colonel Pine Coffin

        12th Parachute Battalion – Lieutenant-Colonel Johnny Johnson

        13th Parachute Battalion – Lieutenant-Colonel Luard

    6th Airlanding Brigade – Brigadier Hugh Kindersley

        A Company, 12th Battalion, The Devonshire Regiment

        2nd Battalion, The Oxfordshire & Buckinghamshire Light Infantry

        1st Battalion, The Royal Ulster Rifles

British 3rd Infantry Division – Major-General Tom Rennie

    8th Infantry Brigade – Brigadier E. Cass

        1st Battalion, The Suffolk Regiment

        2nd Battalion, The East Yorkshire Regiment

        1st Battalion, The South Lancashire Regiment

    9th Infantry Brigade – Brigadier J. C. Cunningham

        2nd Battalion, The Lincolnshire Regiment

        1st Battalion, The King's Own Scottish Borderers

        2nd Battalion, The Royal Ulster Rifles

    185th Infantry Brigade – Brigadier K. P. Smith

        2nd Battalion, The Royal Warwickshire Fusiliers

        1st Battalion, The Royal Norfolk Regiment

        2nd Battalion, The King's Shropshire Light Infantry

        7th Field Regiment, Royal Artillery

        33rd Field Regiment, Royal Artillery

        76th Field Regiment, Royal Artillery

        20th antitank Regiment, Royal Artillery

        92nd Light Anti-aircraft Regiment, Royal Artillery

        53rd Medium Regiment, Royal Artillery (attached for landings)

        2nd Battalion, The Middlesex Regiment (machine-gun)

        3rd Reconnaissance Regiment, Royal Armoured Corps

        101st Beach Sub-Area

            5th King's Regiment (Beach Group)

            1st Oxfordshire & Buckinghamshire Light Infantry (Beach Group)

    1st Special Service Brigade – Brigadier Lord Lovat

        3 Commando

        4 Commando

        6 Commando

        45 Royal Marine Commando

    4th Special Service Brigade – Brigadier B. W. Leicester

        41 Royal Marine Commando

    27th Armoured Brigade – Brigadier G. E. Prior Palmer

        13th/18th Royal Hussars

        1st East Riding Yeomanry

        The Staffordshire Yeomanry

79th Armoured Division – Major-General Sir Percy C.S. Hobart

    30th Armoured Brigade – Brigadier N. W. Duncan

        22nd Dragoons

        2nd County of London Yeomanry (Westminster Dragoons)

        141st Regiment, Royal Armoured Corps

    1st Assault Brigade, Royal Engineers – Brigadier G. L. Watkinson

        5th Assault Regiment, Royal Engineers

heavier firepower from the guns of the 53rd Medium Regiment Royal Artillery; and the swift mobility of Lord Lovat's 1st Special Service Brigade, comprising 3, 4, 6, and 45 (Royal Marine) Commandos. To these were added units to organize the beach landings and traffic movement out of the beachhead – the 101st Beach Area and Port Operating Group. To protect from enemy interference from the air, two more antiaircraft regiments were added. Two specialist field engineer companies were also allocated to help with demolitions and obstacle clearance, while a host of other minor service units took care of various fine details associated with the amphibious landings. All these new arrivals resulted in a doubling in the size of the division, and with these changes and additions the British 3rd Infantry Division became the most powerful division that had ever left England.

The British 6th Airborne Division was given the task of landing east of the River Orne prior to the seaborne landings, in order to protect the left flank of the invasion forces. The division was raised on May 2, 1943, under the command of Major-General Gale, with the specific role of providing airborne troops to assist any invasion against occupied Europe. The division was, therefore, completely new, and it had just one year to train and ready itself for this momentous task. It comprised three brigades – the 3rd and 5th Parachute Brigades and 6th Airlanding Brigade – each containing three battalions. The 3rd Parachute Brigade consisted of the 8th and 9th Battalions, The Parachute Regiment, and 1st Canadian Parachute Battalion; the 5th Parachute Brigade consisted of the 7th, 12th, and 13th Battalions, The Parachute Regiment; and the 6th Airlanding Brigade was made up of 12th Devonshire Regiment, 2nd Oxfordshire and Buckinghamshire Light Infantry, and 1st Royal Ulster Rifles. The 53rd Airlanding Light Regiment Royal Artillery provided artillery support, and the 6th Airborne Armoured Reconnaissance Regiment RAC, 6th Airborne Divisional Engineers, and 6th Airborne Divisional Signals gave specialist support.

GERMAN FORCES

The sector that included Sword Beach and the DZ of the British 6th Airborne Division was held by a single German division, the 716th Infantry Division. The 716th was originally activated under the command of Oberst Otto Matterstock on May 2, 1941, from replacement units raised in Military District VI at Münster. Its soldiers were older men from the Rhineland and Westphalia areas. The 716th was one of the 15 static divisions raised in Mobilization Wave 15, beginning in April 1941, which was specifically organized for occupation and anti-invasion duties in the West and in the Balkans. It was immediately sent to the Caen area for coastal defense duties and, after a brief spell in Soissons and Belgium, returned once again to Normandy in June 1942, where it remained until D-Day.

Initially the division consisted of two regiments, the 726th and 736th Infantry Regiments, each with three battalions. Its artillery support was provided by the 656th Artillery Battalion, containing three batteries of field guns, but this was later supplemented by the arrival of an additional battalion, and the division's artillery unit was upgraded and redesignated the 1716th Artillery Regiment. Being a static formation, the division was without any vehicles for troop movements and what little transport it did have was often horse-drawn.

It was inevitable that the division's static role on the Normandy coastline would be seen as a source of manpower to help make up the German losses in Russia, and many of its soldiers were drafted to the East, to be replaced by lower-quality troops from the occupied territories of Poland and Russia. Little by little, the division's strength and morale was diluted by the influx of foreign soldiers drafted in under the threat of service to the German Army or brutal captivity in concentration camps.

In April 1943 Generalmajor (later Generalleutnant) Wilhelm Richter arrived to take over the division. His task was to improve the defenses and secure the area against invasion, and his responsibility was to hold a front of over 21 miles of coastline. It was a demanding task, particularly when one considers that a good division could reasonably be expected to hold only 6 miles of front. Richter complained that his forces were "beaded along the coast like a string of pearls." The division did, however, have some assistance to help stiffen its defensive role, sited as it was behind the much-vaunted,

German troops mine a bridge over the Dives Canal before the invasion. The River Dives marked the eastern boundary of the proposed landings of the British 6th Airborne Division. (Bundesarchiv, 721/382/32A)

|but still incomplete, concrete emplacements and defenses of the Atlantic Wall. Richter set his men to help in the construction of the coastal defenses and assisted in organizing over 40 fortified centers of resistance in his sector.

As anticipation of an Allied invasion grew, Richter was reinforced by two battalions of *Osttruppen* from the occupied territories of the Soviet Union. These Eastern troops were complete units of about 1,000 men, and one battalion was assigned to each of the regiments – the 441st Ost Battalion went to the 726th Regiment and the 642nd Ost Battalion joined the 736th Regiment. The Osttruppen acted as the fourth battalion for each unit, although their usefulness was considered suspect, as were similar battalions placed in the line elsewhere along the French coastline. As one senior German general scathingly observed: "It is hard to imagine why Russians should fight for the Germans, in France against Americans."

When the Allied blow struck, the German 716th Division became involved in fighting against not only the British at Sword Beach and the 6th Airborne east of the Orne, but also against the Canadians on Juno Beach. Approximately half of the division's strength was dispersed between the two sectors. In the area of Sword Beach, Richter had the first and second battalions of the 736th Regiment holding the coastline, with its third battalion inland acting as a reserve. The Regiment's 642nd Ost Battalion was dispersed behind the coast, mainly in the area east of the Orne.

The armor readily available to counter the landings near Caen amounted to just one division, the 21st Panzer Division, which had its HQ at St-Pierre-sur-Dives, about 20 miles southeast of Caen. There were other Panzer units allocated to resist an invasion along the Normandy coast, but they were stationed well inland, waiting to see where the Allied blow would land. The 12th SS-Panzer Division "Hitlerjugend" was close to Lisieux and the Panzer Lehr Division was in the Chartres area, both within a day's march of Caen. In addition, the 17th SS-Panzergrenadier Division south of Tours, the 2nd Panzer Division east of the Seine, and 116th Panzer Division near Paris could all arrive in the area of the invasion within a matter of days.

The 21st Panzer Division was commanded by the aforementioned Generalmajor Edgar Feuchtinger. It was available for immediate counterattack wherever it was required in Normandy and was under the control of Army Group B. By contrast, the 12th SS-Panzer and Panzer Lehr Divisions were part of the strategic reserve and could only be released by authority of the Supreme Commander, Adolf Hitler. The Führer needed to be convinced that any landing, no matter where it might fall along the Channel coast, was the main invasion and not just a feint to draw off his mobile forces while other larger landings took place elsewhere. The German Supreme Command felt sure that the Allies would land in the Pas-de-Calais and even weeks after the Normandy landings they still expected that fresh assaults would be made in that area.

The 21st Panzer Division was a reconstituted division organized after the original unit was destroyed in Tunisia in May 1943. It was formed at Rennes in July 1943 from veterans of the Eastern Front and those soldiers of the Afrika Korps who had escaped the disaster in Tunisia, together with some from miscellaneous units of the German Seventh Army. These latter troops were often other people's rejects and not always the best of men. General Leo Geyr von Schweppenburg had commented that the 21st Panzers were flawed because they were composed of many undesirable personnel with bad traits, which even thorough and experienced training could never overcome.

The division was composed of the 100th Panzer Regiment and the 125th and 192nd Panzergrenadier Regiments, all of which had two battalions instead of the normal three. The 155th Panzer Artillery Regiment, the 21st Panzer Reconnaissance Battalion, the 220th Panzer Pioneer Battalion, and the 305th Antiaircraft Battalion completed the make-up of this division. Raised in France, its transport was composed mainly of captured French vehicles and it was armed with many obsolete weapons. Its tanks were mostly PzKpfw IVs together with some light tanks of foreign manufacture. Of the ten Panzer and Panzergrenadier divisions in the West in early 1944, the 21st Panzer Division was the only one rated as unfit for service in Russia.

In the air, the German Luftwaffe was only a shadow of the force that had waged war on Britain in 1940. Most of its strength was either engaged in Russia, or committed against the Allied bombing effort that was pounding the industries and cities of the Reich on a daily basis. The German Third Air Force (Luftflotte 3), commanded by Generalfeldmarschall Hugo Sperrle, was responsible for air attacks against any Allied invasion. The Third Air Force covered the whole of France, Holland, and Belgium. To protect this massive area, however, it had only 168 Messerschmitt Bf-109 and Focke-Wulf Fw-190 fighters in II Fighter Corps, and it had just 67 Fw-190F fighter-bombers in II Air Corps to provide air support for ground troops. Nor were all of these aircraft airworthy, with the average unit serviceability at below 50 percent. They were also short of experienced air crews and adequate fuel stocks.

At sea, the Kriegsmarine had also been curtailed in its offensive capability through the superiority of Allied air and sea power. Admiral Theodor Krancke, Commander-in-Chief Naval Group Command West, was responsible for opposing the invasion, but he had few craft in the western Channel with which to counter it. The only vessels that were available in the area on June 6 between Boulogne and Cherbourg were three torpedo boats, one minesweeper, 29 S-boats, 36 R-boats (motor minesweepers), 35 auxiliary minesweepers and patrol boats, 11 gun carriers, and three mine-laying craft. This was all that Krancke had to counter an Allied naval force of over 6,000 vessels.

German Forces, Sword Beach, June 6, 1944

German Supreme Commander – Adolf Hitler

German Commander-in-Chief (West) – Generalfeldmarschall Gerd von Rundstedt

German Army Group B – Generalfeldmarschall Erwin Rommel

German Seventh Army – Generaloberst Freidrich Dollmann

German LXXXIV Corps – General der Artillerie Erich Marcks

German 716th Infantry Division – Generalleutnant Wilhelm Richter

    726th Infantry Regiment

        I Battalion

        II Battalion

        III Battalion

        441st Ost Battalion

    736th Infantry Regiment – Oberst Krug

        I Battalion

        II Battalion

        III Battalion

        642nd Ost Battalion

    1716th Artillery Regiment

        I Battalion

        II Battalion

        716th Reconnaissance Company

        716th Engineer Battalion

German 21st Panzer Division – Generalmajor Edgar Feuchtinger

    100th Panzer Regiment – Oberst von Oppeln-Bronikowski

        I Battalion

        II Battalion

    125th Panzergrenadier Regiment – Oberst Hans von Luck

        I Battalion

        II Battalion

    192nd Panzergrenadier Regiment – Oberstleutnant Rauch

        I Battalion

        II Battalion

        200th Panzer Reconnaissance Battalion

        200th Sturmgeschütz Battalion

        200th Panzerjäger Battalion

    155th Panzer Artillery Regiment – Oberst Huehne

        I Battalion

        II Battalion

        III Battalion

        305th Army Flak Battalion

        220th Panzer Pioneer Battalion

OPPOSING PLANS

ALLIED PLAN

Major-General Gale's 6th Airborne Division had been set a series of tasks aimed at protecting the eastern flank of the seaborne landings and providing of a firm lodgement from which a rapid expansion of the beachhead could be launched when the time was right. Gale had been ordered to seize the bridges over the River Orne and the Caen Canal at Bénouville to allow a link-up between the beaches and the airborne forces. He had also been tasked with destroying the bridges over the River Dives between Caen and the sea to prevent German counterattacks from the east, and to hold the ground in between the Orne and Dives rivers in order to deny it to the enemy. In addition, the gun battery at Merville had to be eliminated before it could interfere with the seaborne landings. Several DZs for paratroops and LZs for gliders had been allocated to receive units of the 6th Airborne. The 5th Parachute Brigade was to land on DZ N north of Ranville; 3rd Parachute Brigade was given DZ V to the northeast near Varaville; 8th Parachute Battalion (from 3rd Parachute Brigade) was to land separately on DZ K to the southeast near Touffréville, while the *coup de main* parties assaulting Bénouville were to land on LZs X and Y close to the bridges. A further LZ, LZ W, was identified on the western side of the Caen Canal near St Aubin to receive the division's follow-up brigade, the 6th Airlanding Brigade, which would land in gliders on the evening of D-Day. The brigade could not be brought over to Normandy sooner because, due to a lack of aircraft, it had to wait until the towing aircraft used during the assault phase had returned to England and been made ready for a second mission.

Sword Beach and the area to the east of the River Orne marked the left-hand section of the British seaborne assault. Just offshore of Sword Beach, most notably opposite Lion-sur-Mer, were large shoals that made the approach to the beaches difficult. These shallows influenced the actual landfall of the assault waves and a decision was made that the initial

A Horsa glider, which displays the three broad white recognition stripes of the Allies, is towed skywards by an Armstrong Whitworth Albemarle tug aircraft. *(Imperial War Museum, H39183)*

landings would take place in the locality of the seaside hamlet of La Brèche. The targeted area had a clear approach from the sea and good access inland, but it was, unfortunately, only wide enough to land one brigade at a time.

Sword Beach was itself composed of four sectors, which were codenamed "Oboe," "Peter," "Queen," and "Roger." These sectors were in turn divided up into three areas ("Green," "White," and "Red"), which represented right-hand, central, and left-hand parts of each beach respectively. The proposed landing site on Sword Beach at La Brèche was in the designated Queen Red and Queen White sectors.

With the landing site identified and confirmed, Allied planners could now concentrate on how they might best gain a secure foothold on the beaches. The 5th Assault Regiment, from 79th Armoured Division, that was to land in support of 3rd Division, had specialized armor in its arsenal with which to overcome the miscellaneous beach obstacles (see below). Major-General Percy Hobart, the innovative commander of 79th Armoured Division, had gathered together a variety of special tanks each with a specific purpose. All were designed to attack some particular type of German defence. There were Sherman "Crab" tanks that had a revolving drum attached to their fronts onto which were connected large steel chains. As the drum rotated, the metal chains smashed into the ground exploding any mines that lay in the tank's path, and thereby cleared a lane through the minefield for following vehicles. There were AVREs modified for specific tasks such as bridge-laying, filling in ditches, crossing antitank walls, and firing large charges against concrete emplacements. Other tanks were modified as flamethrower vehicles, while "Bobbin" tanks – Churchills capable of laying flexible carpets to allow the passage of vehicles over sand and shingle – were also developed. All of these special types of tanks were at the disposal of 3rd Division for its assault.

British 6th Airborne Division – D-Day Operations

At selected locations along the seafront were strongpoints, which were built to give mutual support. These were often given individual codenames by the Allies and specific plans were made for their capture. Along Sword Beach the fortified areas were: "Trout" at Lion-sur-Mer; "Cod" at La Brèche; the "Casino" at Riva Bella; and the "Shore Battery" at Riva Bella/Ouistreham. Inland from the beaches, sited to prevent Allied forces moving off the beach, were other fortified strongpoints: "Sole" southwest of Ouistreham; "Daimler" to the south of Ouistreham; and "Morris" and "Hillman" near Colleville.

The task of transporting Allied forces onto Sword Beach and defending them from enemy interference during the passage was given to the ships of the Royal and Commonwealth navies. Force S, commanded by Rear Admiral Talbot, was part of the Eastern Task Force that supported the British and Canadian beaches of Gold, Juno, and Sword. Force S comprised three Assault Groups: S1, S2, and S3. Assault Group S3 was to be responsible for the initial landing of the assault brigade, followed by Group S2 with the intermediate brigade, while Group S1 would take responsibility for the landings of the reserve brigade. Each of these naval groups would have their own flotillas of various types of landing craft.

Sword Beach, being the easternmost section of the British assault area, was seen as the most vulnerable to enemy attack, both from the heavy guns around Le Havre and from the German vessels based there. For this reason a powerful bombarding force was to be stationed to port of the invasion convoys, to counter such threats. This force was to contain two battleships, a 15in gun monitor, and five cruisers, supported by 13 destroyers and numerous other lighter vessels.

The 3rd British Division was to lead the invasion onto Sword Beach, with its 8th Brigade carrying out the initial assault. It would land two battalions up front, with a reserve battalion following closely behind. The 1st South Lancs would touch down on Queen White, while the 2nd East Yorks would land on Queen Red and the 1st Suffolk Regiment would follow them in. All three battalions were to be conveyed ashore in tiny wooden LCAs, each carrying around 30 fully laden troops. They would be supported at the same time by DD tanks from the 13th/18th Hussars (27th Armoured Brigade). The arrival of these tanks on the beach, coinciding with the arrival of the infantry, would enable enemy strongpoints to be attacked immediately.

Just behind the first wave, and arriving almost simultaneously, specialized armor from the 79th Armoured Division would land in LCTs – comprising the 22nd Dragoons, Westminster Dragoons and 5th Assault Regiment RE. These units were tasked with the role of overcoming beach defenses, clearing minefields, and opening gaps from the beach for the infantry and tanks to pass through.

Next would land the remaining regiments of tanks of 27th Armoured Brigade – 1st East Riding Yeomanry and the Staffordshire Yeomanry – together with the three self-propelled regiments (7th, 33rd, and 76th Field Regiments RA) of the 3rd Division's field artillery. These forces would add punch to the 8th Brigade's move inland.

The immediate objectives for the first assaulting waves were to clear the beach of underwater obstacles, silence local defenses – especially the German strongpoint Cod just behind the shoreline – and secure exits from the beaches. They were then to move inland and attack their designated objectives in order to leave the beach area relatively clear for the follow-up waves of troops and armor. The 1st South Lancs would press inland to take the village of Hermanville, 2nd East Yorks would move on strongpoints Sole and Daimler to the west of Ouistreham, while the 1st Suffolks would advance through Colleville and attack strongpoints Morris and Hillman.

As these units attacked German defenses close to the landing sites, other enemy strongpoints would be sure to interfere with the landing. To the east were two such fortified areas: the Casino at Riva Bella and the Shore Battery on the seafront at Ouistreham. To the west was the strongpoint Trout at Lion-sur-Mer. Warships would bombard these sites during the early hours after dawn, then 4 Commando (from the 1st Special Service Brigade) would land just behind the assault waves and advance inland to capture the eastern

strongpoints from the rear. At the same time, 41 Royal Marine Commando (from the 4th Special Service Brigade) would move to the west to attack Trout.

After the first waves had gained a foothold, other groups would arrive and pass through. Following the reserve battalion of the assaulting brigade would come the remainder of the 1st Special Service Brigade in the shape of 3 and 6 Commandos and 45 Royal Marine Commando. Their task was to move straight off the landing beach and advance to link up with and reinforce the 6th Airborne Division on the eastern side of the River Orne.

All of these landings were programmed to be completed at H-Hour plus 120 minutes. Then came the intermediate brigade, the 185th Brigade, comprising the 2nd Warwickshires, 1st Royal Norfolks, and 2nd King's Shropshire Light Infantry (KSLI). All three battalions would strike out for the vital D-Day objective of Caen with all speed, supported by the tanks of 27th Armoured Brigade. The reserve brigade, 9th Brigade, was to begin its landings at H-Hour + 270 minutes. Its three battalions (2nd Lincolnshires, 1st King's Own Scottish Borderers (KOSB), and 2nd Royal Ulster Rifles), supported by tanks, would drive on Caen along the right flank of the beachhead as soon as they cleared the waterfront.

Commandos from the 1st Special Service Brigade embark onto LCI (S) – Landing Craft Infantry, Small – at Warsash in Southampton Water, England. These small craft would take the commandos across the Channel and set them down right onto the landing beaches. The vessels could carry 96 fully equipped troops below deck. Disembarkation was via four ramps manhandled over bow sponsons. *(Imperial War Museum, H39043)*

Lieutenants Bob de la Tour, Don Wells, John Vischer, and Bob Midwood of the 22nd Independent Parachute Company synchronize watches on the evening of June 5 before boarding their aircraft to lead their advance parties into Normandy. *(Imperial War Museum, H39070)*

GERMAN PLAN

For the German planners, their problem was extremely difficult: they did not know when or where the blow might fall on the hundreds of miles of occupied coastline that they were defending. They had to prepare for all eventualities.

The German plan of defense against an Allied invasion was built around two key principles. First, the assaulting forces must be stopped or disorganized along the waterline itself by impregnable fixed defenses, and second, they must be destroyed by an armored counterattack, either on the exposed beaches, or on suitable ground inland. As we have seen, this latter point provoked prolonged and bitter debate, dividing the Germans into two schools of thought represented by Rommel on the one hand, and von Schweppenburg and von Rundstedt on the other. Rommel was certain that Allied air superiority would foil any attempt to mass Panzer divisions and that such a policy would be doomed to failure. He went so far as to suggest that if the Allies managed to establish a beachhead then the war would have been lost. Hitler, to whom all such arguments were referred for a decision, fudged the issue. He compromised, allowing one Panzer division to be located close to the coast under Army Group B's control for immediate use, while keeping others under his express control further back. In Normandy this compromise resulted in 21st Panzer Division being located south of Caen, and 12th SS-Panzer Division "Hitlerjugend," and the Panzer Lehr Division being held further away, more than 100 miles from the Channel.

Along the length of Sword Beach, the Atlantic Wall offered a significant obstacle to the Allied forces. General Richter, commander of the German division garrisoning this stretch of coastline, had added his improvements to

German Defenses – Sword Beach

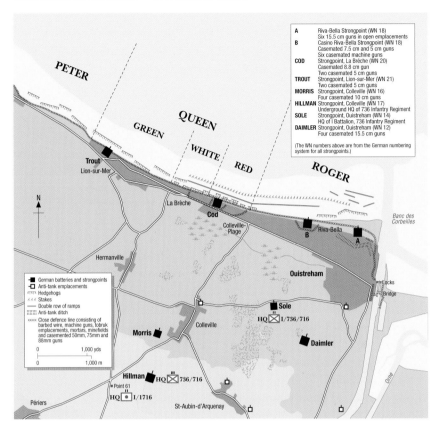

A   Riva-Bella Strongpoint (WN 18)
        Six 15.5 cm guns in open emplacements
B   Casino Riva-Bella Strongpoint (WN 18)
        Casemated 7.5 cm and 5 cm guns
        Six casemated machine guns
COD   Strongpoint, La Brèche (WN 20)
        Casemated 8.8 cm gun
        Two casemated 5 cm guns
TROUT   Strongpoint, Lion-sur-Mer (WN 21)
        Two casemated 5 cm guns
MORRIS Strongpoint, Colleville (WN 16)
        Four casemated 10 cm guns
HILLMAN Strongpoint, Colleville (WN 17)
        Underground HQ of 736 Infantry Regiment
SOLE   Strongpoint, Ouistreham (WN 14)
        HQ of I Battalion, 736 Infantry Regiment
DAIMLER Strongpoint, Ouistreham (WN 12)
        Four casemated 15.5 cm guns

(The WN numbers above are from the German numbering system for all strongpoints.)

Rommel's defensive plan and created a number of interlocking strongpoints to supplement the wall of fortifications.

The first thing that the invasion craft would meet on their run-in to Sword Beach was the fire of long-range artillery. The landing beaches were within range of the heavy guns of batteries away to the east as far afield as Le Havre, with calibres of 150–381mm. Closer to Sword Beach were the smaller artillery positions at Merville, Ouistreham, Riva Bella, and Colleville, housing guns with calibres of 104–155mm. Next on their approach to the beaches, the landing craft would hit underwater defenses, which were placed between high- and low-water marks and consisted of stakes topped by mines, steel hedgehogs made from sections of railway line, mined rafts floating just under the water, steel ramps, and minefields. Once they had managed to maneuver themselves past these obstacles, the landing craft would finally hit the beach. Here they would come under fire from the interlocking machine-gun posts, mortar weapons pits, and antitank pillboxes, whose fire would be sweeping the area. Behind this line of fortifications were antitank seawalls, barbed-wire entanglements, and more minefields.

THE LANDINGS: THE AIRBORNE ASSAULT

As darkness was falling at 2256hrs on June 5, 1944, six Horsa gliders were pulled airborne from the runway at Tarrant Rushton airfield in England by six Halifax bombers. Inside the wood-and-canvas gliders were troops from D/2nd Oxfordshire and Buckinghamshire Light Infantry, part of the 6th Airlanding Brigade of the British 6th Airborne Division. The troops were commanded by Major John Howard and were the *coup de main* party ordered to attack the bridges over the River Orne and Caen Canal at Bénouville in Normandy. Seven minutes later, 70 miles away to the northeast, more planes from No. 38 Group RAF lifted into the sky from Harwell airfield in Berkshire. This time, Albemarle aircraft carried the men of the 22nd Independent Parachute Company, whose task was to drop onto and mark out LZs ready for the main parachute force that was set to arrive 30 minutes after them.

The original Caen Canal lifting-bridge captured by Major Howard and his company during the first minutes of D-Day. It now lies in the grounds of the Airborne Museum at Bénouville, moved there after it was replaced by a more modern structure. *(Ken Ford)*

Major-General Richard Gale is given a present of a tin of treacle by the RAF station commander, Group Captain Surplice, as he boards glider number 70 ready for his passage to Normandy to join the main body of the 6th Airborne Division. *(Imperial War Museum, H39072)*

THE CAPTURE OF THE ORNE BRIDGES

At 0007hrs (British Double Summer Time) on June 6, Sergeant Jim Wallwork cast off his glider from the tug aircraft and began the descent to his designated Landing Zone X close by the Orne bridges. Behind him, following at one-minute intervals, came the other five Horsas carrying the remainder of Major Howard's small force. At 0016hrs Wallwork brought his aircraft to a grinding halt just 60 yards from the bridge over the Orne Canal. Howard and his men quickly crashed their way out of the aircraft's flimsy structure and dashed for the bridge. In the lead was Lieutenant Den Brotheridge. He led his men through the barbed-wire surrounding the bridge and onto the roadway. Behind them, almost silently, the next two gliders swept in and landed just a few yards from Wallwork's plane. The skill of three glider pilots, Sergeants Wallwork, Boland, and Hobbs, had delivered almost 90 men across the Channel to within 100 yards of their objective.

Howard's men now set about the tasks for which they had spent so many months training. The operation worked like clockwork. Lieutenant Brotheridge and No. 1 Platoon were swiftly onto the road and they began running across the bridge to get among the enemy weapons pits on the far side of the structure. On the bridge, striding aimlessly back and forth, were two German sentries. They had not heard the arrival of the gliders above the noise of aircraft and antiaircraft fire and were suddenly startled to see the blackened faces of British troops rushing toward them. One sentry turned

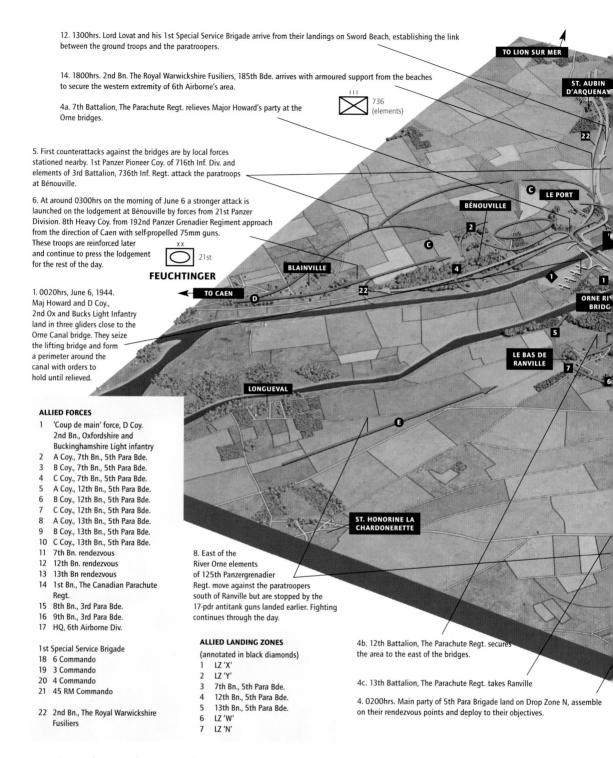

12. 1300hrs. Lord Lovat and his 1st Special Service Brigade arrive from their landings on Sword Beach, establishing the link between the ground troops and the paratroopers.

14. 1800hrs. 2nd Bn. The Royal Warwickshire Fusiliers, 185th Bde. arrives with armoured support from the beaches to secure the western extremity of 6th Airborne's area.

4a. 7th Battalion, The Parachute Regt. relieves Major Howard's party at the Orne bridges.

5. First counterattacks against the bridges are by local forces stationed nearby. 1st Panzer Pioneer Coy. of 716th Inf. Div. and elements of 3rd Battalion, 736th Inf. Regt. attack the paratroops at Bénouville.

6. At around 0300hrs on the morning of June 6 a stronger attack is launched on the lodgement at Bénouville by forces from 21st Panzer Division. 8th Heavy Coy. from 192nd Panzer Grenadier Regiment approach from the direction of Caen with self-propelled 75mm guns. These troops are reinforced later and continue to press the lodgement for the rest of the day.

FEUCHTINGER

21st

1. 0020hrs, June 6, 1944. Maj Howard and D Coy., 2nd Ox and Bucks Light Infantry land in three gliders close to the Orne Canal bridge. They seize the lifting bridge and form a perimeter around the canal with orders to hold until relieved.

TO CAEN

ALLIED FORCES

1 'Coup de main' force, D Coy. 2nd Bn., Oxfordshire and Buckinghamshire Light infantry
2 A Coy., 7th Bn., 5th Para Bde.
3 B Coy., 7th Bn., 5th Para Bde.
4 C Coy., 7th Bn., 5th Para Bde.
5 A Coy., 12th Bn., 5th Para Bde.
6 B Coy., 12th Bn., 5th Para Bde.
7 C Coy., 12th Bn., 5th Para Bde.
8 A Coy., 13th Bn., 5th Para Bde.
9 B Coy., 13th Bn., 5th Para Bde.
10 C Coy., 13th Bn., 5th Para Bde.
11 7th Bn. rendezvous
12 12th Bn. rendezvous
13 13th Bn rendezvous
14 1st Bn., The Canadian Parachute Regt.
15 8th Bn., 3rd Para Bde.
16 9th Bn., 3rd Para Bde.
17 HQ, 6th Airborne Div.

1st Special Service Brigade
18 6 Commando
19 3 Commando
20 4 Commando
21 45 RM Commando

22 2nd Bn., The Royal Warwickshire Fusiliers

8. East of the River Orne elements of 125th Panzergrenadier Regt. move against the paratroopers south of Ranville but are stopped by the 17-pdr antitank guns landed earlier. Fighting continues through the day.

ALLIED LANDING ZONES
(annotated in black diamonds)
1 LZ 'X'
2 LZ 'Y'
3 7th Bn., 5th Para Bde.
4 12th Bn., 5th Para Bde.
5 13th Bn., 5th Para Bde.
6 LZ 'W'
7 LZ 'N'

4b. 12th Battalion, The Parachute Regt. secures the area to the east of the bridges.

4c. 13th Battalion, The Parachute Regt. takes Ranville

4. 0200hrs. Main party of 5th Para Brigade land on Drop Zone N, assemble on their rendezvous points and deploy to their objectives.

TO LION SUR MER
ST. AUBIN D'ARQUENAY
LE PORT
BÉNOUVILLE
BLAINVILLE
ORNE RIVER BRIDGE
LE BAS DE RANVILLE
LONGUEVAL
ST. HONORINE LA CHARDONERETTE

736 (elements)

British 6th Airborne Division – The Eastern Flank

June 6, 1944, 0020hrs–2100hrs, viewed from the southeast showing the parachute and glider assault by British 6th Airborne Division. This included the capture of the two vital bridges near Bénouville across the Orne River and the Caen Canal – 'Pegasus' Bridge. Also shown are the increasingly powerful German counterattacks as the defenders respond to the Allied attack.

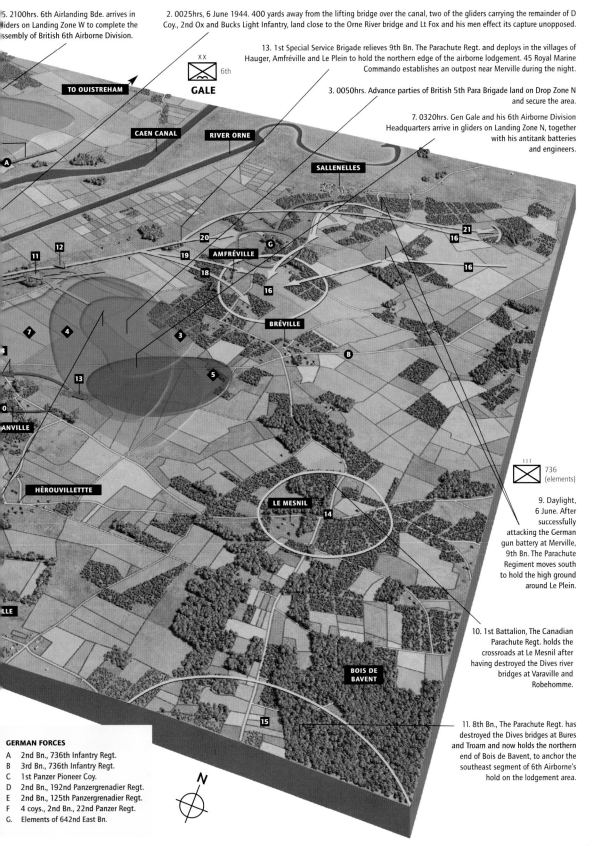

5. 2100hrs. 6th Airlanding Bde. arrives in gliders on Landing Zone W to complete the assembly of British 6th Airborne Division.

2. 0025hrs, 6 June 1944. 400 yards away from the lifting bridge over the canal, two of the gliders carrying the remainder of D Coy., 2nd Ox and Bucks Light Infantry, land close to the Orne River bridge and Lt Fox and his men effect its capture unopposed.

13. 1st Special Service Brigade relieves 9th Bn. The Parachute Regt. and deploys in the villages of Hauger, Amfréville and Le Plein to hold the northern edge of the airborne lodgement. 45 Royal Marine Commando establishes an outpost near Merville during the night.

3. 0050hrs. Advance parties of British 5th Para Brigade land on Drop Zone N and secure the area.

7. 0320hrs. Gen Gale and his 6th Airborne Division Headquarters arrive in gliders on Landing Zone N, together with his antitank batteries and engineers.

XX
6th
GALE

TO OUISTREHAM

CAEN CANAL

RIVER ORNE

SALLENELLES

A

20
19
AMFRÉVILLE
G
18
16
21
16
16
11
12

BRÉVILLE
3
B

7
4
5
13

0
ANVILLE

736
(elements)

9. Daylight, 6 June. After successfully attacking the German gun battery at Merville, 9th Bn. The Parachute Regiment moves south to hold the high ground around Le Plein.

HÈROUVILLETTTE

LE MESNIL
14

LLE

10. 1st Battalion, The Canadian Parachute Regt. holds the crossroads at Le Mesnil after having destroyed the Dives river bridges at Varaville and Robehomme.

BOIS DE BAVENT

15

11. 8th Bn., The Parachute Regt. has destroyed the Dives bridges at Bures and Troarn and now holds the northern end of Bois de Bavent, to anchor the southeast segment of 6th Airborne's hold on the lodgement area.

GERMAN FORCES

A   2nd Bn., 736th Infantry Regt.
B   3rd Bn., 736th Infantry Regt.
C   1st Panzer Pioneer Coy.
D   2nd Bn., 192nd Panzergrenadier Regt.
E   2nd Bn., 125th Panzergrenadier Regt.
F   4 coys., 2nd Bn., 22nd Panzer Regt.
G. Elements of 642nd East Bn.

N

The bridge over the River Orne at Bénouville. This was the second target of Major John Howard's D Company of 2nd Oxfordshire and Buckinghamshire Light Infantry, and it was captured intact in the early minutes of June 6. Its fame and place in history have been long overshadowed by the more glamorous events at Pegasus Bridge over the Caen Canal a few hundred yards away. *(Imperial War Museum, B5230)*

and ran while the other managed to get off a flare to raise the alarm. Almost immediately he was killed by a burst of Sten gunfire from Brotheridge. Next, the lieutenant rushed toward the machine-gun, which was positioned in a sandbagged pit at the end of the bridge, throwing a grenade as he went. The now awakened MG42 crew saw him coming and opened fire on the young officer, killing him instantly. However, the gun was quickly silenced by the troops following behind Brotheridge.

By now the German defenders were fully roused and fighting back. No. 1 Platoon began clearing the enemy from the western side of the canal around the bridge, throwing grenades and firing as they went. On the eastern side of the lifting-bridge, Lieutenant Wood and his No. 2 Platoon broke free from the second glider and cleared the German trenches, machine-gun positions, and a 50mm antitank gun on that side of the canal. The third glider contained No. 3 Platoon commanded by Lieutnant Smith, and had a bumpy landing. Six of the platoon remained trapped in the glider when the lieutenant and the others leapt from the aircraft to join up with Howard. The major directed Smith to take his men over the bridge and help No. 1 Platoon to clear the western canal bank and form a defensive perimeter. As this was happening, sappers began checking the underside of the bridge for demolition charges, cutting any wires that they came across, but they found no explosives in position. (It later transpired that the charges allocated for the bridge were stored in a hut nearby and were only to be put in place when directed by higher authority). The enemy had been caught entirely unprepared for the assault.

Meanwhile, a few hundred yards to the east, Howard's other three platoons were dropping in their gliders toward the bridge over the River Orne. Unfortunately, the leading glider carrying Howard's second-in-command, Captain Brian Priday, had been cast adrift in the wrong place and landed near the River Dives 5 miles away. The other two, however, made a successful landing within a few hundred yards of their objective and the river bridge was captured with little opposition.

The initial operation had been a complete success. Within just 15 minutes both bridges had been captured and made secure with a minimum of casualties. When Howard received news of the capture of the river bridge, he ordered the success signal "Ham and Jam" to be transmitted to signify that he had the intact bridges under his control. It now only remained for him and his company to hold them until they were relieved by the paratroopers of Lieutenant-Colonel Pine Coffin's 7th Parachute Battalion, who were to land on DZ N 30 minutes later.

The pathfinders of the 22nd Independent Parachute Company, who had leapt into Normandy just a few minutes after Major Howard's company had descended on the bridges, did not have such a successful landing. Their drops were scattered and it took a long time for the men to rally. Two aircraft had been allocated to deliver men to each of the three DZs. They were then to set up their Eureka beacons to guide in the main force of paratroopers onto their allocated LZs. This main force was arranged to drop 30 minutes after the

The wrecked gliders that brought Major John Howard and his men to within a few yards of the Caen Canal bridge at Bénouville. The Café Gondrée alongside the canal can be seen in the left background. *(Imperial War Museum, B5233)*

Pegasus Bridge

Lieutenant Den Brotheridge leads No. 1 Platoon into the attack across the canal bridge at Bénouville. With the gliders landing so close to their objective, the paratroopers of the Ox and Bucks Light Infantry were able to get onto the bridge virtually undetected. Close behind Brotheridge was Private Billy Gray, carrying a Bren gun. The two German guards patrolling the bridge were suddenly confronted by the paras rushing toward them out of the night. Schütze (Private) Romer turned and fled, but the other managed to fire off a red flare to raise the alarm. Brotheridge reacted immediately and cut the man down with a burst of Sten gun fire; Billy Gray then joined in with a volley from his Bren gun. The firing alerted the machine-gun crew on the end of the bridge. Brotheridge continued toward them, tossing a grenade as he ran, but was instantly killed by a bullet through the neck. Following closely behind Brotheridge, the men of his platoon concentrated their fire on the German machine-gun post. The grenade thrown by the now dead officer exploded, killing the enemy gun crew. Without pause, the men of the platoon continued their race across the bridge and fanned out on the other side of the canal. In just a few swift seconds the first Allied objective had been captured. The first Allied soldier had been killed in action on D-Day and the first German soldier had died defending Hitler's Fortress Europe. The war continued for the other men on the bridge. Within minutes Romer, a 16-year-old Berliner fresh from training camp, was captured. For Billy Gray and his comrades in D Company, the fighting was only just beginning. After the capture of the bridge the company joined the remainder of the 2nd Oxs and Bucks and went into the line as infantry early on June 7. For the next seven weeks they fought an increasingly bitter war of attrition to protect the left flank of the landings. Little by little the battalion's strength was eroded by artillery, machine-guns, and snipers. By the end of August, Major Howard's D Company was a shadow of its former strength. All of the original sergeants and most of the corporals were gone, and of the officers on D-Day only Howard was left, and he had been wounded twice. Altogether, the company could only muster 40 of the 181 men who began the campaign. *(Howard Gerrard © Osprey Publishing Ltd)* pathfinders. The 5th Parachute Brigade's commander, Brigadier Nigel Poett, arrived with his advance HQ precisely on target on DZ N, close by Ranville with the pathfinders. He was immediately cheered by the sound of the whistle being blown by Major Howard, signaling the successful capture of the bridges.

With so little time to complete their tasks and the failure of the majority of them to land on target, the pathfinders were unable to mark the DZs sufficiently well to ensure that the following paratroopers landed in the correct place. When the aircraft bringing the main force arrived over their various DZs at around 0045hrs, the beacons guiding them onto their targets were giving misleading signals. German antiaircraft fire was also causing many planes to lose formation and direction, so when the order came for the parachutists to drop, they were often released in the wrong places.

On DZ N, the 5th Parachute Brigade was dispersed over a wide area. The 7th, 12th, and 13th Parachute Battalions became intermingled and confused. Some order was restored as the individual groups quickly assembled at their appropriate collection points, but many paratroopers became completely lost and only joined up with their units after many hours or even days trying to get their bearings.

Lieutenant-Colonel Pine Coffin's 7th Parachute Battalion dropped on the Ranville DZ N in some disarray. After waiting at the rendezvous point for a short while for his battalion to rally, the colonel decided to take those men who had arrived and lead them toward Howard's isolated company of the Ox and Bucks at the Orne bridges. He left his second-in-command, Major

Private Frank Gardner, Captain Brian Priday, and Lance-Corporal B. Lambley of D/2nd Oxfordshire and Buckinghamshire Light Infantry. These men were part of the *coup de main* party designated to capture the river bridge over the Orne at Bénouville, but their glider landed 10 miles away from their objective close to the River Dives. It took several days for them to find their way through enemy territory to join up with their battalion. *(Imperial War Museum, B5586)*

Pegasus Bridge over the Caen Canal some time after it was captured. In the foreground, signalers string up telephone wires to provide communications with forward units. In the background are the Horsa gliders that carried Major Howard's *coup de main* party during the assault. *(Imperial War Museum, B5288)*

Baume, to collect any stragglers who might turn up later. The battalion's arrival at the bridges was most opportune, as the enemy was beginning to launch determined counterattacks against Howard's exposed company. Pine Coffin now took over command of the bridges and organized a strong perimeter around the river and canal crossings. Howard's company was withdrawn to the eastern river bridge to act as reserve, while the 7th Battalion's own companies crossed over the Caen Canal and established defensive positions on the western side of the lodgement. A and C Companies blocked the road from Caen, holding the southern part of the village of Bénouville, while B Company moved into place in the tiny hamlet of Le Port and in the small wood alongside it, blocking the approaches from Ouistreham. The battalion was only 200 strong, although other paratroopers filtered in during the night as isolated individuals picked their way through the darkness to join their units.

THE CAPTURE OF THE MERVILLE BATTERY

The 5th Parachute Brigade's other two battalions also had a scattered drop around DZ N. Its 12th Battalion, commanded by Lieutenant-Colonel Johnny Johnson, planned to rendezvous in a quarry alongside the Ranville–Sallenelles road, but the dispersed nature of the drop had meant that many of its men came down in the woods and orchards to the east of the zone. After almost an hour only 60 percent of the unit's strength had arrived at the rallying point. Lieutenant-Colonel Johnson decided that he had enough strength to move and led his men to their appointed task of defending the southwestern point of the landings around Le Bas-de-Ranville. The

13th Parachute Battalion, commanded by Lieutenant-Colonel Luard, was also dispersed over a large area. Nonetheless, within an hour Luard had gathered around 60 percent of his men and advanced from the rendezvous point to capture the important village of Ranville.

To the northeast, on DZ V, Gale's 3rd Parachute Brigade, commanded by Brigadier James Hill, also experienced a somewhat disorganized arrival in Normandy. The brigade's two battalions – 9th Parachute Battalion and 1st Canadian Parachute Battalion – were scattered across woods, fields, and flooded valleys all around the drop zone. Lieutenant-Colonel Terence Otway's men of the 9th Parachute Battalion, tasked with attacking the Merville Battery, were the most dispersed of all.

The gun battery at Merville overlooking Sword Beach was a very important target. Its field of fire dominated the sea lane into Ouistreham, through which the invasion ships would have to pass. The 9th Parachute Battalion had to eliminate the battery before 0500hrs or the cruiser HMS *Arethusa* would attempt to destroy the position with its guns. The battery's weapons were enclosed in an area 700 by 500 yards, surrounded by a double belt of barbed-wire 15ft thick and 5ft high, with minefields dotted between them. The guns themselves were housed in steel-doored concrete emplacements 6ft thick, two of which were covered with 12ft of earth. An antitank ditch barred approach from the seaward side and a total of 15 weapons pits protected all approaches. In addition to the 750 men of the battalion engaged in the operation, Otway was equipped with heavy mortars, an antitank gun, jeeps with trailers full of demolition stores, and flamethrowers, all of which were carried to the LZ in five Horsa gliders. It was planned that, at the time of the assault, three gliders would land a further 50 men directly onto the roofs of the guns within the battery itself.

The aircraft carrying the battalion had found it difficult to identify the DZ through the haze and smoke caused by an RAF bombing raid on the Merville Battery shortly before their arrival. Many of Otway's men were dropped to the east of DZ V in the marshes of the River Dives, some as far away as the high ground between Cabourg and Dozulé. The colonel knew that time was of the essence, for the battery had to be eliminated before the ships of the invasion fleet came within range of the guns. Impatiently he waited for his force to gather, with men appearing out of the night in ones and twos, each cautiously moving through the darkness, evading scattered German infantry as they moved toward the battalion's rendezvous point.

By 0300hrs Otway knew that he would have to go with the men he had if he was to stand any chance of capturing the battery before daylight. He had only 150 of the 750 paratroopers of his battalion with which to carry out the attack. None of the five gliders carrying the jeeps, trailers, and antitank guns allocated to the battalion had appeared, nor had the 3in mortars, demolition engineers, medical teams, or naval bombardment parties. Nonetheless, Otway and his small party set out for Merville, determined to execute the important task that had been set them.

When Otway arrived in the vicinity of the battery he was met by Major George Smith and his party, who had landed earlier to reconnoiter the site. Major Smith told him that the bombing raid had caused very little damage and had mostly missed the objective. Smith did, however, have some good news for Otway, for he and two warrant officers had cut their way through the outer wire of the German strongpoint, passed through the minefield, and arrived at the inner wire, where they observed enemy posts and located German positions, all without arousing the attention of the battery's garrison. A taping party, led by Captain Paul Greenway, had also successfully cleared and marked four routes through the minefield, even though they had no mine detectors or marking tape.

With only 20 percent of his force and no heavy weapons, mine detectors, or mortars, Otway was determined that the attack should still go in, timed to coincide with the arrival of the three gliders directly onto the guns. He was hoping that confusion caused by the two-pronged assault would divert the enemy's attention and hamper an effective reaction. There were not enough men to make the attack through the four paths created through the minefield, so only two of the lanes were used, with one party to go in through the wire and attack the casemates while the remainder of Otway's group attacked the main gate. As the men were preparing to rush the battery, a German machine-gun post spotted the movement and opened fire, alerting the enemy garrison. At the same time the sound of aircraft overhead signaled the arrival of the gliders. Otway ordered the attack to start immediately and the firefight for the possession of the battery began.

Two of the gliders now swooped down toward the fortified area; the third had got into trouble after take-off and had returned to base. Winding up to meet them came the snaking trails of tracer fire as the German defenders brought antiaircraft weapons to bear on the gliders. Both aircraft were hit repeatedly, with the cannon shells ripping through the canvas-and-wood sides of the planes and starting small fires, which were fanned by the slipstream. Otway was unable to illuminate the battery with flares because he had no mortars with which to fire his star shells. Disorientated by the fire and darkness, the gliders both missed the target. One landed 200 yards from the perimeter, while the other came down 2 miles away. Neither group was able to play any role in the assault.

Otway's men pressed through the gaps in the outer wire and onto the entanglements protecting the inner zone. Bangalore torpedoes (metal pipes filled with explosives) blasted a way through this second band and in moments the paratroopers were among the gun emplacements. In the darkness it was difficult to identify friend from foe. The paratroopers received fire from all sides and all angles. One by one the trenches and weapons pits scattered around the site were cleared in hand-to-hand fighting, as the enemy infantry put up spirited resistance. However, their resolve quickly began to crumble when they realized they were being attacked by paratroopers. Up went the cry "Fallschirmjäger!" and the resistance began to melt away. The conscripted foreigners and old men of the 716th Division had no wish to tangle with elite forces in the dark – the outcome could only be certain death. The garrison surrendered. With time running out for Otway and his men before the naval bombardment was due to crash into the battery, demolition teams quickly went among the guns, placing charges in their breeches and spiking each piece. Otway's men were disappointed to discover the guns were relatively small 75mm field guns and not the 150mm coastal guns the paratroopers had expected to find, but the main thing was that the battery had been eliminated as ordered. The job done, Otway rallied his men and withdrew the remnants of his battalion toward the high ground near Le Plein as planned, just as German artillery fire began to pound the area. Of the 150 men who started the assault, only about 80 remained on their feet.

THE DESTRUCTION OF THE BRIDGES OVER THE RIVER DIVES

Dropping with the 9th Parachute Battalion on 3rd Parachute Brigade's DZ V was the 1st Canadian Parachute Battalion, commanded by Lieutenant-Colonel George Bradbrooke. The Canadians were ordered to blow the bridges over the River Dives at Varaville and Robehomme and to eliminate the German garrison at Varaville. As with the other battalions, its drop was scattered and disorganized. Many of C Company's men were dropped 10 miles from the correct zone, some even coming down within 1,000 yards of the landing beaches on the western side of the River Orne. A few, however, were dropped close enough to the DZ to form an assault group to attack the German garrison in Varaville. These men, under the command of Major McLeod, were joined by stragglers from A Company and others from the 8th and 9th Parachute Battalions. It took most of the night for this small band to eliminate the Germans in Varaville, who were mainly grouped around a fortified position near the château. While the Canadians were engaging the garrison, they heard an enormous roar as the bridge over the Dives near the village was blown. A small group of men under Sergeant Davies had managed to assemble enough explosives and had infiltrated through the enemy positions to set about destroying the crossing place as planned.

B Company lost many of its men in the flooded waters and marshy ground of the River Dives. Its objective was the bridge at Robehomme. Only a few paratroopers could be gathered together for the task and these men set off for the river led by Lieutenant Toseland. At the crossing place they

This picture was taken on June 10, four days after the landings. It shows a group of paratroopers from the 12th Parachute Battalion who were dropped in enemy territory far from DZ N and spent the next four days trying to link up with their battalion. They now enjoy a deserved cup of tea. *(Imperial War Museum, B5349)*

found Major Fuller, who had earlier dropped in the River Dives itself. The engineers tasked with the blowing of the bridge had not arrived, nor had their explosives. Each man did, however, have a small amount of explosive with him to make Gammon bombs to be used against tanks, and so the major gathered all of the explosives together to form a single charge of about 30lb. One of the sergeants used this charge to try to blow the bridge, but only succeeded in weakening it. Fortunately, some time later a group of engineers arrived and placed adequate charges on the structure, destroying it completely. With both of these bridges blown, the battalion withdrew to the area of Le Mesnil to take up a position guarding the eastern flank of the airborne lodgement.

Further to the south, the 3rd Parachute Brigade's other battalion, the 8th Parachute Battalion, under the command of Lieutenant-Colonel Alastair Pearson, dropped onto DZ K. It had the most scattered drop of all, for only four of the 37 C-47s carrying the battalion dropped their sticks of paras at the right place. Two hundred and thirty men were dropped on DZ N instead of DZ K. The battalion's task was the elimination of the bridges over the Dives at Bures and Troarn. Lieutenant-Colonel Pearson found the same chaos as elsewhere when he had landed and tried to gather his battalion together. At the rendezvous near a track junction close to Touffréville, he could only find 30 of his men. The colonel waited for more to arrive and by 0330hrs he had assembled 11 officers and 130 other ranks. Time was pressing and he could wait no longer; he decided that this depleted force would have to do, and set about achieving his objectives. He sent a small party off to destroy the railway bridge at Bures and took the remainder of his men toward Troarn. This latter village was the greater problem, for it was thought to be held in force by the enemy and the bridge was on the far side of the built-up area.

Pearson gathered a few more men as he advanced, and deployed what he had of his battalion to command the high ground overlooking Troarn. Meanwhile, other men of his unit and some engineers had been gathering near DZ N, where they had been dropped by mistake. They consisted of two separate parties who had met up near the Bavent Wood. The senior officer was Major J. Roseveare, a Royal Engineer from the 3rd Parachute Squadron RE. The combined party consisted of about 60 paratroopers and 60 engineers, together with 400lb of explosives, demolition equipment, and a jeep and trailer. The major sent the bulk of the engineers and most of the material to blow the Bures bridge, while he and eight others loaded the trailer with as much explosive as they could, piled onto the jeep and headed for Troarn.

Just outside the village they found a barbed-wire roadblock, which took 20 minutes to negotiate. While they were doing so, one of the men shot a German cyclist, rousing the enemy garrison. The whole area came alive with Germans, and the intrepid party once more crammed onto the jeep and trailer and set off down the main street firing as they went. "There seemed to be a Boche in every doorway shooting like mad," recalled Major Roseveare later. The engineers returned fire as best they could while clinging desperately to the swaying vehicle as it careered at speed down the street. Nobody was injured, but the sapper on the rear of the trailer, who had been firing a Bren gun, was missing when they reached the unguarded road bridge. Working as quickly as they could, they laid explosives and blew the charges. When the dust settled, there was a large impassable gap in the middle of the roadway. Job completed, the major and his men abandoned the jeep and made their way on foot back to the battalion's lines, swimming small streams and fording inundated areas as they went.

It was later that morning before Lieutenant-Colonel Pearson received confirmation that both the bridges at Troarn and Bures had been demolished as ordered, although he had heard the tremendous explosions earlier. His battalion was strengthened during the night as more stragglers rejoined the unit. By dawn, the colonel had his men deployed along the ridge down the western side of the Bavent Wood and was overlooking the enemy-held territory to the east.

While the individual battalions of the first two brigades of the 6th Airborne Division were completing their assigned tasks, Major-General Gale and his HQ had arrived with the third wave of the division, landing on DZ N at around 0320hrs. The general had set down with the main glider force, and with him were the heavy equipment, light field-guns, and antitank guns that had been carried over to Normandy in 68 Horsa and four giant Hamilcar gliders. The arrival of Gale and his HQ now meant that the paratroopers could fight as a division, rather than as a collection of separate battalions each fighting their own individual wars.

Just after dawn, information began to filter through to Gale at his HQ. News of the capture of the bridges over the Orne and Caen Canal, the destruction of the Merville Battery and the blowing of all the bridges over the Dives gave the general great heart. His division had achieved all their major objectives; it now remained for his specialist paras to fight as infantry and to hold on to the lodgement against the inevitable German counterattacks.

GERMAN REACTION TO THE AIRBORNE LANDINGS

Generalleutnant Richter, commander of the German 716th Infantry Division, received news of the Allied airborne landings at around 0120hrs. He learned that some of his units were in action against British paratroops in several places east of the River Orne. He also heard that the Orne bridges at Bénouville had been captured intact. He quickly contacted the commander of 21st Panzer Division, Generalmajor Feuchtinger, at his HQ at St-Pierre-sur-Dives and ordered him to get his nearest units to attack the landings. By 0200hrs, the large scale of the Allied operations became apparent and it was clear that it would take a major counterattack to deal with them. Richter asked Feuchtinger to bring forward the whole of his armored division to clear the area east of the Orne of British paratroopers.

Feuchtinger hesitated: while it was true that his division came under the 716th Division as a result of the attack made against that division, he was also aware that the 21st Panzers were a component part of the OKW's armored reserve. To support the coast defense division with localized units was one thing, but to release the whole of his armored division against what might still prove to be a diversionary raid, was something more serious and would have to be confirmed by a higher authority. This approval was very slow in coming, for all the way up and down the chain of command from Feuchtinger to OKW, delay and indecision seemed to dominate. Nobody could agree if the situation warranted the release of the armored reserves. Were the British paratroopers part of an invasion or just a diversion? It took almost 12 hours before anyone could decide. In the meantime, those troops in the area of the landings would have to deal with the invaders unaided.

Closer to the Orne, way down the chain of command, other German officers were reacting more positively. The men of Richter's 736th Regiment had units in action to counter the landings that were taking place among them. The British had also descended close to villages where some of Feuchtinger's Panzer units were garrisoned. These units were in contact with the British not because they had been ordered into action, but because the British paratroopers had landed virtually on top of them.

In the southern part of the LZs, east of the Orne, companies from III./125th Panzergrenadiers, part of 21st Panzer Division, were grouped around Troarn, Sannerville, and Colombelles. These units went into action immediately. In the north, especially near Bavent and Sallenelles, were companies of the 642nd Ost Battalion, which were attached to the 736th Infantry Regiment, and these companies formed the bulk of the troops countering the landing on LZ V. At Merville and on the coast at Franceville-Plage, a company from III./736th Regiment and one from the 642nd Ost Battalion found themselves responding to the attack by Otway and his 9th Battalion.

All of these German units were in the area at the time of the airborne landings, and they were simply reacting to an enemy who had landed among them. The first counterattack by units outside the area came from a hastily assembled force put together under Richter's orders. He knew that the main objective of such a counterattack had to be the recapture of the Bénouville bridges. The closest units on the western side of the Orne were elements of Feuchtinger's II./192nd Panzergrenadiers at Cairon. This battalion moved off toward Bénouville just after 0200hrs under the command of Major Zippe, who was ordered to retake the bridges, cross over the Orne, and attack the British from the west. To assist it, from the north, Richter sent his 1st Panzerjäger Company together with guns from the 989th Heavy Artillery Battalion.

The first of Major Zippe's units into action was the 8th Heavy Company under Leutnant Braats, with its three self-propelled 75mm guns, a 20mm flak troop on armored carriers, and a troop of mortars. They attacked down the road from Caen at around 0330hrs and met Pine Coffin's two companies on the outskirts of Bénouville. The paratroopers defended doggedly, blunting the attack. A and C Companies of the 7th Parachute Battalion were forced back into Bénouville in the process, but their perimeter held. The Germans were incapable of penetrating this defensive ring without armor. The Panzergrenadiers therefore dug themselves in and spent the remainder of the night making localized assaults and pounding the area with machine-gun and mortar fire, waiting for the tanks to arrive. Occasional sorties made against the paratroopers' lines came close to a breakthrough, but the 7th Battalion was determined that it would not be moved. Through the night and throughout most of the following day, Pine Coffin's men held on to this vital bridgehead on the eastern side of the Orne.

The Panzergrenadiers of Feuchtinger's division also attacked on the eastern side of the Orne. Those units of 125th Panzergrenadier Regiment who were close to the landings were engaged in the middle of the night, but the main counterattack came later in the morning. The 12th and 13th Parachute Battalions, which were holding the southwestern flank of the lodgement from the River Orne to Hérouvillette, were attacked by German infantry and self-propelled guns from both battalions of the 125th Panzergrenadiers. The British had very good defensive positions on a reverse slope, well concealed from the enemy with about 1,000 yards of open ground in front, forcing any German attack to cross the crest and expose itself to the waiting paras below.

Successive counterattacks were beaten off by the paratroopers, using their six 6-pdr and three 17-pdr antitank guns, together with some of the division's light artillery. Although this fighting around Ranville and Hérouvillette was often fierce and the enemy did force his way close to the British lines, General Gale was never seriously worried about the situation in this sector.

With the dawn of D-Day and with landing craft closing inexorably on the invasion beaches, Gale could feel pleased with the performance of his division. The southern flank was secured by Poett's 12th and 13th Battalions; Pearson's 8th Battalion was ensconced on the ridge within Bavent Wood; the 1st Canadian Parachute Battalion held the eastern stop line through Le Mesnil; Otway's 9th Battalion held the high ground around Le Plein; and Pine Coffin's 7th Battalion held the perimeter around the Caen Canal bridges through Bénouville and Le Port. Although this last sector was the most precarious, the situation was difficult but not critical. It now remained for Gale and his paratroopers to hold out until the troops landing on Sword Beach came to their relief.

THE LANDINGS: SWORD BEACH

Early in the morning of June 6, 1944, at around 0300hrs, Allied air forces began the final aerial bombardment of Hitler's Atlantic Wall defences and artillery sites along the invasion beaches. Strongpoints close to the shoreline of Sword Beach and fortified areas in the rear were also located and attacked. This softening-up process resumed a few hours later when naval Force S arrived 7 miles offshore and began its bombardment of the same areas. HMS *Warspite* and *Ramillies*, together with the monitor *Roberts*, pounded the German long-range gun batteries at Villerville, Benerville, and Houlgate with their 15in weapons, while the cruisers *Scylla*, *Danae*, *Dragon*, *Frobisher*, *Arethusa*, and *Mauritius* attacked the shore batteries and strongpoints around Sword. In return, the enemy replied in a desultory manner, with few of their shots falling anywhere

A Mitchell medium bomber, complete with Allied recognition stripes, returning from a raid on the invasion coast, passes over a convoy on its way to France. *(Imperial War Museum, CL106)*

An LCT nears Queen Beach at La Brèche carrying the tanks and vehicles of 13th/18th Royal Hussars, part of the 27th Armoured Brigade. The number "10" painted on the turret of the Sherman in the right foreground shows that this tank belongs to the armored battalion's regimental HQ. *(Imperial War Museum, B5110)*

near the naval ships. A little later, when daylight allowed the fall of shot to be observed, the smaller destroyers moved in close to shore to add their weight of fire to the bombardment.

At about 0510hrs, low-flying aircraft from the RAF laid a smoke screen to the east of Force S to help shield its ships from the long-range enemy guns at Le Havre. Unfortunately, torpedo boats from the German 5th Torpedo Boat Flotilla took advantage of this screen to approach the bombarding ships and loosed off a total of 15 torpedoes at the Allied vessels. Most of their torpedoes missed, but the German boats did have one success, with the Norwegian destroyer *Svenner* taking a hit on her port beam immediately under her boiler room. The vessel broke in two but, despite sinking rapidly, most of her crew were saved.

To the starboard of this bombardment fleet, a great convoy of transport shipping arrived at their designated lowering positions and hove to. At 0530hrs soldiers clambered on to the decks of these transport ships and began the long, slow process of boarding the light LCAs that would take them to the shores of Normandy. On board the Landing Ships, Infantry (LSIs) *Glenearn* and *Cutlass*, the assault companies of the 1st South Lancs and 2nd East Yorks clambered down the nets and onto the bobbing craft. At about the same time, eight LCTs moved slowly away from the lowering point toward the shore, carrying the DD tanks of the 13th/18th Hussars.

Six miles offshore a flotilla of LCAs pass by the Assault Force S HQ ship, HMS *Largs*, on their way to Sword Beach. Each of the small craft carries 30 fully laden troops from the assault companies of 8th Brigade. In the foreground is an LCT with five Sherman DD tanks of the 13th/18th Hussars. These amphibious tanks will be launched much closer to shore, at about 5,000yds from the beach. *(Imperial War Museum, A 23846)*

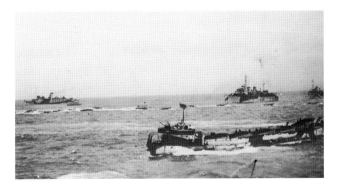

THE RUN-IN TO THE BEACHES

At 0600hrs, with the rising sun still obscured by an overcast sky, the LCAs left their mother ship and set out for Queen Red and Queen White Beaches, along with ten LCTs carrying the assault groups of specialized armor from 79th Division. Fourteen minutes later, flanking the assault force, five Landing Craft, Rocket – LCT(R) – vessels left the lowering position for their run-in to the beaches. Another nine minutes and a further 19 LCTs, containing the three self-propelled artillery regiments of the 3rd Division, followed.

The Landings on Sword Beach

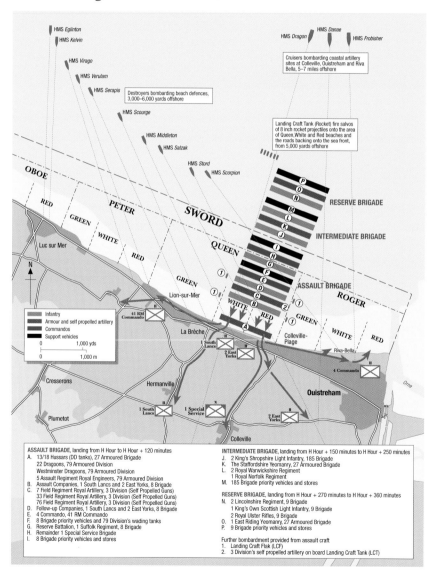

ASSAULT BRIGADE, landing from H Hour to H Hour + 120 minutes
A. 13/18 Hussars (DD tanks), 27 Armoured Brigade
    22 Dragoons, 79 Armoured Division
    Westminster Dragoons, 79 Armoured Division
    5 Assault Regiment Royal Engineers, 79 Armoured Division
B. Assault Companies, 1 South Lancs and 2 East Yorks, 8 Brigade
C. 7 Field Regiment Royal Artillery, 3 Division (Self Propelled Guns)
    33 Field Regiment Royal Artillery, 3 Division (Self Propelled Guns)
    76 Field Regiment Royal Artillery, 3 Division (Self Propelled Guns)
D. Follow-up Companies, 1 South Lancs and 2 East Yorks, 8 Brigade
E. 4 Commando, 41 RM Commando
F. 8 Brigade priority vehicles and 79 Division's wading tanks
G. Reserve Battalion, 1 Suffolk Regiment, 8 Brigade
H. Remainder 1 Special Service Brigade
I. 8 Brigade priority vehicles and stores

INTERMEDIATE BRIGADE, landing from H Hour + 150 minutes to H Hour + 250 minutes
J. 2 King's Shropshire Light Infantry, 185 Brigade
K. The Staffordshire Yeomanry, 27 Armoured Brigade
L. 2 Royal Warwickshire Regiment
    1 Royal Norfolk Regiment
M. 185 Brigade priority vehicles and stores

RESERVE BRIGADE, landing from H Hour + 270 minutes to H Hour + 360 minutes
N. 2 Lincolnshire Regiment, 9 Brigade
    1 King's Own Scottish Light Infantry, 9 Brigade
    2 Royal Ulster Rifles, 9 Brigade
O. 1 East Riding Yeomanry, 27 Armoured Brigade
P. 9 Brigade priority vehicles and stores

Further bombardment provided from assault craft
1. Landing Craft Flak (LCF)
2. 3 Division's self propelled artillery on board Landing Craft Tank (LCT)

As the flotilla of small craft neared the shore, the rocket-carrying LCT(R)s opened fire, concentrating their salvoes of 1,064 5in projectiles on Queen Red and Queen White sectors. Beach obstacles and close defenses began to disappear under masses of flame and smoke. At a range of 7,000 yards, the self-propelled guns of the 3rd Division's field artillery, grouped in fours on their LCTs, opened fire and added their weight of high explosives to the bombardment.

When the LCTs carrying the amphibious Shermans reached a point 5,000 yards from the beaches, they swung round to bring their bows downwind and unloaded their swimming tanks. Slowly the DD Shermans of 13th/18th Hussars began to disembark down the steep ramps and into the choppy sea. Of the 40 amphibious vehicles in the LCTs, 34 were successfully launched. However, almost immediately waves began to slop over their flotation screens. The DD Shermans offered a very low freeboard to the foaming sea and quickly began to take in water. Their pumps worked at full capacity to try to keep the tanks afloat, but two succumbed to the sea and sank, drowning most of their crews. The frail-looking amphibious tanks were almost invisible to the heavy LCTs coming up behind them. Some rockets from the landing craft were starting to fall short, causing the LCTs to take evasive action, veering from their course and plunging among the swimming tanks. One DD Sherman was rammed and sunk, taking most of its crew with it.

In the assault landing craft, the more curious infantrymen peered over the sides to catch a glimpse of the faint shoreline of France looming ahead, only to watch it gradually disappear in a mass of black smoke and belching flame as the Allied bombardment continued to strike home. The choppy seas tossed the small assault boats around and the helmsmen had difficulty keeping station. Men were being seasick everywhere.

A landing-craft approaches the shore close to the extreme right edge of Queen Red sector. A Crab flail tank of the 22nd Dragoons has been hit and is burning fiercely. Other tanks from 79th Armoured Division are on the beach, as is an armored bulldozer. A few men are lying in the surf. In the sea can be seen some of the beach obstacles constructed by the enemy. The two prominent villas in the right background still exist, enabling this shot to be located as to the right of strongpoint Cod. *(Imperial War Museum, B5111)*

The enemy had by now realized that an amphibious landing was taking place and began to retaliate. All along the beachfront the German guns opened up with counter-fire aimed at the approaching landing craft. This began to fall among the leading vessels, forcing them to try to escape the screaming high-explosive shells. Within a few minutes the steady formations of Allied ships closing on the beaches began to break up, with craft weaving in and out of the partially submerged obstacles and trying to dodge enemy fire. Inexorably, the invasion pressed on, closing rapidly on the belt of breaking surf that marked the shoreline.

At 0724hrs the infantry approached the final few yards of the run-in. Alongside and in front of them the first of the DD tanks began to touch bottom and grind their way up the sandy beach. Of the planned 40 tanks, 31 had made it to the shore. Many of these, however, had their engines drowned as their trim changed as they beached, but their guns were, nevertheless, useful against enemy strongpoints until the incoming tide swamped them. At the end of the assault, 23 of the DD tanks had survived the battle. At 0725hrs the infantry hit the beach.

Coincidental with the arrival of the 13th/18th's amphibious Shermans, the LCTs bringing the specialized armor of the assault group from the 79th Armoured Division also landed. These tanks, which were drawn from units of the 22nd Dragoons, Westminster Dragoons, and 5th Assault Regiment RE, were armed with a variety of specialized equipment and their tasks were many. Other equipment such as bulldozers and "Bullshorn" plows also arrived to deal with beach and underwater obstacles.

According to the assault plan, the DD tanks would land just before the infantry and RE teams in order to engage the enemy with their 75mm guns as the others came ashore. However, the heavy seas had slowed down their approach and all three groups arrived more or less together. Watching intently from their concrete emplacements were the enemy troops who had survived the bombardment and, once the barrage lifted to allow the attacking British troops to land, they began to emerge from their shelters. Although they were suffering from the shock of the rocket and shell fire, their casualties seemed to be light. The first waves of the assault infantry from the British 8th Brigade touched down into mounting chaos as the larger LCTs and smaller LCAs vied for an open run-in to the beach. As they stormed ashore, the infantry presented individual targets to the enemy troops and they responded with small-arms and mortar fire. Men began dropping as German machine-gun fire ripped through the bunched groups of troops leaving the landing craft.

A Company of the 1st South Lancs landed to the right on Queen White sector close by strongpoint Cod, which was itself an objective of the 2nd East Yorks who were landing to the left on Queen Red. The company immediately took severe casualties from the German small-arms fire coming

Commandos approach Sword Beach in an LCI(S) that has carried them over the Channel. They will disembark down the stepped ramps in the foreground, which will be lowered from the bows into the shallow water. Ahead, on the beach, drifting smoke helps hide the concentration of stranded armor. Tanks from the 27th Armoured Brigade and 79th Armoured Division cluster at the water's edge; some have been knocked out, while others seek a way off of the beach. *(Imperial War Museum, B5102)*

from the sprawling group of fortifications. The company commander and another officer were killed, but the remainder of the men quickly regrouped and moved to the right toward Lion-sur-Mer, clearing the houses along the shore. C Company, landing alongside them, attacked the strongpoint that was giving so much trouble, helped by the East Yorks who were landing on Queen Red. The follow-up company of the South Lancs, B Company, landed to the left of its assigned position and disembarked directly opposite Cod itself. Its men quickly threw themselves into a frontal assault on the wire fortifications and concrete emplacements surrounding the strongpoint. Resistance was fierce and casualties were heavy. B Company's commander was killed, as was the battalion commander, Lieutenant-Colonel Burbury, when he landed a short while later.

Over to the left, the 2nd East Yorks touched down on Queen Red sector straight into a welter of machine-gun and mortar fire. Even heavier fire criss-crossed the shoreline from 88mm and 75mm guns firing along the length of the beach from the protected confines of their concrete gun emplacements located on the edge of the dunes. Fire was returned by the tanks of 13th/18th Hussars together with the gun tanks of the 22nd Dragoons and the Westminster Dragoons, but they too suffered many direct hits. The East Yorks had landed to the left of strongpoint Cod and keenly felt the intense small-arms fire that came from its fortifications. One company assisted the infantry of the South Lancs in attacking the site, working its way around to infiltrate the area from the rear. After a fierce struggle, Cod was eventually overcome and cleared.

Coming ashore just behind the leading infantry were the obstacle-clearing teams charged with removing beach obstructions to clear the way for the follow-up landing craft. Their work was exhausting and dangerous,

BOMBARDMENT TARGETS

[yellow] Attacks by heavy and medium bombers on the days and weeks prior to the landings.

[red] Bombarded by warships on D-Day from H-Hour-2 until just before the first troops hit the beaches.

[light blue] Rocket attack from LCT(R)s as the assault forces make the final approach to the beaches starting at H-Hour-30 mins.

[blue] Artillery fire from self-propelled guns on board LCTs as they run in to shore.

ALLIED FORCES

8th Brigade
1. 2nd Battalion, The East Yorkshire Regiment
2. 1st Battalion, The South Lancashire Regiment
3. 1st Battalion, The Suffolk Regiment
4. 1st Special Service Brigade
5. 4 Commando
6. Capt Kieffer's men from 10 Commando
7. 41 RM Commando

185th Brigade
8. 2nd Battalion, The King's Shropshire Light Infantry and The Staffordshire Yeomanry
9. 1st Battalion, The Royal Norfolk Regiment
10. 2nd Battalion, The Royal Warwickshire Fusiliers

9th Brigade
11. 1st Battalion, The King's Own Scottish Borderers
12. 2nd Battalion, The Royal Ulster Rifles
13. 2nd Battalion, The Lincolnshire Regiment

GERMAN STRONGPOINTS

(shown in red, annotated in black diamonds)
A. 'Trout'
B. 'Cod'
C. Casino Riva Bella
D. Gun battery Riva Bella
E. 'Sole'
F. 'Daimler'
G. 'Morris'
H. 'Hillman'

GERMAN FORCES
A. HQ, I Bn., 736th Inf. Regt.
B. HQ, 736th Inf. Regt.

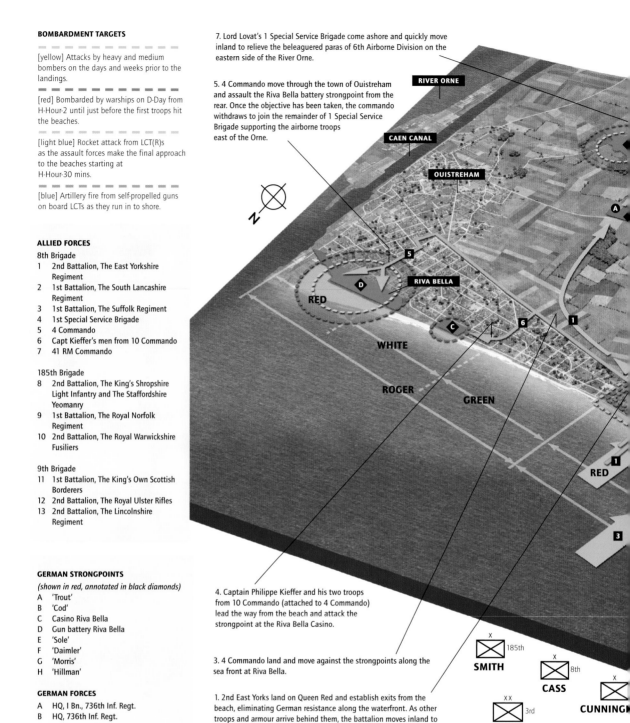

7. Lord Lovat's 1 Special Service Brigade come ashore and quickly move inland to relieve the beleaguered paras of 6th Airborne Division on the eastern side of the River Orne.

5. 4 Commando move through the town of Ouistreham and assault the Riva Bella battery strongpoint from the rear. Once the objective has been taken, the commando withdraws to join the remainder of 1 Special Service Brigade supporting the airborne troops east of the Orne.

4. Captain Philippe Kieffer and his two troops from 10 Commando (attached to 4 Commando) lead the way from the beach and attack the strongpoint at the Riva Bella Casino.

3. 4 Commando land and move against the strongpoints along the sea front at Riva Bella.

1. 2nd East Yorks land on Queen Red and establish exits from the beach, eliminating German resistance along the waterfront. As other troops and armour arrive behind them, the battalion moves inland to attack the further objectives of strongpoints 'Sole' and 'Daimler.

3rd Division on Queen Red and Queen White Beaches

June 6, 1944, 0725hrs–1500hrs, viewed from the northwest showing landings by 8th Brigade, 3rd Division's assault brigade, and the battle to subdue strongpoint 'Cod' and secure the beachhead. As the follow-up brigades land Allied forces push inland expanding the lodgement and attacking a series of German strongpoints.

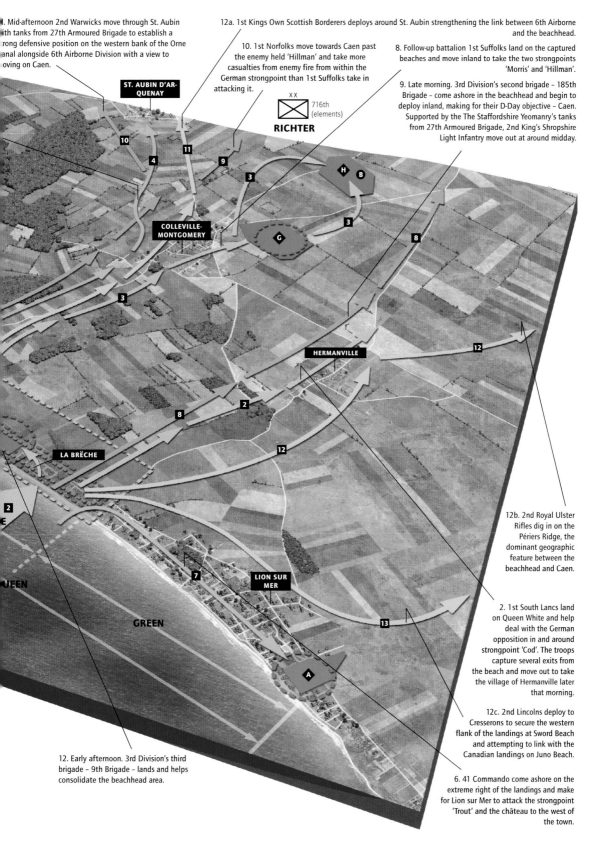

1. Mid-afternoon 2nd Warwicks move through St. Aubin with tanks from 27th Armoured Brigade to establish a strong defensive position on the western bank of the Orne Canal alongside 6th Airborne Division with a view to moving on Caen.

12a. 1st Kings Own Scottish Borderers deploys around St. Aubin strengthening the link between 6th Airborne and the beachhead.

10. 1st Norfolks move towards Caen past the enemy held 'Hillman' and take more casualties from enemy fire from within the German strongpoint than 1st Suffolks take in attacking it.

8. Follow-up battalion 1st Suffolks land on the captured beaches and move inland to take the two strongpoints 'Morris' and 'Hillman'.

9. Late morning. 3rd Division's second brigade – 185th Brigade – come ashore in the beachhead and begin to deploy inland, making for their D-Day objective – Caen. Supported by the The Staffordshire Yeomanry's tanks from 27th Armoured Brigade, 2nd King's Shropshire Light Infantry move out at around midday.

XX
716th (elements)
RICHTER

ST. AUBIN D'AR-QUENAY

COLLEVILLE-MONTGOMERY

HERMANVILLE

LA BRÈCHE

LION SUR MER

GREEN

UEEN

12b. 2nd Royal Ulster Rifles dig in on the Périers Ridge, the dominant geographic feature between the beachhead and Caen.

2. 1st South Lancs land on Queen White and help deal with the German opposition in and around strongpoint 'Cod'. The troops capture several exits from the beach and move out to take the village of Hermanville later that morning.

12c. 2nd Lincolns deploy to Cresserons to secure the western flank of the landings at Sword Beach and attempting to link with the Canadian landings on Juno Beach.

12. Early afternoon. 3rd Division's third brigade – 9th Brigade – lands and helps consolidate the beachhead area.

6. 41 Commando come ashore on the extreme right of the landings and make for Lion sur Mer to attack the strongpoint 'Trout' and the château to the west of the town.

239

Driver R. P. Turnham hangs out his washing behind one of the concrete casemates of the Morris strongpoint near Colleville. The German battery was captured just after midday on D-Day by the 1st Suffolks. *(Imperial War Museum, B5876)*

and the men, who were forced to work in the open, were vulnerable to enemy fire, incoming landing craft, and the swirling surf. They had great difficulty clearing paths through the obstacles, for each ramp, pole, steel hedgehog, and concrete tetrahedron seemed to be armed with a Teller mine or an impact-detonated antiaircraft shell. The obstacle-clearing teams worked feverishly against an incoming tide blown on by high winds. As the minutes passed the water gradually overwhelmed them and their work, and then the next wave of landing forces arrived.

Crashing through the obstacles and dodging landing craft from the assault wave came the 24 landing craft carrying the first of the commandos from Lord Lovat's 1st Special Service Brigade and 41 Royal Marine Commando from Brigadier Leicester's 4th Special Service Brigade. The men of 4 Commando were landed on the extreme left side of Queen Red beach with the objective of clearing the Casino strongpoint at Riva Bella and eliminating the gun battery on the beach at Ouistreham/Riva Bella. Commanded by Lieutenant-Colonel Dawson, 4 Commando landed straight into a barrage of intense small-arms fire, which pinned them to the beach for some moments. By this time the East Yorks should have had the beach clear for the commandos to move through, but opposition from strongpoint Cod and the surrounding dunes had delayed progress. As a result, the commandos had to fight their way off the beach and onto the lateral road leading to Ouistreham, which ran behind the waterfront.

The men of 41 Royal Marine Commando touched down 300 yards to the right of their allocated position on the extreme western end of Queen

White sector. Its task was to eliminate the strongpoint Trout in Lion-sur-Mer and attack the château west of the town. It was also to link up with the remainder of 4th Special Service Brigade who were landing on Juno Beach away to the west, thus joining together the two landing beaches. The elimination of the radar station at Douvres was a secondary objective. The Royal Marine commandos managed to get off Queen White without too much difficulty and then its force split into two groups, one attacking the château, while the other moved against Trout. By the end of the morning it had cleared Lion-sur-Mer – the strongpoint at Trout was deserted – and attacked the château. This latter objective was, however, a difficult proposition, and the group attacking the château lost its commander and two troop commanders killed. Enemy resistance was such that it was found to be impossible to advance westwards from the town to link up with Juno Beach that day. Similarly, 41 Royal Marine Commando did not have the strength to attack the radar station at Douvres.

With the help of the tanks from 13th/18th Hussars and infantry from the newly arrived follow-up battalion, the 1st Suffolks, British 8th Brigade gradually began to clear gaps and open exits from Queen Beach. Flail tanks swept routes through minefields and bridging tanks spanned antitank traps and ditches to allow the infantry to move inland. The division's self-propelled artillery had landed and joined the infantry of 8th Brigade to support the advance. More armor arrived a little later when the next regiment of 27th Armour Brigade, the Staffordshire Yeomanry, began to come ashore. By 0900hrs, the 1st South Lancs had pressed south and secured the village of Hermanville, and the 2nd East Yorks had also moved off the beach, advancing toward the German position Sole.

Sword Beach, Queen Red sector, some time after the initial assault. A medic attends to wounded commandos in the shelter of an AVRE from the 79th Assault Squadron RE, part of the 5th Assault Regiment RE. The tank is a Churchill armed with a "petard" – a 12in caliber weapon capable of firing a 26lb charge of high explosive over 200 yards against concrete emplacements and steel obstacles. In the right background is an M10 Wolverine tank-destroyer, probably from the 20th antitank Regiment RA. *(Imperial War Museum, B5095)*

No. 4 Commando Moves Inland

Troops from 4 Commando moving along the lateral road behind Sword beach, advancing toward the gun battery at Ouistreham/Riva Bella. As they advanced the commandos came under mortar and sniper fire. Captain Phillippe Kieffer's contingent of French commandos led the attack inland and moved ahead to clear the strongpoint at the Ouistreham Casino. To the right of the commandos, a group of the 2nd East Yorks pause briefly during their advance on German strongpoint Sole to shelter behind a DD Sherman tank of the 13th/18th Royal Hussars. By this time resistance along the beach was beginning to wane and enemy troops were withdrawing in the face of the massed Allied infantry coming ashore. The leading elements of the British 3rd Division came under increasing fire from enemy pockets and rearguards. The German 716th Division had lost much of its cohesion and individuals and small groups were retiring toward Caen, attempting to regroup and re-establish contact with their regiment. Captain Kieffer's men were attached to 4 Commando for the invasion, but formed part of No. 10 Inter-Allied Commando, a unit composed entirely of men from countries that were under Nazi occupation. No. 10 Commando included Dutch, French, Belgian, Norwegian and Polish troops, and even had an X-Troop of men from Germany itself. Kieffer's two French Troops joined 4 Commando specifically for the Normandy landings and were given the honor of being the first commandos to land on their home soil. These Frenchmen remained in action throughout June and July when, along with 4 Commando, they crossed over the River Orne to join Major-General Gale's 6th Airborne Division in the defense of the left flank. No. 4 Commando had previously taken part in several raids on enemy-held territory, the most notable of which was the operation at Dieppe in August 1942, when it attacked and destroyed the German battery at Varengeville, the only successful part of the whole operation. It went on to take part in the landings at Walcheren in Holland in November 1944.
(Howard Gerrard © Osprey Publishing Ltd)

With the beach reasonably clear of localized opposition, the 1st Suffolks now began to move inland toward the village of Colleville and the two strongpoints Morris and Hillman. Behind them the incoming tide, made stronger by an onshore wind, had pushed the sea up almost to the dunes. The width of the beach had been narrowed to just a small strip, often only 30 yards wide. With the imminent arrival of more landing craft bringing increasing numbers of troops, tanks, guns, and transport, the water's edge became a scene of chaos and disorder. Traffic jams began to grow at the exits and it took all the skills of the beachmasters to extricate each new unit from the mêlée. As a result, the intermediate brigade of 3rd Division, 185th Brigade, had few tanks available to support its vitally important attack toward Caen when it arrived on Queen sector. In an effort to maintain momentum, 185th Brigade's commander, Brigadier Smith, gave the order for the leading battalion, 2nd KSLI, to start its move without the support of the Staffordshire Yeomanry, hoping that the tanks might extricate themselves from the queues around the beach exits and join them later.

Meanwhile, 4 Commando had moved along the lateral road behind the beach and was attacking its objectives along the seafront at Ouistreham and Riva Bella from the rear. The strongpoint at the Casino was assaulted by two troops from 10 Commando who were attached to 4 Commando. These two troops of Frenchmen commanded by Captain Phillippe Kieffer, were given the independent task of reducing the Casino strongpoint, making the attack a purely French one. They were also given the honor of advancing first, leading 4 Commando off the beach and down the road into Ouistreham. At a rendezvous point behind the dunes they dumped their rucksacks and prepared for their attack.

The seaside Casino at Riva Bella had been completely demolished by the Germans and a strongpoint built around its rubble. It consisted of interlocking defensive bunkers and machine-gun posts, trenches, wire entanglements, and minefields. Most of the site was below ground or in field works, with few structures visible to the attacking commandos. Kieffer split his men into two groups and attacked the fortifications from the rear at two different points. It was a battle of small-arms, hand grenades, and personal antitank weapons. The two groups infiltrated between buildings close by, firing as they went. A large bunker on the left, topped by a steel cupola, proved to be a difficult proposition, while 50mm antitank guns firing through concrete embrasures made the task still more difficult. Nothing that the Frenchmen had in their armory had any effect on these structures and the casemates proved to be a problem during the whole of the attack, as was a water tower on the right, which overlooked the position. After 30 minutes of fighting, and with mounting casualties weakening their firepower, the attack by Kieffer's men stalled. Just as Kieffer had decided to make a last desperate attempt at charging the strongpoint, word came through that there were several DD tanks in the streets of Ouistreham. The young captain went off to search for one to support his attack and later returned riding on top of a Sherman. Under his direction the tank knocked out the antitank guns and water tower and silenced the bunker. With these obstacles removed, the remainder of Kieffer's men were able to clear the enemy out of the trenches and dugouts that made up the strongpoint.

Further away to the east, the remainder of 4 Commando closed on the rear of the gun battery near the mouth of the River Orne. The guns were housed in open emplacements on the beach within a heavily fortified site. The area around the battery was, like the Casino position, thick with minefields, wire entanglements, and trench systems. Machine-guns covered every approach and 50mm antitank guns watched over the landward side of the perimeter. About 100 yards short of the gun positions was an angled antitank ditch. Dominating the whole site was a large concrete tower that housed the control and ranging instruments for the coastal guns. The tower was 56ft high and looked down on every approach, but was not built as an offensive structure and so, apart from the large observation slit on the seaward side at the top, had very few openings through which weapons could be fired. The greatest danger presented by the structure was the showers of hand grenades thrown from the parapet as the commandos passed by underneath. Built to withstand the very worst bombing and shelling, the tower remained intact and was not finally taken until a few days later. The commandos were content to leave it for the follow-up troops, who would have more time to invest in its capture.

The men of 4 Commando attacked the gun emplacements in a series of short firefights linked by bouts of rapid movement, never allowing the

British dead on Sword Beach lie scattered in front of the wire defenses surrounding strongpoint Cod. *(Imperial War Museum, B5118)*

momentum to slacken. They came at the enemy from all angles. Passing from cover to cover through the bomb craters, firing as they ran, they were soon among the trenches, sweeping along them with light machine-gun fire and grenades. Enemy return fire came at the commandos from all directions – from machine-gun posts dotted around the edge of the fortified area and from the observation slit at the top of the tower. As the commandos closed on the artillery emplacements it soon became clear that the sites were empty of weapons. The guns had been removed earlier by the Germans and transported inland. It was, therefore, pointless to continue with the attack and 4 Commando withdrew back into Ouistreham to regroup and join the remainder of 1st Special Service Brigade.

Following behind the landings made by 4 Commando and sandwiched between the arrival of the 8th Brigade's reserve battalion and the 3rd Division's priority vehicles, came the remainder of Lord Lovat's 1st Special Service Brigade. Brigadier Lord Lovat brought his brigade ashore on Queen Red and immediately sent 6 Commando ahead to relieve the British 6th Airborne Division to the east of the River Orne. A signaler had picked up the message that the two bridges over the river and the canal at Bénouville had been captured intact and this boosted the commandos' spirits. They knew that they had to make haste to relieve the beleaguered paratroopers, but the advance was difficult. The commandos had to fight their way through a series of enemy positions, overcoming four strongpoints and a four-gun artillery battery on the way. Nonetheless, they arrived at Bénouville just two-and-a-half minutes behind schedule, to the great joy of Lieutenant-

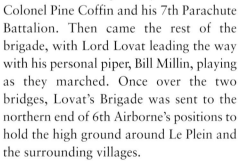

Colonel Pine Coffin and his 7th Parachute Battalion. Then came the rest of the brigade, with Lord Lovat leading the way with his personal piper, Bill Millin, playing as they marched. Once over the two bridges, Lovat's Brigade was sent to the northern end of 6th Airborne's positions to hold the high ground around Le Plein and the surrounding villages.

By late morning, the 3rd Division ad landed the whole of Brigadier Smith's 185th Brigade and two of the three armored regiments from the 27th Armoured Brigade, although some parts of these units were still immobile on the beaches, snarled in massive traffic jams. Smith had brought the leading elements of his brigade south to Hermanville and had sent 2nd KSLI forward on foot, pushing out toward Caen supported by the

Commandos from Lord Lovat's 1st Special Service Brigade dig in close to gliders. The picture was taken on D-Day and probably depicts the scene by Landing Zone N close to Ranville. The troops are, therefore, from Lieutenant-Colonel Peter Young's 6 Commando, who were diverted to the area after they crossed over the Orne bridges. They were sent there by General Gale to add strength to 12th Parachute Battalion, who were being hard-pressed that day by the 125th Panzergrenadiers. *(Imperial War Museum, B5051)*

Lieutenant-Colonel Peter Young, CO of 6 Commando, gives instructions to two of his camouflaged snipers who are going to keep watch on a house on the edge of Breville that overlooks the lines of the 6th Airborne Division. *(Imperial War Museum, B5761)*

self-propelled guns of the 7th Field Regiment. By the time the battalion had reached the lower slopes of Périers Ridge, the tanks of the Staffordshire Yeomanry had caught up. Périers Ridge should have been in Allied hands by then, for the 8th Brigade had originally planned to move onto the feature quite early in the battle, but 1st South Lancs had dug in at Hermanville and halted their advance.

The drive for Caen was supposed to be, after the establishment of a successful beachhead, the most important objective for 3rd Division on June 6. General Montgomery had planned to have Caen under his control by the end of the day. He needed the town to anchor his left flank and provide a stop line that any German armored counterattack would either have to travel through or bypass. The road network converging on the city was of vital strategic importance both for the build-up of strength and for future expansion out of the lodgement areas. The importance of the capture of Caen, however, seems to have been regarded with less urgency by those on the ground, and emphasis appears to have been placed on consolidation rather than expansion. It was an understandable approach, for although a firm foothold had been gained, the situation was still extremely fluid, with some areas seemingly open for the taking, while others had to be fought for against a tenacious and well-entrenched enemy.

The other two battalions of 185th Brigade had also begun their drive on Caen: the 1st Norfolks were passing through the 1st Suffolks strung out in Colleville, and the 2nd Warwickshires were progressing through St Aubin in

This knocked-out concrete gun emplacement has been taken over by the Royal Navy. With the beaches still under occasional shellfire and with the Luftwaffe putting in a few bombing runs, a naval beach group has found it prudent to have some cover over its head. (*Imperial War Museum, B6381*)

the rear of Lovat's Brigade. The 1st Norfolks took heavy casualties when it emerged from Colleville and moved out into open countryside across the eastern flank of strongpoint Hillman. Accurate small-arms and artillery fire from the feature caused the battalion over 150 casualties.

At that time, Hillman was in the process of being cleared by the advance companies of the 1st Suffolks. The battalion had already overcome enemy resistance in Colleville and in strongpoint Morris, and it was now attempting to do the same at Hillman. It was a formidable task, for the subterranean fortified area housed the HQ of Oberst Ludwig Krug's 736th Infantry Regiment. The strongpoint covered an area 600 yards by 400 yards and contained two H605 concrete emplacements topped by steel cupolas, numerous concrete shelters, antitank guns, and Tobruk machine-gun pits. It was surrounded by barbed-wire entanglements and an extensive minefield. Air bombardment and shell fire from warships had done little to dampen its offensive spirit.

The outer wire was breached with bangalore torpedoes by D Company of the Suffolks. Then came the minefield and the inner belt of wire. Eventually the central area was entered by the infantry. Once inside the wire, the steel cupolas were attacked by 17-pdr antitank weapons, but the shells made little impact on the solid round structures. The enemy garrison was bottled up inside the strongpoint in their underground bunkers, but their small-arms fire was very troublesome to the British infantry on the surface. One by one the Suffolks knocked out the antitank guns and eliminated a good number of the surface machine-gun pits, but fire continued to come at them from all directions and from every dip in the ground. Tanks arrived and joined in the action, enabling the infantry to close on the trench systems, but it was a slow process to overcome each enemy infantryman in his well-concealed hiding place. Mopping up and eliminating every emplacement went on for hours. In some cases the bunkers had to be blown out with heavy charges placed right up against their entrances by the battalion's pioneers. It took until 2015hrs that evening before Oberst Krug and his men were finally winkled out of their underground bunkers. By then it was too late for the Suffolks to move any closer toward Caen, so they consolidated where they were for the night.

The reserve brigade of the 3rd Division was the 9th Infantry Brigade, which landed in the early afternoon but took a considerable time to extricate itself from the log jam on the beaches and move inland. The three infantry battalions advanced from the seafront on the right of the lodgement with the intention of concentrating in the area of Plumetot, close by Périers Ridge. Brigadier Cunningham's orders were to take his brigade straight down the right flank toward Carpiquet airfield and Caen, but when he met the divisional commander, Major-General Rennie, and I Corps' commander, Lieutenant-General Crocker, on the outskirts of Hermanville, he was told that the role of his brigade had changed. Because of the pressure being applied to the 6th Airborne by the 21st Panzer Division, his brigade was to move over to the left and assist Major-General Gale's beleaguered paratroopers.

The armor allocated to support the 9th/1st East Riding Yeomanry from 27th Armoured Brigade had not yet landed, so Rennie told Cunningham to wait until these tanks were ashore before moving. The brigadier then warned the 1st KOSB of the change of plans and returned to his brigade HQ to await

A stranded Sherman Crab flail tank from the 22nd Dragoons, 79th Armoured Division, on Queen White Beach. To its left can be seen a Summerfield track of wire mesh, which has been laid over the sand to provide a firm roadway. *(Imperial War Museum, B5192)*

The Capture Of Strongpoint Hillman

Men of the 1st Suffolks pass a knocked-out 5cm KwK in an open emplacement. The crew are dead around it, killed by artillery fire earlier in the attack. The Germans mounted large numbers of these former tank guns in defenses along the coast. The gun had a range of around 7,000 yards with a rate of fire of between 15 and 20 rounds per minute. The main problem faced by the Suffolks in silencing the strongpoint was that virtually all of it was housed underground. Surface emplacements could be attacked with support weapons, but the machine-guns housed in well-protected subterranean fortifications were a more difficult nut to crack. Once through the outer wire and minefields and onto the surface of the strongpoint, the troops were exposed to concentrated small-arms fire from almost impregnable positions. Once a route through the minefields had been cleared for the armor, the tanks enabled the infantry to close with the emplacements and attack them with explosives. It was still a difficult task, however, as the shells from the Sherman Fireflies' 17-pdr guns had little effect on the concrete structures and just bounced off the two fixed steel cupolas. The Suffolks could not simply blow the doors off and invite the enemy inside to surrender – they had to go in and winkle them out. While some of the German defenders surrendered swiftly once the underground corridors were raked with British small-arms fire, others resisted to the last and had to be blown into oblivion with heavy explosive charges. Deep within Hillman was the headquarters of Oberst Ludwig Krug's 736th Infantry Regiment, part of Generalleutnant Richter's 716th Infantry Division. By the early evening of June 6, the Suffolks had got inside the subterranean passages and were closing on the German colonel and his HQ staff. Krug telephoned his commander and said to the hard-pressed Richter: "Herr General, the enemy are on top of my bunker. They are demanding my surrender. I have no means of resisting and no contact with my own men. What am I to do?" Richter paused for a moment. He had received nothing but bad news all day as the British and Canadians ripped his division apart. All order had been lost; the 716th Division was no longer a cohesive fighting unit. At last Richter spoke quietly into the telephone: "Herr Oberst, I can no longer give you any orders. You must act on your own judgment. Auf Wiedersehen." Oberst Krug had little choice. Abandoned by his commander and with no means of escape, he surrendered his garrison to Lieutenant-Colonel Goodwin of the Suffolks.
(Howard Gerrard © Osprey Publishing Ltd)

the arrival of his armor. Once there, he had the misfortune to be wounded by a stick of mortar bombs which also killed six of his staff and injured another five. The brigade's second-in-command was not readily available, as he was liaising with the Airborne Division and so continuity of command was lost at a crucial time. Lieutenant-Colonel Orr eventually assumed command of the brigade and found that the enemy on the right flank was more active than originally thought, so the 9th Brigade would once again need to be involved there. As a result, the 9th Brigade did little to help in the advance on Caen that day. The 2nd Lincolns consolidated a position facing the enemy in Cresserons to the right of Hermanville, the 2nd Royal Ulster Rifles dug-in just outside of Hermanville on the lower slopes of the ridge, and the 1st KOSB moved across to hold the village of St Aubin.

The advance by the 185th Brigade on Caen, which had begun with the move from Hermanville by the 2nd KSLI without its tanks, developed into a powerful thrust when the Shermans of the Staffordshire Yeomanry joined up with the infantry, together with the self-propelled artillery of the 7th and

The assault and follow-up troops of the invasion have moved inland and have left just a few troops dug-in on the edge of the beach at La Brèche to hold the rear. *(Imperial War Museum, B5180)*

33rd Field Regiments, the antitank guns of the 41st antitank Battery, and a heavy machine-gun platoon from the 2nd Middlesex Regiment. Commanded by Lieutenant-Colonel Maurice, the 2nd KSLI advanced up the left side of Périers Ridge, just to the right of the battle for the possession of strongpoint Hillman. On the reverse slope of the ridge, near Point 61, the battalion came into contact with an established battery of German artillery, which also housed the HQ of I./1716th Artillery Regiment and its commander, Major Hoff. The enemy put up a spirited fight, and the position was only taken after a good deal of resistance. Now feeling rather vulnerable, with his right flank exposed to open country along Périers Ridge, Maurice decided to leave B Squadron of the Staffordshire Yeomanry on the high ground to protect his advance from enemy interference from that quarter. With his position more secure, Maurice continued with his move on Caen, taking the villages of Beuville and Biéville and sending a company of infantry supported with tanks into Lebisey Wood close to the outskirts of the city.

THE GERMAN REACTION TO THE LANDINGS

German opposition to the landings on Sword Beach came from troops of Richter's 716th Infantry Division. The sector was manned by I./736th Infantry Regiment around Ouistreham and III./736th Infantry Regiment in and behind Lion-sur-Mer. The guns in the area were crewed by troops from the division's I./1716th Artillery Regiment. Many of these units contained a high percentage of foreign, mainly Eastern, volunteers who fought surprisingly well. Resistance everywhere in the invasion zone was quite stiff, especially when the defenders were protected by concrete and steel fortifications. German regulars and NCOs bolstered the resolve of these troops to the extent that almost every strongpoint and gun emplacement had to be seized by force, but the greater strength and firepower of the British troops engaged on Sword inevitably wore down the static defenses. It might have been much worse if the German positions had been completed to the standard that Rommel would have liked. If more time and effort had been put into the building of the Atlantic Wall sooner, then the possibility of the British establishing a foothold on the coast of Normandy would have been in doubt.

When news of the airborne landings began to filter back to the German HQ during the night, the High Command was uncertain whether the reported parachute activities were the start of the actual invasion or just a diversion to shift attention away from a larger force arriving elsewhere, probably in the area of the Pas-de-Calais. When details came of the size and scale of the seaborne landings, von Rundstedt knew that the long-awaited Allied invasion was taking place. He immediately asked Hitler for the release of the Panzer divisions that were being held specifically to counter this event. However, permission was slow in coming because Hitler and his Supreme

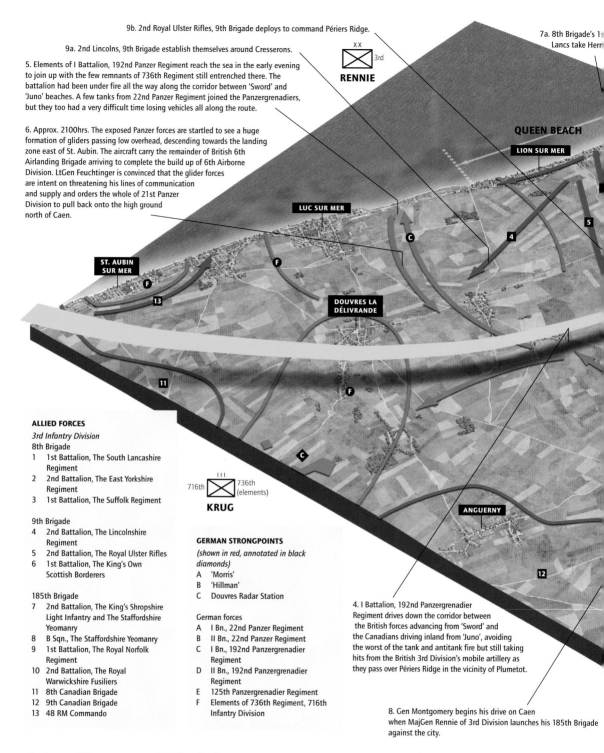

9b. 2nd Royal Ulster Rifles, 9th Brigade deploys to command Périers Ridge.

9a. 2nd Lincolns, 9th Brigade establish themselves around Cresserons.

5. Elements of I Battalion, 192nd Panzer Regiment reach the sea in the early evening to join up with the few remnants of 736th Regiment still entrenched there. The battalion had been under fire all the way along the corridor between 'Sword' and 'Juno' beaches. A few tanks from 22nd Panzer Regiment joined the Panzergrenadiers, but they too had a very difficult time losing vehicles all along the route.

6. Approx. 2100hrs. The exposed Panzer forces are startled to see a huge formation of gliders passing low overhead, descending towards the landing zone east of St. Aubin. The aircraft carry the remainder of British 6th Airlanding Brigade arriving to complete the build up of 6th Airborne Division. LtGen Feuchtinger is convinced that the glider forces are intent on threatening his lines of communication and supply and orders the whole of 21st Panzer Division to pull back onto the high ground north of Caen.

7a. 8th Brigade's 1
Lancs take Herr

XX
3rd
RENNIE

QUEEN BEACH

LION SUR MER

LUC SUR MER

C

4

5

ST. AUBIN SUR MER

F

F

13

DOUVRES LA DÉLIVRANDE

F

11

F

ALLIED FORCES

3rd Infantry Division
8th Brigade
1   1st Battalion, The South Lancashire Regiment
2   2nd Battalion, The East Yorkshire Regiment
3   1st Battalion, The Suffolk Regiment

9th Brigade
4   2nd Battalion, The Lincolnshire Regiment
5   2nd Battalion, The Royal Ulster Rifles
6   1st Battalion, The King's Own Scottish Borderers

185th Brigade
7   2nd Battalion, The King's Shropshire Light Infantry and The Staffordshire Yeomanry
8   B Sqn., The Staffordshire Yeomanry
9   1st Battalion, The Royal Norfolk Regiment
10   2nd Battalion, The Royal Warwickshire Fusiliers
11   8th Canadian Brigade
12   9th Canadian Brigade
13   48 RM Commando

C

716th
736th
(elements)
KRUG

ANGUERNY

12

GERMAN STRONGPOINTS
(shown in red, annotated in black diamonds)
A   'Morris'
B   'Hillman'
C   Douvres Radar Station

German forces
A   I Bn., 22nd Panzer Regiment
B   II Bn., 22nd Panzer Regiment
C   I Bn., 192nd Panzergrenadier Regiment
D   II Bn., 192nd Panzergrenadier Regiment
E   125th Panzergrenadier Regiment
F   Elements of 736th Regiment, 716th Infantry Division

4. I Battalion, 192nd Panzergrenadier Regiment drives down the corridor between the British forces advancing from 'Sword' and the Canadians driving inland from 'Juno', avoiding the worst of the tank and antitank fire but still taking hits from the British 3rd Division's mobile artillery as they pass over Périers Ridge in the vicinity of Plumetot.

8. Gen Montgomery begins his drive on Caen when MajGen Rennie of 3rd Division launches his 185th Brigade against the city.

21st Panzer Division's Counterattack

June 6, 1944, approx 1600hrs–2100hrs, viewed from the southwest showing the attack against the beachhead by LtGen Edgar Feuchtinger's 21st Panzer Division, including 192nd Panzergrenadier Regiment's drive to the coast near Lion sur Mer. With the support of its own self-propelled guns and elements of 27th Armoured Brigade, British 3rd Division blunts the attack and inflicts heavy casualties on the Panzer formations.

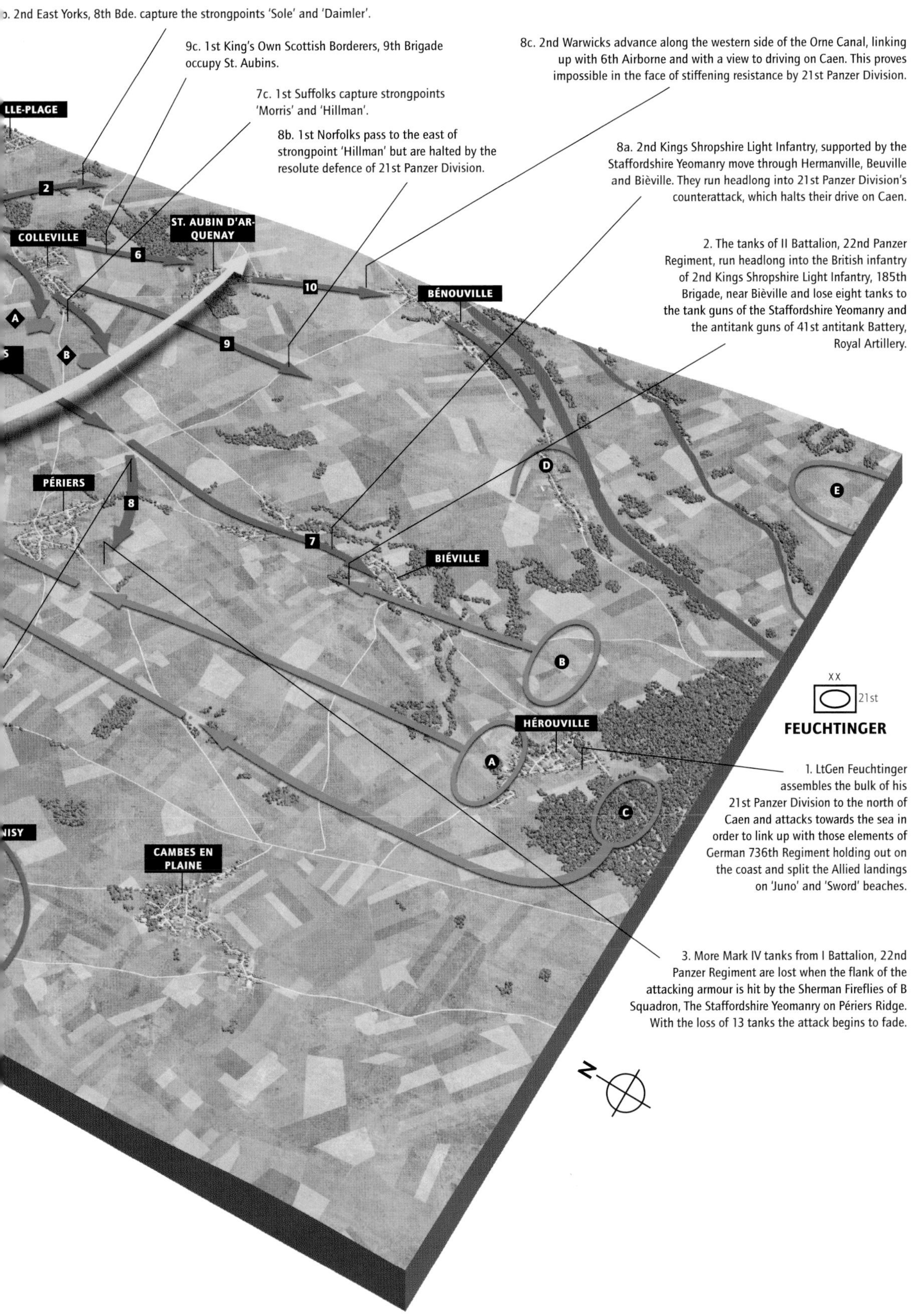

b. 2nd East Yorks, 8th Bde. capture the strongpoints 'Sole' and 'Daimler'.

9c. 1st King's Own Scottish Borderers, 9th Brigade occupy St. Aubins.

7c. 1st Suffolks capture strongpoints 'Morris' and 'Hillman'.

8b. 1st Norfolks pass to the east of strongpoint 'Hillman' but are halted by the resolute defence of 21st Panzer Division.

8c. 2nd Warwicks advance along the western side of the Orne Canal, linking up with 6th Airborne and with a view to driving on Caen. This proves impossible in the face of stiffening resistance by 21st Panzer Division.

8a. 2nd Kings Shropshire Light Infantry, supported by the Staffordshire Yeomanry move through Hermanville, Beuville and Bièville. They run headlong into 21st Panzer Division's counterattack, which halts their drive on Caen.

2. The tanks of II Battalion, 22nd Panzer Regiment, run headlong into the British infantry of 2nd Kings Shropshire Light Infantry, 185th Brigade, near Bièville and lose eight tanks to the tank guns of the Staffordshire Yeomanry and the antitank guns of 41st antitank Battery, Royal Artillery.

LLE-PLAGE

2

COLLEVILLE

ST. AUBIN D'AR-QUENAY

BÉNOUVILLE

6

10

A

9

B

5

PÉRIERS

8

7

BIÉVILLE

D

E

B

HÉROUVILLE

A

C

XX
21st

FEUCHTINGER

1. LtGen Feuchtinger assembles the bulk of his 21st Panzer Division to the north of Caen and attacks towards the sea in order to link up with those elements of German 736th Regiment holding out on the coast and split the Allied landings on 'Juno' and 'Sword' beaches.

NISY

CAMBES EN PLAINE

N

3. More Mark IV tanks from I Battalion, 22nd Panzer Regiment are lost when the flank of the attacking armour is hit by the Sherman Fireflies of B Squadron, The Staffordshire Yeomanry on Périers Ridge. With the loss of 13 tanks the attack begins to fade.

Command HQ were convinced that the Normandy landings were just a feint. They did not think that it was time to release the Panzer reserves and told von Rundstedt to deal with the situation with the forces of Army Group B that were present in the region and the two Panzer divisions already in Normandy, the 12th SS and Panzer Lehr Divisions.

Rommel, commander of Army Group B, was at his home in Germany when he received news of the invasion and he was, therefore, not in a position to present his views to Hitler himself. Had he done so, he might have been able to convince the Führer that all available Panzer forces should attack the beaches and sweep the invaders back into the sea before they became established. As it was, the only tank force available to be used locally to counter the landings on D-Day was Feuchtinger's 21st Panzer Division, located to the south of Caen. By the time the armor of this division began to move against the beaches it was already mid-morning and Allied aircraft were patrolling the sky, pouncing on any German road convoys.

German prisoners wait patiently on board a beached LCT for the craft to be floated by the incoming tide. They will be taken to prisoner-of-war camps in Britain. *(Imperial War Museum, B5135)*

COUNTERATTACK BY GERMAN 21ST PANZER DIVISION

Sword Beach lay in the sector of German LXXXIV Corps, commanded by General Marcks. He immediately saw that the main threat to the German defense of Normandy was the British capture of Caen, and he urged that an armored counterattack be launched. The intention was to reach the sea between the landings on Sword and Juno and then to sweep along the beaches to eliminate the Allied landings. Feuchtinger was ordered to send all available units of the 21st Panzer Division round to the northern edge of Caen to be assembled near Lebisey ready for the attack. This was the very point that the British 2nd KSLI were moving on, and at around 1600hrs the two sides met.

Up on the hill above Lebisey, Marcks told the commander of 100th Panzer Regiment, Oberst von Oppeln-Bronikowski: "Oppeln, if you don't succeed in throwing the British back into the sea, we shall have lost the war." The young colonel then mounted his tank and ordered the advance to begin. Feuchtinger had assembled the two tank battalions of 100th Panzer Regiment and the infantry of I./192nd Panzergrenadier Regiment as his strike force. The tanks advanced on the right, while the mounted Panzergrenadiers took the left flank. Almost immediately the German advance ran into trouble.

Lieutenant-Colonel Maurice had been alerted to enemy tank movements ahead by Y Company of his 2nd KSLI, who had moved into Lebisey Wood. The colonel quickly took steps to prepare for a counterattack, placing A Squadron of the Staffordshire Yeomanry on his left and lining his front with his own 6-pdr antitank guns and the self-propelled guns of 41st antitank Battery. When it began, the German attack came straight at him, with 40 or so PzKpfw IVs from the 100th Panzer Regiment's II Battalion charging across his front. These tanks were met by a hail of fire that immediately knocked out four of them and damaged others. Reeling from such fierce resistance, the armor of the 21st Panzers veered away to their left, but here they had the misfortune to encounter the Staffordshire Yeomanry's 17-pdr guns of B Squadron's Sherman Fireflies. More German tanks were knocked out. Still further over to the left, the regiment's I Battalion ran into the 105mm Priest self-propelled guns of the 7th Field Regiment RA and still more hits were taken. After a short while the German armored attack was in chaos. Thirteen tanks had been completely destroyed, while many more were damaged and coordination was lost.

The 192nd Panzergrenadiers fared slightly better. Advancing on the extreme left flank of the attack, the 192nd's route took it away from the main strength of the 185th Brigade's guns, and it was able to cautiously pick its way over the western end of Périers Ridge, passing through the gap between the British 3rd Division and the Canadian landings on Juno Beach. Some of its strength was lost during the advance, but elements of I Battalion actually made their way to the sea to meet up with isolated pockets of the 736th Infantry Regiment, who were holding out near Lion-sur-Mer. These men were joined a little later by a few tanks of I./100th Panzer Regiment. By this time it was early evening and these exposed units waited expectantly for fresh orders that would exploit their remarkable advance.

No new orders came, however, because Feuchtinger had been alarmed by a new development taking place in the sky above him. At 2100hrs the air was filled with over 250 gliders and their tug aircraft carrying the 6th Airlanding Brigade to their LZ near St Aubin. This landing was bringing General Gale's follow-up brigade to strengthen his hold east of the Orne. Feuchtinger was convinced that these air landings in the rear of his exposed division would eventually lead to its annihilation, and he gave the order for all units to consolidate north of Caen and produce a defensive line ringing the city. The new plan meant the withdrawal of the small force that had reached the sea and an end to the armored counterattack against the landings.

The appearance of German armor in front of the 185th Brigade caused some concern in 3rd Division's HQ. The counterattack and the ability of the enemy to reach the sea made the lodgement look increasingly vulnerable. It was evident that an advance on Caen was out of the question that day, and General Rennie decided that he needed to regroup before a new attack could be made. All units were told to dig in for the night and be prepared for enemy counterattacks.

HOLDING AND EXPANDING THE BRIDGEHEAD

The initial reaction by the Allies to the events of D-Day was one of great satisfaction. There had not been the bloodbath that so many pundits had envisaged and the British airborne landings had been completely successful, with General Gale's troops having seized all their objectives. The American airborne operations had been more scattered than the British, but they had not suffered the 50 percent casualties that had been predicted in some quarters. American seaborne landings on Utah and Omaha had secured a foothold in Normandy and while those on Omaha were precarious, they were at least ashore. The British and Canadian landings over the beaches of Gold and Juno

A troop of commandos from the 1st Special Service Brigade cross over a wire entanglement on the edge of the beach to move up to an assembly area prior to the long march to join up with the airborne troops on the eastern side of the River Orne. In the background a Churchill AVRE tank from the 79th Armoured Division is carrying a small box girder bridge across the beach ready to lay it across an obstacle. *(Imperial War Museum, B5071)*

Commandos of the 1st Special Service Brigade move off in single file, skirting a minefield as they go. The picture was taken at around 1000hrs on D-Day, just after the troops had assembled in groups and were moving inland to join up with the airborne soldiers. *(Imperial War Museum, B5063)*

had allowed troops to get well inland and they were in little danger of being repulsed. In addition, the British 3rd Division's operations through Sword Beach had advanced over 6 miles toward Caen. Certainly, this first day of the invasion could be seen as a great success. A sound foothold had been gained and reinforcements were due to arrive over the next few days at a rate that would match anything the enemy could bring forward over roads harassed by Allied fighter-bombers. But there had been one major failure that day, one which would come back to haunt Montgomery over the next six weeks. His troops had failed to capture Caen.

The city of Caen was one of Montgomery's key objectives for June 6. With Caen and its road network in Allied hands, the British would be able to advance from the beachhead into the good tank country around Falaise and the Germans would find it more difficult to counterattack the lodgement. Caen would also act as a cornerstone to the Allied defenses, allowing the build-up of strength prior to a break-out into northern France. Yet the 3rd Division's 185th and 9th Brigades did not make it to Caen on the first day of the invasion, and the enemy was determined that they never would. It was probably unreasonable to expect that such a small force, supported by just two tank battalions, could advance to and hold such a large objective, especially against local troops and a powerful German armored unit in the shape of the 21st Panzer Division. The element of surprise had now been lost, and the British move toward Caen was an objective that was clear to the enemy. General der Artillerie Erich Marcks was adamant that his LXXXIV Corps, supported by Panzer forces, would never again allow the enemy to gain the initiative by surprise.

Troops of the British 8th Brigade move inland from the beaches past a Sherman tank of the 13th/18th Royal Hussars. On the road, supporting the move, are M10 Wolverine tank-destroyers. *(Imperial War Museum, B5080)*

The main concern facing Montgomery on June 7 was whether his armies could achieve their build-up before the German Panzer divisions met them head-on in a full counterattack against the beachhead. The Allies had superiority in the air and the battlefield was well within the range of the big guns of the warships, but Monty needed infantry ashore to help absorb the armored blow that was bound to fall. The two closest reserve Panzer units were 12th SS-Panzer Division and Panzer Lehr Division, both fully equipped and of the highest caliber. Montgomery knew that these two divisions would soon be thrown against his beachhead and the prospect was quite alarming, but indecision in the German High Command would soon ease some of his immediate worries.

When news of the landings reached Rommel in Germany, he started back for Normandy at once, reaching his HQ that night. He immediately ordered that the American landings be sealed off by infantry and that a concerted armored counterattack be made from Caen against the British. The task of counterattacking was assigned to the newly formed 1st SS-Panzer Corps which, when complete, would contain the 21st Panzer, 12th SS-Panzer, and Panzer Lehr Divisions. The corps, which was to be commanded by Obergruppenführer Sepp Dietrich, was ordered to start the attack immediately on June 7, with Feuchtinger's 21st Panzers and those elements of the 12th SS-Division that had reached the area. There was no time to wait for the arrival of Panzer Lehr, who were not expected to congregate at Caen before June 8.

The direction of the attack would be between the British and Canadian lodgements, aimed at linking up with the German strongpoint at Douvres and those elements of 716th Division that still held out in Luc-sur-Mer. Soon

A group of German troops rest by the side of the road. The surprise gained by the invasion and the rapid disintegration of German resistance on the beach often resulted in pockets of the enemy retreating inland with no clear orders about where or how to regroup. *(Bundesarchiv, 720/324/28A)*

after midnight, Standartenführer Kurt Meyer met with Generalleutnant Richter and Generalmajor Feuchtinger in a bunker near La Folie to plan the attack. Meyer, commander of the 25th SS-Panzergrenadier Regiment of the 12th SS-Panzer Division, was dismayed to hear that the 716th Division had been virtually wiped out and that Feuchtinger had only about 70 serviceable tanks left in his division after his abortive attack the previous day. Meyer, however, was confident that his troops, the pick of the Hitler Youth, could smash the British landings, predicting that he would throw the "little fish" back into the sea.

The 12th SS-Panzer Division "Hitlerjugend" was untried in battle, but was composed of fanatical young men from the Hitler Youth, led and strengthened by experienced officers and NCOs, many of whom came from the veteran 1st SS-Panzer Division "Leibstandarte Adolf Hitler."

Meyer's regiment, which contained three infantry battalions, was the only one that had arrived in the area, but he was reinforced with the division's II Panzer Battalion and III Artillery Battalion. This Kampfgruppe had about 90 PzKpfw IVs at its disposal which, together with those of the 21st Panzers, would pitch around 160 tanks against the British and Canadians. (In the event, however, not all of the Mark IV tanks of the 12th SS arrived in time and only 50 were in place by 1400hrs on June 7.)

The plan of attack was for the 21st Panzers to once again advance toward Lion-sur-Mer, while Meyer's SS troops attacked northwest from the area of Carpiquet airfield through the gap between the British and Canadians. The attacks, however, failed to progress as planned. Both divisions had to react

A Panzer IV from 12th SS-Panzer Division on its way forward to Normandy. The tank is part of a convoy, but large intervals have been left between vehicles to minimize casualties from Allied aircraft. The divisional sign can be seen on the left front of the tank. *(Bundesarchiv, 493/3355/10)*

to the actions of the British 3rd and Canadian 3rd Divisions. With daybreak, Allied fighter-bombers began to harass the movement of Kampfgruppe Meyer, slowing down its concentration. Before Meyer could deploy his units for the joint attack, Feuchtinger's division once again found itself trying to stem the advance of the British 3rd Division through Lebisey Wood. Major-General Rennie had resumed his move on Caen that morning and was committing both his 185th and 9th Brigades against the city. The 185th Brigade's attack on Lebisey, led by 2nd Warwicks, was halted almost immediately, but amid heavy fighting. The Panzergrenadiers had spent the night reinforcing the area, preparing for their own attack and were well sited to repulse the British move. The 185th Brigade later tried again, with the 1st Norfolks joining in the assault, but it was once more unable to gain entry into Lebisey itself.

Over on the 3rd Division's right, the 9th Brigade began its advance on Caen with a move by the 1st Royal Ulster Rifles and 1st King's Own Scottish Borderers along the axis Périers–Mathieu–Le Mesnil, toward Cambes. These infantry battalions had to fight their way through more units of Feuchtinger's division. Again the British were stopped by well-entrenched Panzergrenadiers, and by mid-afternoon the advance had stalled. The attacks had brought some success, for they had forced the 21st Panzer Division to commit itself in a defensive role. The division was no longer able to disengage and regroup for its own counterattack in support of Kampfgruppe Meyer.

Similar events were taking place over on the German's left flank. The Canadian 3rd Division was advancing straight toward Meyer's assembly area with the result that he too became committed to action before he was ready to attack. The "Hitlerjugend" troops fought exceptionally well, halting the Canadians in a bloody battle around Authie. Meyer's battlegroup had stopped the Allied advance and prevented the capture of the strategically important Carpiquet airfield, but it had to commit the whole of its strength to do so, leaving nothing left with which to stage its own planned counterattack against the beachhead.

On the eastern side of the British lodgement, Gale's paratroopers had also been in action that day. The arrival of the 6th Airlanding and 1st Special Forces Brigades late the previous day had strengthened Gale's hold on the left flank of the landings. He was able to deploy these brigades in the north and south of his lodgement and give himself the satisfaction of holding a good all-round defensive position. His task was to defend his ground against enemy attempts to break through toward the Allied beachhead, and this is exactly what he did. Apart from some localized attacks to consolidate its position, the British 6th Airborne Division assumed a defensive role. Gale first "tidied up" his sector by sending Brigadier Lovat's commandos to clear the enemy out of Franceville-Plage in the north, and he used Brigadier

The Allied Lodgement – Night, June 6

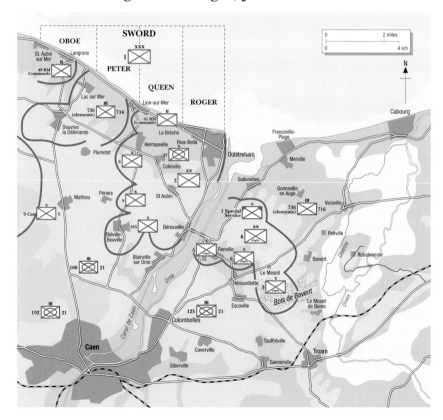

Expanding the Beachhead and the Battle for Caen

1st Special Service Brigade commandos move through Colleville on their way to meet up with the paratroopers over on the eastern side of the River Orne. All have replaced their steel helmets with green berets. *(Imperial War Museum, B5067)*

Kindersley's airlanding brigade to push back the enemy in the south. This done, the 6th Airborne Division's paras and Lovat's commandos set about tightening their grip on the area to the east of the Orne – a task that remained theirs until the great break-out from Normandy in August.

By the end of the second day, Sword Beach looked secure. The British 3rd Division was close to Caen, with the frontline pushed forward almost 8 miles from the coast. Its left flank was secured by the 6th Airborne, its right by the Canadians. In the skies over Normandy, Allied air forces had total command of the air. To its rear, the warships of the Royal Navy secured the sea lanes and dominated inland areas with their massive guns. Supplies and follow-up divisions were coming ashore to bolster the lodgement. It was now time for Montgomery to exploit the landings and push inland, always prepared for the inevitable confrontation with Rommel's gathering forces.

PART IV
GOLD AND JUNO BEACHES

OPPOSING FORCES

BRITISH FORCES

On Gold Beach, the attacking force was the British 50th Division, a veteran of the Gazala and El Alamein battles in North Africa in 1942; on Juno, it was the untried Canadian 3rd Infantry Division that made the assault. These two divisions were the strike force of their respective corps: the British 50th Division was part of the British XXX Corps and the Canadian 3rd Division formed part of the British I Corps. I Corps also contained the assault division attacking Sword Beach – British 3rd Division. Landing behind these divisions was the remainder of the two corps. In XXX Corps, the 7th Armoured Division came ashore after the initial landings, with the 49th Division following on behind. On I Corps' front, the 51st Highland Division followed up the D-Day landings.

The British 50th Division was originally composed of territorial battalions from Northumberland and Durham. Its divisional badge was two capital "Ts," representing the two great regional rivers, the Tyne and the Tees, in red on a black square. The division had seen plenty of action, having fought in France in 1940, in the North African desert in 1942 and in Sicily in 1943. In early 1944, Montgomery brought the division back from the Mediterranean to the UK to join Second Army for the invasion. In June 1944 the division comprised three infantry brigades: 69th Brigade with the 5th East Yorks and the 6th and 7th Green Howards; 151st Brigade containing 6th, 8th, and 9th Durham Light Infantry; and 231st Brigade with the 1st Hampshires, 1st Dorsetshires, and 2nd Devonshires. Also under command for the invasion was the 56th Infantry Brigade. This was an independent brigade that contained the 2nd South Wales Borderers, 2nd Gloucestershires, and 2nd Essex. The brigade stayed and fought with the division until August 20, when it was transferred to the 49th Division. Also attached to the division for the attack was the 8th Armoured Brigade, containing the 4th/7th Dragoon Guards, the 24th Lancers and the Sherwood Rangers, and 47 Royal Marine Commando, from 4th Special Service Brigade, was also part of the initial assault.

PREVIOUS PAGE:
Men of 47 Royal Marine Commando land on Jig sector from LCAs. The tank landing craft behind them are carrying support from the engineers of the 79th Armoured Division. At left a bulldozer is towing a trailer filled with fascines, while another waits to exit LCT858. *(Imperial War Museum, B5246)*

The commander of 50th Division was Major-General Douglas Graham. He had served in World War I and finished the conflict as a captain, having won both the Military Cross and the Croix de Guerre. Between the wars he was gradually promoted through regimental appointments and served as a brigadier in North Africa. In 1942 he was promoted to major-general and took command of 56th (London) Division. In September 1943 his division carried out an assault landing at Salerno as part of the invasion of Italy. Graham was wounded during the battle and returned to England. In January 1944 he took command of 50th Division with orders to train it for the invasion of France.

On Juno Beach responsibility for the assault was given to the Canadian 3rd Division. The division had left Canada for England in July 1941 to join with the 1st and 2nd Canadian Divisions and form I Canadian Corps. For the next two years it carried out an extensive program of training. When, in 1943, the corps left for the Mediterranean, the 3rd Division remained behind. It had been earmarked for the invasion of France and continued training specifically for this role. Its commander was Major-General Rodney Keller. He had been commissioned in 1920 and served in a number of roles, gradually gaining promotion through staff appointments. In June 1941 he was given a battalion and then made brigadier just six weeks later. He took over the 3rd Division in September 1943.

The division consisted of three infantry brigades: 7th Brigade with the Royal Winnipeg Rifles, the Regina Rifle Regiment, and the Canadian Scottish Regiment; 8th Infantry Brigade with the Queen's Own Rifles of Canada,

A Bren gunner of the British 50th (Northumbrian) Infantry Division. His division's formation badge on his sleeve, a red "TT" on a black square, refers to the division's "home" in the area of Tyneside and Teesside, two of the great rivers of the northeast of England. Its 151st Brigade contained the 6th, 8th, and 9th battalions of the Durham Light Infantry, also from England's northeast. *(Imperial War Museum, B5382)*

Le Régiment de la Chaudière, and the North Shore (New Brunswick) Regiment; and finally 9th Brigade containing the Highland Light Infantry of Canada, The Stormont, Dundas and Glengarry Highlanders, and the North Nova Scotia Highlanders. Armored support for the attack was provided by the Canadian 2nd Armoured Brigade, consisting of 6th Armoured Regiment (1st Hussars), 10th Armoured Regiment (The Fort Garry Horse), and 27th Armoured Regiment (the Sherbrooke Fusiliers). Also attached to the division for the assault was 48 Royal Marine Commando.

Allied Forces, Gold and Juno Beaches, June 6, 1944

Allied Supreme Commander – General Dwight D. Eisenhower

British 21st Army Group – General Sir Bernard Montgomery

British Second Army – Lieutenant-General Sir Miles Dempsey

British I Corps – Lieutenant-General John Crocker

Canadian 3rd Infantry Division – Major-General R. F. L. Keller

7th Infantry Brigade – Brigadier H. W. Foster

The Royal Winnipeg Rifles

The Regina Rifles Regiment

The Canadian Scottish Regiment

8th Infantry Brigade – Brigadier K. G. Blackader

The Queen's Own Rifles of Canada

Le Régiment de la Chaudière

The North Shore (New Brunswick) Regiment

9th Infantry Brigade – Brigadier D. G. Cunningham

The Highland Light Infantry of Canada

The Stormont, Dundas and Glengarry Highlanders

The North Nova Scotia Highlanders

Artillery

12th, 13th, 14th, and 19th Field Regiments, Royal Canadian Artillery

3rd Antitank Regiment, Royal Canadian Artillery

4th Light Antiaircraft Regiment, Royal Canadian Artillery

Support

17th Duke of York's Reconnaissance Regiment

The Cameron Highlanders of Ottawa (Machine Gun Battalion)

2nd Canadian Armoured Brigade – Brigadier Wyman

6th Armoured Regiment (1st Hussars)

10th Armoured Regiment (The Fort Garry Horse)

27th Armoured Regiment (The Sherbrooke Fusiliers Regiment)

British 5th Assault Regiment, Royal Engineers (from 79th Armoured Division)
 26th Assault Squadron, Royal Engineers
 77th Assault Squadron, Royal Engineers
 79th Assault Squadron, Royal Engineers
 80th Assault Squadron, Royal Engineers
B Squadron, 22nd Dragoons
A Squadron, Westminster Dragoons

British XXX Corps – Lieutenant-General Gerard Bucknall

British 50th Infantry Division – Major-General D. A. H. Graham
 56th Infantry Brigade – Brigadier E. C. Pepper
  2nd South Wales Borderers
  2nd Gloucestershires
  2nd Essex
 69th Infantry Brigade – Brigadier F. Y. C. Knox
  5th East Yorkshires
  6th Green Howards
  7th Green Howards
 151st Infantry Brigade – Brigadier R. H. Senior
  6th Durham Light Infantry
  7th Durham Light Infantry
  9th Durham Light Infantry
 231st Infantry Brigade – Brigadier Sir A. B. G. Stanier
  2nd Devonshires
  1st Hampshires
  1st Dorsets
 Artillery
  74th Field Regiment, Royal Artillery
  86th Field Regiment, Royal Artillery
  90th Field Regiment, Royal Artillery
  124th Field Regiment, Royal Artillery
  147th Field Regiment, Royal Artillery
  102nd Antitank Regiment, Royal Artillery
  25th Light Antiaircraft Regiment, Royal Artillery
 Support
  61st Reconnaissance Regiment, Royal Armoured Corps
  2nd Cheshire Regiment (Machine Gun Battalion)
 8th Armoured Brigade – Brigadier Anstey
  4th/7th Dragoon Guards
  24th Lancers
  The Sherwood Rangers Yeomanry
  12th Kings Royal Rifle Corps
 British 6th Assault Regiment, Royal Engineers (from 79th Armoured Division)
  81st Assault Squadron, Royal Engineers
  82nd Assault Squadron, Royal Engineers
  B Squadron, Westminster Dragoons
  C Squadron, Westminster Dragoons

Major-General R.F.L. Keller, Commander, Canadian 3rd Infantry Division, is made a Commander of the British Empire (CBE) by King George VI in Normandy. Keller had taken over the division in September 1943 and trained it especially for the invasion. On his sleeve, below his Canada shoulder title, is his divisional insignia, a patch of French gray cloth. *(Imperial War Museum, B5617)*

GERMAN FORCES

Defending the areas of Gold and Juno Beaches was the previously described German 716th Infantry Division, commanded by Generalmajor Richter. Gold Beach marked the boundary between Richter's 716th Division and Generalmajor Kraiss's 352nd Division. Just before D-Day, the 726th Regiment was attached to the 352nd Division. The 1st and 3rd battalions held the coast from near Le Hamel toward Omaha, while its 2nd battalion was located to the rear of Omaha Beach at Château Jacuville, acting as the regimental reserve. Along Gold Beach itself, the 441st Ost Battalion garrisoned the defenses, with its HQ in La Rivière. Occupying Juno Beach were elements of 441st Ost Battalion and II./736th Regiment. The bulk of this regiment was also defending Sword Beach and the area just across the River Orne attacked by the British 6th Airborne Division. The guns and men of the 716th Division's 1716th Artillery Regiment were spread throughout the division's sector, sited mainly in mobile batteries inland from the coast.

The area inland from the Gold and Juno beaches was dominated by just one major town, Caen, with Feuchtinger's 21st Panzer Division located just west of the town. The armored divisions of the strategic reserve were in an altogether different class to 21st Panzer Division. The 12th SS-Panzer Division "Hitlerjugend," as we have seen, was a fully equipped and superbly trained division, comprising the 12th Panzer Regiment and 25th and 26th Panzergrenadier Regiments, supported by a full artillery regiment and reconnaissance, antiaircraft, and antitank battalions. The large numbers of young men who had volunteered to join this elite unit resulted in its manpower being higher than required, at around 20,000. It was equipped with the best weaponry and equipment available and led by a widely respected commander, Gruppenführer Fritz Witt, and supported by senior commanders who had gained impressive reputations in action on the Eastern Front: men like Standartenführer Kurt "Panzer" Meyer and Obersturmbannführer Max Wunsche, distinguished Waffen-SS officers in their own right. Meyer and Wunsche, both holders of the Knight's Cross, had shown themselves to be courageous and capable commanders. Meyer commanded 25th Panzergrenadier Regiment and Wunsche led the 12th Panzer Regiment. Gruppenführer Fritz Witt was an early volunteer to the elite "Leibstandarte," Hitler's bodyguard formation, and had risen from company commander in Poland in 1939 to a regimental commander of 1st SS-Panzergrenadier Regiment in Russia. He had also seen active service in France, Yugoslavia, and Greece. The energetic divisional commander soon raised his men to a peak of fitness and confidence, believing it to be far more important to train them in realistic field exercises with live ammunition than to bore them with the finer points of military drill. When the division finally went into action it quickly earned a fearsome reputation among the Allied troops who encountered it.

Panzer Lehr Division was an elite formation consisting originally of units from the various armored training schools. Raised in January 1944 with the specific role of resisting Allied landings in France, like the "Hitlerjugend" Division, the Panzer Lehr Division was composed of experienced and superior quality men and equipped with the good tanks, mostly PzKpfw V Panthers. In June 1944 it comprised the 901st and 902nd Panzergrenadier Regiments and the 130th Panzer Regiment. The division was commanded by Generalmajor Fritz Bayerlein, who had served with both Guderian and Rommel, as well as having commanded the 3rd Panzer Division on the Eastern Front. A holder of the Knight's Cross with Oakleaves, Bayerlein was a highly respected armor commander. In June 1944, Panzer Lehr was at full strength and based just over 125 miles from the Channel, posing a serious threat to the Allied landings.

Gruppenführer Fritz Witt (center) confers with two of his regimental commanders, Obersturmbannführer Max Wunsche (left) and Standartenführer Kurt Meyer. Witt commanded the 12th SS-Panzer Division "Hitlerjugend," a newly raised tank division composed of members of the Hitler Youth. Although untried in battle before the invasion, the division fought with remarkable zeal and determination in Normandy. *(Bundesarchiv, 146/88/28125a)*

A PzKpfw VI Tiger tank passing through a Normandy village. The concept of using armored forces against a seaborne invasion was a hotly debated subject. The Commander-in-Chief (West), Generalfeldmarschall von Rundstedt, wanted to mass available Panzer divisions and make a strong thrust against any lodgement, destroying Allied forces inland on ground of his choosing. Rommel thought that any invasion should be attacked by armor immediately it arrived, while the troops were still on the beaches. *(Bundesarchiv, 101/301/1951/24)*

German Forces, Gold and Juno Beaches, June 6, 1944

German Supreme Commander – Adolf Hitler

German Commander in Chief (West) – Generalfeldmarschall Gerd von Rundstedt

German Army Group B – GFM Erwin Rommel

German Seventh Army – GenObst Friedrich Dollmann

German LXXXIV Corps – General der Artillerie Erich Marcks

German 716th Infantry Division – Generalleutnant Wilhelm Richter

   726th Infantry Regiment – Oberst Korfes (Attached to 352nd Division on D-Day)

      I Battalion

      II Battalion

      III Battalion

      441st Ost Battalion

   736th Infantry Regiment – Obst Krug

      I Battalion

      II Battalion

      II Battalion

      642nd Ost Battalion

   1716th Artillery Regiment

      I Battalion

      II Battalion

      716th Reconnaissance Company

      716th Engineer Battalion

German 352nd Infantry Division – Generalmajor Dietrich Kraiss
    914th Grenadier Regiment – Oberstleutnant Heyna
        I Battalion
        II Battalion
    915th Grenadier Regiment – Oberstleutnant Meyer
        I Battalion
        II Battalion
    916th Grenadier Regiment – Oberst Göth
        I Battalion
        II Battalion
        352nd Division Fusilier Battalion
    352nd Artillery Regiment – Oberstleutnant Ocker
        I Battalion
        II Battalion
        352nd Antitank Battalion
        352nd Engineering Battalion
        352nd Field Replacement Battalion

German 21st Panzer Division – Generalmajor Edgar Feuchtinger
    100th Panzer Regiment – Oberst von Oppeln-Bronikowski (later
    designated 22nd Panzer Regiment)
        I Battalion
        II Battalion
    125th Panzergrenadier Regiment – Oberst Hans von Luck
        I Battalion
        II Battalion
    192nd Panzergrenadier Regiment – Oberst Rauch
        I Battalion
        II Battalion
        200th Panzer Reconnaissance Battalion
        200th Sturmgeschütz Battalion
        200th Panzerjäger Battalion
    155th Panzer Artillery Regiment – Oberst Huehne
        I Battalion
        II Battalion
        III Battalion
        305th Army Flak Battalion
        220th Panzer Pioneer Battalion

OPPOSING PLANS

BRITISH XXX CORPS PLAN

The British 50th Division would land on Gold Beach at 0725hrs on June 6. Gold was the westernmost beach of the British landing area, stretching 10 miles across from Port-en-Bessin to La Rivière. Much of Gold was useless for landings, as the shoreline from Port-en-Bessin to well east of Arromanches was dominated by high chalk cliffs. The length of seafront chosen for the assault was the stretch of beach from Le Hamel to La Rivière, which included the areas known as "Jig" and "King." The division's 231st Brigade was to land two battalions abreast on the western sector, Jig, with the 1st Hampshires on the right and the 1st Dorsets on the left. The 2nd Devons were the follow-up battalion landing after the assault formations had moved inland. King sector was the landing beach for 69th Brigade. Again the initial attack was to be on a two-battalion front, with 6th Green Howards on the right and 5th East Yorks on the left. The 7th Green Howards was the reserve battalion that would follow the assault waves ashore.

Port-en-Bessin marked the westernmost point of the British sector and this small port became the objective of 47 Royal Marine Commando. Its task was twofold: first, it was charged with capturing the harbor and town itself, and second, it was to make contact with the US army over on Omaha Beach to link up the British and US landings. The Commando was to land behind the assault waves of the 231st Brigade on Jig Beach and move immediately inland in a wide encircling movement to approach Port-en-Bessin from the rear. Speed was of the utmost importance and it was instructed not to get caught up and delayed in the fighting. It was ordered to avoid contact with the enemy wherever possible until it made its attack upon the port.

The assault waves of infantry landing across the open beaches were to be heavily supported every step of the way. Prior to the landings, almost right up until the moment the landing craft beached, known strongpoints were to be bombed by heavy and medium bombers, continuing the program of destruction that had been in progress over the preceding weeks. Soon after dawn, naval warships would add the power of their guns to the destruction of the enemy when they opened fire on gun batteries, strongpoints, and beach defenses. Royal Navy cruisers would concentrate on eliminating the gun batteries at Mont Fleury, Ver-sur-Mer, Arromanches, Vaux-sur-Aure, and Longues. Closer inshore, Fleet and Hunt class destroyers would bombard beach defenses. As the LCAs loaded with men made for the beaches, LCT(R) vessels would each fire over 1,000 5in rockets, plastering the area behind the beaches with high explosive. Added to this deluge of fire would be the shells of the divisional artillery from the self-propelled guns of the 86th Field Regiment carried in LCTs.

Once they hit the beaches, the infantry would have more support from the tanks of the 8th Armoured Brigade. The 4th/7th Dragoon Guards supporting 69th Brigade and the Sherwood Rangers supporting 231st Brigade were equipped with DD Shermans. They were timed to arrive just before the infantry at 0720hrs to give close armored support to the troops just when it was needed. Landing immediately behind the assault waves were LCTs carrying a variety of specialized armor from the 79th Armoured Division, including "Crab" flail-tanks, "Crocodile" flamethrowing tanks, and AVREs. On Gold Beach, the 79th Armoured Division provided B and C Squadrons of the Westminster Dragoons with their flail tanks, while the AVRE tanks came from 6th Assault Regiment RE.

A direct Allied assault on a major port was not practical. The German demolition of the facilities at Cherbourg and Brest, combined with their determined defense of the other major ports of northern France, denied them to the Allies. Anticipating this problem the Allies manufactured two artificial harbors codenamed "Mulberry," which were towed across to Normandy and assembled within days of the landings. The one shown here was located opposite Arromanches on the western edge of Gold Beach, the other was located off the American Omaha Beach. *(Imperial War Museum, BU1029)*

A Landing Craft Tank (Rocket) armed with 1,064 5in rockets. These craft followed the assault waves toward the shore and fired their salvoes of rockets over the heads of the other landing craft while still 5,000 yards out to sea, plastering the beach and the area immediately behind the shoreline with a deluge of high explosive. *(Imperial War Museum, B5263)*

Following the two assault brigades ashore were the two reserve brigades. The 56th Infantry Brigade would land on Jig Beach, pass through 231st Brigade, and make for Bayeux. From King Beach, the 151st Brigade would advance southwest to seize the Caen road and railway between Bayeux and the River Seulles.

BRITISH I CORPS PLAN

Crocker's British I Corps was to land on two beaches: the Canadian 3rd Division was to assault Juno Beach, while the British 3rd Division was to attack Sword Beach. Juno Beach stretched for 6 miles from just outside La Rivière in the west to St Aubin in the east. The shallows in front of Juno Beach allowed approach through only two narrow channels: one into the port of Courseulles and one off Bernières-sur-Mer. The Canadian 3rd Division would use these to launch their two-brigade attack. The Canadian 7th Brigade would land on a two-battalion front either side of the harbor entrance at Courseulles: one battalion on Mike Beach, the other on Nan Green Beach. The Canadian 8th Brigade would also land two battalions: one at Bernières in sector Nan White and one on Nan Red Beach close to St Aubin. Once a beachhead had been established, both brigades would land their follow-up battalions. The reserve brigade, the Canadian 9th Brigade, would come in next and land over Nan Beach.

The Canadian 7th Brigade's landings were scheduled for 0735hrs. The Regina Rifles were to assault the town beach in front of Courseulles and then clear and hold the town, most of which was on the eastern side of the harbor, while the Royal Winnipeg Rifles were to attack on the right and to advance and occupy the village of Graye-sur-Mer, which lies about a mile inland. Behind them, the follow-up battalion of the Canadian Scottish Regiment was to land behind the Winnipegs and strike out for the villages of St Croix and Creully to meet up with the British 50th Division, linking Gold and Juno beaches.

At 0745hrs on Nan Beach, the Canadian 8th Brigade would land two battalions in front of and to the east of Bernières: the Queen's Own Rifles of Canada on the right would assault and clear the village, while the North Shore (New Brunswick) Regiment would attack on the left, clear St Aubin, and advance on Tailleville. Behind would come the follow-up battalion, La Régiment de la Chaudière, which was to make for Bény-sur-Mer. From this position, the reserve brigade landing over Nan Beach would launch its drive on Caen and the airfield at Carpiquet with the North Nova Scotia Highlanders, the Highland Light Infantry of Canada, and the Stormont, Dundas and Glengarry Highlanders. Landing after the assault battalions would be 48 Royal Marine Commando, which would come ashore on Nan Red and move east to attack the strongpoint at Langrune, then link up with Sword Beach.

To support the landings on Juno, the Canadians had specialized armored assistance from B Squadron, 22nd Dragoons, A Squadron, Westminster Dragoons, and part of 5th Assault Regiment RE, all from the British 79th Armoured Division. The Canadian 3rd Division also had its own dedicated armored support from Canadian 2nd Armoured Brigade to help the attack once it was ashore, with DD tanks from 6th and 10th Armoured Regiments landing with the assault waves.

An area of Juno Beach just to the east of Bernières showing the white spotted mosaic pattern caused by the explosions of over 1,000 5in rockets, fired by an LCT(R) out at sea. *(Imperial War Museum, MH24332)*

GERMAN PLAN

The men of the German 716th Division were responsible for manning the fortifications of the Atlantic Wall along the stretch of coast designated Gold and Juno Beaches by the Allies. The Wall along this part of the coast followed a common pattern. Along the beach, between the low- and high-water marks, were the sea defenses. These consisted of a variety of steel, wooden, and explosive obstacles designed to damage or destroy approaching landing craft. Above the high-water mark were minefields and wire entanglements to delay the advance of the assaulting infantry. This killing zone was swept by machine-guns and mortars located in concrete pits and casemates for protection. At intervals larger guns dominated long stretches of beach, and these were able to fire high explosives against vessels and armored vehicles. These were housed in thick concrete bunkers designed to shield the guns from naval bombardment. Finally there were the *Widerstandsnester*, or resistance points, sometimes sited on the beaches and sometimes positioned inland, but always well placed to dominate the chokepoints around the exits from the beaches with interlocking fire.

THE LANDINGS: GOLD BEACH

Force G, containing the ships carrying the assault waves to Gold Beach, arrived at the point from which the landing craft were to be launched just before dawn on Tuesday June 6. At 0535hrs HMS *Bulolo*, with Commodore Douglas-Pennant, the Naval Commander of Force G, on board, dropped anchor 7 miles out from the beach amid a great armada of vessels. At the heart of this fleet of ships were the eight large infantry landing ships, LSI(L)s. Each of these converted merchant ships, ranging in size from 10,000 to 14,000 tons, carried 18 LCAs slung from their davits. Almost immediately, troops began to fill the craft and prepare for the landings. Closer to shore, the cruisers *Orion*, *Ajax*, *Argonaut*, *Emerald*, and *Flores* adjusted their positions and swung their turrets southwards, fixing a bead on the German coastal batteries that were their targets. The coastline was quiet; complete tactical surprise had been achieved.

In the first few minutes after dawn, just as the sun rose into an overcast and storm-laden sky, medium and heavy bombers droned overhead to begin their bombing runs on the strongpoints of Hitler's Atlantic Wall. Sheets of yellow flame and billowing clouds of smoke and dust began to mark the shoreline and the rumble of huge detonations rippled across the sea. The bombardment was now taken up by the cruisers and their 6in and 8in guns began to add their weight of shell to the destruction of the German defenses. Then, one by one, the flotilla of small vessels began to assemble and make for the shore, with spray flying over their blunt bows from the choppy sea. In the lead were the tank landing craft carrying the DD tanks, with the smaller assault landing craft weaving among them. On the flanks were rocket-firing craft and tank landing craft with 4.7in guns. Protecting the flotillas from air attack were LCT(F)s, the cannon-firing antiaircraft flak ships, and as the ships closed inexorably on the beaches, they too switched their attention to the beach defenses.

During and immediately after the landings, while the fighting was within range of warships at sea, the Royal Navy provided Forward Observation Bombardment Officers inland to coordinate naval gunfire with the troops on the ground. This party of seamen, all from the Royal Navy, are wearing army-type battledress. On their sleeve they show the "Combined Operations" gun, anchor, and eagle badge and a "Royal Navy" shoulder title. The sergeant is spotting enemy positions, the officer is plotting them on a map, and the signaler is passing coordinates back by landline to a transmitter in the rear, where they will be relayed on by radio to the warship at sea. *(Imperial War Museum, A14342)*

At 0730hrs, the leading waves hit the beach. The DD tanks, which were to be launched 5,000 yards out and become the vanguard of the landings, were released much closer to the shore because of the rough seas; other landing craft took their charges all the way in and landed them straight onto the beach. The changes of plan caused confusion and delayed their arrival. They reached the beach at about the same time as the infantry and almost simultaneous with the LCTs carrying the specialized armor of 79th Division. All of these craft jostled together for landing space and weaved alarmingly through the underwater obstacles which had broken through the surface of the water. The orderly lines of craft that had plowed relentlessly toward the French shore for the past 6 miles now broke up as each vessel made its own final run-in and attempted to touch down safely. Here and there craft hit mines mounted on poles and great waterspouts shot up from beneath the ships. Others swung crazily over as steel hedgehogs ripped jagged holes in their hulls. All around them the air zipped and cracked with bullets as the Germans opened fire on the invaders.

231ST BRIGADE'S LANDINGS

On Jig Green sector, the leading waves of the 231st Brigade came toward the shore intent on landing on a 900-yard stretch of sand immediately to the east of Le Hamel. The 1st Hampshires were on the right, the 1st Dorsets on the left. The two battalions were ordered to capture the beach and move inland, the Hampshires swinging westwards to take the strongpoint and villages of Le Hamel and Asnelles, while the Dorsets attacked the beachfront strongpoint of La Cabane-des-Douanes (Customs House) and made a wide sweeping movement toward the high ground overlooking Arromanches.

An LST loaded with medical personnel and transport from the British 50th Division approaches the Normandy shore. These very large craft with a loaded displacement of over 3,700 tons were able to beach for unloading. They were capable of carrying 300 troops and 60 tanks or vehicles. A number of them were fitted for casualty evacuation; this was probably one of them. *(Imperial War Museum, A23891)*

As the landing craft approached the beach, it soon became clear that something had gone badly wrong.

The 231st Brigade should have landed on a beach whose major German strongpoints had been knocked out by aerial bombing, but the hail of fire that met the Hampshires and Dorsets that morning clearly showed that the aerial attack had been a failure. None of the German defenses had been silenced and they now unleashed a torrent of machine-gun, mortar, and shellfire. Worse was to come, for the DD tanks that should have already been ashore attacking the enemy were still struggling free of their landing craft or wading through the surf dodging obstacles. The firepower from the Royal Marine Centaur tanks was also missing. Of the 16 craft that should have arrived on Gold Beach with the leading elements, only two came ashore; all the others had been delayed or had turned back because of rough weather. Another complication for the infantry was that the beach-clearing team of flail and AVRE tanks from the 79th Division soon became bogged down or knocked out from the heavy shellfire that now raked the beach.

The fire coming from Le Hamel together with the steady easterly current tended to push the assault waves to the left of their intended landing places. Both the Hampshires and the Dorsets landed well to the east of their intended positions. This resulted in the assault wave of the Hampshires landing close to Les Roquettes and almost on top of the strongpoint of La Cabane-des-Douanes. Thus it fell to the assault companies of the Hampshires to attack the initial objective of the Dorsets.

A Company landed in the thick of very heavy fire coming from the strongpoint. It was rapidly pinned down on the beach, unable to get forward to cut its own path through the minefields and wire, and move westwards to attack the strongpoint at Le Hamel. B Company landing alongside was caught

HMS *Ajax* bombarding German gun positions on the Normandy Coast

The cruiser HMS *Ajax* joins in a long-range gun duel with the German 152mm gun battery at Longues to the west of Port en Bessin. The guns at Longues had been in action since first light when they engaged the French cruiser *Georges Leygues* and the American destroyer *Emmons* at 0537hrs. HMS *Ajax* bombarded the battery as part of Force G's pre-arranged fire plan. The cruiser was able to bring all eight of her 6in guns to bear on the German position, firing 112lb shells at the rate of between four and six rounds per minute. Her maximum effective range was 24,800 yards and her gunnery control so effective that she actually put a shell right into one of the casemates. After completing her initial D-Day counterbattery mission, HMS *Ajax* turned her guns to support the infantry advance inland. Communications with the 50th Division were via naval Forward Observation Bombardment Officers who landed with the leading troops and were able to radio back the coordinates of enemy positions and areas of resistance to the cruiser. Men of the assault companies of the 1st Hampshire Regiment pass in front of *Ajax* on their way to Jig sector of Gold Beach. This was the third assault landing to be made by the 1st Hampshires. As part of the 231st Brigade it had already carried out amphibious landings in Sicily and Italy. The battalion had had a long war. It was in Egypt when war was declared in September 1939, took part in General Wavell's campaign in North Africa in 1940 and then undertook garrison duties in Malta until 1943. After Sicily and Italy it was called home in November 1943 to prepare for Operation Overlord. This was the first time the battalion had been back in England for 23 years. The men are wearing the recently introduced Mark III steel helmet, which was issued to assault units of the 21st Army Group for D-Day. Of basically the same pattern as used in Word War I, the earlier Mark I and II helmets were designed to give the men in the trenches protection from shellfire and missiles falling from above. The Mark II helmet gave somewhat improved all-round protection. The troops are carried in LCAs, small wooden boats each capable of transporting 30 fully laden infantrymen from their landing ship to the shore. With a top speed of just 6 knots, the craft were vulnerable to enemy fire. The Royal Navy manned these LCAs, but many others during the operation had Royal Marine crews. In fact, Royal Marines manned almost two-thirds of landing craft used in the D-Day landings. The LSI in the background was the armed merchant ship that carried the Hampshires across the channel along with the LCAs. The assault craft were launched fully loaded with men from davits along the ship's side. LCIs came in a variety of sizes and were often small liners or cross-Channel ferries varying from 10,000 to 14,000 tons. *(Kevin Lyles © Osprey Publishing Ltd)* in the same way. Immediately in front of the troops were two pillboxes and concealed machine-gun posts and behind them the beach was being swept by fire from Le Hamel. It was clear to the exposed infantry that they had to get off the beach to stand any chance of survival. On the left a platoon managed to work its way onto the flank of the pillboxes and silenced them, allowing others to storm the wire perimeter of the strongpoint. Point-blank fire eliminated the small garrison and the Hampshires began to force their way off the beach and inland. The sanatorium at the center of the position at Le Hamel proved to be the greatest of the Hampshires' problems. The strengthened and heavily defended building controlled a powerful array of weapons. Down on the seafront, a massive H612 casemate with a 75mm gun swept the beach with concentrated shellfire. It had already knocked out several tanks and withstood all of the naval gunfire attempting to destroy it. Its aperture faced eastwards, with the long barrel of its gun pointing along the length of Jig sector. Its reinforced concrete sides, which faced seaward, resisted even the largest-caliber shell. Around the sanatorium and the casemate were several Tobruk positions housing mortars and machine-guns. Their occupants were safe behind reinforced concrete and their weapons commanded wide arcs of fire. It was a formidable strongpoint to assault from any direction.

The 75mm gun at Le Hamel continued to add to its tally of kills. It had already knocked out two flail tanks and they were shattered and burning at the water's edge. It had also shot off the bows of a landing craft, trapping its complement of tanks inside. B Squadron of the Sherwood Rangers supporting the Hampshires lost four tanks on the beach and three "drowned" during the run-in to shore. A flail tank from B Squadron, Westminster Dragoons, commanded by Sergeant Lindsay, managed to beat a path through the dunes as far as the lateral road, but was knocked out by the 75mm when it turned right and headed for Le Hamel. This close-range German fire was now supported by artillery further inland, especially from the clifftops to the west of Le Hamel. Shells from 88mm guns began to land among the troops and tanks, showering the beaches with high explosives and red-hot splinters of shrapnel. At this point, the second wave of assault craft swept onto the beach and into the inferno.

Twenty minutes behind the assault wave of the Hampshires came its other two companies, with C Company landing on the right and D Company on the left. Chaos greeted the troops as they left the landing craft. Every man had to run the gauntlet over an open beach swept by fire. Weighed down by their packs and sniped at by the enemy, the few hundred yards of distance from the water's edge to the dunes seemed like miles. It was inevitable that casualties mounted to alarming proportions. The Hampshires' CO, Lieutenant-Colonel Nelson Smith, was hit twice and evacuated. Also wounded were the forward observation officer for the supporting ships and a battery commander from the field artillery, thus leaving the battalion without the means of calling down

An LCT stranded high and dry on Gold Beach. The craft has taken several direct hits from German shellfire and has been knocked out. The sign, with its dire warning, shows that the ship is salvageable and will probably see more action during its lifetime. *(Imperial War Museum, A23948)*

support from the destroyers or from the self-propelled artillery of 147th Field Regiment in their landing craft circling offshore. The battalion's second-in-command, Major Martin, had not yet landed, so Major Warren took over command. When Major Martin did eventually get ashore two hours later, he was immediately killed by a sniper.

Major Warren could see that it was impossible to make a direct attack on Le Hamel from along the beach, for the minefields fronting the defenses were too deep and too well covered by enemy fire, and so he grouped his men behind the strongpoint at La Cabane-des-Douanes and decided to assault the sanatorium from the rear. Nevertheless, it took several hours for the Hampshires to push through Les Roquettes and along the lateral road to the west to arrive behind Le Hamel, so fierce was the opposition.

The 1st Dorsets had landed to the east of their intended position, fortunately away from their original objective, the strongpoint at La Cabane-des-Douanes. The opposition was still very troublesome, however. Like the Hampshires, their sector was strafed by the guns in Le Hamel, and like the Hampshires their tank support was in disarray. C Squadron of the Sherwood Rangers had lost five tanks swamped during the run-in and a further two on the beach. The AVRE tanks from 6th Assault Regiment RE and the flails from the Westminster Dragoons both met with difficulties as they tried to create an exit from the beach. The first Crab flail tank struck a mine that its chains had failed to detonate and the AVRE following behind also struck a mine trying to get past the disabled flail, and blocked the lane. Nearby, another Crab trying to clear an additional path became bogged down in the clay and the AVRE following behind was knocked out by shellfire.

British Assault on Gold Beach

The Dorsets were able to get off the beach much sooner than the luckless Hampshires. By landing further east than their intended position, and by not having to immediately attack the strongpoint at La Cabane-des-Douanes, they were able to move inland across the marshes and form up behind Les Roquettes in reasonable order. Once clear of the shoreline, enemy resistance became less concentrated, but still limited any open movement by large bodies of troops. The Dorsets bypassed Le Hamel and advanced toward the enemy position at Buhot, clearing several machine-gun posts and fortified areas as they went. Once Buhot had been taken, they moved on to clear the enemy from Puits d'Hérode. As the morning wore on, the Dorsets were able to complete their wide sweeping advance to the west and got themselves on the high ground south of Arromanches. Here they came under fire from the German-held heights either side of the town.

With the Hampshires all ashore, the 231st Brigade's follow-up battalion, the 2nd Devons, was due to arrive. The battalion landed at 0815hrs onto a beach still very much alive with German fire; offshore obstacles were still intact and Le Hamel remained unsubdued. The Devons had a hazardous time landing and a difficult time getting clear of the beach. One company joined with the Hampshires to stiffen their attack on the sanatorium complex, while the remainder of the battalion moved round Asnelles and advanced inland 2 miles toward the important village of Ryes.

Landing just behind the Devons was 47 Royal Marine Commando, with its own special task. The unit was not tasked to assist the initial assault on the beaches, but merely to pass through the landings on the way to seize its particular objective, the town and harbor of Port-en-Bessin, and link up with the Americans landing on Omaha. Lieutenant-Colonel Phillips had been told to avoid contact with the enemy wherever possible and to press on to his objectives regardless. The Commando had a rough time on the run-in to the beaches, losing four of its 14 landing craft on the way. Three of them hit mines near the surf and the fourth was sunk by shellfire; casualties were considerable. It landed at H-Hour +90 minutes further east than planned onto a beach crowded with LCTs and other craft, scattered with drowned and burnt-out vehicles and littered with dead bodies. A company of enemy infantry blocked the Commando's route to its rendezvous point at the church in Le Hamel.

Reinforcements coming ashore across Gold Beach. In the right foreground are some of the hedgehog beach obstacles made of angled steel that were placed in the water below the high-water line to rip out the bottoms of light landing craft. (Imperial War Museum, A23947)

289

The Commando had to put in an attack against this position, suffering around 40 casualties in the process, but capturing about 60 German prisoners. It then took some time for the unit to reorganize. Much of its equipment had been lost in the sea and some key personnel were missing. Among the three officers and 73 marines that failed to make the rendezvous was the colonel. His craft had been sunk and he was forced to swim for the shore. Nonetheless, the Commando pressed on with the men it had, gathering German weapons as it went.

The route took the commandos on a wide detour around Le Hamel. Led by X and B Troops they made their way across country avoiding all villages and major roads. The first real opposition to their advance came in the afternoon at La Rosière to the south-west of Arromanches, where they were held up by machine-gun fire from two concealed posts. By early evening they had reached the high ground to the south of Port-en-Bessin and dug in for the night around Point 72.

69TH BRIGADE'S LANDINGS

On the eastern sector of Gold, along the beach designated King Red, the 69th Brigade came ashore with its leading elements, touching down at H-Hour, 0730hrs. The DD tanks of 4th/7th Dragoon Guards who were to support the brigade were due to be launched 5,000 yards off the beach at H-Hour -50, giving them 50 minutes to swim ashore to arrive alongside the infantry. C Squadron was to support the 5th East Yorks on the left, while B Squadron would similarly stiffen the attack by 6th Green Howards on the right. The follow-up battalion, 7th Green Howards, landing 50 minutes later, would be supported by A Squadron. Specialized armor was again provided by 79th Armoured Division with C Squadron, Westminster Dragoons, providing Crab flail tanks and the 81st Squadron from 6th Assault Regiment RE supplying AVREs.

The stormy weather of the previous days had left the sea very choppy and it proved too rough to launch the DD tanks. It was decided to land them directly on the beach and as the LCTs carrying the armor approached the shore the formation changed from two divisions in line ahead to a single line abreast. Resistance was fairly light as the craft prepared to beach, with none of the concentrated fire that was experienced further west on Gold Beach. However, once the tanks began leaving their landing craft, things began to heat up considerably. On the far east flank of the landings, a large casemated gun sited on the edge of La Rivière opened fire along the beach. Like its opposite number at the other end of Gold at Le Hamel, this H677 casemate was protected on its seaward side by massive reinforced concrete walls, rendering it impervious to naval gunfire. Its large 88mm gun fired along the beach, sited so as to enfilade any landings. The flails and AVREs of 79th Division, together with the DD tanks of 4th/7th Dragoon Guards, now began to fall prey to the gun.

Landing among the increasing chaos on the beach was the infantry. The 5th East Yorks came ashore just to the west of the strongpoint at La Rivière. Here they found the worst of the enemy fire and were forced to seek cover beneath the seawall at the top of the beach. Any attempts to get over the wall met a strong enemy response. The situation improved when a flail tank from the Westminster Dragoons managed to approach close enough to the strongpoint's main casemate to fire a shell through its aperture, knocking out the deadly 88mm gun and demoralizing its crew. Naval support was called for to occupy the defenders in the rear of the strongpoint, while the East Yorks crossed over the seawall and onto the lateral road running parallel with the beach. Infantry gradually closed on the wire defenses and minefields around La Rivière and got into the interconnecting dug-outs and fortified houses of the village to begin clearing them of the enemy. An AVRE, firing massive petard charges as it moved, led a group of DD tanks into the village and the remainder of the morning was spent flushing out the enemy. One by one the tanks bombarded the German positions and the infantry then rushed in to clear them. One company made a wide movement inland and came at the village from the rear, after first having attacked the strongpoint around the Mont Fleury lighthouse to the south. The East Yorks took 45 prisoners, but it cost them six officers and 84 other ranks killed and wounded to gain their precarious foothold in Normandy.

A Sherman Crab flail tank of the Westminster Dragoons, knocked out on Gold Beach during the assault phase. The metal chains on the revolving drum at the front of the tank were designed to beat a path through minefields, detonating the charges as the vehicle went forward. *(Imperial War Museum, B5141)*

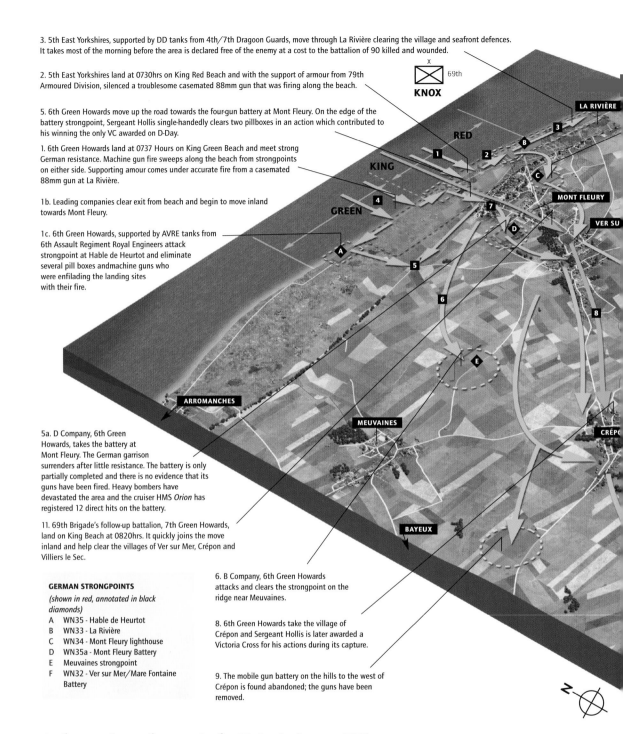

3. 5th East Yorkshires, supported by DD tanks from 4th/7th Dragoon Guards, move through La Rivière clearing the village and seafront defences. It takes most of the morning before the area is declared free of the enemy at a cost to the battalion of 90 killed and wounded.

2. 5th East Yorkshires land at 0730hrs on King Red Beach and with the support of armour from 79th Armoured Division, silenced a troublesome casemated 88mm gun that was firing along the beach.

5. 6th Green Howards move up the road towards the four-gun battery at Mont Fleury. On the edge of the battery strongpoint, Sergeant Hollis single-handedly clears two pillboxes in an action which contributed to his winning the only VC awarded on D-Day.

1. 6th Green Howards land at 0737 Hours on King Green Beach and meet strong German resistance. Machine gun fire sweeps along the beach from strongpoints on either side. Supporting armour comes under accurate fire from a casemated 88mm gun at La Rivière.

1b. Leading companies clear exit from beach and begin to move inland towards Mont Fleury.

1c. 6th Green Howards, supported by AVRE tanks from 6th Assault Regiment Royal Engineers attack strongpoint at Hable de Heurtot and eliminate several pill boxes and machine guns who were enfilading the landing sites with their fire.

5a. D Company, 6th Green Howards, takes the battery at Mont Fleury. The German garrison surrenders after little resistance. The battery is only partially completed and there is no evidence that its guns have been fired. Heavy bombers have devastated the area and the cruiser HMS *Orion* has registered 12 direct hits on the battery.

11. 69th Brigade's follow-up battalion, 7th Green Howards, land on King Beach at 0820hrs. It quickly joins the move inland and help clear the villages of Ver sur Mer, Crépon and Villiers le Sec.

GERMAN STRONGPOINTS

(shown in red, annotated in black diamonds)

A   WN35 - Hable de Heurtot
B   WN33 - La Rivière
C   WN34 - Mont Fleury lighthouse
D   WN35a - Mont Fleury Battery
E   Meuvaines strongpoint
F   WN32 - Ver sur Mer/Mare Fontaine Battery

6. B Company, 6th Green Howards attacks and clears the strongpoint on the ridge near Meuvaines.

8. 6th Green Howards take the village of Crépon and Sergeant Hollis is later awarded a Victoria Cross for his actions during its capture.

9. The mobile gun battery on the hills to the west of Crépon is found abandoned; the guns have been removed.

69th Brigade, 50th Division, King sector, Gold Beach

June 6, 1944, 0730hrs–1500hrs, viewed from the southwest showing the landings by 5th East Yorkshires and 6th Green Howards, the assault battalions of 69th Brigade, and 7th Green Howards, the follow-up battalion. A series of coastal strongpoints at La Rivière, Mont Fleury lighthouse and Meuvaines are subdued amid fierce fighting and the gun batteries at Mont Fleury and Ver sur Mer eliminated before the drive inland for the Bayeux–Courseulles road begins.

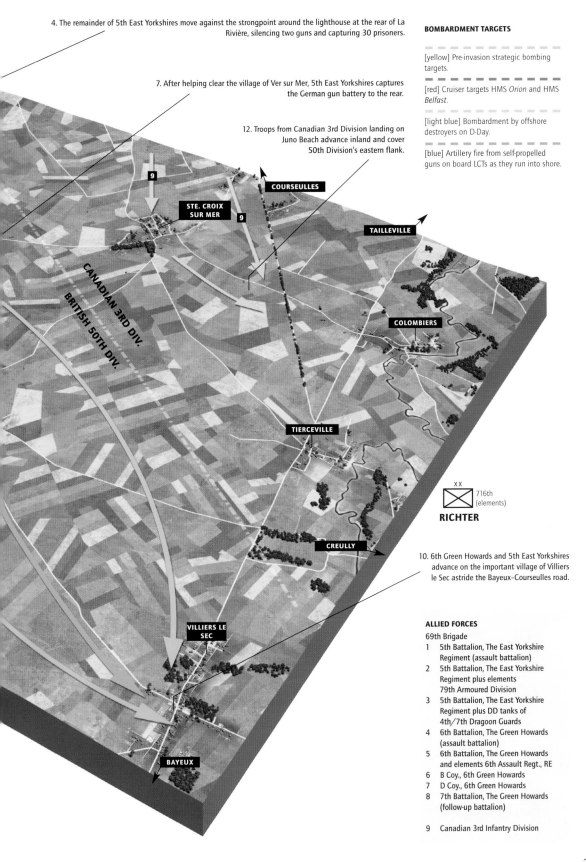

4. The remainder of 5th East Yorkshires move against the strongpoint around the lighthouse at the rear of La Rivière, silencing two guns and capturing 30 prisoners.

7. After helping clear the village of Ver sur Mer, 5th East Yorkshires captures the German gun battery to the rear.

12. Troops from Canadian 3rd Division landing on Juno Beach advance inland and cover 50th Division's eastern flank.

COURSEULLES

9

STE. CROIX SUR MER

9

TAILLEVILLE

CANADIAN 3RD DIV.

BRITISH 50TH DIV.

COLOMBIERS

TIERCEVILLE

XX
716th
(elements)

RICHTER

CREULLY

10. 6th Green Howards and 5th East Yorkshires advance on the important village of Villiers le Sec astride the Bayeux–Courseulles road.

VILLIERS LE SEC

BAYEUX

BOMBARDMENT TARGETS

[yellow] Pre-invasion strategic bombing targets.

[red] Cruiser targets HMS *Orion* and HMS *Belfast*.

[light blue] Bombardment by offshore destroyers on D-Day.

[blue] Artillery fire from self-propelled guns on board LCTs as they run into shore.

ALLIED FORCES

69th Brigade

1 5th Battalion, The East Yorkshire Regiment (assault battalion)
2 5th Battalion, The East Yorkshire Regiment plus elements 79th Armoured Division
3 5th Battalion, The East Yorkshire Regiment plus DD tanks of 4th/7th Dragoon Guards
4 6th Battalion, The Green Howards (assault battalion)
5 6th Battalion, The Green Howards and elements 6th Assault Regt., RE
6 B Coy., 6th Green Howards
7 D Coy., 6th Green Howards
8 7th Battalion, The Green Howards (follow-up battalion)

9 Canadian 3rd Infantry Division

To the west, the 6th Green Howards received a rather more subdued welcome. Although the shellfire was not as intense, a great deal of machine-gun and small-arms fire from the enemy position at Hable-de-Heurtot had raked their landings. The supporting armor was close at hand and immediately began helping them silence the strongpoint. Captain King with three AVREs under his command closed on the pillboxes while the infantry of A Company of the Green Howards kept the defenders bottled up with small-arms fire. A petard charge wiped out the first of the enemy's concrete emplacements and then the Green Howards stormed the others, silencing the strongpoint completely. D Company forced a way directly off the beach and made its way cautiously toward the four-gun battery at Mont Fleury.

In the meantime, a group of Crabs was flailing exit paths from the beach. While two of these were soon blocked by mined and bogged-down tanks, the easternmost exit was opened by a single Crab, commanded by Lieutenant Pear, which then went on to reach the lateral road, turned east toward La Rivière for a short way, and then south along a track, beating a path as it went. It traversed the antitank ditch that barred the way inland by using the German crossing place, which had not been blown, and then proceeded to clear a path up toward the Mont Fleury battery on the hill overlooking the beach. Just past a large house wryly named "Lavatory Pan Villa" because of the circular shape of its driveway, Pear's Crab was halted by a crater in the road. An AVRE with a bridge was quickly despatched to the site and a crossing was placed over the large depression, allowing the advance to resume. The way was now open for vehicles to drive toward Ver-sur-Mer.

The Green Howards and the tanks of 4th/7th Dragoon Guards now quickly took up the advance. With an exit from the beach fully open, streams of troops and vehicles were able to get clear of the shore. Twenty minutes after the first wave, B and C Companies began to land and all of the Green Howards' main objectives could now be attacked.

D Company had by this time closed on the gun battery at Mont Fleury and cleared the area with little resistance. The heavy bombing of the site and the bombardment laid down on the battery by HMS *Belfast* had knocked the fighting spirit out of its garrison. Completely demoralized, the battery did not seem to have fired a shot at the landings. B Company now attacked the trench system and machine-gun posts on the Meuvaines Ridge to the southwest, clearing the enemy from a small quarry on the way. After a stiff firefight the ridge was cleared. C Company meanwhile pressed on to occupy Point 52 to the west of Ver-sur-Mer and cover the main push inland by the tanks of the 4th/7th Dragoon Guards toward Crépon.

Forty-five minutes after the 6th Green Howards had landed, its sister battalion, the 7th Green Howards, also touched down on King sector. This follow-up battalion completed the landings of the 69th Brigade. The 7th Green Howards quickly found a way off the beach, but had some difficulty finding

Rhino ferries bring follow-up vehicles and reinforcements to Gold Beach. These flat blunt-ended rafts transported all kinds of loads to the shore from larger ships anchored in deeper water. The scene shows King Beach near the exit toward Mont Fleury. The group of trees in the left background marks the area of the lighthouse behind La Rivière and the prominent house to the right of center is "Lavatory Pan Villa." *(Imperial War Museum, CL57)*

a suitable route inland. Eventually they advanced up the hill, past Lavatory Pan Villa and the Mont Fleury battery, and gained the open ground beyond. The battalion's first task was to attack the gun battery at Ver-sur-Mer. This they did and found that it was completely out of action, with its garrison retired into concrete shelters. These demoralized Germans soon surrendered to the aggressive persuasion of the Green Howards and over 50 prisoners went into captivity.

With the two assault brigades of British 50th Division landed, the reserve brigades were due to come ashore in support. At around 1100hrs, both brigades began to land on beaches still raked by enemy fire, but it was only a fraction of the intensity that had met the assault waves. Le Hamel had still not been subdued so the 56th Brigade, which was due to land on Jig sector behind 231st Brigade, landed further to the east instead and came ashore near Hable-de-Heurtot. The 151st Brigade set down on King sector in the rear of 69th Brigade. Throughout the remainder of the morning more troops came ashore through exits and pathways cleared by the engineers. With these troops came a vast tail of support vehicles carrying stores and ammunition. No sooner had the chaos and disorder caused by enemy fire been cleared, than it was replaced by the chaos and disorder of traffic jams and bogged-down vehicles. But from this confusion there emerged a steady stream of infantry and tanks that inexorably forced their way inland.

By the end of the morning the 24th Lancers had joined the 4th/7th Dragoon Guards and the Sherwood Rangers to complete the landings of 8th Armoured Brigade. This new regiment immediately went forward to join in the advance. The Dorsets and Devons had by then cleared a wide area behind Jig beach to allow the 56th Brigade to pass through and continue its move toward Bayeux. On the extreme right, however, the 1st Hampshires were still trying to force their way into the strongpoint around the sanatorium at Le Hamel.

Gold Beach, H-Hour +15 Minutes

Armored vehicles from the British 79th Armoured Division and Sherman DD tanks from the 4th/7th Dragoon Guards, part of the 8th Armoured Brigade, arrive on Gold Beach to support 5th East Yorks during the assault phase of the landings. The specialized armor of British 79th Armoured Division provided all of the British and Canadian beaches with direct-fire support. It was a unique formation; its constituent units never fought together as a division but provided heavy firepower and special expertise to whichever division or brigade required it. Each of the tanks had specific tasks to perform, but once they landed and began to take casualties, confusion reigned. These troops are attacking the area around German strongpoint WN33 on the extreme left of King sector at La Rivière. The strongpoint is grouped around the type-H677 casemate containing an 88mm Pak 43/41 gun. French houses within the strongpoint's perimeter have been reinforced with concrete and small-arms and machine-gun fire from these positions raked the beach. The elimination of the large German gun became the most important priority for the men and armor landing in front of it. The AVREs confronting the enemy casemate were standard Churchill tanks modified for particular tasks. They were armed with a 12in spigot mortar known as a "petard," which could deliver a massive 26lb charge of high explosive – known as the Flying Dustbin – up to a range of 230 yards, although the effective range was about 85 yards. The tanks were capable of destroying the fortification with devastating effect if they could get close enough. The first AVRE tank from 81 Squadron, 6th Assault Regiment RE, was knocked out by the German 88mm gun. A second AVRE later succumbed to the same gun. On the extreme left is a Sherman Crab flail tank from C Squadron, Westminster Dragoons. This type of tank was fitted at the front with a revolving drum with attached lengths of chain. As the name suggests, this flailed the ground as it advanced, exploding buried mines. The 88mm gun in strongpoint WN33 was eventually knocked out a short time later by a Crab tank commanded by Captain R. F. Bell, whose 75mm gun put a shell right through the embrasure of the casemate at short range. On the right a DD Sherman from 4th/7th Dragoon Guards is attacking an enemy pillbox supported by men from the East Yorks. These Sherman tanks were fitted with canvas flotation screens, giving them an amphibious capability. They were propelled by twin screws at the rear. Once they had touched down on the beach, their screens were dropped and the propellers disengaged, converting the DDs back into normal track-driven tanks. Cooperation between tanks and infantry was difficult. Once they were in close contact with the enemy the infantry usually went for cover and the tank crews battened down their hatches. The only way to communicate with the tank crew was via the telephone housed on the outside of the vehicle, which left the infantryman vulnerable to enemy fire. A tank commander was just as disinclined to put himself at additional risk by opening his hatch to communicate with the infantry. *(Kevin Lyles © Osprey Publishing Ltd)*

Royal Navy Beach Group command post on Gold Beach organizing the landing of follow-up units, stores, and reinforcements. These are Royal Navy personnel, wearing army Commando battledress complete with Combined Operations badges. They proudly display the White Ensign above their control post and the two officers retain their naval headdress. *(Imperial War Museum, A24092)*

The Hampshires were off the beach and behind the village, but were unable to close on the outer defenses of the strongpoint because of the intensity of the enemy's small-arms and mortar fire. Battalion HQ was set up in Asnelles while a new approach to the problem was considered. At 1345hrs a concerted effort was made to reach the strongpoint. B and C Companies advanced to the lateral road south of Le Hamel, but it took over an hour for the infantry to get into a position from which to make the final attack. At 1500hrs, B Company crossed over the lateral road and advanced grimly on the houses surrounding the sanatorium. The infantry got to within 50 yards of the main building, but were stopped by a torrent of fire. In a stroke of luck, at this critical moment the troops were joined by an AVRE tank which came down the road from Asnelles. With small-arms fire peppering its sides, the tank closed on the sanatorium and began firing huge bunker-busting petard charges at the building. This momentarily stopped the enemy machine-gun fire and, during a pause, C Company managed to get into the strongpoint. The building was gradually cleared amid fierce hand-to-hand fighting, with few of the German defenders surrendering. The enemy retreated house-by-house, firing as they withdrew toward the western end of the village. Additional attacks were made on the shrinking enemy garrison by B Company and by 1600hrs all active resistance in the area had been subdued. The great casemate and its 75mm gun that had caused so much havoc on Jig sector eventually succumbed to a petard charge fired through the rear door of the blockhouse.

While the attack on Le Hamel was in progress, the remainder of the Hampshires had moved westwards along the coast and had cleared the gun positions of WN38 at St-Côme-de-Fresné and captured the radar station on the cliffs to the east of Arromanches. This now left the 231st Brigade overlooking the town from both the south and east. At the same time, from the high ground on the other side of Arromanches, German fire began to interfere with the build-up of troops and naval gunfire was called for to put a stop to it. Patrols were sent down into Arromanches late that afternoon and met little resistance, so an artillery program was arranged to give supporting fire and the town was entered by the Hampshires and captured later that evening.

By this time the Dorsets were occupying Ryes and the Devons had continued westwards toward the great gun battery at Longues. The guns at Longues had first opened fire on the invasion fleet approaching Gold Beach at around 0605hrs. Prior to that the battery had been subjected to both heavy bombing and bombardment from other warships. At 0537hrs, the French cruiser *Georges Leygues* had targeted the battery. This fire was then taken up by the American battleship USS *Arkansas*. Longues battery replied by firing its 152mm naval guns at the battleship and the US destroyer *Emmons*. Then another French cruiser, the *Montcalm*, joined in the skirmish. At 0605hrs the guns were turned on a closer target when the battery opened fire on the flotilla of ships anchored off Gold Beach. The first to feel the effects of the German coastal weapons was the HQ ship HMS *Bulolo*. So accurate were the initial salvos that *Bulolo* was forced to weigh anchor and move out of range. At this time the cruiser HMS *Ajax* began its bombardment plan and concentrated all of its guns on Longues. A long-range duel now began that was to last 20 minutes. At a distance of 12,000 yards the two adversaries swapped shell for shell. Victory went to the *Ajax* as the battery fell silent at 0620hrs. This was only a temporary respite, however, and at around 0700hrs it opened up once more on the Americans landing at Omaha. Once again *Ajax* pounded the battery, joined by HMS *Argonaut*. This time the action was decisive: with astonishing precision the two cruisers managed to knock out three of the four guns.

That should have been the end of Longues, but its one gun resumed firing later that afternoon, threatening Allied shipping and the landing beaches. Throughout the afternoon and into the early evening the lone gun kept up intermittent fire on the invaders. Finally, at 1900hrs it fell silent. The next day, June 7, the garrison of 184 men, led by their commanding officer, surrendered peacefully to the 2nd Devons.

THE MOVE INLAND

With the beachhead relatively secure, the 50th Division could now push forward and attempt to secure the remainder of the day's objectives. The whole of the division was ashore just after midday and the 56th Brigade was ordered to make its move on Bayeux and beyond to the River Drôme. In the early afternoon it advanced through the 231st Brigade's gains and set out into open country. The leading troops of the South Wales Borderers passed through La Rosière and turned southwards astride the road to Bayeux. As they approached the radar station at Pouligny, the enemy set fire to it and withdrew. The advance continued to Vaux-sur-Aure and a crossing point over the river was secured. The nearby gun battery was found to be deserted. It had been bombed by heavy bombers and shelled by the cruiser HMS *Argonaut* earlier that day and it appeared that the garrison had simply abandoned the position. Meanwhile, on the left, the 2nd Essex had reached St Sulpice and the 2nd Gloucestershires had followed behind and occupied Magny, both meeting only light enemy resistance on the way. Here the brigade halted and made preparations to hold the position for the rest of the night. Its progress had been slow, advancing just 4 miles in five hours and then stopping and digging in. It did send patrols as far as Bayeux,

Gold Beach, King sector, mid-morning June 6. The left foreground shows the track running inland from the beach up to the Mont Fleury battery through the antitank ditch. The extreme right of the picture shows the beach curving into Jig Sector, at about the position of strongpoint WN35 at Hable de Heurlot. *(Imperial War Museum, MH 24333)*

A Cromwell tank leads a line of armor from the 4th County of London Yeomanry inland from Gold Beach. The tanks, from the 7th Armoured Division, have just crossed the antitank ditch at the rear of King Beach and are driving up toward "Lavatory Pan Villa" and the site of the German gun battery at Mont Fleury. *(Imperial War Museum, B5251)*

but the D-Day objective remained untaken. One reason for the brigade's lack of urgency may have been the absence of its commander, Brigadier Senior. He had been ambushed south of Crépon, wounded in the arm and had been forced to lie up to avoid capture. He rejoined the brigade the next day, but his injuries were severe enough for him to be repatriated to England.

To the left of the 56th Brigade, the 151st Brigade moved forward in two groups, supported by the self-propelled guns of the 90th Field Regiment RA. Its objective was to seize the Caen–Bayeux road and railway between the Bayeux and the River Seulles. The brigade had come ashore over King Beach and had concentrated around Meuvaines. In the middle of the afternoon, the right-hand group, led by the 9th Durham Light Infantry, advanced along the line of the Crépon–Bayeux road. On their left the other group, led by the 6th Durham Light Infantry and a squadron of Sherman tanks of the 4th/7th Dragoon Guards, pushed south from Crépon toward Villiers le Sec and then westwards on the road toward Bayeux. The move was not without incident, and between Bazenville and Villiers le Sec the brigade was subjected to a determined enemy counterattack, but after some fierce fighting the Germans retired.

The division's fourth brigade, the 69th Brigade, moved out from its beachhead and secured the extreme left flank of Gold Beach's lodgement. The 6th Green Howards continued its advance past the Mont Fleury battery on to another field battery further inland. The advance troops found this empty – the Germans had hitched their 88mm guns to their tractors and had retired. At Crépon the battalion concentrated, ready to move with the rest of the brigade toward the River Seulles at Creully. By 1500hrs the brigade was in Villiers le Sec where 5th East Yorks had to beat off a strong enemy counterattack. The squadron of 4th/7th Dragoon Guards that was supporting the move then went forward over the River Seulles and entered Creully. By nightfall the whole brigade had crossed the Seulles and had established itself in the villages of St Gabriel, Rucqueville, and Coulombs. It had also made contact with the Canadians who had landed on Juno Beach.

During the day, Colour Sergeant-Major Stanley Hollis of 6th Green Howards had made history. His was an eventful day that had begun when he landed on King Beach with the assault waves. His company exited the beach and advanced up the road that led toward Mont Fleury battery past Lavatory Pan Villa. His company commander noticed that two pillboxes near the villa had been bypassed and remained untaken. Hollis went forward to investigate and the machine-guns inside opened up on him. He rushed the first pillbox firing his Sten gun as he ran. He poked his gun through its aperture and sprayed the inside with his Sten, then jumped on the roof and tossed a grenade inside, killing the occupants. He then cleared a nearby trench of Germans and accepted the surrender of the other pillbox. Later that day in Crépon, he attacked a German field gun with a PIAT and then created a diversion so that two of his stranded men could be evacuated. Throughout the day, wherever there was action, Hollis was in the thick of it. His bravery and valor earned him the award of the Victoria Cross, the only one granted during the whole of D-Day.

Once the 50th Division was completely ashore, the beaches were given over to the arrival of transport, stores, and reinforcements. During the remainder of the day advance elements of the 7th Armoured Division arrived over the beaches. As night fell these new units gathered at their rendezvous points ready to join in the advance the next day.

GERMAN REACTION TO THE LANDINGS ON GOLD BEACH

In the early hours of June 6, German commanders in the Normandy area had been alerted to the fact that something unusual was taking place when news reached their various headquarters of Allied airborne landings east of the River Orne and west of the River Vire. With the arrival of Allied warships off the Normandy coast just after dawn, it was clear that an invasion of some considerable size was actually taking place. The commander of 716th Division, Generalmajor Richter, became involved in countering British paratroopers during the night. The British 6th Airborne Division had landed among the easternmost elements of his division and his men had been in action since the early hours. Richter's difficulties increased markedly when he was given news later that morning that the British and Canadians had landed on three beaches, all of them within the sector defended by his division.

Richter's untried static division, made up primarily of old men, foreign conscripts, and exhausted veterans, was having to resist the landings of three full-strength, well-trained, and well-equipped infantry divisions. There really was no contest. Once the Allied assault infantry and tanks had penetrated the fixed defenses along the coast and chased the German troops out of their concrete shells, the 716th Division had practically nothing left with which to resist them. The backbone of its defense had been the concrete and steel shelters. When forced to retreat into open country, their will to resist evaporated. Behind Gold Beach, Richter had just the 441st Ost Battalion of press-ganged Russian auxiliaries and elements of his 726th Regiment holding the coast. Behind these troops, field positions manned by the 352nd Artillery Regiment, from the 352nd Infantry Division, covered the beach. The shock of British 50th Division's landings quickly disrupted all cohesion in the German line, leaving just isolated islands of resistance with which to deny the Allies a lodgement. When these were captured one by one, the battle quickly became a rout. Those German forces that were able to retired as quickly as possible, falling back to other centers of resistance established behind them, but unable to provide any but token resistance to the British advance.

As early as 0900hrs, the HQ of the adjacent German 352nd Division learned that British tanks were in operation around the area of Meuvaines. The division's commander, Generalmajor Kraiss, viewed this news with alarm, for a breakthrough by British armored troops from Meuvaines to the south would make it possible for them to turn to the west without great difficulty, capture Bayeux, and roll up the 352nd Division's sector from the rear. The bulk of Kraiss's division was in action against the Americans on Omaha Beach and the airborne landings around the River Vire. The divisional reserve, Meyer's Kampfgruppe of the reinforced 915th Infantry Regiment, was also the corps' reserve and was employed under the control of General Marcks and his LXXXIV Corps. It had already been committed against American paratroopers in the western part of the division's sector near Carentan since the early hours. Kraiss now requested the return of the battlegroup from Marcks so that he could send it against the British. With the Americans bottled up on Omaha and their paratroopers strung out and disorganized, Marcks agreed that the greatest threat was now in the east from the British.

Orders were given for the 915th Infantry Regiment's Kampfgruppe to reverse its advance westwards and head east past Bayeux, form up at Villiers le Sec, and attack toward Crépon. The Kampfgruppe consisted of the two grenadier battalions of the 915th Regiment and 352nd Fusilier Battalion, but before it had even reached Bayeux, it had to relinquish its I Battalion to the 914th Regiment to counter the American landings on Omaha Beach.

The column was then reinforced with ten self-propelled 75mm guns from the 1352nd Assault Gun Company and was promised the support of a railway artillery battery at Torigny. When it was in position at Villiers le Sec, the remnants of 441st Ost Battalion and the surviving elements of II./1716 Artillery Regiment were also to come under command.

Sometime after midday, the clouds dispersed and the sun came out, and with the brighter weather came the Allied fighter-bombers. The column was harried all the way to its rendezvous point at Villiers le Sec, finally arriving near the village in the late afternoon. By then the British 69th Brigade was through Crépon and closing on the German assembly area. However, before Kampfgruppe Meyer could deploy to begin the counterattack, it clashed with the British. A stiff battle ensued as the tanks and guns of the 69th Brigade made contact with the Germans. Four tanks from 4th/7th Dragoon Guards were knocked out by the assault guns, but British pressure was such that the bulk of the Kampfgruppe was broken up in small defensive actions. Meyer radioed back to 352nd Division's HQ that the enemy had anticipated his

German Defenses – Gold Beach

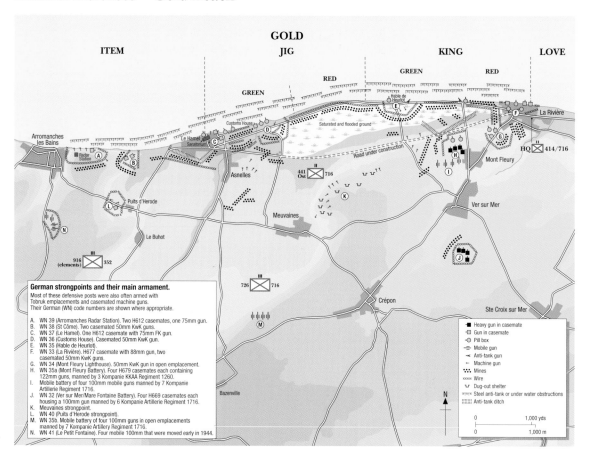

German strongpoints and their main armament.

Most of these defensive posts were also often armed with Tobruk emplacements and casemated machine guns. Their German (WN) code numbers are shown where appropriate.

A. WN 39 (Arromanches Radar Station). Two H612 casemates, one 75mm gun.
B. WN 38 (St Côme). Two casemated 50mm KwK guns.
C. WN 37 (Le Hamel). One H612 casemate with 75mm FK gun.
D. WN 36 (Customs House). Casemated 50mm KwK gun.
E. WN 35 (Hable de Heurtot).
F. WN 33 (La Rivière). H677 casemate with 88mm gun, two casemated 50mm KwK guns.
G. WN 34 (Mont Fleury Lighthouse). 50mm KwK gun in open emplacement.
H. WN 35a (Mont Fleury Battery). Four H679 casemates each containing 122mm guns, manned by 3 Kompanie KKAA Regiment 1260.
I. Mobile battery of four 100mm mobile guns manned by 7 Kompanie Artillerie Regiment 1716.
J. WN 32 (Ver sur Mer/Mare Fontaine Battery). Four H669 casemates each housing a 100mm gun manned by 6 Kompanie Artillerie Regiment 1716.
K. Meuvaines strongpoint.
L. WN 40 (Puits d'Herode strongpoint).
M. WN 35b. Mobile battery of four 100mm guns in open emplacements manned by 7 Kompanie Artillerie Regiment 1716.
N. WN 41 (Le Petit Fontaine). Four mobile 100mm that were moved early in 1944.

Heavy gun in casemate
Gun in casemate
Pill box
Mobile gun
Anti-tank gun
Machine gun
Mines
Wire
Dug-out shelter
Steel anti-tank or under water obstructions
Anti-tank ditch

0   1,000 yds
0   1,000 m

attack and had overrun his spearhead with tanks supported by fighter-bombers. Close-quarters fighting was taking place and the British could not be held. Then things went quiet. Meyer was killed and the commanders of the 352nd Fusilier Battalion and the 1352nd Assault Gun Company were both then posted as missing. The Germans had suffered heavy casualties and had begun retreating. Out of the entire Kampfgruppe only about 90 men escaped. An attempt was made to recover Meyer's body, as he had been carrying a map containing exact details of German dispositions along the coast, but it fell into British hands.

By this time, Kraiss knew that he could not force the British back to the sea, but only try to contain their advance and prevent Bayeux falling into their hands. He subordinated the remnants of the 915th Regiment to the 726th Regiment for the night and ordered that a defensive line be established from Coulombs to Esquay then across to Bazenville and on to Asnelles. The reality was, however, that most of this proposed line had already been overrun by the British 50th Division. To man the line, Kraiss ordered forwards all troops present in Bayeux and, together with III./352nd Artillery Regiment, the remainder of the 915th battlegroup, and elements of the 726th Regiment, they were to be concentrated into combat groups and employed in preventing any further advance toward Bayeux. To further bolster his line, Kraiss was also given LXXXIV's 30th Mobile Brigade, which was on its way northwards from Coutances on bicycles, but was not expected to arrive until early the next day.

THE LANDINGS: JUNO BEACH

The 3rd Canadian Infantry Division was designated to land on Juno Beach as part of British I Corps. The beach stretched from La Rivière in the west to St Aubin in the east, a distance of about 5½ miles. The coast here was low lying with a sandy beach edged by dunes, protected by an offshore reef of rocks that was exposed at low tide.

At the center of Juno Beach lay the small port of Courseulles on the estuary of the River Seulles. To the east of Courseulles were the seaside villages of Bernières-sur-Mer and St-Aubin-sur-Mer, small holiday centers with a few large villas strung out between them. Juno Beach was divided into three sectors: Love Beach from La Rivière to a point half-way toward Courseulles, Mike Beach from there to the harbor entrance, and Nan Beach from the center of Courseulles to St Aubin. German defenses along this section of the coast quite naturally concentrated on denying an invader access to the harbor at Courseulles. Both sides of the seaward entrance to the port were heavily fortified.

CANADIAN 7TH BRIGADE'S LANDINGS

Naval Force J, commanded by Commodore G. N. Oliver in his HQ ship HMS *Hilary*, anchored 6½ miles off Juno Beach just before dawn. The two groups of ships carrying the attack waves of infantry, Group J1 with the Canadian 7th Brigade and J2 with the Canadian 8th Brigade, anchored in their lowering positions a little further inshore. Closer still were the bombarding group of naval ships that were to deluge the German strongpoints along the beaches with high-explosive fire. The cruisers *Belfast* and *Diadem* were to target gun batteries and the Hunt and Fleet class destroyers were to concentrate on beach defenses. *Diadem* was programmed to fire at the German battery at Bény-sur-Mer, well inland from the beaches, and *Belfast*, after dealing with

German Defenses – Juno Beach

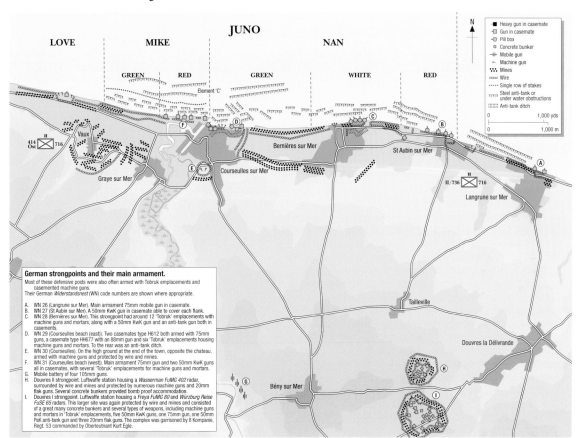

German strongpoints and their main armament.

Most of these defensive posts were also often armed with Tobruk emplacements and casemented machine guns.
Their German *Widerstandsnest* (WN) code numbers are shown where appropriate.

A. WN 26 (Langrune sur Mer). Main armament 75mm mobile gun in casemate.

B. WN 27 (St Aubin sur Mer). A 50mm KwK gun in casemate able to cover each flank.

C. WN 28 (Bernières sur Mer). This strongpoint had around 12 'Tobruk' emplacements with machine guns and mortars, along with a 50mm KwK gun and an anti-tank gun both in casements.

D. WN 29 (Courseulles beach (east)). Two casemates type H612 both armed with 75mm guns, a casemate type HH677 with an 88mm gun and six 'Tobruk' emplacements housing machine guns and mortars. To the rear was an anti-tank ditch.

E. WN 30 (Courseulles). On the high ground at the end of the town, opposite the chateau, armed with machine guns and protected by wire and mines.

F. WN 31 (Courseulles beach (west)). Main armament 75mm mobile gun and two 50mm KwK guns all in casemates, with several 'Tobruk' emplacements for machine guns and mortars.

G. Mobile battery of four 105mm guns.

H. Douvres II strongpoint. Luftwaffe station housing a *Wasserman FuMG 402* radar, surrounded by wire and mines and protected by numerous machine guns and 20mm flak guns. Several concrete bunkers provided bomb proof accommodation.

I. Douvres I strongpoint. Luftwaffe station housing a *Freya FuMG 80* and *Würzburg Reise FuSE 65* radars. This larger site was again protected by wire and mines and consisted of a great many concrete bunkers and several types of weapons, including machine guns and mortars in 'Tobruk' emplacements, five 50mm KwK guns, one 75mm gun, one 50mm PaK anti-tank gun and three 20mm flak guns. The complex was garrisoned by 8 Kompanie, Regt. 53 commanded by Oberleutnant Kurt Egle.

Ver battery behind Gold Beach, was to turn her attention to targets in the rear of Juno Beach. The destroyers *Kempenfelt*, *Faulknor*, *Venus*, *Fury*, *Vigilant*, *Bleasdale*, *Algonquin*, *Glaisdale*, *Sioux*, *Stevenstone*, and *La Combattante* were each given targets on the beachfront from La Rivière to Langrune.

As on Gold Beach, the early morning light brought with it the heavy and medium bombers of the RAF and USAAF. Areas that had been bombed for weeks prior to the invasion now received a final deluge of intense bombing. Very soon the faint coastline visible from the ships at sea disappeared beneath clouds of dust and smoke, lit intermittently with great flashes of red and yellow flame. Then, as individual targets reappeared through the gradually dispersing cloud, the naval guns began their own bombardment of the concrete defences of Hitler's Atlantic Wall with their large-caliber weapons.

H-Hour on Juno was slightly later than on Gold and Sword. A greater depth of water was needed by the landing craft to clear the offshore reef, so it was decided that extra minutes would be required to allow the incoming tide to cover it with sufficient draught of water. The initial assault wave

Canadian troops coming ashore from a LCI(L) – Landing Craft Infantry (Large) – on Nan White Beach near Bernières. An AVRE has placed a span bridging the seawall, enabling tanks to get off the beach. The picture was taken in the late morning and the incoming tide has reduced the width of the beach to just a few yards. As more landing craft came in bringing the follow-up brigade, Canadian 9th Brigade, this small strip of sand became hopelessly clogged with traffic. *(Imperial War Museum, A23938)*

would go in ten minutes later than on Gold, at 0745hrs, while J2 Group would arrive ten minutes after that at 0755hrs. The strong swell and choppy seas meant the launch of the amphibious DD tanks was delayed until they were much closer inshore. Those supporting Canadian 7th Brigade were launched about 1,000 yards out and partly swam and partly waded ashore. Those on Nan White and Red sectors supporting 8th Brigade were not launched at sea, but landed on the beaches with the LCTs bringing the AVRE tanks.

The later arrival of the assault waves onto the beach meant that their landing craft touched down among the beach obstacles instead of ahead of them. On Juno this problem was unavoidable; the combination of rocks, beach obstacles, and tide meant there was no perfect time to land. If the invasion was made at low tide underwater obstacles would be exposed and useless, but infantry and tanks would have to cross hundreds of yards of open beach and rocks swept by German fire before they could get to grips with the enemy's defenses. If the landings were made at high tide, the assault waves would have less exposed ground to cover, but the landing craft could be ripped to pieces by underwater obstacles. The timing of the landings was therefore a compromise. The craft would touch down at midway between high and low tides, allowing the greatest number of beach obstacles to be visible and therefore avoidable, while giving the infantry and tanks the shortest area of open beach to cross.

The Canadian 7th Brigade, commanded by Brigadier H. W. Foster, landed on Mike Red and Nan Green sectors, either side of the Seulles estuary, to a barrage of German fire. The bombing by medium and heavy bombers, the naval bombardment, the salvoes of 5in rockets, and the artillery fire from

Canadian troops coming ashore from an LCI(L). It is now high tide and the beach has virtually disappeared, with the water now lapping against the collapsed seawall . *(Imperial War Museum, B5261)*

field guns at sea in LCTs, all failed to silence the opposition. Ensconced in concrete and steel bunkers, German defenders were impervious to high explosives. The Royal Navy later admitted that, at most, only 14 percent of positions fired at were put out of action by its guns. Those German infantry and artillerymen in open emplacements had for the most part taken shelter from the storm of Allied fire and only emerged to man their weapons when the landing craft actually approached the beach. Then, at short range, they raked the frail wooden assault craft with small-arms and mortar fire. Heavier weapons concentrated on the LCTs following behind. Hits were taken and ships began to swerve out of line, dodging enemy shells and the mine-topped spikes pointing menacingly out of the water.

On Mike Red and Green sectors to the right of the mouth of the River Seulles, the Royal Winnipeg Rifles arrived before the first of their supporting armor at 0749hrs. The tanks should have landed five minutes before the infantry but they were late. The DD tanks of A Squadron from the 1st Hussars were delayed in arriving because of the change in launching plans. The Crab flail-tanks of B Squadron, 22nd Dragoons, and the AVREs from 26th Squadron, 5th Assault Regiment RE, both from the British 79th Armoured Division, were late because of navigational problems during the crossing. All of this armor should have been on the beach attacking the German defenses when the infantry landed, giving covering fire to the exposed troops as they came off their craft, but the initial assault waves of the Winnipeg Rifles had to fight their own way ashore, dealing with the pillboxes as best they

Canadian 3rd Division Landings on Juno Beach

could. Casualties among the exposed infantry were significant. The LCTs carrying AVREs were up to 30 minutes late in arriving.

B Company of the Winnipegs landed on the right on Mike Green and moved along the beach to deal with the group of concrete casemates forming a strongpoint whose fire enfiladed the landings. On this sector of the beach there was no sign of supporting armor, so the infantry stalked the concrete pillboxes on foot. Enemy small-arms fire was concentrated and accurate and the Canadians suffered as a consequence. The other assault company,

This was the sector of Nan Red where the commandos of 48 Royal Marine Commando landed. The men were under concentrated machine-gun, mortar, and sniper fire when they came ashore and they suffered considerable casualties, but they took their greatest losses just offshore when two of their LCI(S)s hit obstacles and sank. Many of the fully laden commandos were swept away and drowned in the offshore currents. By the time the Commando had reached its first objective at Langrune, it could only muster 50 percent of its original strength. *(Imperial War Museum, B5225)*

D Company, landed on the left and immediately started trying to fight its way off the beach inland, through a maze of concealed machine-gun posts and "Tobruk" emplacements. The two great concrete emplacements that dominated the entrance to the harbor were taken amid tough, prolonged fighting, most of which was at close quarters. Only seven of the DD tanks from A Squadron, 6th Armoured Regiment (1st Hussars), had got ashore and many of them were later swamped by the incoming tide as they stopped in the surf firing at the pillboxes.

Once the emplacements on the beach had been captured, the two companies topped the sand dunes and moved inland. Immediately behind Mike Red Beach, the course of the River Seulles curved round in a great semicircle, forming a three-sided "island." B Company crossed a small bridge, got onto the island and began clearing it of the enemy. This area was in fact the western part of Courseulles and was covered with oyster beds and harbor installations. D Company also moved away from the beaches crossing the minefield in front of La Vallette and advancing toward the village of Graye-sur-Mer beyond it.

On the extreme right of Mike Green Beach, C Company of the Canadian Scottish Rifles, which was attached to the Winnipegs, landed against lighter opposition. Its main objective on the beach was a concrete casemate housing a 75mm gun. When the infantry closed on the position they found it had been already knocked out by naval gunfire. Within a short time the company was off the beach and moving inland, dealing with the wire and minefields in front of Vaux and advancing across open land toward St-Croix-sur-Mer. Twenty minutes after the assault waves, the reserve companies landed. The beaches were still under heavy mortar and machine-gun fire, but the

A crowded scene on Juno Beach as Canadian reinforcements come ashore. Naval beach parties wearing steel helmets with a white band try to bring some order out of the chaos. The tide is now high and only a narrow strip of beach is available on which to maneuver men, tanks, and vehicles. *(Imperial War Museum, MH3097)*

immediate vicinity was clear of the enemy. A Company pushed straight over the dunes and also made for St-Croix-sur-Mer, while C Company advanced on Banville.

On the beaches, the late arrival of the specialized armor and the rapidly incoming tide, blown on by a stiff breeze, had caused chaos all along the water's edge, for neither of the two exits planned for Mike Beach were open. When the flails and AVREs of B Squadron, 22nd Dragoons, and the 26th Assault Squadron RE, landed late at 0830hrs, the beach was less than 100 yards wide. The LCTs carrying the tanks had drifted to the east and all the specialized armor was landed close to the No 2 gap that the division hoped to make. The teams from 79th Armoured Division were hoping to clear two exits from the beach: the first, No. 1 gap, on the extreme right of the beach, led on to a lane that went inland toward Vaux, while No. 2 gap on the left joined with the lane leading back to La Valette.

No. 2 gap was seen as the priority and was tackled first. Two Crabs flailed a lane up to and over the dunes, but both were disabled when they struck mines just as they were turning. A third Crab continued and cleared a single track along the lane to a point 150 yards inland. There it was halted by a crater 60ft wide and 12ft deep, left by a demolished culvert. The broken drain had flooded the area and the Crab became bogged down. An AVRE Churchill came forward with a fascine and dropped the great wooden roll into the water-filled crater, but then itself slipped into the hole. Now a sitting duck to enemy gunners, the crew baled out. In making their escape, three of the tankers were killed by enemy fire and the other three were wounded. A second AVRE came forward with a fascine and pushed it into the crater. Then an SGB bridge was brought up to cover the gap. The bridge was placed across the top of the stranded AVRE and the abandoned tank was used as a support. A Crab now came forward and continued to flail the lane up to the lateral road, thus opening an exit from the beach. The time was 0915hrs.

This unusual and unorthodox bridge remained in use for the next three hours, as traffic and tanks streamed off Mike Beach. Just after midday, when all enemy resistance had been cleared, the crater was filled in with rubble and a permanent crossing established over the culvert. The AVRE tank remained entombed under the road for the next 32 years until a party of Royal Engineers dug it out in 1973 and restored it. Gap No 1 proved to be a less complicated affair, with the major obstacles to its completion coming from enemy fire. Mines proved to be the only field defenses and the lane was opened for traffic at 0930hrs.

The Canadian 7th Brigade's other assault battalion, the Regina Rifle Regiment, landed its troops on Nan Green on the other side of the mouth of the River Seulles straight onto the town beach at Courseulles. In front of them, and very much alive, was the German strongpoint WN29, comprising two H612 casemates armed with 75mm guns and an H677 containing an 88mm gun. These were supported by the small-arms and mortar fire from six concrete machine-gun posts and four Tobruk emplacements. Bombing and naval bombardment seemed to have done little to silence the enemy and the landing craft were shelled all the way to the shoreline. As on Mike sector, the supporting armor from the British 79th Armoured Division was late arriving, but B Squadron of the Canadian 6th Armoured Regiment (1st Hussars) landed just before the first waves of infantry. Nineteen DD tanks had been launched about 2,000 yards from shore and swam in. Fourteen of them reached the beach and were wading through the surf blasting the enemy defenses as the assault landing craft bringing the Regina Rifles weaved their way among them.

The advance wave of infantry, A and B Companies, arrived at around 0810hrs. A Company landed immediately in front of the German strongpoint and met heavy resistance; B Company landed further to the east. Ahead of them was 200 yards of exposed beach, swept by German fire. Each man leaving the craft had to wade through tumbling surf and then make a mad dash for cover at the top of the sandy shoreline. But the only cover to be had on that exposed sea front was under the guns of the strongpoint. For the infantry on the beach it was like running into the mouth of a dragon. Help was on hand from the supporting armor, and one by one the DD tanks closed on the concrete emplacements and machine-gun nests, sweeping the area with their own machine-guns and firing armor-piercing rounds at close range.

While all of these enemy positions had received numerous direct hits on their concrete sides from naval gunfire, none ceased firing for more than a brief period. One of the 75mm guns had over 200 empty shell cases around it when finally captured, evidence of its effectiveness even after the

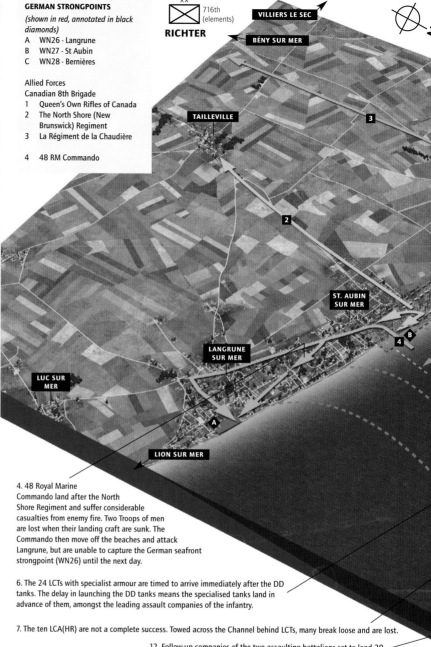

ALLIED FLEET

Destroyers
1. HMS *Bleasdale*
2. HMS *Glaisdale*
3. HMS *Sioux*
4. HMS *Algonquin*
5. HMS *Vigilant*
6. HMS *Kempenfelt*

LCS(M) Landing Craft Support (Medium) providing close support with machine guns and smoke. These craft also contain Forward Observation Officers to check the fall of shot of supporting guns and rockets and radio back adjustments to the fire plan.

LCT(3) Landing Craft Tank (Mk. III) of 11th LCT Flotilla. These craft carry the DD tanks of 'B' and 'C' Sqns, Canadian 10th Armoured Support Regiment.

LCG(L) Landing Craft Gun (Large) of 331st Flotilla providing artillery support against identified targets with their two 4.7in. guns.

LCT(HE) Landing Craft Tank (High Explosive) of 590th Assault Flotilla. Each carries one Sherman and two Centaur tanks from 2nd Royal Marine Armoured Support Regiment.

LCT(4) Landing Craft Tank (Mk. IV) from 22nd and 30th LCT Flotillas carrying the AVRE tanks from 79th Armoured Division.

LCT(CB) Landing Craft tank (Concrete Buster) from 106th LCT Flotilla, each carrying two 17-pdr tanks able to provide high-velocity fire against concrete emplacements.

LCA(HR) Landing Craft Assault (Hedgerow) from 590th Assault Flotilla armed with spigot mortars capable of firing 24 x 60lb bombs to blast lanes through wire and mines.

LCA Landing Craft Assault from various Landing Ships Infantry carrying the assault companies of the Canadian North Shore Regiment and the Queen's Own Rifles of Canada.

LCF Landing Craft Flak from 331st Assault flotilla providing anti-aircraft and close-support fire from their eight 2-pdr and four Oerlikon guns.

LCT(R) Landing Craft Tank (Rocket) from 320th LCT(R) Flotilla, each armed with 1,000 5in. rockets.

LCT(4) Landing Craft Tank (Mk. IV) from 22nd and 30th LCT Flotillas carrying the self-propelled artillery of Canadian 3rd Division.

LCA Landing Craft Assault from various Landing Ships Infantry carrying the reserve companies of the Canadian North Shore Regiment and the Queen's Own Rifles of Canada.

LCI(S) Landing Craft Infantry (Small) of 202nd LCI(S) Flotilla carrying 48 RM Commando.

LCH 167 Landing Craft Headquarters 167, the HQ ship of the assault area's senior officer.

GERMAN STRONGPOINTS

(shown in red, annotated in black diamonds)
A   WN26 - Langrune
B   WN27 - St Aubin
C   WN28 - Bernières

Allied Forces
Canadian 8th Brigade
1   Queen's Own Rifles of Canada
2   The North Shore (New Brunswick) Regiment
3   La Régiment de la Chaudière

4   48 RM Commando

4. 48 Royal Marine Commando land after the North Shore Regiment and suffer considerable casualties from enemy fire. Two Troops of men are lost when their landing craft are sunk. The Commando then move off the beaches and attack Langrune, but are unable to capture the German seafront strongpoint (WN26) until the next day.

6. The 24 LCTs with specialist armour are timed to arrive immediately after the DD tanks. The delay in launching the DD tanks means the specialised tanks land in advance of them, amongst the leading assault companies of the infantry.

7. The ten LCA(HR) are not a complete success. Towed across the Channel behind LCTs, many break loose and are lost.

12. Follow-up companies of the two assaulting battalions set to land 20 minutes after the assault waves.

Canadian 8th Brigade on Nan White and Red Beaches

June 6, 1944, 0755hrs to mid-afternoon, viewed from the northeast showing the assault on St Aubin and Bernières by the Queen's Own Rifles of Canada and the Canadian North Shore Regiment respectively. 48 Royal Marine Commando land on Nan Red and move to attack the strongpoint in Langrune. With the coastal defences subdued the drive inland towards Tailleville and Bény sur Mer begins.

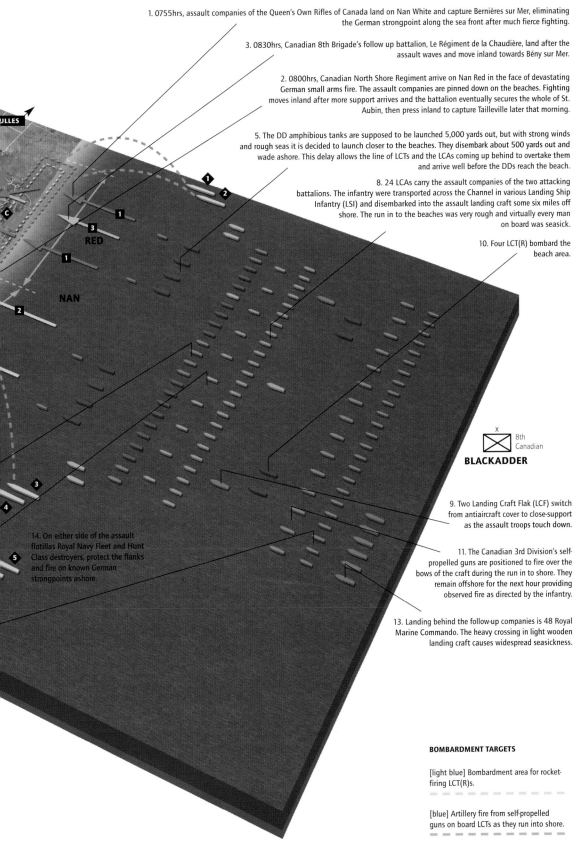

1. 0755hrs, assault companies of the Queen's Own Rifles of Canada land on Nan White and capture Bernières sur Mer, eliminating the German strongpoint along the sea front after much fierce fighting.

3. 0830hrs, Canadian 8th Brigade's follow up battalion, Le Régiment de la Chaudière, land after the assault waves and move inland towards Bény sur Mer.

2. 0800hrs, Canadian North Shore Regiment arrive on Nan Red in the face of devastating German small arms fire. The assault companies are pinned down on the beaches. Fighting moves inland after more support arrives and the battalion eventually secures the whole of St. Aubin, then press inland to capture Tailleville later that morning.

5. The DD amphibious tanks are supposed to be launched 5,000 yards out, but with strong winds and rough seas it is decided to launch closer to the beaches. They disembark about 500 yards out and wade ashore. This delay allows the line of LCTs and the LCAs coming up behind to overtake them and arrive well before the DDs reach the beach.

8. 24 LCAs carry the assault companies of the two attacking battalions. The infantry were transported across the Channel in various Landing Ship Infantry (LSI) and disembarked into the assault landing craft some six miles off shore. The run in to the beaches was very rough and virtually every man on board was seasick.

10. Four LCT(R) bombard the beach area.

ULLES

RED

NAN

x
8th
Canadian

BLACKADDER

9. Two Landing Craft Flak (LCF) switch from antiaircraft cover to close-support as the assault troops touch down.

11. The Canadian 3rd Division's self-propelled guns are positioned to fire over the bows of the craft during the run in to shore. They remain offshore for the next hour providing observed fire as directed by the infantry.

13. Landing behind the follow-up companies is 48 Royal Marine Commando. The heavy crossing in light wooden landing craft causes widespread seasickness.

14. On either side of the assault flotillas Royal Navy Fleet and Hunt Class destroyers, protect the flanks and fire on known German strongpoints ashore.

BOMBARDMENT TARGETS

[light blue] Bombardment area for rocket-firing LCT(R)s.

[blue] Artillery fire from self-propelled guns on board LCTs as they run into shore.

315

bombardment. It was finally knocked out by a direct hit from a tank shell, which pierced its gun shield and killed all of the crew. All of the guns in the strongpoint were eliminated by direct fire from tanks at short range and for a while the beach quietened down, save for the fire from snipers and isolated machine-guns. But this respite did not last, for once the immediate German resistance was subdued, other weapons opened up from further inland, showering the beach with artillery and mortar fire. This continued throughout the morning until each German battery was identified and eliminated by naval guns or artillery fire from those guns still in landing craft offshore. Several positions were overrun by advancing Canadian troops.

By the time the specialized armor arrived on Nan Green, 40 minutes behind schedule, the local German opposition had been subdued and the exit teams immediately began opening up lanes off the beach. Crabs flailed lanes over the dunes and up to the antitank ditch behind the strongpoint. Fascines were then brought up and the ditch was crossed with few problems. An armored bulldozer carved out two lanes and around 0900hrs two exits were open for business. Tanks moved inland through the streets of Courseulles helping the Regina Rifles to clear the town.

Landing 15 minutes after the assault wave, the two follow-up companies of the Regina Rifles came ashore. C Company quickly moved off the beach and began clearing its assigned area of the town. Courseulles itself had been divided into 12 numbered blocks, with each company designated to clear certain squares. Prior to the invasion, the battalion had spent several months perfecting its street-fighting techniques. Unique among all the

By the late afternoon Courseulles was finally cleared of the enemy and Canadian armor began moving inland to support the drive on Caen. *(Imperial War Museum)*

assaulting infantry who landed on D-Day, the Regina Rifles faced the formidable task of making an assault landing and then clearing the streets of an enemy-held town.

The landing craft bringing D Company in had the misfortune of running into a number of obstacles close to shore. Many of the light vessels hit mines or struck underwater obstructions. Explosions blew some craft out of the water and others were ripped apart by steel hedgehogs. By the time the company was ashore and at its rendezvous point, only 49 men of the unit were available to execute its mission.

The capture of Courseulles involved a bitter and prolonged struggle. Each house had to be individually assaulted and cleared of the enemy. Snipers were everywhere, slowing the Canadian advance and picking off the unwary. At the top of the town, just behind the château, was German strongpoint WN30, which looked down on the streets and houses of Courseulles. The position contained machine-guns and mortars and guarded the route inland along the road toward Reviers. By mid-morning many tanks were in the streets helping the infantry break up and crush enemy resistance. The entire battalion was now involved in the street fighting and the sheer numbers and weight of firepower grinding inexorably through the town began to tell. By midday Mike and Nan sectors had linked up and formed a continuous front along the northern part of the town, all the houses were eventually cleared, and strongpoint WN30 was outflanked and taken. By the early afternoon, troops and tanks were clear of the built-up area and were pushing south toward Reviers.

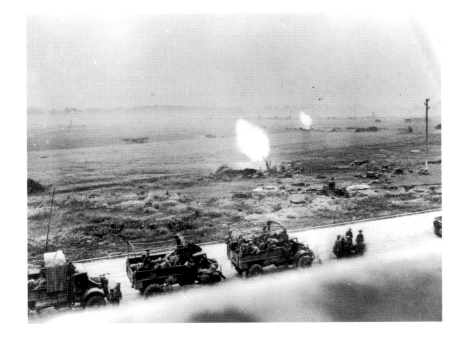

Canadian troops move inland past a battery of 5.5in medium guns firing in support of the advance. *(Imperial War Museum, MH3093)*

The Canadian 7th Brigade's follow-up battalion was the Canadian Scottish Regiment and it landed over Mike Beach at around 0830hrs. Some resistance was encountered during the run-in and the leading troops suffered mortar fire on the beach. The brigade was delayed while an exit was cleared through a minefield, but by 0930hrs the Canadian Scottish was moving out across open fields. C Company had already landed with the Winnipegs in the assault wave and was by then on its way toward St-Croix-sur-Mer. The rest of the battalion now moved up behind its advance company and closed on the village, picking up C Company on the way. German machine-guns in field emplacements caused casualties throughout the march. St Croix was reached and cleared of isolated snipers and then the advance continued. A short distance further on, the battalion passed through the Winnipeg Rifles in Colombiers and reached Pierrepont late in the afternoon. The battalion could have pressed on, but were ordered simply to hold in place, pushing ahead with nothing larger than patrols.

CANADIAN 8TH BRIGADE'S LANDINGS

The 8th Brigade carried out the left-hand landings of the Canadian 3rd Division, assaulting on a two-battalion front between Bernières and St Aubin. The DD tanks of the Canadian 10th Armoured Regiment (Fort Garry Horse) together with A Squadron, Westminster Dragoons, and the 80th Assault Squadron RE, from the British 79th Armoured Division, provided armored support.

The Queen's Own Rifles of Canada landed on Nan White sector at 0755hrs. Once again, as on Mike Red and Nan Green, the DD tanks were late arriving. They were launched much closer to shore than elsewhere and more or less waded to the beach, arriving just after the leading waves of infantry had disembarked from their landing craft. Two companies of the Queen's Own led the assault. Both had a difficult time during the first 15 minutes ashore. B Company suffered on the beach from the attentions of the enemy strongpoint in front of Bernières. A Company succeeded in crossing the beach only to encounter difficulties crossing the open fields behind.

B Company landed 200 yards to the east of its planned position, directly in front of WN28. As the troops left their landing craft, they faced 200 yards of open beach, their route inland blocked by a high seawall, and a cluster of concrete pillboxes staring down at them. As the troops began to scatter and make for the shelter of the seawall, the enemy's machine-guns and mortars opened fire in earnest. Within the first few minutes the company had taken 65 casualties. Its best hope was to cover the loose sandy ground as quickly as possible and get to grips with the enemy. Those who stumbled, fell, or hesitated were lost, for the German defenders swept the beach with fire and homed in on any static target. Once under cover of the wall, the Canadians could close on the pillboxes, keeping low to avoid the mutually supporting fire from the other enemy emplacements. The concrete structures were attacked with grenades and Sten guns. With the first pillbox overcome, the men of the Queen's Own moved on to silence the other emplacements in the strongpoint one by one from close range. Behind them the beach was littered with the bodies of those who did not make it.

On the right, A Company stormed ashore and its men made the same mad dash across the beach to the cover of the seawall. The same machine-gun and mortar fire picked many of them off as they ran, but the intensity of it was much less as the enemy in the strongpoint concentrated most of their fire on the troops of B Company who were rushing straight at them. Most of A Company got off the beach over the seawall and into the fields behind. It had been a hard race as each man sought his own route to safety, but there was little security to be found on the open ground behind the beach. It was there that their worst troubles began: the area was covered in mines and being sprayed with machine-gun fire. Mortars had the eastern approach to Bernières covered and each time the troops attempted to regroup or push forward, they were forced to ground by concentrated fire or suffered casualties from the mines. Units became disorganized and individuals found it difficult to link up with their sections. This first 15 minutes of action had cost A Company 50 percent casualties.

Things improved a little when the tanks came ashore, for they quickly helped B Company mop up the strongpoint and allowed the infantry to push into Bernières. This in turn eased the pressure on A Company and its men gradually worked across the open ground and entered the western part of the village. Then the follow-up companies landed. D Company lost a few of their landing craft to mines during the run-in, but had an easier time getting off the beach. C Company came ashore to sporadic small-arms fire and made

Canadian troops from the 9th Brigade land on Nan White Beach to the west of Bernières. This part of the beach was the site of the assault landings made by A Company of the Queen's Own Rifles of Canada three hours previously. *(Imperial War Museum, A23939)*

swift progress into Bernières. As more and more Canadians pushed into the village, the pressure on the German defenders increased, allowing the Allied troops to press ahead and clear the southern edge of the village.

By the time the specialized armor of the 79th Division arrived, the beaches were clear of all but long-range enemy fire. The first Crab ashore flailed a path up to the seawall and an AVRE following behind quickly laid a bridge across it. Another AVRE started to cross, but promptly hit a mine and blocked the exit. An armored bulldozer was called forward to push the broken tank aside. A few moments later the bulldozer hit a mine and its driver was killed. Another exit was made over a damaged part of the seawall and flail tanks created a lane linking the two exits. The Crabs then cleared the fields behind the beach of mines, allowing troops and vehicles to move off the shoreline and inland. Two more exits were created later to the east of Bernières.

Le Régiment de la Chaudière, the brigade's reserve battalion, began to land at around 0830hrs. It came ashore directly in front of Bernières and was pinned down by the seawall for some time while the assault companies cleared the strongpoint. About two hours later it was in its assembly area to the south of the village waiting for orders to advance. In fact, it waited there until after midday before it started to attack toward Bény-sur-Mer supported by the tanks of the Fort Garry Horse, and it was not until mid-afternoon that this, the first of 8th Brigade's inland objectives, was taken.

Next ashore were the self-propelled field guns of the division. The 14th and 19th Field Regiments, Royal Canadian Artillery (RCA), arrived between 0910 and 0930hrs and were ready and in action on the outskirts of Bernières at 1030hrs. By this time the incoming tide was eating up the available beach and access to the exits was limited. Incoming landing craft brought their loads into a crowded and chaotic mêlée of troops, tanks, and vehicles. Every tank, jeep, carrier, and gun had to use the bridges over the seawall and their passage was very slow and ponderous. Once off the beach they entered the narrow streets of Bernières and jammed the place solid. Movement inland was delayed. Matters were made even worse a little later at 1050hrs, when Nan White Beach was also made available to the reserve brigade. The Canadian 9th Brigade now joined in the crush and virtually choked the area with traffic for several hours. Just when speed and movement were most vital to seize the division's D-Day objectives, the spearhead earmarked for the great advance was trying to extricate itself from an immense traffic jam along the seafront.

The Canadian 8th Brigade's other assault battalion landed on Nan Red at 0800hrs. The North Shore (New Brunswick) Regiment attacked with A Company on the right and B Company on the left, just to the west of St Aubin. German strongpoint WN27 in the seaside village swept the beach with fire from a casemated 50mm gun mounted on the top of the seawall

and from machine-guns and mortars in positions along the edge of the beach. Several seaside villas had been fortified and turned into strongpoints. As in Bernières, the beach was lined with a high seawall, with few natural breaks. This formed the first barrier to the troops as they stormed ashore.

A Company made its landing against relatively light opposition. The troops dashed through small-arms fire to the seawall and dispersed inland to clear the way to the lateral road running east–west behind the beach. B Company's first task was to deal with WN27. Its landing craft beached as planned and then the infantry swung eastwards to attack the strongpoint. The naval bombardment failed to silence the fortified position and its guns did great damage on the beach. The first two DD tanks to land were immediately knocked out, followed by two AVREs when they came ashore. It took almost the whole of the morning for B Company to silence the post. It was later helped in its task by the guns of two DD tanks and an AVRE. The Royal Engineers' AVRE used its petard to hurl great explosive charges at the strongpoint and blasted the infantry inside. At 1115hrs, strongpoint WN27 was finally silenced.

Canadian infantry of the 8th Brigade working their way forward in St Aubin. The troops are approaching the seafront to the south of strongpoint WN27. The piles of logs and steel girders in the road are part of the roadblock protecting the approaches to the strongpoint. Bombing and shellfire has created a complete tangle of rubble and debris through which the Canadians must attack. (Imperial War Museum, B5228)

321

Fritz Witt and Kurt "Panzer" Meyer leaving Ardenne Abbey, June 8, 1944

Gruppenführer Fritz Witt, commander of the 12th SS-Panzer Division "Hitlerjugend," leaves the northern entrance of the HQ of 25th SS-Panzergrenadier Regiment in a motorcycle combination driven by the regimental commander Kurt "Panzer" Meyer. Both of these men were highly decorated veterans of many campaigns. They were young, unconventional officers who liked to keep in close contact with their troops in the line. In this scene Meyer is personally taking his divisional commander forward to consult with his battalion commanders prior to launching his attack against the Canadians at Bretteville L'Orgeilleuse. Witt had joined the SS in 1931, choosing a career aligned to the ruling Nazi Party. In 1933 he was among the first 120 men who volunteered to join the elite "Leibstandarte SS Adolf Hitler" (LSSAH) bodyguard formation. Witt commanded a company during the Polish campaign and later fought in France and Holland. In 1941 he campaigned in Yugoslavia, Greece, and Russia with the LSSAH Division, rising to command its 1st SS-Panzergrenadier Regiment in 1942. In early 1943, Witt was given the honor of raising the 12th SS-Panzer Division "Hitlerjugend." At the age of just 35 years he became the second-youngest divisional commander in the German armed forces. Witt was killed by Allied naval shellfire at his HQ at Venoix on June 14, 1944. Kurt "Panzer" Meyer was also a veteran of the LSSAH Division and like Witt had been awarded both classes of the Iron Cross and the Knight's Cross with Oak Leaves. In 1943 he was transferred from LSSAH Division to lead the 25th SS-Panzergrenadier Regiment in Witt's division. On Witt's death Meyer took command of the "Hitlerjugend" Division and fought with it until he was captured during the collapse of the German Seventh Army in August 1944. He was then the youngest divisional commander in the German Army. Meyer's headquarters were located in Ardenne Abbey, a large walled enclosure housing a medieval church and a range of domestic buildings. The site covered several acres and provided cover for hundreds of troops with their vehicles. Advance elements of Meyer's regiment had arrived at the abbey late on June 6 and were ready to attack the Canadians the next day. Meyer was confident that he could throw the "little fish" back into the sea, but his first contact with the Allies on June 7, just a few hundred yards from the abbey grounds, resulted in a very sharp repulse. The counterattack made by Meyer's 25th SS-Panzergrenadier Regiment met the Canadian 3rd Division's advance head-on and Meyer watched the encounter from the tower of the abbey church. In the stiff fighting that followed neither side was able to seize the initiative. During June, while his regiment was based in Ardenne Abbey, Meyer tacitly allowed his men to execute a total of 27 Canadian prisoners of war in cold blood in the small garden behind the courtyard. After the war he was prosecuted for this crime and sentenced to death. This was commuted to life imprisonment on appeal. He was released in September 1954 and died in 1961 at the age of 51. *(Kevin Lyles © Osprey Publishing Ltd)*

By the time these commandos from the HQ of the 4th Special Service Brigade arrived, the worst of the enemy fire that had been raking the beach had subsided. They landed on Nan Red sector behind 48 Royal Marine Commando, but suffered few casualties. *(Imperial War Museum, B5218)*

When C and D Companies came ashore they had a reasonably clear run. D Company cleared the southern part of St Aubin, while C Company set out for the village of Tailleville, 2 miles away. Its advance was relatively free of enemy opposition until it neared the village. Here enemy troops were well dug in and they fought with the tenacity of seasoned campaigners. Even when C Company was later joined by other infantry, Tailleville remained an awkward proposition and it was not until late afternoon that it was finally cleared with the help of tanks.

Behind the North Shore Regiment, landing over Nan Red from the six Landing Craft Infantry (Small) in which they had crossed the Channel from the River Hamble in England, were the men of 48 Royal Marine Commando. The commandos suffered badly during the landing: two of the craft struck mines and were destroyed. Loss of life was considerable. Things got even worse when they discovered the Canadians had not subdued their section of Nan Red. Snipers and small-arms fire picked off the marines as they tried to get inland and they were pinned behind the shelter of the seawall while the situation stabilized.

Eventually the commandos extricated themselves from the debacle on the beach and set off to the east on their twin missions. Lieutenant-Colonel Moulton's marines were first to capture strongpoint WN26 at Langrune and then make contact with 41 Royal Marine Commando coming from Sword Beach to link the two landings made by British I Corps. They achieved neither that day. Langrune proved to be a very difficult proposition for the lightly armed marines. It consisted of a street of fortified houses along the sea front, all connected by internal passageways and by an external trench system. The two side roads at either end were blocked by 6ft-high, solid concrete walls. On the seaward side, jutting out from the promenade were two concrete emplacements housing a 75mm gun and a 50mm antitank gun. Machine-guns covered every approach and a minefield protected the inland flank; WN26 was a veritable fortress. Despite their best efforts, Moulton's men were unable to get to grips with the strongpoint. Tanks proved to be of little help, for the first of the two Royal Marine Centaurs that came to their assistance was knocked out by mines and the second could make little impact on the solid concrete barriers with its gun. Warships out at sea had also done little damage to the position during their prolonged bombardment. The Germans in WN26 were content to sit tight and let the shells bounce off their impregnable shelters. By the end of the day, 48 Royal Marine Commando had suffered over 50 percent casualties and had achieved very little. It also failed to achieve its other objective, as when its advance guard reached its rendezvous with 41 Commando, there was no one to be seen; 41 Commando had suffered heavily since landing on Sword Beach and could not advance to close the gap.

GERMAN REACTION TO THE LANDINGS ON JUNO BEACH

The arrival of the Canadians on Juno Beach added to the worries plaguing the commander of the German 716th Division, Generalleutnant Richter. Since the early hours his men had been forced to contend with the parachute landings made by the British 6th Airborne Division east of the River Orne. Then, at 0730hrs, the British 3rd Division had landed on Sword Beach near Ouistreham. At 0745hrs British 50th Division arrived on Gold Beach and now, at 0800hrs, the Canadians had come ashore on Juno. The realization that four Allied divisions had descended on his sector made Richter's position seem hopeless. And it was, for there were no immediate reserves to hand to bolster his unit or plug any breaks in the line. Once the division's outer defensive crust had been penetrated along the coastline, there was little strength in depth with which to avert a complete rout.

Panzergrenadier units of Feuchtinger's 21st Panzer Division had been in action against the paratroopers since before daylight. The airborne landings had descended on top of them and they had no choice but to fight. Later in the morning permission was given for the division to attack the seaborne landings. The delay was caused by indecision at army level whether or not the landings were indeed the invasion proper or just some feint to draw

Situation at Midnight, June 6

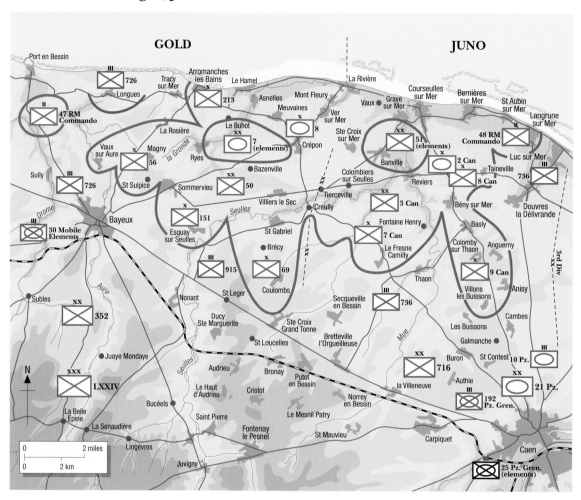

troops away from more landings elsewhere. It was not until mid-afternoon that a sufficiently clear picture of Allied intentions was formed. General Marcks, commander LXXXIV Corps, realized that the gap between the British landings near Ouistreham (Sword Beach) and the Canadians at Courseulles (Juno Beach) offered the best prospects for a successful counterattack. If Feuchtinger could get his tanks down to the sea between Lion- and Luc-sur-Mer he would split the landings and could then roll up the invasion beaches on either side.

At around 1600hrs the 21st Panzer Division attacked. It was only able to launch its thrust to the sea with part of its strength, for some of its units were still involved in countering the paratroopers and could not be disengaged. The strike force consisted of the two tank battalions of 100th Panzer Regiment and I Battalion of the 192nd Panzergrenadier Regiment. No sooner had the

Panzers begun their advance than they ran into trouble. The advance units of the British 3rd Division met them head-on and did great damage with their antitank guns and 17-pdr Sherman Fireflies. Feuchtinger's tanks and personnel carriers were battered all the way down the Périers Ridge to the sea. Some isolated parties of Panzergrenadiers actually made it to the coast, but were soon recalled to help deal with the arrival of a new wave of gliderborne Allied infantry. Some were unable to get back to their lines and diverted to the fortified radar station at Douvres in front of the Canadians and bolstered the garrison there for the night. In fact, on June 7 the Canadians surrounded the radar station and the Panzergrenadiers remained there until the strongpoint was taken several days later.

By the evening of D-Day German reaction to the landings had been minimal. The attack by 21st Panzer Division had come to nothing, immediate reserves to counterattack the beachhead were almost non-existent, and German High Command had released the Panzer forces far too late for them to be effective. Rommel knew that the great opportunity to crush the Allied landings on the beaches had been lost.

CONCLUSION *with Stephen Badsey*

By the end of June 6, the Allied Supreme Commander, General Eisenhower, and the Commander 21st Army Group, General Montgomery, could feel very satisfied with the results of the first day of the invasion. Although none of the major inland objectives had been taken – Caen and Bayeux remained in enemy hands – and all forces were still short of their proposed phase lines, the beachhead was in place, there had not been the bloodbath that had been predicted in some quarters, and men and matériel were pouring across the beaches in ever-increasing quantities. The landings were by no means secure, but what the day before had seemed a great gamble now looked achievable. Everything would now depend on the battle of the build-up. Eisenhower would have to assemble his forces at a faster rate than the enemy could bring his forward and Montgomery would have to steel his commanders to be ready for the German armored counterattack when it came.

On Gold Beach, the British 50th Division had stopped for the night short of its objectives. The encounter with Kampfgruppe Meyer had caused its brigades some consternation and the decision was taken to dig in and gather strength. The German 352nd Division had committed its only reserve and the 50th Division had taken this as a show of strength. On June 7, the division continued its advance, comforted by the news that the 7th Armoured Division was landing behind it. Resistance was sporadic, but dogged. What the enemy 352nd Division lacked in numbers was made up for in determination. The remnants of the 441st Ost Battalion and 726th Regiment were grouped in defensive outposts and resisted for as long as possible before retiring, but their interpretation of "as long as possible" was often a very brief period indeed.

The 69th Brigade advanced across the Bayeux–Caen road at St Léger keeping pace with the Canadians on their left flank. The 8th Armoured Brigade moved through the 69th Brigade to exploit southwards through Audrieu and captured the high ground above Tilly, 10 miles south of Bayeux, the next day. Enemy Panzer units countered this movement and the advance to the south was brought to a dramatic halt. On the right, the

A gaggle of young German prisoners performs a double-take as their famous adversary, General Montgomery, passes in a jeep. For the early stages of the Allied invasion, from June 6 to August 1, Montgomery commanded all land forces. *(Imperial War Museum, B5179)*

56th Brigade took Bayeux and the 151st Brigade took the high ground between the Seulles and Aure rivers. Nearer the coast 231st Brigade pushed westwards and captured the German battery at Longues. Two miles further west, 47 Royal Marine Commando captured Port-en-Bessin after a stiff fight and then met up with the Americans, forming a continuous Allied beachhead from the River Vire to the east of the River Orne.

On Juno Beach, the Canadians had advanced just over halfway toward their objectives on D-Day. The Canadian 3rd Division had planned to get to the Caen–Bayeux railway line and capture the airfield at Carpiquet, but had only reached the line Creully–Villons les Buissons by nightfall and had dug in. Not surprisingly, the attack by 21st Panzer Division that swept down its left flank during the evening had caused some alarm, but by then the movement inland was becoming overstretched because of the late start by the Canadian 9th Brigade.

On June 7 the advance continued and almost immediately ran into trouble. The 9th Brigade, led by the Canadian 27th Armoured Regiment and the North Nova Scotia Highlanders, moved southwards down the road from Villons les Buissons to Authie, on its way to Carpiquet. At Authie it came under prolonged and accurate artillery fire and halted, only to be met immediately by even fiercer resistance when it was attacked by the 12th SS-Panzer Division "Hitlerjugend." The division had finally been released by German High Command and sent forward against the invasion. Progress from its holding area around Évreux had been slow and only its 25th SS-Panzergrenadier Regiment had arrived near Caen in time to launch the counterattack alongside 21st Panzer Division. But the advance by the Canadian 3rd Division and the

A wounded Panzergrenadier from 12th SS-Panzer Division "Hitlerjugend" resting outside the northern entrance to Ardenne Abbey. The attacks against the Allied landings were the division's first taste of battle. Raised in 1943, the division was a mixture of seasoned veterans from other SS armored divisions and members of the Hitler Youth. The average age of its troops was just 18 years. *(Bundesarchiv, 146/84/11/15a)*

British 3rd Division caught these Panzer units off balance as they prepared to launch their own counterattack. A very stiff battle ensued that resulted in stalemate. The Allies were stopped dead, unable to close on Caen and the Panzer force's attack was blunted and the last chance of actually pushing the Allies back into the sea was lost.

Over the next few days both sides clashed all along the front, each hoping to hold the other while they gathered sufficient strength to give them a decisive advantage. Each day, and more especially each night, over roads swept by Allied fighter-bombers, the Germans brought new units forward in a vain attempt to concentrate for their big push. And each day these new units were thrown into the line to help plug some gap that the Allies had opened up. For Montgomery the goal of seizing Caen dominated his thinking. The capture of the town, with its network of roads, was a prerequisite to launching his main drive to the south. Rommel realized this and concentrated the bulk of his armor in defense of the town.

The British XXX Corps gradually built up strength and pushed forward south of Bayeux. The 50th Division, together with 7th Armoured Division, advanced toward Tilly. Here they met the Panzer Lehr Division and the move southward stopped. The close Normandy countryside, the *bocage*, turned the Allied advance into a nightmare. The small fields, high hedges, and sunken lanes that criss-crossed the area were ideal for waging a defensive war. It was an infantryman's battle. Tanks were of limited use in the close terrain and horribly vulnerable to German antitank guns or tank-hunting teams with Panzerfaust antitank weapons. It took just a few well-sited antitank guns to hold up an entire armored battalion. It is thus hardly surprising that the advance through the *bocage* slowed almost to a standstill and casualties began to mount alarmingly.

Behind the advancing troops, the priority at Gold and Juno Beaches became the landing of stores, reinforcements and supplies of every description. The Royal Navy had secured the seaways and great convoys of ships arrived unmolested to discharge prodigious amounts of matériel over the open beaches. New roads were built, fuel dumps established, and assembly areas carved out. Then came the air forces. Airfields were bulldozed through open fields and steel matting laid for runways. With little more than a tent from which to control operations and a fuel truck, these airfields were operational within days of the landings. The RAF no longer had to make a cross-Channel flight to reach the battlefield and could now have rocket-firing Typhoons and Spitfires patrolling the air above Normandy throughout the hours of daylight.

Cherbourg and Le Havre were the great ports of Normandy and the German High Command knew that the Allies would soon need a large harbor through which to land their supplies. They therefore fought tenaciously to prevent any advance toward these towns. The Allies had realized this well before the invasion and had decided that they would bring their own ports over to Normandy with them. Two artificial harbors, one off Omaha Beach and one centered on the town of Arromanches, were transported piecemeal over the Channel and then erected *in situ*. These British-designed and built harbors, codenamed "Mulberry," were each intended to have a capacity of over 7,000 tons of stores a day. Each harbor enclosed an area of 2 square miles. Outer floating breakwaters sheltered an inner fixed breakwater made of huge concrete caissons five storeys high and of 6,000 tons displacement. These were towed into position and then sunk into place. The whole harbor was a prodigious feat of engineering. It had 4 miles of piers, 6 miles of floating roadways, and 15 pier heads linked to the shore. The first components of the Mulberries were taken across to Normandy on June 7 and by June 18 both artificial ports were in use. The American port off Omaha was destroyed in a gale between June 19 and 21, but the British Mulberry at Arromanches, although damaged in the same gale, remained in use for the next ten months, by which time it had landed 2,500,000 men, 500,000 vehicles and 4,000,000 tons of supplies.

While the Canadians concentrated on defending their line against enemy Panzer forces, a few miles behind them one German garrison still stubbornly held out in the face of hopeless odds. The fortress of steel, concrete, and wire which made up the defenses of the Douvres radar station contained a motley collection of troops from the Luftwaffe, the 716th Division, and the 192nd Panzergrenadiers, and they were determined not to surrender. When the Canadians came ashore over

Four days after the landings, members of a tank crew from C Squadron of the 13th/18th Hussars sit beside their Sherman and write letters home or just take the opportunity to catch up on some sleep. The squadron had been in action with the airborne division near the Bénouville bridges, helping to deal with counterattacks by the 125th Panzergrenadier Regiment. *(Imperial War Museum, B5425)*

Juno Beach on D-Day, the radar station was too strongly defended to be taken by the assault troops available. With the urgent need to capture Caen uppermost in their thoughts, the Canadians bypassed the strongpoint and left it for the follow-up troops to deal with. Its garrison was contained by aggressive patrols and was watched by the tanks of the 80th Assault Squadron from the 79th Armoured Division, while a plan was formulated for its capture. Several units kept watch on the site over the next week: the Canadians on D-Day, 48 Royal Marine Commando afterwards, 5th Black Watch from the 51st Highland Division when they came ashore and then, finally, 41 Royal Marine Commando.

On June 17 the radar station was attacked. The plan was for several feints to be made toward the strongpoint from the south and west by the 77th Assault Squadron RE, while four assault teams, each comprising two Crabs and one troop of AVREs from the 22nd Dragoons and 26th Assault Regiment RE, attacked from the north. Other Crabs would give covering fire from the nearby woods. Once the Allied troops broke into the strongpoint, 41 Royal Marine Commando would mop up the various emplacements.

After an initial bombardment by heavy artillery, the tanks rumbled forwards in the late afternoon. The Crabs flailed paths through the minefields, the AVRE crews shelled shelters and concrete emplacements, and 70lb "Beehive" charges were placed against underground entrances. Several tanks were lost to mines and some to antitank guns, but the determined crews in the others pressed on among the bunkers, silencing each of them in turn. The explosions inside

The landing beach on Gold is now given over to the arrival of stores and reinforcements. It came as some surprise to the naval planners how easy it was to beach fairly large ships for unloading on the sandy seabed and then refloat them without damage on the next high tide. Millions of tons of supplies were landed in this way over the following months. (Imperial War Museum, A24012)

Floating roadway leading from the Mulberry harbor to Arromanches. Two of these artificial harbors were built and both were hit by a great storm, which began on June 19 and blew for three days. The American Mulberry off Omaha was completely destroyed and abandoned, but this one at Arromanches, although badly damaged, was repaired and continued in service for ten months. *(Imperial War Museum, A24360)*

the concrete tombs were colossal and the noise reverberated around the underground passageways, striking fear into the defenders. When the commandos entered the underground corridors and began spraying Bren gun fire along the walls, the garrison knew that the end had come. Two hundred defenders surrendered and marched out into captivity.

By the end of D-Day, the US Army had a firm toehold on Omaha Beach, clinging to a ragged line about a mile inland from the beach. This fell far short of the plan but was, in view of the serious underestimation of German strength, a significant accomplishment. A total of about 34,200 troops landed at Omaha Beach on D-Day. In spite of the large numbers of troops landed much of this force was still congregated on or near the beach at the end of the day. The assault forces south of the beach were too scattered, disconnected and weak to make a push forward until the next day. The senior US commanders had not expected the landings at Omaha Beach to be difficult. The decisive action would come when the Germans launched a violent counterattack within a day or two of the landings. In the event, the landings proved to be more costly than expected, but the German counterattack never materialized.

Precise US casualties for D-Day will never be accurately determined. V Corps history places the total at 1,190 for the 1st Infantry Division, 743 for the 29th Division, and 441 for V Corps troops for a total of 2,374. Of these, 694 were killed, 331 missing, and 1,349 wounded. No breakdown is available by rank, but from written reports the casualties among the combat leaders – the young majors, captains, lieutenants, and sergeants – had been disproportionately high. The 1st Division later reduced their casualty figures as the missing were gradually located, and a total of about 2,000 army casualties is the generally accepted figure for Omaha Beach on

D-Day. This exceeded the casualties of all the other beaches combined. There has been a tendency to exaggerate these losses in recent years, especially in view of the difficulty of the assignment. As dreadful as they were it should be remembered that the US Army suffered an average of 1,200 casualties a day during the fighting in Normandy in July 1944. What marked out Omaha Beach from later Normandy fighting was the high level of losses among the first assault waves in such a short period of time. Yet the bloodletting should not obscure the fact that Hitler's vaunted Atlantic Wall had withstood the Allied onslaught for less than a day. The sacrifice at Omaha was the foundation for the forthcoming liberation of France.

The reasons for the high casualties are not difficult to identify. Omaha Beach was more heavily defended than any other beach and its high bluffs posed a much more substantial defensive obstacle than the relatively flat beaches elsewhere. A classified wartime British study noted that the three beaches in the British/Canadian sector were defended by an average of nine antitank guns per beach compared to 30 antitank and field guns at Omaha, four mortars per beach compared to six at Omaha, and 21 machine-guns compared to 85 at Omaha. In addition, Omaha was subjected to fire from two artillery battalions, compared to a battalion or less at most of the other beaches. Finally, the preparatory bombardment of Omaha Beach was shorter than those at the neighboring British/Canadian beaches, in some cases by as much as an hour, as the Omaha landing took place earlier due to tidal variations.

Although the initial bomber attack on Omaha Beach had been a failure, the activity of the Allied air forces over Normandy on D-Day had been extremely effective. The most important consequence of Allied air superiority

A grim reminder of the enormous human toll at Omaha Beach became evident when the tide again receded in the early afternoon. More than a third of the 1,450 men in the first assault wave were casualties. *(NARA)*

over the beach was that it gave free rein to Allied bombers and fighter-bombers to isolate German reserves from the beachhead. Movement by any type of motorized transport became difficult or impossible. The US Eighth Air Force conducted 1,729 heavy bomber missions on D-Day and IX Bomber Command added a further 823 medium bomber attacks for a combined total of 5,037 tons of bombs delivered. The Eighth Air Force conducted 1,880 fighter sorties on D-Day and the Ninth Air Force a further 2,065 fighter-bomber missions.

The performance of the US Navy at Omaha Beach had been exemplary. The US Navy, US Coast Guard, and Royal Navy crews of the landing craft had contended with fearsome difficulties through the day and had landed the force in the face of intense fire. When the landings appeared to falter, the young destroyer skippers skillfully maneuvered in shallow water to bring their vital firepower to bear on the German fortifications. These actions helped turn the tide of the D-Day fighting and Omaha Beach was a combined-arms battle in the fullest sense of the term.

The German perspective at the end of D-Day was far more pessimistic than in the afternoon, when it appeared that the invasion had been thwarted on Omaha. General Kraiss retained little hope of stemming the Allied forces unless substantial reinforcements arrived. Casualties on D-Day had not been particularly high compared with US losses – about 1,000 men. But his artillery was out of ammunition, his units were thinly spread, and no units remained in reserve. He was primarily concerned about the breakthrough by British armor at Gold Beach next to Omaha. The counterattack by Kampfgruppe Meyer near Bazenville during the afternoon and evening of D-Day had been decisively smashed by the British. Oberstleutnant Meyer had been killed and his three battalions reduced to fewer than 100 effectives. This destruction

A Hawker Typhoon operating from a Normandy airstrip. The total Allied domination of the skies over France created immense difficulties for the Germans in their attempts to reinforce their forces in Normandy and enabled the Allies to win the race to build up forces. *(Imperial War Museum CL472)*

consumed the LXXXIV Corps reserve except for the 30th Mobile Brigade, which was being fed in piecemeal to cover gaps in the line. Kraiss did not have a firm idea of the status of Omaha Beach, since communication had been lost with most of the forward strongpoints, and his forces along the coastal highway received contradictory stories from the stragglers retreating back from the beachhead strongpoints. Nevertheless, his defensive line opposite Omaha Beach appeared to be holding, which was far better than could be said for the situation on either side of Omaha Beach. The following day, he sent his operations officer to the surviving WN76 strongpoint on Pointe-et-Raz-de-la-Percée. The trip took five hours instead the usual 30 minutes due to Allied aircraft. Oberstleutnant Fritz Ziegelmann later wrote: "The view from WN76 will remain in my memory forever. The sea was like a picture from the Kiel review of the German fleet. Ships of all sorts nestled close together on the beach, and echeloned at sea in depth. And the entire concentration remained there intact without any real interference from the German side! I clearly understood the mood of the German soldier who was pleading for the Luftwaffe. That the German soldiers fought here hard and stubbornly is, and remains, a wonder."

The Luftwaffe, battered by months of Allied air action, played practically no role in the fighting. The commander of Luftflotte 3, Generalfeldmarschall Hugo Sperrle, did not authorize the "Impending Danger West" signal until mid-morning on June 6, 1944, even though his reconnaissance aircraft had spotted the Allied fleets before dawn. As a result, the many fighter units that had been moved inland to avoid Allied fighter sweeps did not return to the forward fields near the Channel until the evening of D-Day. The only Luftwaffe aircraft over the beaches on D-Day were a pair of Fw-190s from I./Jagdgeschwader 26 led by the squadron commander, Oberstleutnant Josef "Pips" Priller, which took off from Lille around 0800hrs and made a fast pass over the Normandy beaches before landing, out of fuel, at Creil. The units near the coast were able to launch only about 100 daylight sorties on D-Day, of which 70 had been by fighters. The Luftwaffe fighters claimed 24 Allied aircraft, but lost 16 fighters in the process. One attempted raid on the beaches by a dozen Junkers Ju-88 bombers led to the entire force being shot down. The Luftwaffe attempted to redeem itself with a concerted night attack by the bombers and torpedo-bombers of Fliegerkorps IX, but few of the 175 sorties managed to reach the Allied fleets due to Allied night-fighters and antiaircraft fire. The Kriegsmarine had even less effect on the landings and its warships and coastal artillery played no role whatsoever at Omaha Beach.

The reaction by higher German commands on D-Day was tentative and indecisive. There was the belief through most of the day that the Normandy landings were a diversion, and not the main invasion. Hitler was reluctant to commit the Panzer reserves and insisted that the landings be crushed with local resources. This indecision would linger through much of June. Rommel

began moving the Panzer divisions under his control against the Allied beaches, but none of this force was directed against Omaha Beach. Nor did the Panzers have a decisive impact once deployed over the next few days. Not only was it difficult to move the Panzer divisions forward due to air attack, but the area of coastal farmland behind the beaches, the *bocage*, was broken up by thick hedges and constricted by a poor road network that made maneuver impossible.

The US V Corps gradually expanded the Omaha beachhead, finally reaching the River Aure and the D-Day objectives two days late. The 352nd Infantry Division continued to offer stiff resistance but the advantage was clearly shifting to the growing American forces. On June 9, V Corps launched its first offensive out of the beachhead, a three-division attack that pushed 12 miles inland and seized the dominating terrain at the Cerisy forest. On June 12 the attack was resumed and the Utah and Omaha beachheads joined by seizing Carentan. By June 13 V Corps had pushed 20 miles beyond the beachhead, linking with both Utah and Gold beaches on either flank. In the neighboring Utah Beach sector, Collins' VII Corps faced far less formidable defenses and reached the seaport of Cherbourg on June 20. But the Germans had demolished the harbor facilities, rendering it a hollow victory.

Flying control at an RAF airstrip in Normandy. Work building these landing grounds began immediately after the initial assaults. Within days of the landings, RAF servicing commandos and engineers moved onto a suitable site, bulldozed a primitive landing strip, laid down a steel mesh covering for a runway, and opened for business. Amenities were sparse: tented accommodation for the aircrews, road tankers as bunkering facilities, and packing cases for a control tower. *(Imperial War Museum, CL162)*

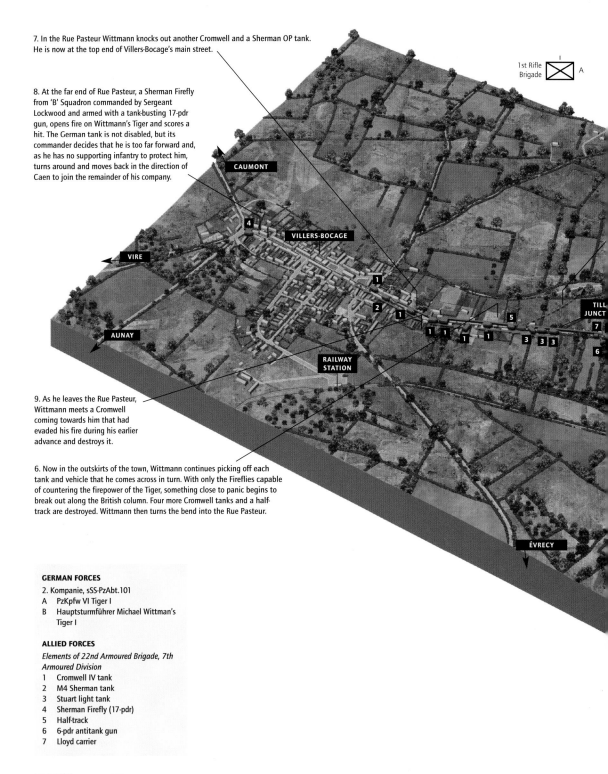

7. In the Rue Pasteur Wittmann knocks out another Cromwell and a Sherman OP tank. He is now at the top end of Villers-Bocage's main street.

8. At the far end of Rue Pasteur, a Sherman Firefly from 'B' Squadron commanded by Sergeant Lockwood and armed with a tank-busting 17-pdr gun, opens fire on Wittmann's Tiger and scores a hit. The German tank is not disabled, but its commander decides that he is too far forward and, as he has no supporting infantry to protect him, turns around and moves back in the direction of Caen to join the remainder of his company.

9. As he leaves the Rue Pasteur, Wittmann meets a Cromwell coming towards him that had evaded his fire during his earlier advance and destroys it.

6. Now in the outskirts of the town, Wittmann continues picking off each tank and vehicle that he comes across in turn. With only the Fireflies capable of countering the firepower of the Tiger, something close to panic begins to break out along the British column. Four more Cromwell tanks and a half-track are destroyed. Wittmann then turns the bend into the Rue Pasteur.

1st Rifle Brigade A

CAUMONT

VILLERS-BOCAGE

VIRE

AUNAY

RAILWAY STATION

TILL JUNCT

ÉVRECY

GERMAN FORCES

2. Kompanie, sSS-PzAbt.101

A   PzKpfw VI Tiger I
B   Hauptsturmführer Michael Wittman's Tiger I

ALLIED FORCES

Elements of 22nd Armoured Brigade, 7th Armoured Division

1   Cromwell IV tank
2   M4 Sherman tank
3   Stuart light tank
4   Sherman Firefly (17-pdr)
5   Half-track
6   6-pdr antitank gun
7   Lloyd carrier

Villers-Bocage

June 12, 1944, 0855hrs–0910, viewed from the southeast showing 2. Kompanie, schwere SS-Panzer Abteilung 101's devastating attack on the leading elements of 22nd Armoured Brigade, around the small market town of Villers-Bocage.

10. Near the junction with the road to Tilly, men of the 1st Rifle Brigade have got one of their 6-pdr antitank guns working and fire a shot at Wittmann's Panzer. The shell hits the Tiger's running gear and immobilises it, forcing Wittmann and his crew to abandon the tank. They make off to the north towards the Panzer Lehr Division's positions near Orbois.

5. Wittmann's Tiger reaches the junction with the road to Tilly after devastating the line of transport vehicles backed up along the highway. His tank's high-explosive shells have smashed through eight half-tracks, four personnel carriers and two 6-pdr antitank guns. Near the junction he goes on to attack and destroy three Stuart light tanks.

1. Tanks from 'A' Squadron, 4th County of London Yeomanry, and mobile infantry from 'A' Company, 1st Rifle Brigade, advance towards Point 213 along the Villers-Bocage–Caen road.

4. Wittmann knocks out a Sherman Firefly and a Cromwell tank and then turns south, driving down the road attacking a line of infantry transport as he goes.

11. Around Point 213, the remaining Tigers from Wittmann's company deal with the tanks and men of 4th County of London Yeomanry, knocking out five Cromwells and a Sherman Firefly and capturing 30 men. 'A' Squadron has been completely wiped out.

ILLY SUR SEULLES

4th CLY A Sqn.

POINT 213

CAEN

LES HAUTS VENTS

LA CIDÉRIE

3. 0900hrs, Wittmann decides to attack and breaks cover heading for the vehicles on the main road while four other Tigers from his company attack the British around Point 213. One Tiger remains immobile with engine trouble.

sSSPzAbt 101 2

WITTMANN

2. From their camouflaged positions Hauptsturmführer Michael Wittmann and the crews of his six Tiger tanks from 2. Kompanie, schwere SS-Panzer Abteilung 101, watch the leading elements of British 22nd Armoured Brigade as they pass by barely 200m away.

N

A knocked-out Tiger tank from Hauptsturmführer Möbius's 1st Company, schwere Panzer-Abteilung 101 in Villers-Bocage. After Obersturmführer Michael Wittmann's 2nd Company had destroyed the armored column, Möbius attacked the town with four of his Tigers and some PzKpfw IVs from Panzer Lehr Division. This attack was blunted by the antitank guns of the British 22nd Armoured Brigade and many of the German tanks were knocked out. After this short battle the British withdrew from Villers-Bocage and then subjected the town to intense bombing. (Bundesarchiv, 1011/494/3376/12)

By the middle of June the lodgement was secure in every way. Enemy attacks could be broken up with the aid of naval gunfire as the front line was still within 10 miles of the beaches. Overhead the Allied air forces dominated the sky and pounced on any German troop concentrations. But on the ground things were moving much slower than was desirable. Caen was still untaken and constituted a large thorn in the side of the 21st Army Group's commander.

Unable to make a direct thrust through to Caen with I Corps, Montgomery tried to outflank the city by sweeping around from the Gold Beach sector with XXX Corps. The plan was to advance through Villers-Bocage to attack Caen from the southwest. This gamble failed when an armored column from 7th Armoured Division was destroyed by a handful of PzKpfw VI Tiger tanks commanded by the Panzer ace Michael Wittmann as it emerged from the town of Villers-Bocage. Over the next few weeks Montgomery tried with ever-larger set-piece attacks to take Caen the hard way. Operation *Epsom* attempted to put troops across the River Orne and to threaten the city from the southwest, but failed after small gains had been made at great cost. The Canadians then tried charging down the road from the north in the immediate aftermath of a massive carpet-bombing raid by RAF heavy bombers in Operation *Charnwood*. This offensive was only partly successful, with the Canadians breaking into the northern part of the city. Monty had another go at the end of July with a massive armored thrust out of the airborne bridgehead and onto the Falaise Plain in Operation *Goodwood*, but the drive came to a shuddering halt to the southeast of Caen, stopped by the German guns on the Bourguébus Ridge. By then the city was one huge pile of rubble and charred

Cromwell tank of A Squadron, 4th County of London Yeomanry, knocked out during the battle of Villers-Bocage, when an entire column from the British 7th Armoured Division was destroyed by Obersturmführer Michael Wittman's six PzKpfw VI Tigers. *(Bundesarchiv 1011/738/269/7)*

ruins, eventually taken by the Canadians at the climax of the operation. It was a hollow victory, for although Caen was taken, the roads to the south were still blocked by massed German armor.

It took several more battles and the American breakout in Operation *Cobra* before the British and Canadians moved beyond the confines of the Normandy *bocage*. At the end of August, a wide encircling movement by American mobile forces combined with a British, Canadian, and Polish drive toward Falaise to trap the German Seventh Army and annihilate it. Those German forces that escaped the collapse rapidly retreated to the Seine and beyond, the Allied armies snapping at their heels. The German rout did not stop until the Allies reached the German border in late September.

On September 1, 1944, Eisenhower took over formal command of all SHAEF ground forces in Europe from Montgomery, to the latter's intense frustration. In compensation, Churchill promoted Montgomery to field marshal, one rank higher than Eisenhower, for whom the new five-star rank of General of the Army was then quickly invented. Meanwhile, the Allied spearheads were advancing virtually unopposed toward Germany. The Third US Army liberated Châlons-sur-Marne on August 29, and on August 31 its leading tanks crossed the River Meuse at Verdun. On September 3, the Second British Army liberated Brussels, with Antwerp following a day later. Commanders talked with some optimism of ending the war in one or two months.

Eisenhower was faced at once with a difficult decision. German garrisons still held the ports of Brittany and the Pas-de-Calais, and all Allied supplies were still coming across the Normandy beaches. Logistics planners advised that the available supplies could not support all four armies at such a rate of advance. The original *Overlord* strategy of a broad front had been based on the fear that the Germans might counterattack a narrow thrust. Montgomery now pressed Eisenhower, to the verge of insubordination and beyond, to abandon this strategy, halt the Third US army, and give priority to a northern drive to be made by the Second British Army with FUSA in support. Within a week, Patton, with Bradley's support, was pressing for the opposite strategy, to give priority to his own Third US Army driving into eastern France. Both hoped to get across the Rhine and into the German industrial heartland of the Ruhr before Christmas.

It was not apparent to Eisenhower, however, that Allied supplies could support even one army on such a drive. For reasons of coalition solidarity and safety he took the politically correct but strategically controversial decision to continue the broad-front strategy. The normally cautious Montgomery, trying to force Eisenhower's hand, attempted to seize a bridgehead over the Rhine in Operation *Market Garden* on September 17, in which three divisions of the First Allied Airborne Army dropped to form a "carpet" through northern Holland along which XXX British Corps could advance to Arnhem. The operation was a disastrous failure – Montgomery's first and only defeat in a major battle. Characteristically, he described it as 90 percent success. By the end of September lack of fuel had slowed the whole Allied advance, giving the Germans time to strengthen their lines, and it was not until a renewed campaign in the spring that the Rhine was finally crossed. But after the battle of Normandy, the only question was how soon the war would end, not who would win it. Germany surrendered unconditionally to the Allies on May 8, 1945.

Too much discussion on Normandy has centered on the controversial decisions of the Allied commanders. It was not good enough, apparently, to win such a complete and spectacular victory over an enemy that had conquered most of Europe unless it was done perfectly. Most of the blame for this lies with Montgomery, who was foolish enough to insist that it *had* to be done perfectly, that Normandy – and all his other battles – had been fought according to a precise master plan drawn up beforehand, from which he never deviated. It says much for his personality that Montgomery found others to agree with him, despite overwhelming evidence to the contrary. His handling of the battle of Normandy was of a very high order, and as the person who would certainly have been blamed for losing the battle, he deserves the credit for winning it. Credit should also go to Eisenhower for his skill as a political leader. (In 1952 he was to be elected President of the United States and to serve two terms of office.) Those German commanders who survived the war were happy to blame their defeat on Adolf Hitler. Some, with incredible arrogance, even tried to lecture the men who had so thoroughly defeated them on how they themselves might have done better.

Could the Germans have won the battle of Normandy? They might have had better intelligence, to see through Operation *Fortitude*. They might have rationalized their command structure and improved their supplies and training. The Allies would not have invaded without air superiority, but it has been suggested that the Germans could have won at least air parity after D-Day by producing and employing as fighters a significant number of their Messerschmitt Me-262 jet aircraft, which were already in service. The Germans might have mixed armor in their weaker infantry formations, raising the overall standard at the expense of a few "showcase" divisions. They might have built the submarines or surface vessels to cut the vital sea link across the English Channel. There is much that they might have done. But in the actual circumstances of the battle as it developed, there was nothing they could have done to win it. At the level that the battle of

The toll of war. A temporary grave for one of the Rangers killed on Pointe-du-Hoc created among the litter of war. *(NARA)*

Normandy was fought, the art of generalship consisted of not letting such circumstances arise. The dispute between Rommel and von Rundstedt over a rigid or flexible defensive strategy was a massive irrelevance. Nor did any of their replacements have anything better to suggest. In truth, German generalship in Normandy was of a low order throughout the battle. Patton, who was killed in a road accident in 1945, could have given them all lessons in inventiveness, and in how to get results by disobeying orders.

Below the highest command level, Allied air power and artillery were the key factors in winning the battle of Normandy, but they did not win it alone. Cutting off supplies and reinforcements to the German frontline was only of value if, at the same time, the Allies were attacking and forcing the Germans to use up their reserves. Inferior in quality to the best German troops, likely to identify every tank they saw as a Tiger, the Allied infantry and tank crews showed great courage in maintaining the offensive. A large part of the German strength, however, came from the country in which they were fighting. Like the trenches of World War I or the jungles of the Pacific, the *bocage* itself became a formidable enemy. It is noteworthy that the Germans themselves had rather less success attacking through it than the Allies, and once without its protection they collapsed at great speed.

It is commonplace that an army reflects its society. Having seldom lost at a war, the British Army, in false modesty, likes to praise its opponents and denigrate itself. "They were almost the best troops in the world," the attitude seems to suggest, "what a pity they were facing us." The American style is more of self-praise at the expense of all others, conceding merit to an opponent before a rival. The German approach turns war into a morality play, the tragic defeat of mere mortals struggling with superhuman strength against the impersonal forces of the machine. If the Americans had been as good as they said they were, the British as bad as they said they were, and the Germans as good as everyone said they were, the battle of Normandy could not have been fought as it was.

THE NORMANDY BEACHES TODAY

Due to their dramatic history, the Normandy beaches have become a popular tourist attraction, with many preserved artifacts. The drive through the Norman countryside is very picturesque and Normandy is accessible from the Channel ports or Paris. The area around the Normandy beaches is still rural, so the road network becomes restricted near the coast. There are numerous markers and orientation maps along the beach, although it is a good idea to obtain one of the many guidebooks available to better appreciate the significance of many of the locations. A good map is essential, as some of the more significant sites can easily be overlooked. In addition, some areas are privately owned and wandering tourists are not welcome.

The D-Day beaches are also within easy reach of each other by car, so if time is limited it is useful to determine in advance which sites are of special interest. Some of the museums located near the other beaches are dedicated to the D-Day landings in general and should not be overlooked. For readers interested in uniforms and military equipment, many of these contain an interesting display of preserved artifacts. Much of this equipment is not original to the battle, but was brought to the area later. There are, however, some veteran pieces of equipment that actually took part in the assault, though these are rare. For example, the private Musée Sous-Marins at Commes contains one of the DD tanks recovered from offshore along with other equipment sunk on D-Day.

Many of the bunkers and other shore fortifications have been removed or altered over the years. For example, none of the *Panzerstellung* turreted tank bunkers are still preserved, and other bunkers have been sealed up. Casual tourists should not wander into bunkers at Omaha Beach or elsewhere along the Normandy coast, except for those clearly intended for tourist visits. Many have ammunition sub-basements at the bottom of the access stairs that present a serious hazard to the unwary as the doors have often been removed or rotted away.

OMAHA BEACH

The landing areas at Omaha Beach stretch for about 3 miles so the beach can be visited on foot in one day, depending on the amount of time spent at the many sites. One of the most impressive sites is Pointe-du-Hoc, which remains little changed from 1944, still pockmarked with bomb craters. The site has become overgrown with grass and weeds over the years, but the sense of the devastation there in 1944 is still obvious. Most of the concrete bunkers remain, cleaned up a bit and the debris removed. The view over the cliff is a vivid reminder of the courage of the Rangers. Pointe-du-Hoc is separated from the main landing beaches by the Pointe-et-Raz-de-la-Percée promontory and so is best reached by car before or after visiting the landing beaches. It is readily accessible from the coastal road (D.514).

Probably the best known of the sites at Omaha Beach is the US military cemetery located on the bluffs near St Laurent, and most ceremonies dedicated to the US forces on D-Day have been held here. More than 9,000 GIs are buried in the cemetery, mostly from the fighting after D-Day, and the row upon row of markers stand as a very tangible reminder of the cost of the Normandy campaign. There are numerous memorials located along and above the beach dedicated to units that took part in the D-Day landings or during later fighting in France.

The beach itself has seen many changes since 1944, as Normandy remains a popular seaside attraction in France. Most of the smaller beach obstructions have long since been cleared away, although there are remains of the Mulberry harbor near the Vierville draw. Since the Vierville draw was the primary route from the Mulberry harbor off the beach, it was heavily reworked by US engineers in 1944, and so bears little resemblance to the defensive position of June 1944. The National Guard memorial was placed on the location of the 75mm gun casemate of the WN72 strongpoint. Some of the other draws are less important for access to the beach and so remain closer to their original condition. Many of the concrete casemates located in the draws are still in place, some of them dedicated as monuments to the fighting. The antitank gun casemate of the WN65 strongpoint has been preserved.

UTAH BEACH

In contrast to Omaha Beach, where most of the combat action occurred on the beach itself, the fighting for Utah Beach was over very quickly. The most intense D-Day fighting in this sector consisted of small skirmishes by the paratroopers scattered in the farmland behind the beach. There is a museum near the beach itself, and a significant number of German fortifications remain, including some preserved artillery emplacements. The Musée de Débarquement d'Utah Beach is located in Ste-Marie-du-Mont adjacent to the beach and includes many exhibits of weapons and equipment associated with the landing. The area behind the beach that was flooded at the time of D-Day has long since been drained and is now farmland.

Of all the sites connected with the paratrooper actions, Ste-Mère-Église is no doubt the most popular, due in no small measure to the dramatic depiction in the well-known film *The Longest Day*. None other than John Wayne depicted (the much younger) Lieutenant-Colonel Benjamin Vandervoort. The images of Red Buttons in the film, portraying Private John Steele hanging by his parachute from the church steeple, is one of the most memorable in the movie. For years, the church in Ste-Mère-Église has had a mannequin hanging from a parachute draped from the roof to commemorate the airborne landings. The church also contains a stained-glass window commemorating the 505th PIR, which was added on the 25th anniversary. There is a large museum in the town, the Musée des Troupes Aéroportées, devoted to the airborne landings.

The countryside around Ste-Mère-Église is dotted with dozens of small markers, monuments, shrines, and plaques. Some of these are memorials to various units that took part in the fighting, while some commemorate individuals, such as a plaque at the site where General Pratt was killed. It is helpful to have a guidebook or map to seek out these memorials, as many are remote from the main roads. La Fière bridge still exists, though it is still as inconspicuous as in 1944. Nearby is the famous "Iron Mike" monument to the paratroopers. There are markers nearby showing the depth of the water of the flooded farm fields, but it takes some imagination to recall how difficult the fight along the causeway must have been.

The 82nd Airborne Division Museum at Ft Bragg has preserved one of the few surviving Waco CG-4A gliders. In spite of their canvas covering, their tubular fuselage construction proved to be relatively robust for such a light airframe. The canvas bench seat for the glider infantry can be seen in the left foreground. *(Steven J. Zaloga)*

The numerous concrete fortifications erected by the Germans along the coast in many cases still exist, as the larger bunkers are so difficult and costly to remove. Some of the most impressive fortifications are the Crisbecq and Azeville batteries and there is a museum (La Batterie d'Azeville) open in the summer months nearby. Cherbourg has been heavily rebuilt since the war, and the Fort de Roule has been converted into the Musée de la Libération.

American servicemen killed in action were interred in the American Cemetery and Memorial, located in Colleville-sur-Mer near the St Laurent draw on Omaha Beach. There are two German military cemeteries near Utah Beach, the Orglandes cemetery about 7 miles from Ste-Mère-Église and the larger cemetery at La Cambe, which is about 17 miles southeast of Ste-Mère-Église.

SWORD BEACH

Sword Beach and the area of the British 6th Airborne's operations east of the River Orne lie in a part of Normandy now popular with holidaymakers. In the summer the area swarms with visitors, most of whom are intent on enjoying the delights that a seaside resort can bring, particularly the magnificent wide sandy beaches that are so common in this part of France. But visitors to Normandy seeking evidence of the area's recent violent history will, likewise, not be disappointed.

At Bénouville the original lifting-bridge across the Orne Canal has been removed to make way for a larger modern structure, but the new bridge's similar shape gives the visitor a good impression of the site as it was in 1944. Still there alongside the bridge, dispensing refreshment to the traveler, is the Café Gondrée, once used as a dressing station during the battle and the first house in France to be liberated. Opposite the café is a real veteran of the landings in the shape of a Centaur tank. It came ashore with 5th (Independent) Battery of the Royal Marine Armoured Support Group at La Brèche on Sword Beach, but was knocked out shortly after landing. On the eastern side of the bridge, there is a gunpit housing the 50mm antitank weapon that was present during Major Howard's raid. It has been renovated and re-sited, but remains largely as it was when captured. A few hundred yards to the east is the Airborne Museum, which houses relics of the landings. In its grounds is the original Pegasus Bridge over which D Company of the 2nd Oxs and Bucks stormed during the first minutes of June 6.

Most impressive of the airborne locations is the Merville battery. Its four casemates, set in quiet green fields, now form part of an excellent museum complex. No. 1 casemate was renovated by Royal Engineers in 1982 and now houses a display of artifacts associated with its capture. Within the battery grounds the German command bunker and personnel shelters can also be seen.

Pictured a month after the invasion, the Caen Canal bridge has been officially labeled "Pegasus Bridge." Howard's glider still overlooks the site, but Café Gondrée, on the right, looks to be closed for business. *(Imperial War Museum, B7032)*

On Sword Beach, along the seafront at La Brèche, many of the seaside villas that were present in 1944 have been rebuilt and can often be identified from wartime photographs. Today these villas, which are no longer isolated from each other by large gardens, merge with modern holiday homes and housing estates to form a continuous ribbon of development all the way along the beach eastwards to Ouistreham/Riva Bella. The rear of the flat beach is still edged by sand dunes, held together by grassy knolls, behind which the assault waves of the British 3rd Division sheltered from enemy fire. Strongpoint Cod has been buried by houses, but its site can be traced by a network of quiet roads that mark the perimeter of the fortified area. The point where Lovat's 1st Special Service Brigade came ashore is celebrated by a memorial located opposite a concrete casemate that once housed a 75mm gun.

At Riva Bella, the Casino area captured by Captain Kieffer and his French commandos has been built over. The modern Casino sits squarely on the site of the old. There are a few tangible remains of the German strongpoint, such as the antitank "dragon's teeth" that run between beach huts to the rear of the site, and a casemate topped by an armored cupola that forms the base of the monument to the commandos. A good depiction of the capture of the strongpoint can be found in the Commando Museum opposite the present Casino.

Further along the seafront is the site of the six-gun battery at Ouistreham, which was captured by 4 Commando. This was an open construction defended by machine-gun posts and wire. Although little of the physical

Rising 55ft above the tree-lined streets of suburban Ouistreham is the concrete monolith that once housed the German fire-control post for the area. It now contains an excellent museum dedicated to the sea defenses of Hitler's Atlantic Wall, easily one of the very best of all of the visitor attractions along the Normandy coastline. *(Ken Ford)*

structures remain, the sites of the guns can still be traced. Just behind this area is one of the best examples of a modern museum being housed in a contemporary building, in this case a building that actually played its part in the D-Day battles. Standing 55ft high among suburban streets and gardens, with only a large observation slit visible to the outside, is the German fire-control post for the defenses of the River Orne estuary. The building's equipment supplied range and direction information to the surrounding artillery batteries. On June 6 the post received a lucky direct hit from the cruiser HMS *Frobisher*, which put it out of action. The troops inside still remained active, however, and even interfered with the attack made on the Ouistreham battery by 4 Commando. At the time, Lovat's men were occupied on other tasks and did not attempt to capture the structure. It was not until June 9 that its garrison surrendered to a Royal Engineers officer and three men. Lieutenant Bob Orell and his team blew in the armored door and invited the Germans to come out. Fifty artillerymen gave themselves up. Today the post houses a museum devoted to Hitler's Atlantic Wall. It contains excellent exhibitions on each of its levels. On the top floor, looking out through the narrow observation slit, is a working German optical rangefinder, from which one can gain an excellent view of Sword Beach.

Of the land battles fought to extend the lodgement, virtually all of the German field works that defended inland positions have been erased, but there is still much to be seen of the fortified complex known as Hillman lying just to the southwest of Colleville-Montgomery. The strongpoint was captured by the 1st Suffolks on D-Day, and there is a memorial to the battalion on a concrete bunker close to the road. Behind this, spread

The Commonwealth War Graves Commission's cemetery close by the church at Ranville. More paratroopers are buried just inside the wall of the churchyard. *(Ken Ford)*

throughout a series of grassy meadows, are the visible remains of many other defensive structures and steel cupolas that fortified the site. It should be remembered that, like an iceberg, what you see on the surface is only a small part of the huge network of bunkers and passages that lie underground.

Perhaps the most pertinent of the memorials that remind us of the great sacrifices made during D-Day are the cemeteries that mark the area. In the Commonwealth War Graves Commission cemetery at Ranville, Major-General Gale's fallen paratroopers lie side by side with the dead of the later battles for Caen and many of their German opponents. Alongside, in the walled enclosure of Ranville church, are the graves of more of the 6th Airborne's heroes, including that of Lieutenant Den Brotheridge, the first British soldier to be killed in the invasion. Many of the dead who fell during the Normandy battles can be found in the other British cemeteries at Douvres La Déliverande, Cambes en Plaine, and Hermanville. Please pay them a visit and honor the sacrifice made by the heroes of Operation *Overlord*.

GOLD AND JUNO BEACHES

Most of Gold Beach is unchanged, and it is possible to walk along the beach from Le Hamel to La Rivière and see only a handful of modern additions. Behind the beach the old road, which followed the shoreline, is now abandoned and modern traffic now passes by a few hundred yards inland. Between the beach and the new road the ground is unencumbered by modern development – low, marshy, and unvisited, a haven for local wildlife. Rising gently behind it is the Meuvaines Ridge from the top of which the machine-guns of the 726th Regiment poured down such a weight of fire on the 50th Division. At the western end of La Rivière is the great H677 casemate of WN33, which housed the 88mm gun that destroyed the tanks supporting the 5th East Yorks. It is now used as a store for the local sailing club. A few hundred yards to the west is the road leading up from the beach along which the 6th Green Howards advanced; follow it for about a half of a mile and it will lead you past Lavatory Pan Villa to the long-abandoned casemates of the Mont Fleury battery.

At Le Hamel at the other end of Gold Beach stands the gun emplacement that wrought such havoc with the Hampshires. Nearby in the car park and built into the seawall are Tobruk emplacements that contained the machine-guns of WN37 that swept the beach with such deadly fire. To the west, on top of the hill overlooking Arromanches, is the site of the radar station, now a visitor center with a 360° cinema showing films relating to the history of the area. There is a good view to be had from the hill of the remains of the Mulberry harbor, many pieces of which remain in place, defying the sea's efforts to obliterate them. In Arromanches itself is one of the better D-Day museums, with an emphasis on the construction and use of the artificial harbor.

Continue westward and make a point of visiting the Longues battery, without doubt the most significant and best-preserved of all of the sites along this coast. It still has its powerful weapons *in situ* in their casemates – the guns that fired defiantly on the invasion fleet and took so long to be silenced. On the top of the cliffs nearby is the observation and ranging bunker and contained within the perimeter of the battery is a visitor center. Further west still is the tiny harbor at Port-en-Bessin, captured on D-Day +1

The control bunker for the German guns at Longues. It was built on the edge of the cliffs with a clear view out to sea. The two-storey bunker served as the battery command post. On the upper level was the observation deck. On the lower floor was the map room, officers' room, and the range-finder room with its observation slit looking out to sea through a radius of 220º. (Ken Ford)

by 47 Royal Marine Commando. Just inland from the port near Escures, close by Point 72 where 47 Commando holed up for the night on D-Day, is an unusual private museum devoted to the wrecks that have been salvaged from the sea along the D-Day coast. This has a fascinating display of original hardware together with poignant relics from the tanks and ships that were sunk during the invasion.

Juno Beach is more developed than Gold, but still retains much of its D-Day past. Courseulles is a popular destination for the sun lovers, who now crowd the town beach where the Regina Rifles came ashore. The strongpoint on the beach has gone and the whole of the seafront has been redeveloped. At the mouth of the harbor are two originals from D-Day: a DD tank from the Canadian 6th Armoured Regiment salvaged from the seabed and now restored to its 1944 condition, and a restored German 50mm antitank gun with its battered shield showing its invasion battle scars. To the west, on the other side of the harbor entrance, several casemates are still visible, now sinking slowly in the shifting sands. Along the first exit from the beach made by the specialized armor of 79th Armoured Division stands one of its Churchill AVREs. This vehicle, mentioned earlier, is a genuine veteran of the landings – it had been buried in the crater into which it had fallen and spent the next 30 years helping to support the roadway that led inland from the beach.

At Bernières, the strongpoint on Nan White that was built into the seawall opposite where the Queen's Own Rifles of Canada landed retains its concrete casemate and Tobruk emplacements. Along the road eastwards can be seen remnants of WN27, including its original 50mm gun in a casemate at St Aubin. Inland from Juno is the site of the radar station at Douvres.

German war cemetery at La Cambes, one of three German cemeteries in Normandy. Over 20,000 German soldiers are buried here, killed in the fighting between D-Day and the breakout. *(Ken Ford)*

It has a visitor center (visitors should check opening times) and numerous casemates and shelters remain visible, giving some indication of the great strength of this underground fortress that held out against superior forces for so long. A German Würzburg radar antenna now stands on one of the original concrete bases, not a veteran of the war, but one brought from the Observatoire de Paris to form part of the radar museum.

Closer to Caen, just past the tiny village of Authie where the Canadian 3rd Division met the 12th SS-Panzer Division "Hitlerjugend" head-on, is the medieval Ardenne Abbey. On the night of D-Day the regimental headquarters of Kurt Meyer's 25th SS-Panzergrenadier Regiment was located here. Its domestic range is now a private dwelling closed to the public, clustered around a courtyard close by the abbey church. The buildings are surrounded by a high stone wall and the site remains as it was in 1944. Through an archway in the corner of the courtyard a gate leads to a small garden. In that garden is a memorial to the 27 Canadian soldiers who were murdered there in cold blood by the 12th SS-Panzer Division. It serves as a poignant reminder of the barbarity of the regime that so many Allied soldiers fought and died to overthrow.

FURTHER READING

The D-Day landings have proven to be one of the most popular topics of World War II history, and there are hundreds of titles on this subject, of varying quality. There was a flood of new books around the time of the 1994 anniversary. The list below is by no means exhaustive and consists mainly of more recent titles that the authors have found to be particularly useful. Apart from the commercially published books, there are a number of limited-circulation books by US Army commands that are particularly useful for those looking for more in-depth coverage, and can be found in specialist military libraries. The two most relevant are the FUSA and V Corps report of operations. There are also many after-action reports on the D-Day landings that are more difficult to find except in archives. The authors consulted the collections at the Military History Institute at the Army War College at Carlisle Barracks, Pennsylvania, and the US National Archives and Records Administration (NARA) at College Park, Maryland. Some of the better reports include the "Operation Report *Neptune*: Omaha Beach" by the Provisional Engineer Special Brigade Group, and "Amphibious Operations: Invasion of Northern France: Western Task Force June 1944" by the US Fleet HQ. There are also numerous after-action reports by the various US Army units located in Record Group 407 at NARA, College Park.

Ambrose, Stephen E., *D-Day, June 6, 1944* (Simon & Schuster, 1994)

Ambrose, Stephen E., *Pegasus Bridge* (Allen and Unwin, 1984)

Anon., *Operation "Neptune" Landings in Normandy, June 1944* (HMSO, 1994)

Anon., *Airborne Forces* (Air Ministry, 1951)

Anon., *The Story of the 79th Armoured Division* (Privately Printed, 1946)

Balkoski, Joseph, *Beyond the Beachhead: The 29th Infantry Division in Normandy* (Stackpole, 1989)

Bando, Mark, *101st Airborne: The Screaming Eagles at Normandy* (MBI, 2001)

Berger, Sid, *Breaching Fortress Europe* (Society of American Military Engineers, 1994)

Bernage, George, *Omaha Beach* (Heimdal, 2002)

Bernage, George, *Premiere Victoire Americaine en Normandie* (Heimdal, 1990)

Bernage, George, *Debarquement à Utah Beach* (Heimdal, 1984)

Carell, Paul, *Invasion - They're Coming!* (George Harrap, 1962)

Chazette, Alain, *Le Mur de L'Atlantique en Normandie* (Heimdal, 2000)

Clay, Ewart, *The Path of the 50th* (Gale & Polden, 1950)

Collins, J. Lawton, *Lightning Joe* (LSU Press, 1979)

Crookenden, Napier, *Dropzone Normandy* (Ian Allen, 1976)

Ellis, Major L. F., *Victory In The West* (HMSO, 1962)

Esvelin, Philippe, *D-Day Gliders: Les Planeurs Americains du Jour J* (Heimdal, 2002)

Ewing, Joseph, *29 Let's Go! A History of the 29th Division in World War II* (*Infantry Journal* 1948; Battery Press reprint 1979)

Gale, Lieutenant-General Richard, *With The Sixth Airborne Division in Normandy* (Sampson, Low, Marston, & Co, 1948)

Gawne, Jonathan, *Spearheading D-Day* (Histoire & Collections, 1998)

Golley, John, *The Big Drop* (Janes, 1982)

Harclerode, Peter, *"Go To It!"* (Caxton Editions, 2000)

Harrison, Gordon, *Cross-Channel Attack* (US Army Center for Military History, 1951)

Hastings, Max, *Overlord* (Michael Joseph, 1984)

Isby, David, *Fighting the Invasion: The German Army at D-Day* (Greenhill, 2000)

Isby, David, *Fighting the Invasion: The German Army from D-Day to Villers Bocage* (Greenhill, 2001)

Kilvert-Jones, Tim, *Omaha Beach* (Leo Cooper, 1999)

Knickerbocker, H. R., et. al., *Danger Forward: The Story of the First Division in World War II* (1947, Battery Press reprint 2002)

Koskimaki, George, *D-Day with the Screaming Eagles* (1970, Casemate reprint 2002)

Lewis, Adrian, *Omaha Beach: A Flawed Victory* (University of North Carolina, 2001)

Masters, Charles J., *Glidermen of Neptune* (Southern Illinois University Press, 1995)

McDougall, Murdoch C., *Swiftly They Struck* (Odhams, 1954)

McNish, Robin, *Iron Division* (Ian Allan, 1978)

Meyer, Hubert, *The History of the 12th SS Panzer Division "Hitlerjugend"* (J. J. Fedorowicz, 1994)

Mitcham, Samuel W., *Hitler's Legions* (Leo Cooper, 1985)

Morgan, Lieutenant-General Sir Frederick, *Overture To Overlord*
(Hodder & Stoughton, 1950)

Morison, Samuel E., *The Invasion of France and Germany 1944–1945*
(Little, Brown, 1957)

Omaha Beachhead (US Army Center for Military History, 1945,
numerous reprints)

Ramsey, Winston, *D-Day Then and Now, Vol II* (After the Battle, 1995)

Rapaport, Leonard, and A. Northwood, *Rendezvous with Destiny*
(*Infantry Journal*; Battery Press Reprint)

Reignier, Stéphane, *The German Battery at Longues-sur-Mer*
(Memorial Editions, 1999)

Ruge, Friedrich, *Rommel in Normandy* (Presidio, 1984)

Saunders, Hilary St George, *The Green Beret* (Michael Joseph, 1949)

Scarfe, Norman, *Assault Division* (Collins, 1947)

Scott Daniell, David, *Regimental History of the Royal Hampshire
Regiment, Vol III* (Gale & Polden, 1955)

Shilleto, Carl, *Utah Beach: Ste-Mère-Église* (Leo Cooper, 2001)

Stacey, C. P., *The Canadian Army 1939–1945* (Canadian Ministry
of National Defence, 1948)

Stillwell, Paul, *Assault on Normandy* (US Naval Institute, 1994)

Synge, Captain W., *The Story of the Green Howards*
(Privately Printed, 1952)

Taylor, Daniel, *Villers-Bocage Through The Lens* (Battle of Britain
Prints International, 1999)

Utah Beach to Cherbourg (US Army Center for Military History, 1946;
many reprints)

Wilmot, Chester, *The Struggle For Europe* (Collins, 1952)

Wolfe, Martin, *Green Light: A Troop Carrier Squadron's War from
Normandy to the Rhine* (Univ. of Pennsylvania Press, 1983)

INDEX

Figures in **bold** refer to illustrations.

A

air support, allied 34, 69, 72, 95, 126, 189,
203, 265, 276–277, 281, 304, 305, 307,
308, 330, 334–335, **335**, 344
see also Royal Air Force; US Army Air
Force (USAAF)
airborne landings
British 196, 214–229, **216–217**
German reaction to 229–231
US 114, 123, 128, 132–151, **138**, 166–167
aircraft
Hawker Typhoon **335**
Mitchell medium bomber **232**
Ajax, HMS 281, **284–285**, 299
Albany, Mission 132–135, **135–141**
Algonquin, HMCS 307
allied commanders 24–28, 42–44, 116–117, 197
shortcomings in chain of command 26
allied naval forces
see also Royal Navy; US Navy
Task Force 'G' 281
Task Force 'J' 306
Task Force 'O' 46–47, 66–67, 68, 69
Task Force 'S' 199, 209, 233
Task Force 'U' **6**, 157
amphibious landings exercises **9**
amphibious trucks (DUKW) **82**, 98, 106, 107

amtracs(amphibious tractors) 50
antitank weapons 34, **55**, 57, **57**, 58, **58**,
60–61, 94, 95, 109, 119, 149, 164, 176,
184, 185, 191, 231, 325, 330
Anvil, Operation 15
Arcadia Conference 9, 24
Ardenne Abbey **322–323**
Arethusa, HMS 224, 232
Argonaut, HMS 281, 299, 300
Arkansas, USS 299
Arnhem 342
Arromanches 282, 299, 331, **333**
artificial harbors 114, 127, **277**, 331, **333**
artillery 120, 130, 200
British
5.5in medium **317**
German
105mm 120
Atlantic Wall **13**, 30–32, 36, 54–59, 114,
167, 184
antitank ditches **43**
beach obstacles **44**, **54**, 54–55, 280, 282,
289, 308
coastal batteries and strongpoints **37**, **38**, **352**
at Gold and Juno Beaches 277, 280,
285–286, 290–291, 294, 298–299,
309, 311, 313, 315–316, 318–319,
320–321, 324–325
at Omaha Beach 53, **55**, **57**, 58–59, 64,
95, **99**, 105

U